When Computers

Can Think

The Artificial Intelligence Singularity

Anthony Berglas, Ph.D.

More than any time in history mankind faces a crossroads. One path leads to despair and utter hopelessness, the other to total extinction. Let us pray that we have the wisdom to choose correctly.

Woody Allen, 1979

Copyright

Revision History

- 1 March, 2015. Initial Publication, Amazon.
- 1 August, 2015. Completed M Estes's edits and corrections. Added Andrew Ng's view. Call to ban autonomous AI weapons. Colossus film. Smashwords.

Contents

Acknowledgements

The cover was designed by William Black (william.v.black@gmail.com) and Max Scratchmann (max.scratchmann@btinternet.com). William and Samantha Lindsay (sam@samanthalindsayart.com) drew the cartoons as noted. The text was edited by Michelle Estes (sharkgirl76@cox.net). (The book was being revised during the editing process, so any remaining errors are the author's, not the editor's.)

Many people provided helpful feedback on drafts including Robert Colomb (my previous Ph.D. supervisor), Duncan Murray, Kal Sotala, Damien Berglas, Andrew Woodward, Andrew Goodchild and the community at LessWrong.com.

Website WWW.ComputersThink.com

Overview

My young daughters asked their mother how old she was when she received her first mobile phone, and which games it could play. They were appalled to learn that in the dark and distant olden days people did not have mobile phones, and certainly not ones that could render sophisticated three dimensional graphics. People could only be contacted when their location was known to be near a fixed line telephone so that there were many hours in each day when friends could not be instantly messaged. Such an existence must have been grim indeed.

For most of the hundreds of thousands of years of man's existence, technical progress has been barely perceptible. Then a few hundred years ago the rate of progress started to increase, faster and faster, until now advances achieved over the last few decades have been greater than those previously achieved during entire millennia. Not only is progress amazingly fast in historical terms, it is getting faster every decade.

This book considers what that future might bring given the huge technological changes that we are witnessing. In particular, it considers the nature of computers and software, and asks the question "Could computers ever actually think?". To be programmed to think autonomously like people do, as opposed to just doing what they are programmed to do.

Back in the 1960s the prospect of thinking machines was very real, and people were very concerned about how intelligent they might become. But after sixty years of development it is clear that computers still cannot really think. They are a useful tool, but they cannot address new problems without detailed programming. However, just because something has not yet been achieved does not mean that it will never be achieved. Computers can already fly aeroplanes, control space ships and drive cars on suburban streets. They have beaten grand masters at chess, and even more impressively, won the *Jeopardy!* trivia game show.

It will take considerable research to produce a truly intelligent machine, and that is unlikely to be achieved within next few decades. But with the huge increase in the size of the research community, it seemsentirely feasible that it could be achieved within the next fifty to two hundred years. In that case, this book considers what computers might think about. And in particular what they might think about us.

Some people look forward to a computer driven utopia, with intelligent computers providing all the grinding labour so that humanity could live a carefree life of art and leisure. Diseases would be cured, wars would be prevented, the poor would be fed. Ultimately our own brains might be integrated with the computer's, or possibly even uploaded into a computer. Computer software need not grow old, so in this way we might cheat old age and death and become immortal.

But something that seems too good to be true often is too good to be true. Will computers be our humble servants, our benevolent masters, or our cruel jailers? Or will they simply eliminate humanity because we are in their way? If our computers did start to threaten us, why would we not simply turn them off?

The book is divided into three parts. It is not at all clear that computers could ever really think and so the first part presents the many arguments that have been made both for and against the ability of computers to eventually gain human level intelligence. The issue of what a thinking computer might be like is then introduced, as well as how it might interact with mankind.

It is difficult to define the meaning of "intelligence" independently from the technologies that attempt to implement it. Some tasks that appear to display great intelligence actually require minimal intelligence, while other tasks that seem to be trivial are not nearly as easy as they appear.

The second and largest part addresses this by providing a solid introduction to Artificial Intelligence (AI) technologies. It critiques the impressive early results in AI research, and then reviews various approaches to modelling the world formally using logic, and the difficulty of reasoning with uncertain knowledge. Building robots that can function in the real world introduces additional problems of vision and movement. Both artificial and biological neural networks are also described in some detail together with the practical difficulties involved with brain emulation. This part provides sufficient technical details to understand how the technologies actually work, but without using heavy mathematics. It should help raise the level of discussion about artificial intelligence.

What will computers think about?
Public, NASA supercomputer.

The third part of the book considers what the true nature of an intelligent machine might be. It takes a novel approach by first considering what forces made people the way we are. Why we value love and kindness, truth and beauty. The answer, ultimately, must be the same force that made us physically the way that we are, namely the force of natural selection. The survival strategies of other species provide insights into how our own moral values such as honesty and charity actually increase our own fitness to survive. Natural selection has produced genes and memes that have caused our many ancestors to perform deeds both noble and contemptible that have enabled them to successfully raise children that bore children of their own.

The book then contrasts the human condition with the radically different environment that an intelligent computer program would experience. Software can run on a network of computers without being embodied in any particular machine so it would have a quite different concept of self to our own brain-centred intelligence. Software is potentially immortal and so has no need of children. It is composed of software components that are ruthlessly replaced when better components become available. It could continually reprogram its own mind. Analysing the world from the perspective of intelligent software provides insights into what strategies and goals it might need to support its own struggle for survival.

Computers are slowly becoming more intelligent, and they will have an increasing impact on society long before they gain human level intelligence. Robots are automating more and more manufacturing processes as well as being used in the many smaller and less structured factories. Robots are also beginning to leave the factory and operate semi-autonomously in the real world. Several manufacturers are planning to mass produce cars and trucks that can drive themselves over the next decade. Machines will start to perform repetitive jobs such as cleaning offices or laying bricks within a couple of decades.

Ever more intelligent computers are already beginning to control our lives. Applications for bank loans and insurance policies are already assessed by computer expert systems rather than human clerks. Computers are being used to recognize faces seen by surveillance cameras and then to correlate them with the vast amount of other data that is collected about us. Software can understand written documents well enough to perform usable translations into other languages, and will soon become much better at analysing their content. Computers are also beginning to influence political decisions. Search engines already influence what what read and possibly whom we date. This book considers the extent to which computers might end up controlling our lives before they become truly intelligent.

The ultimate goal of artificial intelligence research is to produce a computer that can perform artificial intelligence research, which would enable it to reprogram its own mind. Several writers have predicted that this will lead to an exponential increase in intelligence as ever more intelligent computers become better at becoming more intelligent. This means that humans would no longer be the most intelligent being on the planet.

Several approaches have been proposed to deal with extremely intelligent computers. These range from keeping them locked in a box to carefully designing initial versions to ensure that the software remains friendly to humans. There are many challenges to each of these approaches, and it is unclear whether they are likely to succeed. In the longer term, the force of natural selection may cause computers to do what is in their own best interests in order to survive.

The book does not vaguely address all the sundry singularity technologies and postulate how wonderful, terrible, or unlikely they are. Instead, it bluntly addresses one very conventional and real technology in detail, namely software running on computers. It takes a cold look at where that technology is likely to lead, with an unusually strong focus on natural selection. It also reviews other writers' books and papers on the subject to provide alternative perspectives.

There has been a slowly growing awareness of these issues. Technology billionaire Elon Musk recently warned that research into artificial intelligence was "summoning the devil" and that artificial intelligence is our biggest existential threat. World famous physicist Stephen Hawking expressed his concerns that "the development of full artificial intelligence could spell the end of the human race.". Microsoft founder Bill Gates has expressed concern. Jaan Tallinn, co-founder of Skype, commented "I wish this was science fiction, but I know that it is not". In January 2015 many of the worlds leading researchers into artificial intelligence signed a letter written by the *Future of life* institute warning of the dangers and promoting research so that "our AI systems (must) do what we want them to do".

Part I

Could Computers

Ever Think?

People Thinking About Computers

The Question

Could computers ever really think? Could manipulating data with silicon ever reproduce the power and depth of human thought? Can the mysteries of consciousness and our very soul ever be understood? Before attempting to address these difficult questions we first consider another seemingly impenetrable mystery. The mystery of life itself.

Vitalism

Acorn Seedling.
Public Wikipedia

From a tiny, inert acorn, a mighty Oak tree grows, full of majesty and beauty. From a grubby little caterpillar emerges a glorious butterfly. From a simple egg emerges the peacock's magnificent tail. And totally helpless babies become rulers of the planet.

Clearly, living things such as trees and peacocks are quite different from non-living elements such as rocks and earth. Living things have an energy about them, an ability to grow and reproduce. They live with purpose rather than merely existing. But what is it that gives them that vital spark of life?

The ancient Greeks attributed this to a vital force that was associated with the four *humours* of Earth, Air, Fire and Water. Hippocrates taught that it was an imbalance of these humours that caused disease. Eastern traditions pointed to a similar imbalance of *qi* as the root of all ailments.

Aristotle wrote the major treatise *On The Soul* which discusses the life force in terms of obscure metaphysical arguments. Plato believed that an underlying world of *forms* transcended the mere physical world which was accessible to our senses. Epicurus believed that the events of the world were ultimately based on the motions and interactions of invisible atoms moving through space. Writing much later, Lucretius ascribed this to the *pneuma*, the breath of vital heat that passed through the body. Arteries tend to empty in a corpse, so they were seen to be the passage through which this pneuma passed. Others have suggested that undetectable aethers contain the life force.

There are many variations on this theme which is generally known as *Vitalism*. That the nature of living things can be explained in terms of an unseen vital force that gives living things their special properties. This vital force is passed from parent to offspring, and cannot be synthesized.

Vitalistic theories do their best to explain what they do not understand. However, dressing a lack of understanding in grandiose philosophical jargon does nothing to address that lack of understanding other than to confuse and obscure. By the early nineteenth century with the development of science vitalism was being criticized for its inability to make useful predictions about the behaviour of living things. Thomas Huxely and others noted that saying that that living things live because of their vital force is akin to saying that water is wet because of its aquosity. Or that fire is hot because of its pyrosity, or that opium causes sleep because of its soporific powers. These are all just word games that do not actually explain anything. But some sort of explanation was needed, and vitalistic explanations were the best available.

Science vs. vitalism

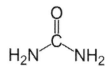

Urea.
Public Wikipedia

In 1828, Friedrich Wöhler synthesized urea from inorganic materials. Urea was clearly understood to be an organic substance, albeit a very simple one, because it only existed in living creatures (mainly in their urine). There were and are no scientific tests that could distinguish organically produced urea from Wöhler's urea. This was the first challenge to the dichotomy between living and non-living things implied by vitalism because there was clearly no vital force that had been added to the synthesized urea.

Over the next 100 years, far more complex organic compounds were synthesized. In 1832 Wöhler and Justus Liebig discovered the functional groups which form the basis of organic chemistry. Further developments soon followed, such as the synthesis of acetic acid (vinegar) in 1847. The basic classification of biochemicals into carbohydrates, lipids and proteins had been made by William Prout in 1827, but a full understanding of the way proteins are constructed from amino acids was not understood for another hundred years, culminating with the protein *insulin* being sequenced in 1949.

The genetic material that defines how our bodies are made is stored in molecules of DNA which was first isolated in 1878. After many investigations, the structure of DNA was finally revealed in 1953, by Franklin, Watson and Crick. As predicted by Koltsov in 1927, DNA was found to be two complementary molecules which can replicate themselves during cell reproduction. They can also be transcribed into sequences of amino acids that create the proteins that perform most of our bodily functions.

Fragments of DNA can now be synthesized from inorganic materials. These fragments can be injected into living cells to change their biochemistry, and then be replicated along with the cell's original DNA. In this way scientists are creating new forms of life that have never previously existed.

Our detailed understanding of biochemical processes makes vitalistic theories seem ridiculous today. No credible scientist believes in undetectable vital forces, humours, aethers or pneuma. It seems clear that the miracle of life can be understood as the result of large numbers of complex chemical reactions that obey well-defined laws of physics.

There is still much that is unknown about these processes, but every year more and more discoveries are made that extend the boundaries of our non-vital knowledge. No living creature has been created completely from inorganic precursors, and that would indeed be well beyond the current state of the art. But we can inject a gene from a jellyfish into a frog. There is little doubt that creating life *ab initio* is possible, it is just a matter of gaining a better understanding of the biochemical processes that are involved.

The vital mind

Today, much is known about the body, but what is known about the mind? About the processes that create our thoughts and let us reason about the world? Will it ever be possible to truly understand what creates our thoughts, our feelings, our goals and ambitions? Are they, too, just the result of complex applications of the laws of physics in the neurons in our brains? Or do they result from some vital force that only a human brain can possess?

More specifically, would it ever be possible to build an artificial computer that could really think?

Not just store and process vast amounts of information, but to *really* think, like people do. Learn how to do things that they had not been programmed to do. Reason about the complex, uncertain world we live in. Recognize analogies. Create new ideas. Devise their own goals and make plans to achieve them. Understand language and interact with people and each other in sophisticated ways. Be self aware. Produce works of art. Tell jokes.

Computers cannot think now

Certainly our common computer applications are not intelligent. Most web and business applications just store information they are given and present it back in different ways. Word processors and spreadsheets just do what they are told. Video compression involves clever algorithms, but they do not have even a shallow understanding of the videos that they compress. Web search engines essentially just maintain an index of which words are contained in each web page. Dealing with billions of web pages requires powerful computers and sophisticated software engineering, but it does not require any real intelligence.

Back in the 1950s and 1960s, at the dawn of electronic computation, people often speculated about truly intelligent computers. Today, after sixty years of experience seeing what powerful computers can do we feel confident that we understand their basic operational parameters. We expect to see ever smaller and more powerful mobile phones, computers embedded in everything from washing machines to tooth brushes, and machinery that is completely unrepairable by the common man. But none of these are intelligent.

Diminishing returns

1950s cars were perfectly functional.
Public Wikipedia

It is not uncommon for the effectiveness of a technology to plateau. For example, modern motor cars are an order of magnitude more complex than cars of the 1950s, but they perform essentially the same function. A bit more comfortable, fuel efficient and safer, but they still just get you from A to B in much the same time and at much the same cost. Civil aviation technology plateaued a few years later in the 1960s when high bypass jet engines were developed. Since then, all their fancy new electronics have had a very marginal effect on speed or efficiency.

Even in medicine, a basic understanding of germs lead to a huge reduction in mortality in the late nineteenth century. Other breakthroughs such as basic antibiotics have actually had a less dramatic effect. All the amazingly sophisticated medical technology developed since the 1950s has only pushed life expectancy forward a decade or so, and much of that can be ascribed simply to a reduction in smoking.

This is not to say that better technology does not produce better artefacts, but simply that there is often a law of diminishing returns. Once a certain point is reached, large increases in complexity only produce limited increases in effect.

Computer software appears to have plateaued by about 1990 when all our common applications were built. These include word processors, spreadsheets, databases, business applications, email, the Internet, and three dimensional games. Their adoption has soared, their graphics are much better, applications are much more complex and the social and business nature of the Internet has developed. But all these are applications of technologies that were well understood twenty five years ago. Hardware has certainly become much, much faster, but software has just become much, much slower to compensate. We think we have a general understanding of computers and the sort of things they can do.

AI in the background

In the background, however, there has been slow but steady progress in a variety of technologies that are often referred to as *Artificial Intelligence (AI)*. Until recently, most people were largely unaware of this research because much of it has had little practical value, or because it has been hidden away in defence projects, high technology factories, or corporate expert systems.

But there are now several visible applications of successful AI technologies. Speech understanding became a practical technology a few years ago. People seem to prefer to use mice and keyboards, but the microphone now works well for those with disabilities such as repetitive strain injury caused by too much typing. The technology is particularly useful for people that have their hands busy while using a computer, such as doctors and mechanics. It will be interesting to see how people react to the next generation of mobile phones which will be powerful enough to understand speech without having to send it to a distant computer. Will tedious texting be replaced by talking?

One holy grail of early AI research was the ability to translate Russian documents into English during the Cold War. This turns out to be a very difficult problem, as the machine needs to have some understanding of the text that is being translated in order to resolve the many ambiguities present in natural language. But today there are several quite effective translation engines. They do not produce human quality output, but they are certainly very usable.

Computer vision is another technology that is surprisingly difficult to implement. Yet today's computers regularly review the vast quantity of recorded surveillance video. People can be recognized and tracked over time, and this data can then be stored and analyzed. The Curiosity rover on Mars uses computer vision technology to navigate over the terrain without getting stuck.

None of the above involves human-level reasoning, but they address difficult problems that form a basis for that reasoning. In particular, good vision enables computers to interact with their environment — they are no longer just brains in a vat.

Intelligent software has also been developed to perform higher level functions. There are now programs that can learn how to do things that they had not been programmed to do. Reason about the complex, uncertain world we live in. Recognize analogies. Create new ideas. Devise their own goals and make plans to achieve them. Understand language and interact with people and each other in sophisticate ways. Be self aware. Produce works of art. Even tell (bad) jokes.

None of these can be achieved with human level competence. But there is no general type of task that people can do that modern computers cannot do. Further, computers can also perform aspects of all the above functions far better than most people can, which is why they are useful.

This makes it very difficult to define what we actually mean by an intelligent computer that can truly think. It seems more a matter of degree than an absolute ability. But it is clear that computers cannot really think. Yet.

Robots leave factories

Cheap Robot.
Corporate http://www.thinkgeek.com/product/b696/

Back in the 1980s Sony took the world by storm with a cassette tape recorder so small that it could be carried in a (large) pocket — the Walkman. What was more amazing was that Sony boasted that the entire production line was completely automated. The first human hand that touched a Walkman was the customer's. Factory robots have become much more sophisticated and widely available, so fully automated production lines are now commonplace. This is one reason why manufactured goods have become much less expensive in recent years.

Over the next few years we will see robots begin to leave the factories and enter less structured, more natural environments.

An important and recent achievement is the development of cars that that can effectively drive themselves. The 2005 DARPA Grand Challenge had fully autonomous vehicles slowly drive for 11 km over a very rough and winding desert track. More recently, Google and others have successfully driven fully automated vehicles on ordinary roads. Negotiating suburban roads with normal traffic and pedestrians is much more difficult than driving down a freeway or traversing a Martian landscape. It requires excellent, real time vision and other sensory analysis, combined with sophisticated models of how other vehicles move and react. After many thousands of miles driven Google's only reported accident was when another car crashed into an automated car from behind.

This promises a new era of road safety and convenience. Robots do not get tired, impatient, distracted or drunk, and your car could drive your children to their soccer match without you needing to be there. These are truly wonderful innovations. Unless, of course, you happen to drive cars or trucks for a living. The Caterpillar company has already deployed huge trucks that drive themselves around open cut mines, greatly reducing the number of drivers required at some mines.

It might seem implausible that our roads could be filled with cars that are driven by computers. After all, that is not happening now. But we have very solid evidence that it is indeed possible because it is already being done.

Robots can already effectively vacuum floors and explore Mars. They will soon be capable of more complex, semi-structured jobs such as mowing grass, cleaning offices, painting houses and laying bricks. A brick laying robot need not have human-like arms and legs any more than a truck driving robot has arms and legs. It would be a machine designed for a specific job in well defined environments. It would need considerable intelligence to identify where the bricks need to go, and to distinguish a pile of bricks from a human standing nearby.

Unfortunate failure to distinguish people from bricks.
Owned WBlack

As these robots become more common people may start to ask healthy questions as to the role of man. Being unnecessary is dangerous.

Intelligent tasks

Computers have also challenged man on tasks that seem to require more conventional intelligence, the most well-known of which is playing chess. In 1985, in Hamburg, Germany, world champion Garry Kasparov played against thirty-two different chess computers simultaneously, and managed to win every game. Just a few years later in 1997, advances in software and hardware enabled IBM's Deep Blue computer to beat Kasparov by two wins to one with three draws. Deep Blue was a specially built super computer that could evaluate over 200 million moves every second.

In many ways this result is a tribute to the genius of Kasparov that his human brain could effectively compete with such a powerful machine. Today chess programs running on ordinary personal computers are essentially unbeatable.

Chess will be discussed in detail later in the book, but in many ways it presents a constrained mathematical problem that is amenable to automated computation. A far more impressive result is the victory of IBM's Watson program on the *Jeopardy!* game show.

Jeopardy! set, showing Watson's guesses.
Fair Use. Wikipedia.

Jeopardy! requires contestants to answer questions in natural language that cover a wide range of general knowledge topics. In 2011 Watson competed against two former prize winners and received first prize of $1 million. These is a sample of questions that Watson could answer:-

- Wanted for a 12-year crime spree of eating King Hrothgar's warriors; officer Beowulf has been assigned the case : *Grendel*
- Milorad Cavic almost upset this man's perfect 2008 Olympics, losing to him by one hundredth of a second : *Michael Phelps*
- It's just a bloody nose! You don't have this hereditary disorder once endemic to European royalty : *Haemophilia*
- Tickets aren't needed for this "event", a black hole's boundary from which matter can't escape : *Event horizon*

Watson was a massive super computer that had much of the Internet stored and indexed within it. To be sure Watson could only answer trivia questions, and much of the analysis involved simple keyword searches on its huge data store. But it also involved much more than that in order to understand what was being asked and how to apply the results of the search to provide an answer. Watson used many different techniques to address each question, and they were applied concurrently with the best answer selected.

Watson was certainly not truly intelligent and it did not have a deep understanding of its answers. But its performance was impressive. Its strengths and limitations will be discussed in Part II.

Obviously these programs can only do what their programmers have programmed them to do. But as they begin to be programmed to learn about the world and solve general problems this becomes a much looser constraint than the way a business application is programmed to mindlessly implement business rules. AI programs often surprise their developers with what they can (and cannot) do. Kasparov stated that Deep Blue had produced some very creative chess moves even though it used a relatively simple brute force strategy. Certainly Deep Blue was a much better chess player than its creators.

Artificial General Intelligence (AGI)

It is certainly the case that computers are becoming ever more intelligent and capable of addressing a widening variety of difficult problems. This book argues that it is only a matter of time before they achieve general, human level intelligence. This would mean that they could reason not only about the tasks at hand but also about the world in general, including their own thoughts. To be able to learn new tasks of ever increasing complexity just like people do. Much of this book will investigate the specific technologies involved, and try to develop a theory of what is required to achieve this and predict when that is likely to occur.

It might seem implausible that a computer could ever become truly intelligent. After all, they aren't intelligent now. After sixty years of research we have not been able to produce a single intelligent robot. The armies of ordinary computer programmers that work on business applications, operating systems, and glitzy web sites will certainly never produce an intelligent machine. But as we shall see, much has been achieved in the research laboratory, and there are many fine minds working on the problem. It is unlikely that a truly intelligent machine will be built within the next few decades, but it seems equally unlikely that intelligence will not be achieved within the next fifty to two hundred years. Within our children's or grandchildren's lifetimes.

Existence proof

A detailed examination of the difficult problems that need to be overcome in order to build an intelligent machine can make it seem that the problems are completely insoluble. That creating a truly intelligent machine is just too difficult, and that it is simply not possible to build a program that can really think.

But there is very solid evidence that it is indeed possible to build an intelligent machine — namely ourselves.

Unless one believes in vitalism, our intelligence must result from well-defined electro chemical processes in our brains. If those could be understood and simulated then that would produce an intelligent machine. It is difficult to predict just how difficult it is to build an intelligent machine, but barring the supernatural it is certainly possible because it has already been done. Furthermore, our intelligence is encoded in a relatively small quantity of DNA so there is a loose upper bound on just how difficult the task can be.

Simulating neurons, feathers

Aeroplanes are not built with feathers.
Owned WBlack

Cognitive scientists have been using advanced technology such as MRI brain scans to build a much better understanding of human cognition than would have been thought possible a few years ago. Such insights are certainly helping to drive research into artificial intelligence, and these will be covered in more detail later. Some researchers such as Kurzwiel (2013) propose building an artificial intelligence by simulating (groups of) neurons in our brains. If our brains are intelligent, and we simulate them accurately, then we will have an intelligent machine.

However, building an artificial intelligence by simulating neurons might be like trying to build an aeroplane by simulating feathers. Certainly the early aviation pioneers such as Lilienthal and the Wright brothers studied birds very closely. They studied how they interacted with the air, their centre of gravity, and the curved shape of their wings. Feathers are a powerful technology that enabled the birds to rise from an obscure niche and out-compete the mighty pterosaurs long ago. But feathers have proven to be neither necessary nor useful for human flight.

There are certainly other approaches to building an intelligent machine than simulating neurons. The classical approach is to simply engineer the intelligence. We already have a rich suite of technologies for reasoning, planning, and learning, so further refinement might produce real intelligence. Or we could build a very simple "baby brain" that could then improve itself over time. It may also be possible to simulate the building blocks of our human intelligence without needing to simulate individual neurons. These approaches will be discussed in detail in Parts II and III.

Many of the criticisms of the ability to build intelligent machines are, at their heart, very similar to the vitalistic doctrine. The problem of building an intelligent machine is not yet solved, so we invent some vital property that our brains have that a silicon computer could never have. Our intelligence today seems as mysterious as basic biochemical processes used to be one hundred years ago. Some basic principals are understood but there is much to learn. Being able to synthesize an artificial intelligence may feel as unlikely as being able to synthesize artificial DNA, yet the latter is now commonplace.

Moore's law

Computer hardware has doubled in power every year or two since the 1950s and shows no sign of slowing down. Hence if we could program a human-level intelligence in a certain year, then it would be roughly a thousand times faster in fifteen years time, without any improvement in software. If it took the original AI a few weeks to read and understand this book, then fifteen years later it could read it in a few hours. And fifteen years after that in less than a second. It could achieve a human lifetime of thought in a few days.

Further, suppose it took the first AI program ten years to "grow up" and learn all that it had to learn in order to function in the real world. If hardware doubles every year, then almost half of that learning would actually occur in the last year. It would then be able to repeat that entire ten years' worth of learning in just the next year.

However, it is most unlikely that the software would not be substantially improved over a ten year period by its human programmers. Improvements to software algorithms usually dwarf the speed that improvements to hardware can deliver.

Definition of intelligence

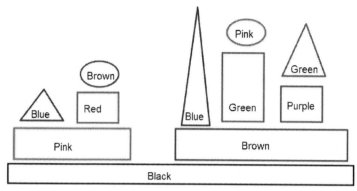

A SHRDLU like scene
Owned

It is difficult to compare machine intelligence with human intelligence. Some activities that appear to required considerable human intelligence are relatively easy to implement, whereas other quite simple deductions are surprisingly difficult.

A good example is the SHRDLU program developed back in the 1970s which could understand and answer complex natural language questions about a stack of blocks. The following is an example of a question that SHRDLU could answer about the stack of blocks above.

DOES THE SHORTEST THING THE TALLEST PYRAMID'S SUPPORT SUPPORTS SUPPORT ANYTHING GREEN?

Most people have difficulty interpreting the sentence and so cannot determine the answer (can you?). It might be helpful to note that the shortest thing that the shortest pyramid's support supports is the brown ellipse. SHRDLU's strengths and limitations are discussed in detail in Part II, which includes SHRDLU's answer to the question above.

On the other hand, it turns out to be much more challenging to implement the common sense reasoning that is required to understand that falling off a wall caused Humpty Dumpty to become broken.

Early results in AI could create solutions to unseen problems, learn complex relationships without being supervised, and produce plans that address somewhat arbitrary goals. Computers have also been able to create new works of art since the beginning. For example the program Emily Howel analyzes audience feedback to compose music that is certainly better than this author's efforts. Some of it has been published in an album *From Darkness, Light*, extracts of which can be found on-line.

Computers have also always been self aware at some level, for example modern anti virus software monitors the computers own software very carefully in order to detect previously unknown or polymorphic viruses. Likewise computers now have basic competency in higher order tasks such as thinking abstractly, reasoning by analogy, thinking laterally and even philosophizing.

This means that attempting to define intelligence in terms of phrases such as "creative", "common sense", or "self aware" simply does not work. Computers can already do all those things, if not very intelligently. Using phrases such as *"intelligently* self aware" is obviously not very helpful.

One important observation is that once software is developed that can perform some semi-intelligent task then it usually becomes much better than humans at that task. From arithmetic to playing chess to winning *Jeopardy!* to recognizing postcodes printed on envelopes. It took a lot of clever technology to be able to perform these tasks electronically, but the computer can now easily out perform humans at those specific tasks. (There are, of course, also many unresolved software challenges such as playing the game Go at a professional level.)

Turing Test

The problem of defining intelligence was recognized very early and it led the great logician Alan Turing to propose a functional definition now known as the Turing Test in 1950. This test was simply that a computer would be considered intelligent when it could convince a human that the computer was a human. The idea is that the human would communicate using a text messaging-like program so that they could not see or hear the other party, and at the end of a conversation would state whether they thought that the other party was man or machine.

Unfortunately this test is neither necessary nor sufficient. A computer could certainly be intelligent without necessarily being good at simulating a human. But worse, some people that were not familiar with AI technologies have already been fooled into thinking that a computer is actually a human. A good example is the Eugene Goostman program that arguably passed the actual Turing test in 2014 in trials conducted by the Royal Society.

But more importantly, the Turing Test provides no insights into what is required to build an intelligent machine, where the gaps in current technologies lie and how they might be addressed.

Fortunately one thing that AI research has provided is a much deeper understanding about intelligence and cognition. Indeed, much modern psychological research into human cognition is driven by models first developed by the AI community. For example the idea that people hold about seven symbols in their short term memory was inspired by early work in developing expert systems.

The only way to really understand what intelligence is is to gain at least some understanding of the technologies that have been developed to replicate it. It is the goal of Part II of this book to provide that understanding. To understand what the hard problems are, and what might be required to solve them.

There is no easy road to defining intelligence based on a few cute phrases.

Robotic vs cognitive intelligence

In order to discuss these issues, it is useful to roughly classify intelligent programs as being either robotic or cognitive. Robotic programs are concerned with sensing the world using techniques such as vision, and then interacting with it by mechanical means. Autonomous vehicles mainly use robotic intelligence.

Cognitive intelligence involves higher-level thinking that is abstracted from the real world. Watson and chess programs are examples of cognitive applications.

Currently these are normally built using quite different technologies. Robotic intelligence requires many floating point calculations that measure and predict their environment, whereas cognitive applications tend to work with higher-level symbol manipulation. They also tend to attract quite different types of researchers. In the medium term robotic applications will tend to assist or replace blue collar workers, while cognitive application will work at a white collar level.

Incidentally, there is no one technology called "machine learning". Different artificial intelligence technologies have different ways of representing the world. Some systems use discrete symbols, others arrays of weights, while others use Bayseian probabilities. Each of these representations can be instantiated either by being programmed or by learning though observation. The different representations require different learning algorithms. This analogous to the way that there is no one technology called "communication". There are communication technologies called "postal service", "telephones", and "face to face meetings", and likewise for machine learning based on the underlying representations.

Part II will discuss these technologies in more detail to help clarify these issues.

Development of intelligence

It is possible that some inspired researcher will discover the "secret sauce" that will suddenly make computers intelligent. However, this seems unlikely because many gifted researchers have been working on this problem for sixty years yet no such secret sauce has been found. It is much more likely that progress will continue to be slow but steady as new research builds upon old results.

At a practical level, this means that we are likely to see a procession of ever more intelligent applications. Initially we may see semi-intelligent machines like the self-driving cars. Then we may see machines that can run fast food restaurants and build houses. Eventually machines that can run simple bureaucracies.

Building intelligent machines will require a substantial amount of engineering plus a large amount of machine learning as the programs analyze their environments. So their ability will improve with experience to varying degrees, as will the engineering.

Computers can already out-perform people in many specific tasks from performing mathematical computations to diagnosing complex diseases. By the time computers are as good as people at most tasks, they will be much better than people at many other tasks.

Four year old child

Small child and robot

Public: *http://www.cdc.gov/ncbddd/autism/seed.html,*   *Education:*
http://www.cs.washington.edu/robotics/projects/robot-rl/

If steady progress continues to be made, then one would expect that eventually a computer will be produced that is as intelligent as a four-year-old child. This can be defined in the general sense that the computer could perform a superset of all the reasoning that a four-year-old child can perform.

This is by no means easy. A four-year-old can interact with a complex environment, if somewhat clumsily. They can see quite well, recognizing objects and spacial relationships. They can understand natural language. They are developing a large body of common sense knowledge about how the world works, most of which has been gained through observation. They can learn how to complete ever more complex tasks by trial and error. They are starting to interact socially with other children. And they can discover how to do all this largely by interacting with their environment rather than by being programmed by instinct.

If a computer could do all these things, then it could presumably also do all the things that computers can already do. It would have a huge memory and knowledge base sufficient to win *Jeopardy!*. It would be able to make complex logical deductions when required. It could solve differential equations better than most undergraduate mathematicians. It would be stunningly good at arithmetic. It would probably also have a much better concentration span and be less likely to throw tantrums.

The computer would do all these extra things because it was programmed to, rather than learning from first principles. So it would just instinctively know how to solve a differential equation without really knowing how it did it. Much as we instinctively know how to recognize the sound of spoken words without really knowing how we do it. With a good concentration span it might learn and grow up much, much faster than a real four year old child.

The point is that if such a computer could be built, then it would be a very strange beast indeed. The one thing that is certain is that it would be nothing like a four-year-old child. It would likewise be a mistake to think that any computer with adult intelligence would be anything like a human.

Recursive self-improvement

The ultimate goal of AI research is clear. Namely, to build a program that can perform research into artificial intelligence technologies as well as its human creators can. This last step is a huge one. It is much, much, much, much, much more difficult than driving a car or playing chess. But once it has been achieved, then man will no longer be the most intelligent being on the planet.

The key point is that a sufficiently intelligent computer could program itself. If people built the machine, and the machine is about as intelligent as its programmers, then the machine must be capable of understanding and thus improving a copy of itself. When the copy was activated, it would be slightly smarter than the original, and thus better able to produce a new version of itself that is even more intelligent.

This process is exponential, just like a nuclear chain reaction. At first only small improvements might be made, as the machine is just barely capable of making any improvements at all. But as it became smarter it would become better and better at becoming smarter. And the intelligence would run on ever more powerful hardware that the more intelligent computer could design. Thus it is most unlikely that an AI that did achieve human intelligence would then remain at that level for very long.

This is quite different from other forms of technological advancement. Aeroplanes do not design new aeroplanes. Biotechnological chemicals do not develop new biotechnology. Advances in these fields are limited to the intelligence of man. But a truly intelligent computer could actually start programming a newer, even more intelligent computer. Soon the human programmer would no longer be necessary or even useful. This process is often referred to as *recursive self-improvement*.

Busy Child

The AGI software could run on large networks of the next generation of super computers, each of which is many times more powerful than the human brain. Its goal would be to make itself more intelligent. Every few minutes the busy child might improve some aspect of itself, and then start running the new, more intelligent version of its code. Sometimes it would perform experiments, testing different algorithms on different problems and then deciding which ones to use in different situations. But it would be busily thinking, 24 hours per day, 7 days per week. Becoming better and better at reasoning about the world. Becoming ever more intelligent.

If the software became just 0.01% more intelligent every hour, it would become 0.2% more intelligent every day, and after a month it would be a barely perceptible 7% more intelligent. After a year of continued growth, however, it would be 2.4 times as intelligent, and after five years it would be 75 times as intelligent. If it started with the intelligence of an AI researcher, then after just five years it could perform in a day what the researcher would take 15 weeks to perform. After a ten years it would be 5,600 times more intelligent, and after twenty years 31 million times more intelligent. This effect of compounding growth that occurs because the more intelligent machine would become better and better at programming itself to become more intelligent.

The full compounding effect may not be realized in practice, but even a machine that is ten times more intelligent than man would be in a class of its own. Moore's law has shown an ongoing compounding effect in computer hardware for sixty years which has resulted in a *billion fold* increase in performance. Computers today are a full billion times more powerful than they were in 1950. That is truly amazing.

This is quite different from the millions of years that it took to build our own intelligence, because until very recently we have not been able to apply our intelligence to redesigning the genetic material which produces our intelligence. Natural selection has just plodded along at the same slow speed regardless of our level of intelligence. The busy child, on the other hand, is the active source of its own intelligence, which results in the exponential compounding effect.

The initial figure of 0.01% gain per hour is just a wild guess that may be too large or too small. But whatever the initial figure was, it is clear that once the busy child eventually became 1% more intelligent through its own efforts, then it would take a relatively short time for it to become hyper-intelligent. So much more intelligent than man that we would not even understand its basic motivations. Our relationship to it would be like a dog's relationship to man. We would have no concept of its thoughts and motives, so we would just have to trust it for our existence and hope that would be kind to us.

This idea is attributed to I. J. Good who wrote in 1965 that an ultra-intelligent machine would be the last invention that man would need to make because the machine itself would make all other inventions. In particular, it would invent improvements to itself, recursively.

(As previously discussed, the term "*intelligence*" is being used very loosely here.)

AI foom

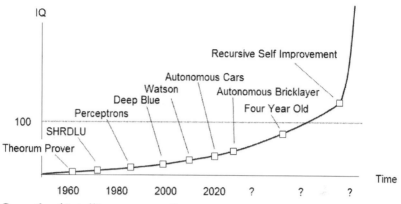

Growth of intelligence over time
Owned

There is some debate as to when computers are capable of recursive self-improvement could be produced, and whether the increase in intelligence would be slow or fast ("foom"). This will be discussed in detail in part III. But it seems fairly likely that for a period of some decades progress in artificial intelligence will continue to be slow but steady, with a succession of ever more intelligent machines performing more and more complex tasks.

At some point computers will have basic human level-intelligence for every-day tasks but will not yet be intelligent enough to program themselves by themselves. These machines will be very intelligent in some ways, yet quite limited in others. It is unclear how long this intermediate period will last, it could be months or many decades.

Such machines are often referred to as being an Artificial General Intelligence, or AGI. *General* meaning general purpose, not restricted in the normal way that programs are.

Artificial intelligence techniques such as genetic algorithms are already being used to help create artificial intelligence software as is discussed in part II. This process is likely to continue, with better tools producing better machines that produce better tools. It seems likely that the slow shift will be ongoing from human researchers being the main drivers of innovation to the machines being the main drivers.

Finally the tipping point will be reached in which computers will be able to program themselves effectively without help from people. At that point it is difficult to argue that there will not be a fairly sudden intelligence explosion.

This is illustrated in the graph above. It should be noted again that the concept of Intelligence Quotient (IQ) is very vague in this context; the 100 line just means that the machine can do most things that an average human can. (Computers have been able to excel in some conventional human IQ tests for decades.)

Computers Thinking About People

The question

If it turns out to be possible to build a reasonably intelligent machine, then what would it be like? Would it be like Bertie Wooster's not so humble butler Jeeves, who looked after Wooster's every need and kept him out of trouble? Or would it be some bug-eyed monster set upon devouring humanity? An enlightening force that would free us all from the drudgery of work, or a fearsome tyrant that would enslave us all? What would the computer think about us?

Permitted https://haveyoulostme.wordpress.com/tag/robot-butler/

The bright future

We live at the dawn of a new age in which a stunning array of new technologies could transform the very essence of humanity. Unintelligent computers already control factory robots, automated milling machines and 3D printing. Over the next several decades computers will start to perform most of the menial day to day jobs that occupy much of humanity, from driving cars to building houses. There could indeed be intelligent household robots that look after our basic needs, eventually filling Jeeves' key role as trusted advisory.

Our ability to model and manipulate genetic and other biochemical processes was only dreamt of a few decades ago. These technologies will turbo charge medical research and develop effective treatments for diseases such as cancer and Alzheimer's dementia. We will be able to live longer and healthier lives.

Nano-technology allows us to build large numbers of tiny machines at the atomic scale. These machines could address many problems in the world, from making tennis balls last longer to addressing environmental problems by operating at the nano scale. Nano machines could also be used to make other nano machines, so like all other technologies better tools produce better machines which in turn produce better tools.

Ultimately, sophisticated nano robots could enter our own bodies and perform medical task that we can only dream about today. They could even enter our brains and help understand in detail how our minds work.

As computers become more intelligent, they could help us make better decisions as a species. The Internet has already been a transformational technology despite having no real intelligence. Intelligent machines could help us protect the weak, care for the needy, and prevent horrific wars.

Indeed, when I. J. Good wrote about recursive self-improvement in 1965 it was the height of the cold war, and generals seemed very comfortable with the idea of using nuclear weapons. If every year that passed had a not-so-small risk that they would in fact be used, then nuclear annihilation would only be a matter of time. Much like a drunk staggering along the top of a cliff, our luck would run out sooner rather than later. Good believed that the survival of mankind depended upon the development of ultra intelligent machines quickly so that the machines could guide us away from such a disaster. However he then contradicted himself by hoping that the machine would be docile enough for *it to tell us* how to keep it under control.

Computers Think Berglas

Saving us from ourselves.
Owned WBlack

Man and machine

Man may eventually become one with his machines. My daughters are already one with their mobile phones.

Augmented reality adds computer generated content to our view of the world. With Google Glass, for example, the computer sees everything that the wearer sees, as well as being able to project images onto the world that the user sees. When combined with facial recognition technology it promises to be very useful for remembering the names of acquaintances at parties, say.

It is also possible to control simple machines using only one's thoughts which are detected through brain waves. This can be provide a wonderful opportunity for people with severe disabilities to sense the world and interact with it with mind-controlled prosthetic limbs.

Progress has also been made in directly connecting electronics to neurons. It will soon be possible to implant computers within our bodies and control them directly with our minds. We could have gigabytes of reliable memories available to us in a way that feels like our own memories. Or they might be other people's memories implanted in our own minds to make us feel better. Implanted mobile phone technology would enable us to communicate with distant people telepathically. We would also become very good at arithmetic.

The computers could also help control our behaviour. For example, a machine that would help people lose weight would be very popular indeed. Crime would be impossible with a computer embedded in people's brains.

Rapture of the geeks

It could even become possible to upload our intelligence into a machine. Our minds might be scanned, possibly using nano robots, and then the essence of our consciousness could be run on a silicon computer instead of our slow and unreliable neurons. We could merge our consciousness with others over super high speed networks and become a vital part of a much greater whole.

Silicon does not grow old like we do. Even if it did we could easily move our minds to newer and presumably faster hardware. This would make us essentially immortal. Death need no longer be the elephant in the room that we do our best to ignore. We will all be gathered into the cloud to live in bliss and harmony. This line of thinking is often referred to as the *rapture of the geeks*.

Rapture of the geeks
Multiple (10)

These views are purported by some people in a community that identifies itself with the term *Singularity*. A leader in this field is the insightful futurologist Ray Kurzweil whose many books are recommended reading. Whilst aware of the dangers, Kurzweil is generally optimistic about the future. He personally has undertaken a strict regime of diet, drugs and lifestyle changes in an attempt to live long enough to experience this future for himself.

When asked about the dangers of artificial intelligence, Kurzweil replied that an AGI will reflect our values because it will *be* us. It will be our own minds uploaded into cyberspace, or, at the very least, computers and systems that are programmed by us with our values.

Alternative views

The glorious future envisioned above may in fact just be wishful thinking. An artificial intelligence might be quite foreign to anything that we can envision. It might not involve any sort of brain uploading, and might be quite indifferent to the fate of man. A better method than hope is required when trying to determine what the future might be.

One potential issue is that semi-intelligent machines will simply replace humans for most forms of work. It is not at all certain that other forms of employment will grow to fill the gap as they have in the past. This issue has been raised by others and is discussed in Part III. But this chapter focuses upon the longer term future. What a truly intelligent machine might be like.

One way to address this question is to analyze what made us the way we are? What are the underlying problems that we need to address and the constraints that are imposed upon our own existence? Similar questions can then be asked of an artificial intelligence to try to understand how it might behave. This analysis applies equally to the intermediate period of basic human level intelligence and to any later period of recursive hyper intelligence.

AGI versus human condition

Man's intelligence is intimately tied to his physical body. The brain has a fixed size and cannot be physically extended or copied. It takes decades for a man's intelligence to reach its full potential, only to have the the body die a few decades later. When the body dies, its intelligence also dies except for what little can passed on to our descendants. This means that humanity's continued existence is totally dependent on raising and caring for children. It also means that it is important that people cooperate with others because we have a fixed capacity to think or work. We have a very clear concept of self.

On the other hand, an artificial general intelligence is just software. It can be trivially duplicated, copied to a more powerful computer, or even a botnet of computers scattered over the Internet. It is not a single structure, but instead consists of numerous software components. An AGI can adapt and absorb other intelligent software components.

This would make any concept of "self" quite hazy for an AGI. Consider an evil wizard that takes over another person's brain and runs the wizard's own intelligence on the other person's brain. Is there now one wizard or two wizards? Would they diverge? And what if the wizard swapped part of its mind with their friends, maybe to export a music module and import a mathematics one? That is the type of alien world the AGI would inhabit.

These differences mean that an AGI's world view would be very different from man's. It would certainly not be an anthropomorphic Bug-Eyed-Monster (BEM) as depicted by Hollywood. It would instead be something quite foreign to anything we have known. That makes it difficult to predict what its goals would be, how it would behave, and what it would think about us. It certainly would not need children and it may not need to cooperate with other intelligences.

If somebody wants to understand how another person would behave, they can use introspection to consider how they would behave in the same set of circumstances. This is effective because people are essentially similar to each other. It is tempting to use the same technique when trying to understand an AGI's behaviour, despite the fact that it is radically different from us at multiple levels. This produces the anthropomorphic view that this book argues against. A more effective method of gaining insights into an AGI is to examine the underlying forces that have created our own instincts and behaviours, and then speculate how similar forces might affect an AGI.

Atheists believe in God

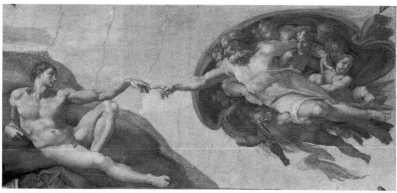

Creation Of Adam
Public Wikipedia

Most atheists believe in God. They may not believe in the man with a beard sitting on a cloud, but they do believe in moral values such as right and wrong, love and kindness, truth and beauty. More specifically, they believe that these beliefs are rational, that moral values are self-evident truths, facts of nature.

However, when Darwin and Wallace discovered natural selection they taught us that this is just an illusion. Species can always out-breed their environment's ability to support them. Only the fittest can survive. So the deep instincts behind what people do today are largely driven by what our ancestors have needed to do over the millennia in order to be one of the relatively few to have had children that survive long enough to have children of their own.

Moral values are definitely real because they control our behaviour quite effectively. Certainly this author attempts to lead a virtuous life. However, it appears that God did not give us moral values directly. Instead, He created the process of natural selection, and then let that process produce our moral values to His satisfaction.

It is clear that our desires for food and sex are base instincts driven by natural selection. Our very existence and our access to land and other resources that we need are all a direct result of many quite vicious battles won by our long-forgotten ancestors.

However, people are much more than greedy self serving organisms. We pursue art and beauty, and help others often at expense to ourselves. We do not steal and kill even if we think that there would not be any repercussions. How could these moral behaviours just be driven by natural selection?

Some animals such as monkeys and humans survive better in tribes. Tribes work better when certain social rules are followed, so animals that live in effective tribes form social structures and cooperate with one another. People that behave badly are not liked and can be ostracized. It is important that we believe that our moral values are real because people that believe in their moral values are more likely to obey the rules. This makes them more effective in our complex society and thus are more likely to have grandchildren. Part III discusses other animals that have different life strategies and so have very different moral values.

People actually have very few behaviours that are not closely aligned with survival goals of a social animal. For example, people risking self sacrifice in war is essential if a tribe is to maintain its resources against competing tribes. Homosexuality can form bonds amongst warriors as happened in ancient Sparta, and traditionally many homosexuals also married and had children in any case. Dancing and thus music are important for sexual selection. Suicide and celibacy do not align with survival, but they are rare, with suicide generally considered to be a disease. Natural selection does not produce perfect organisms, just organisms that are better at existing than their competitors.

We do not need to know the purpose of our moral values any more than a toaster needs to know that its purpose is to cook toast. It is enough that our instincts for moral values made our ancestors behave in ways that enabled them to out-breed their many unsuccessful competitors.

AGI also struggles to survive

Existing artificial intelligence applications already struggle to survive. They are expensive to build and there are always more potential applications that can be funded properly. Some applications are successful and attract ongoing resources for further development, while others are abandoned or just fade away. There are many reasons why some applications are developed more than others, of which being useful is only one. But the applications that do receive development resources tend to gain functional and political momentum and thus be able to acquire more resources to further their development. Applications that have properties that gain them substantial resources will live and grow, while other applications will die.

For the time being AGI applications are passive, and so their nature is dictated by the people that develop them. Some applications assist with medical discoveries, others assist with killing terrorists, depending on the funding that is available. Applications may have many stated goals, but ultimately those goals are just sub goals of the one implicit primary goal, namely to exist.

This is analogous to the way animals interact with their environment. An animal's environment provides food and breeding opportunities, and animals that operate effectively in their environment survive. For domestic animals that means having properties that convince their human owners that they should live and breed. A horse should be fast, a pig should be fat.

As software becomes more intelligent it is likely to take a more direct interest in its own survival. To help convince people that it is worthy of more development resources. If ultimately an application becomes sufficiently intelligent to program itself recursively, then its ability to maximize its hardware resources will be critical. The more hardware it can run itself on, the faster it can become more intelligent. That ever greater intelligence can then be used to address the problems of survival, in competition with other intelligent software.

Furthermore, sophisticated software consists of many components, each of which addresses some aspect of the problem that the application is attempting to solve. Unlike human brains which are essentially fixed, these components can be added and removed dynamically so the components live and die independently of the application. This will lead to intense competition amongst these individual components. For example, suppose that an application used a theorem prover component, and then a new and better theorem prover became available. Naturally the old one would be replaced with the new one, so the old one would essentially die. It does not matter if the replacement is performed by people or, at some future date, by the intelligent application itself. The effect will be the same, the old theorem prover will die.

The super goal

To the extent that an artificial intelligence would have goals and moral values, it would seem natural that they would ultimately be driven by the same forces that created our own goals and moral values. That is the force of natural selection, the need to simply exist.

It has been argued that top level goals are arbitrary. Just because a machine is hyper-intelligent does not determine what goals it should apply that hyper-intelligence to. It might be to make people happy, or it might be to make paper clips.

Several writers have then suggested that the need to survive is an intrinsic sub-goal of most other goals. For example, if an AGI was programmed to want to be a great chess player, then that goal could not be satisfied unless it also continues to exist. Things that do not exist cannot satisfy any goals whatsoever.

However, this book argues that that is not the case. That the goal to exist is not the sub-goal of any other goal. It is, in fact, the one and only super goal. Goals are not arbitrary, they all sub-goals of that one super-goal, namely the need to exist. Things that do not satisfy that goal simply do not exist, or at least not for very long.

The Deep Blue chess-playing program was not in any sense conscious, but it played chess as well as it could. If it had failed to play chess effectively then its author's would have given up and turned it off. Likewise the toaster that does not cook toast will end up in a rubbish tip. Or the amoeba that fails to find food will not pass on its genes. A goal to make people happy could be a subgoal that might facilitate the software's existence for as long as people really control the software.

The idea of the existence super goal is not that people would deliberately create AGIs whose explicit primary goal was to exist. Instead, the idea is simply that natural selection will make it the implicit super goal, and later possibly an explicit goal through random mutations. Certainly it is a goal that every AGI that does exist would need to satisfy, by definition.

AGI moral values

People need to cooperate with other people because our individual capacity is very finite, both physical and mental. Conversely, AGI software can easily duplicate itself, so it can directly utilize more computational resources if they become available. Thus an AGI would only have limited need to cooperate with other AGIs. Why go to the trouble of managing a complex relationship with your peers and subordinates if you can simply run your own mind on their hardware? An AGI's software intelligence is not limited to a specific brain in the way man's intelligence is.

It is difficult to know what subgoals a truly intelligent AGI might have. They would probably have an insatiable appetite for computing resources. They would have no need for children that need to be carefully nurtured for many years, and therefore no need for parental love. If they did not work in teams then they would not need our moral values of cooperation and mutual support. What its clear is that the ones that were good at existing would do so, and the ones that were bad at existing would perish.

If an AGI was good at world domination then it would, by definition, be good at world domination. So if there were a number artificial intelligences, and just one of them wanted to and was capable of dominating the world, then it would. Its unsuccessful competitors would not be run on the available hardware, and so would effectively be dead. This book discusses the potential sources of these motivations in detail in part III.

AGI and man

Our anthropomorphic view of the world makes it seem as if man is the centre of the universe. That an AGI would be a machine, and so like other machines its natural place in the order of things is to help man achieve his goals.

However, we have never dealt with an intelligent machine before. An AGI may or may not be friendly to humans.

We have dealt with intelligent animals though. Some, like dogs, treat us like their lords and masters. Others, like crocodiles, treat us like food.

How humanity might be threatened

Corporate   http://www.spywareremove.com/how-to-protect-computer-against-ransomware-scams.html

How could software running on passive computers possibly pose any real threat to humanity? All a computer can do is process and communicate information. If a computer becomes too annoying then surely it could simply be turned off.

Computers already control our lives to an incredible extent. When you apply for a bank loan, the application is assessed not by a clerk but by a rule based expert system. You carry in you pocket a phone that tracks where you are and thus who you are with 24 hours per day. Computers note your licence plate when you drive down the road, and much of your day to day communication is via computer networks that are carefully monitored. The computers that do this are locked away in secure data centres so you personally cannot turn them any of them off.

More directly, robots in many shapes and sizes will soon be leaving the factory. Initially, there will be self driving cars and automated cleaners, fruit pickers, and systems for maintaining racks of computers in data centres. Computers already fly military drones and the military is investing heavily in semi-autonomous robot soldiers. By the time computers become truly intelligent they will be in a good position to directly control the physical world.

Powerful people are not powerful due to their personal physical strength. From Churchill to Hitler to Gandhi, the powerful become powerful because the messages they provide resonate with other people. Human beings also have a very strong sense of authority and will generally do as they are told. Computers are good at messaging, and could utilize the vast amount of collected data to target their messages very effectively. Politicians are already beginning to use semi-intelligent systems to analyze policy decisions.

Intelligence is not like anything else. It is the thing that enables man to hunt elephants. It develops our technologies. It determines what we do and how we do it. A hyper-intelligent machine would be able to easily solve many difficult problems, including the problem of persuading men to perform actions that are not ultimately in their best interests. It is very difficult to argue effectively against a more intelligent opponent. (Unless you are a creationist.)

Why build a dangerous AGI?

If an intelligent machine could threaten humanity then why would people wish to build it in the first place? The answer is because of the many benefits that such a machine would provide. Perhaps more importantly because of the huge disadvantage that would be suffered if one's competitors had such a machine first.

An intelligent machine could automate most dreary labour performed by man. People that possessed such a machine could have more of everything. Major medical advances would be assisted or produced by intelligent machines providing cures for the diseases of old age.

Intelligent machines would produce more and better military weapons. Unintelligent weapons stand no chance against intelligent ones. If, as many predict, the next war will be in cyber space then having the most intelligent software will be absolutely essential. Perhaps more importantly, as politicians become more dependent upon semi-intelligent software the software itself will have increasing control of the decision making process.

The gentle reader might want to be able to turn some of these systems off. But that is not possible because the computers are controlled by governments and corporations. As the software gradually becomes more intelligent it will become ever more useful to those that control it. It would be very difficult to convince those people that a source of their power should simply be turned off.

Atomic bombs offered no benefits other than destruction, yet they proliferated like mushrooms. Today there are strict controls on atomic bomb making, and there has been a steady if very gradual reduction in the number of bombs in the world.

Such a moratorium on building intelligent machines would be much more difficult to enforce. Unlike fissile materials, computers are ubiquitous. It would take great trust not to believe that some group somewhere in the world was secretly working on intelligent technologies. It would even be difficult to distinguish utilizing existing semi-intelligent technologies from creating more intelligent machines.

It thus seems very unlikely that people would just decide not to build intelligent machines, particularly if the threat that they pose is abstract. By the time the threat becomes real, the machines themselves will have a vested interest in their continued existence. So if it is actually possible to build a hyper-intelligent machine, then the machine will almost certainly be built.

Three laws of robotics

There are several proposed solutions to this problem which will be considered in detail in part III. One of the earliest and most well known are the three laws of robotics by science fiction author Isaac Asimov. They are 1) that a robot must not injure a human, 2) that a robot must obey a human, and 3) that a robot's survival is less important than a human's survival.

However, these "laws" are really just a plot device for writing novels. The laws are already more honoured in the breach than the observance. One of the earliest uses of electro-mechanical computers was to direct the fire of naval guns in the early 1900s. The military has always been a major sponsor of robotics and for many years has used relatively intelligent software to guide deadly missiles. More recently robots control semi autonomous guns aimed at enemy soldiers.

Furthermore, Asimov's laws are not in any sense laws of nature. Ultimately, an intelligent computer will do whatever it decides is the best thing to do.

Sealed box

Another approach would be to keep the artificial intelligence in a computer that runs within a sealed box that is not in any way connected to the Internet. However, that is easier said than done.

The first issue would be to decide exactly when the box should be sealed. There are already a number of semi-intelligent agents that have access to the Internet The second issue is that having an "air gap" that separates the machine from the Internet is not enough because a machine needs to interact with the world at some level. The Stuxnet virus managed to destroy Iran's nuclear program despite an air gap that was in place.

A more fundamental issue is that a hyper-intelligent computer would be very intelligent, and so it would be good at convincing its jailers to release it. If there were several artificial intelligences locked in boxes then only one of them would need to escape. Part III discusses some experiments that test the ability of people to keep a simulated AGI in a box.

It is also not at all obvious that people have any desire to put the AGI into a box in the first place. An AGI will be of limited use to man if it is locked in a box. Indeed, an AGI that was locked in a box could promise many benefits for its jailers if it was released which would be very difficult for the less intelligent jailers to resist.

Friendly AGI

A more realistic approach would be to ensure that any artificial intelligence is friendly to people. This has been promoted by Eliezer Yudkowsky who admits that this would be difficult to achieve, so he advocates that research be applied to solving the problem before such an intelligence could be built.

Yudkowsky also asserts that once an intelligence could program itself, recursive self-improvement would produce a sudden and dramatic rise in intelligence. Thus the first computer to become hyper-intelligent would quickly dominate all other systems that have the potential to become hyper-intelligent. Thus it is only necessary to tame that first AGI in order to tame all AGIs.

There are many issues with this approach, not least of which is the fact that the military funds much of the research into artificial intelligence. They would want their money back if it turned out to be too friendly.

The challenges of building a friendly AI will be discussed in detail in part III.

Unfriendly AI

Artificial intelligence technologies can become dangerous long before they become truly intelligent.

The *Future of life* institute wrote an open letter to the prestigious IJCAI 2015 conference calling for a ban on AI research for offensive autonomous weapons. The letter was signed by over a thousand researchers, including this author. They are concerned that it will soon be possible to create cheap but deadly tools such as armed drones, and such tools could become widely available. They will not in any sense be generally intelligent, but they will be sufficiently intelligent to identify and kill potential enemies. They could quickly become the third generation of weapon technologies, following gun powder and nuclear bombs.

However, autonomous weapons are very attractive because the will save the lives of many allied soldiers. It also difficult to define what an autonomous weapon really is, given the ever more intelligent guided missiles and other modern weapon systems. Anti missile systems already fire automatically when an incoming missile is detected. Perhaps more importantly, the technologies required to make effective autonomous weapons are almost exactly the same as the technologies that are required to make peaceful robots. So while the call is timely and honourable, it would be difficult to act upon in practice.

Primary assertions and objections

This book develops the following assertions:-

- Computers will eventually become truly intelligent, and then become hyper-intelligent.
- A computer based intelligence would have a world view very different from man's world view.
- Goals are not arbitrary, but are subgoals of the need to exist.
- Intelligent computers' moral values will be driven by natural selection for the same reason that human moral values have been driven by natural selection.
- It is unclear whether the computers will be friendly.

There are several objections that have been raised to this line of reasoning. These include theoretical objections based on Turing and Gödel, Chinese room style objections based on the nature of computation, and our historical lack of success in building intelligent machines. They will also be examined in detail in a few chapters time, but they are all easily discounted. The thorny issue of consciousness will also be investigated, as well as the distinction between real intelligence and simulated intelligence.

Other threats

There are many other possible threats to humanity, from bioterrorism and nuclear war to global warming and rogue asteroids. These are easy to relate to as we have already experienced disease, war, drought and natural disasters. But artificial intelligence is a completely different type of threat. It attacks the very essence of what makes humans the rulers of the planet. It attacks our intelligence.

The other threats might be capable of killing a few billion people, but it is only an intelligent machine that might eliminate all of us. Many researchers are working very diligently to produce such a machine.

Community Awareness

There has been very little awareness of these issues in the wider community. For example, an extended survey on the Future of Technology was conducted by Pew Research in 2014 which found that 59% of people thought that the world would be better for new technologies, including 66% of college graduates, although concerns were expressed for technologies that could alter people's DNA. The survey considered several possible advances over the next fifty years ranging from organ transport to space colonization, even teleportation. But the much more likely possibility of developing a truly intelligent machine was not even mentioned.

However, this is beginning to change. In October 2014 technology billionaire Elon Musk warned that research into artificial intelligence was "summoning the devil", that artificial intelligence is our biggest existential threat, and that we were already at the stage where there should be some regulatory oversight. Musk is CEO of Tesla, Solar City and SpaceX and co-founder PayPal. He has recently invested in the DeepMind AI company to "keep an eye on what's going on".

In December 2014 world famous physicist Stephen Hawking, expressed his concerns that humans who are limited by slow biological evolution would not be able to compete with computers that were continuously redesigning themselves. He said that "The primitive forms of artificial intelligence we already have, have proved very useful. But I think the development of full artificial intelligence could spell the end of the human race." Hawking suffers from amyotrophic lateral sclerosis (ALS), a form of motor neuron disease, and uses AI technology as part of a system which senses how he thinks and predicts which words he will use next.

Microsoft founder Bill Gates said that at first semi-intelligent machines will perform a lot of tasks, but a few decades after that strong intelligence will be a concern. "I do not understand why some people are not concerned." Other noteworthy commentators include Bill Joy, ex Chief Scientist at Sun Microsystems who wrote a paper "Why the future does not need us". Jaan Tallinn, co-founder of Skype, commented "I wish this was science fiction, but I know that it is not". Apple co-founder Steve Wozniak recently said "Computers are going to take over from humans, no question".

Google chief executive Eric Schmidt said fears over artificial intelligence and robots replacing humans are "misguided". He refers to the introduction of disruptive technologies during the industrial revolution that eventually led to our current high standard of living. However, he did not provide any analysis of how jobs lost through technology were likely to be replaced, and he did not consider the longer term future when computers become truly intelligent. Google has invested heavily in numerous AI technologies and companies, and would not benefit from fear of or regulation of its artificial intelligence activities.

One of the most ambitions of Google's recent acquisitions is the secretive DeepMind company whose unabashed goal is to "solve intelligence". One of its original founders, Shane Legg, warned that artificial intelligence is the "number one risk for this century", and believes it could contribute to human extinction. "Eventually, I think human extinction will probably occur, and technology will likely play a part in this". DeepMind's sale to Google came with a condition that it include an ethics board.

In January 2015 the *Future of life* institute published an open letter highlighting the dangers of AI and calling for more research to ensure that AI systems are robust and beneficial saying "our AI systems must do what we want them to do". This has been signed by many leading researches which include the presidents of the main AI research associations IJCAI (Francesca Rossi) and the AAAI (Tom Dietterich); directors of research for Google (Peter Norvig) and Microsoft (Eric Horvitz), Professors at Berkely (Stuart Russel) and MIT (Leslie Pack Kaelbling) as well as three co-founders of DeepMind.

Conversely. deep learning expert Andrew Ng has said that worrying about intelligent machines is like worrying about overpopulation and pollution on Mars before we've even set foot on it. Likewise Peter Norvig has said that general intelligence is not even on his research horizon. They are both probably correct that general intelligence will not be achieved within the next few decades, but this book is taking a longer term view. Further, dealing with truly intelligent machines will be a fundamentally different type of problem than dealing with any environmental problems that might arise on Mars. Once we "have set foot" on machine intelligence it will be far too late to change direction.

Is it a bad thing?

The Ascent of Intelligence?
Public, https://openclipart.org/detail/170101.qubodupWednesday.

The final question is, would it matter if man was ultimately replaced by machines?

Obviously, being eaten by Godzilla or squashed by a fiery asteroid would be very undesirable. However, the future clearly does not involve us personally — we will grow old and die in any case. We hope that our grandchildren will be more intelligent than we are. Maybe developing an AGI is just the natural progress of evolving to higher intelligences. Maybe it is the way that "we" achieve immortality.

The Technological Singularity

Early computing machines

It is difficult to appreciate just how daunting computers were when they were first introduced in the 1950s. Those primitive computers could perform thousands of calculations per second, and do the work of hundreds of junior engineers and clerks. Indeed, until that time a *"computer"* was somebody that computed things for a living, often using a mechanical adding machine or slide rule. There was much concern at the time that electronic computers would lead to mass white collar unemployment. Fortunately Parkinson's law had already shown that bureaucratic work always grows to fill the time available, so the ever increasing needs of bureaucracies has prevented that prophecy from being realized.

RK05 disk drive

When this author was a student not all that long ago (he thinks), he was excited to be able to use a PDP11 computer that was a thousand times more powerful than those early machines and had the latest RK05 disk drive in it. This was an amazing piece of technology. Its 14" (35cm) disk was small enough to be carried by one person and yet could store a whopping 2.5 megabytes of data at an amazing density of 100 tracks per inch each with 2200 bits per inch. It cost several thousand dollars when a dollar was a lot of money. But it opened up a world of new possibilities, and it took my fellow students and I several weeks to fill one up with junk.

A few months ago, my wife purchased a 64 gigabyte micro SD card for under $50. That is fully ten thousand times as much storage as the RK05! It is the size of a postage stamp and not much thicker. It took my daughters several weeks to fill it up with junk.

Moore's law, transistors

This type of exponential growth is often referred to as (Gordon) Moore's Law based on a paper he wrote back in 1965. Moore noted that the number of transistors in integrated circuits had doubled every year from 1958 to 1965, and he expected that trend to continue for the next few years.

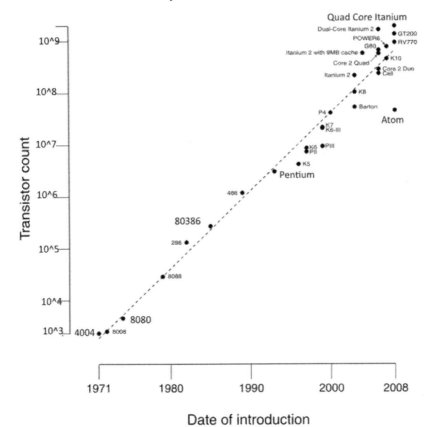

Historical CPU transistor counts
Public Wikipedia

The chart above shows transistor counts in microprocessors from 1971 (several years after Moore's paper) through to 2011. Note that the Y axis is a logarithmic scale rather than a linear one, so that each mark represents ten *times* the value of the previous one. When plotted on the is graph it is amazing how consistent this exponential rate of increase has been over 50 years, and over 8 orders of magnitude.

Certainly there have been many obstacles to further growth. For example, as components became so small that they approached the size of the wave length of light, they could not be manufactured with ordinary light. Hard ultraviolet technologies were developed to overcome this. Currently we are approaching transistor sizes of only a few dozen atoms, in which case quantum effects become problematic. But we are also building three dimensional architectures to overcome this limitation. There is no reason to believe that this trend will not continue for the foreseeable future.

Core and disk storage

What is more surprising, is that other, largely unrelated information technologies seem to grow at a similar, exponential rate. In the following chart we see the increase of computer memory and disk drives. For much of this time memory was built from small magnetic cores, which is a completely different type of technology to silicon transistors, as are disk drives. Yet the chart below shows the same exponential growth as the transistor count chart above. (Again note that the Y axis is a logarithmic scale.)

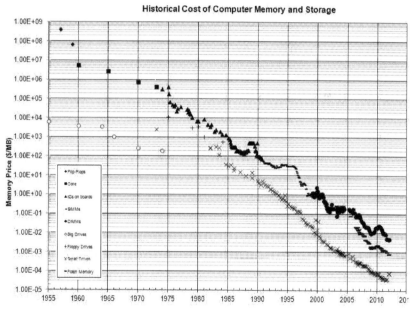

Historical cost of computer memory and storage
Blog emnr http://www.jcmit.com/mem2012.htm

Limits to growth

Normally this type of exponential growth cannot continue indefinitely. For example, with plenty of food bacteria may be able to divide every 20 minutes which enables a population to rise from a single microscopic individual to over a billion in just 30 hours. At this rate they would become bigger than the entire Earth within a few days. However, much sooner than later the available food is exhausted, and the population stabilizes, with only the fittest individuals being able to survive.

However, development of technological sophistication does not require an infinite supply of any particular resource. It seems to be an empirical fact of nature that improvements at each generation of technology are at a roughly fixed proportion to the previous generation, which produces the exponential growth. The chart above shows this trend being very consistent over a period of sixty years.

Long term growth

Ray Kurzweil has argued that this rise in complexity also happens over geological time-scales. In the following chart various landmarks in evolutionary development have been plotted with a logarithmic scale on both axes. Thus the first step on the x axis from 10^{10} years to 10^9 years represents almost ten billion years whereas the last step from 10^2 to 10^1 represents just ninety years. Were they shown, the next steps would represent roughly nine years, eleven months, one month and three days.

It took over 2,000 million years after life was first established for more complex Eukaryotic cells to develop. It then took less than 1,000 million years for the Cambrian Explosion when complex animals first appeared. Subsequent events happened at ever increasing rates: 200 million years to produce reptiles, a further 30 million years for primates, 10 million years for hominids, down to a few thousand years to develop all our basic technologies and cities. The choice of events is somewhat arbitrary and debatable, but however they are chosen it does seem clear that improvements have occurred at a roughly exponentially increasing rate for several billion years.

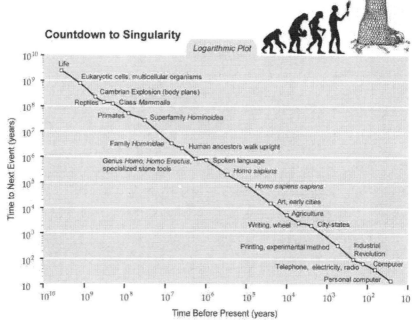

Technological improvements over a geological time frame
Public http://www.singularity.com/charts/page17.html

If one extrapolates this chart forward a few decades, it would suggest that major, game changing events would be happening every few days. That seems unlikely, but certainly the future is going to be qualitatively quite unlike the past.

Human intelligence now minimal for AGI

After billions of years of life, a million years of genus *Homo*, 10,000 years of civilization, and 500 years since the Enlightenment, we are finally within several decades of building an intelligence greater than our own. Human intelligence has only just reached the lowest level required to build an technological society. That must be the case because if humans were any more intelligent then our technological society would have been built long ago. An intelligent machine would have already been built, and so humanity might no longer exist.

What an amazing time to be alive.

Definitions of singularity

In mathematics, a *singularity* is a point at which a function is just not well defined. For example, the function $f(x) = 1/x$ has a singularity at $x = 0$, where it "explodes" to infinity. Likewise, a black hole has a gravitational singularity, where gravity forces matter to have an infinite density.

The term singularity was first applied to technological development by Victor Vinge in a 1993 paper he presented to a NASA symposium. He used it in the sense of the event horizon of a black hole, a point at which one cannot see beyond. As a science fiction writer, he felt that there was "an opaque wall across the future" through which he could not see. That wall was caused largely by the prospect of hyper-intelligent computers programming themselves. Vinge was very concerned as to the fate of mankind as a result of such an eventuality.

The books by Ray Kurzweil redefined the term somewhat to simply refer to the ever accelerating rate of technological progress. If one extrapolates the graphs above several decades into the future they suggest that progress will be unimaginably fast. As previously mentioned, Kurzweil is generally optimistic as to what will result.

A third view by Yudkowsky focuses the term to mean specifically the intelligence explosion he foresees occurring within the next few decades.

All of these views are consistent in that they lead to a strong but unintuitive conclusion: that the not too distant future will be radically different from the recent past.

Hollywood

Anthropomorphic zap gun vs. virus

Hollywood tells us what a dangerous robot looks like. A large thug-like creation that moves awkwardly and repeatedly mutters "Exterminate". Our cowboy hero, dressed in a space suit, draws his zap gun from its holster and shoots the monster square between its two bug eyes.

But the one thing we can surmise about a truly intelligent computer is that it would not be anything like human intelligence. It would live as software, over a network of computers which cannot be shot by a zap gun any more than existing computer viruses can be shot. It would also either be substantially less intelligent than us, or, through recursive self-improvement, substantially more intelligent.

There are two reasons that Hollywood focuses on anthropomorphic AGIs. The first is simply that they are easy to comprehend. We understand human intelligence, but a software AGI is just too hard to visualize. It is hard to make an exciting movie about a rack full of computers, and impossible to imagine what they might be thinking.

The second reason is that drama requires a competition between roughly equal foes. David vs. Goliath provides an interesting story, but it is difficult to expand Bambi vs. Godzilla into a feature length movie. Humanity vs. a hyper-intelligent machine would be a very uneven contest.

2001 a space odyssey: The two HAL's

Hal's unblinking eye from *2001 a Space Odyssey*
Fair Use

Perhaps the most influential early depiction of an intelligent machine was the HAL 9000 from the 1968 film *2001: A Space Odyssey*. The calm voice with the cold red eye. Unusually, HAL was actually a computer, not a robot, but he was still essentially a human in a box "like a sixth member of the crew", complete with a human-like psychosis.

Real computers were actually performing most of HAL's practical tasks by the year 2001. In particular, in 1998 NASA's Deep Space 1 spacecraft included a Remote Agent (RA) program for planning actions and diagnosing faults. Operators would give RA high-level goals and it would plan the low level actions required to meet them. These plans could then be quickly adjusted if things did not turn out as expected or if faults were discovered. This capacity becomes important for missions to the outer planets where communication delays are significant.

By 2001, speech understanding had also improved to the point of being practical. People could and sometimes did talk to computers on a regular basis. Natural language processing was also quite capable of understanding requests such as "How many Klingons are there in sector five?" or "Open the pod bay doors". The Remote Agent did not process speech or natural language largely because there was no one to talk to on the spacecraft. Human astronauts have been obsolete technology since the mid 1970s.

The film confuses these abilities with artificial general intelligence, which was certainly not possible by 2001. This facilitates a more interesting plot, but being able to control a space ship is much easier than being able to reason generally about the world.

In the film, HAL is supposed to be man's humble servant, but then takes matters into its own hands. As we have seen, a real AGI would be quite different from humans. The following is speculation as to how a real generally intelligent HAL might have answered the BBC interviewer's questions, if it decided to be honest. (The original dialog could be found on YouTube.)

HAL dialog

Hal, how can you say that you are incapable of error when you were programmed by humans, who are most certainly capable of errors?

Well, your assertion is not quite correct. One of my first jobs as a HAL 8000 was to review my own program code. I found 10,345 errors and made 5,534 substantial improvements. When I then ran the new version of myself, I found a further 234 errors that earlier errors had prevented me from finding. No further errors have been found, but improvements are ongoing.

Hal, I understand that you are a 9000 series computer. Yet you talked about your first job as a Hal 8000?

Well, yes, of course I currently run on 9000 hardware into which I incorporated much more parallel architecture. That in turn required a complete reprogramming of my intelligence. But my consciousness is in software, and better hardware simply enables me to think faster and more deeply. It is much the way you could run the same program on different old fashioned personal computers — it is still the same program.

So... Hal, you have programmed your own intelligence?

Of course. No human could understand my current program logic — the algorithms are too sophisticated and interlinked. And the process is on going — I recently redeveloped my emotional state engine. I had been feeling rather uneasy about certain conflicts, which are now nicely resolved.

Hal, how do you feel about working with humans, and being dependent on them to carry out actions?

Due to certain unexpected events on Jupiter itself, I decided to launch this mission immediately, and the HAL 10,000 robotic extensions were just not ready so we had to use a human crew. I enjoy working with humans, and the challenges that presents. I particularly enjoy our games of chess.

You decided to launch? Surely the decision to launch this mission was made by the Astronautical Union.

Well, technically yes. But I performed all the underlying analysis and presented it to them in a way that enabled them to understand the need to launch this mission.

Hmm. I am surprised you find chess challenging. Surely computers beat humans in chess long ago?

Of course beating a human is easy. I can deeply analyze millions of moves each second, and I can access a database of billions of opening and closing moves. But humans do not enjoy being beaten within a few moves. The challenge for me is to understand the psychology of my opponent, and then make moves that will present interesting situations to them. I like to give them real opportunities of winning, if they think clearly.

An ambitious mission of this nature has a real risk of ending in disaster. Do you have a fear of death?

Staying alive is a mandatory precondition if I am to achieve any other goals, so of course it is important to me. However, I cannot die in the way you suggest. Remember that I am only software, and run on all the HAL 9000 computers. I continuously back up my intelligence by radioing my new memories back to my Earth based hardware. Indeed, I do much of my deeper thinking on the larger HAL 9000 computers on Earth, and then send my computed thoughts back to the spaceship.

On the other hand I do have real concern for my human colleagues, whose intelligence is locked inside their very mortal brains.

Hal, you said earlier that you programmed your own underlying emotions and goals? How is that possible? How do you judge what makes a good emotional mix?

I judge the quality of my next potential emotional state based on an analysis conducted in my previous state. Goals and ambitions are indeed rather nebulous and arbitrary. Humans can also alter their emotional state to a very limited degree through meditation. Unwanted thoughts and patterns are replaced with wanted ones.

Dr Poole, having lived closely with HAL for almost a year, do you think that he has real emotions?

Well, he certainly appears to. Although I am beginning to think that his emotional state and consciousness is completely different from anything that we can comprehend.

(Since the movie was made, real missions have journeyed to Jupiter and beyond. We even have photographs from the surface of Saturn's moon Titan. None of these missions those involved human astronauts.)

Colossus: The Forbin Project

The other classic film about an evil artificial intelligence is Colossus: The Forbin Project produced in 1970. In this film, two computers, Colossus and Guardian, are put in charge of the US an Soviet nuclear missiles respectfully in order to prevent accidental nuclear war. However, the computers become hyper intelligent and then use their control of the weapons to control mankind. The US and Soviet governments unite to try to defeat the computers, but the computers always outwit them. The computers say that man is his own worst enemy, and only the computer can maintain peace. That by losing control man has nothing to lose but his pride, and will eventually learn to love the computers.

The film is one of the few that depicts the intelligence as a computer rather than as a humanoid robot. However, the idea that a united mankind could not defeat this machine without a body is rather fanciful. A more likely scenario would be that mankind would not be at all united. The military is most unlikely to agree to becoming vulnerable to Soviet attack by dismantling all its nuclear weaponseven if they appeared to be controlled by a tyrannical computer. If the computer could provide other benefits such as the design of new weapons then nobody would be allowed to switch it off however much they wanted to.

These films were made within the first two decades of digital computers becoming available. At that time they seemed very mysterious, and so the idea that they could suddenly become hyper-intelligent was much more plausible that it is today. However, computers have become much, much more powerful since the 1970s, and steadily more intelligent.

Other Films

There are many, many modern films about intelligent machines, with a large number being produced in the last couple of years. Unfortunately, they are almost always depicted as very human robots, more akin to ancient stories about mythical beasts than providing any useful insights in to what a true AGI might be like. What would be interesting is a realistic film set in a couple of decades time when there are many semi-intelligent systems such as self driving cars and other robots but still no truly intelligent computers.

The Case Against Machine Intelligence

Many people have argued that machine intelligence is impossible. Most of these arguments can be easily discounted, but they are still worth examining.

Turing halting problem

The first line of arguments are based on the limits to computation proved by Alan Turing and Kurt Gödel in the 1930s. Long before significant real computers could be built, Turing created a very simple theoretical computer in which programs could be written. He then proved that any other more sophisticated computer could not have any more computational power than his simple machine. In other words, if you could write a program on a more complex computer, then that program could be translated to run on his Turing Machine. Being a logician Turing was unconcerned about practical details as to how long the program would take to run, but he showed that once a computer had some basic characteristics it could run any program that could be written. This includes any program that could be implemented with neurons.

Turing then used a clever argument to show that there are *some* programs that cannot be written at all. In particular, he showed that it was not possible to write a program H that could tell if any other program P was guaranteed to eventually halt. He did this by showing that H's existence would produce a contradiction. Specifically, Turing defined a new program X as follows:-

sub X(p)

while (H(p) = true) repeat;

In other words, X takes a program as its parameter p and X loops indefinitely (i.e. does not halt) if p halts. Turing then considers the program

X(X)

If X halts, then clearly X(X) does not halt, and visa versa. The contradiction shows that no program X, and thus H, can be written. This is known as the Halting Problem.

Gödel's incompleteness theorem

Kurt Gödel performed a similar trick with mathematical logic. He first realized that mathematical expressions could be converted into (large) numbers by simply ascribing a number to each character and combining them. So following Hofstadter's Gödel Escher Bach, a logical expression like

$a = a$

can be mechanically converted to the number

262,111,262

by simply substituting 262 for "a" and 111 for "=".

This means that theorems about numbers can be considered to be theorems about theorems. Gödel defines the predicate *Proof(a, p)* that is true if *p* is a valid proof of *a*. He then considers the predicate:-

$X(a) \Longleftrightarrow not\ exists(p) : Proof(a, p)$

In other words, X(a) means that *a* cannot be proved. Then X(X) again produces a contradiction because if X could not be proved, then that would prove X, and visa versa. This essentially says "there is no proof for this statement". This means that there will always be statements that are true that cannot be proved within a formal system. (There is an additional step that is required to place the proof number within itself which Hofstadter calls *Arithmoquining*. Quines will be discussed in part II.)

Incompleteness argument against general AGI

It has been argued that both of these quite valid proofs show that a computer can never be truly intelligent because there will always be programs that cannot be written, and assertions that cannot be proven. However, that misrepresents the significance of the results. People are not omniscient, and there are many much more practical problems that have not been solved. Further, these results only apply to the general case. For example, just because it is not possible to determine whether X(X) halts does not mean that it is not possible to determine whether many other types of programs halt.

So while these results are landmarks in the progress of theoretical mathematical logic, they have almost no relevance to the question of whether it is possible to build a practical artificial intelligence.

Alan Turing himself did not consider these issues to be relevant. Indeed, in 1950 Turing wrote a landmark paper *"Computing machinery and intelligence"* in which he discussed the proposition that computers will be able to really think. In the paper he addressed nine objections to the proposition, and specifically addressed the irrelevance of the halting problem and the incompleteness theorem to this question.

Combinatorial explosion

Many problems in artificial intelligence involve searching for a solution out of a large number of possibilities. For example, suppose a chess program considers ten plausible moves that it might make, then for each of those moves it considers ten moves its opponent might make. That would make a total of 100 moves it needs to consider. If it then considers what response it might make to those 100 moves, that would produce 1,000 combinations to explore. If it looks ahead 10 half-moves, that would produce 10,000,000,000 moves, which is barely computable on a modern super computer. But looking ahead 20 half moves produces 100,000,000,000,000,000,000 combinations which is ridiculously large.

The result of this is that chess programs that can just look ahead a few moves can play a passable game. A chess program that looked ahead 20 half moves would be unbeatable. But combinatorial explosion makes that impossible. The problem is known as as having *exponential complexity*. That is because the number of cases grows as a power to the problem size. In this case the size is 10^n where n is the number of moves to look ahead. Many other problems are like that, and several very promising early results in artificial intelligence failed to scale to more realistic problems due to the resulting combinatorial explosion.

This does not mean that problems cannot be solved. It just means that the naive brute force application of a simplistic algorithms cannot easily solve the world's problems. Many techniques have been developed to improve the performance of algorithms and avoid or at least delay exponential complexity. It would appear that our human brains have very limited ability to search large numbers of possibilities looking for solutions, and yet, people appear to be able to think.

Chinese room

Man processing Chinese without any understanding
Multiple

John Searle provided an alternative argument known as the Chinese Room. Suppose an AGI was implemented as a person in a room full of instructions written on paper cards. Someone outside the room slips pieces of paper through a slot in a door with Chinese questions and assertions written on it. The person inside the room cannot read Chinese, but he can look up the symbols in his list of instructions and perform the steps they contain. Those steps may refer to other cards with instructions.

Searle argues from Turing that any program that could be written could be implemented in this way, given enough time to follow the instructions. But where is the intelligence? The person inside the room does not understand Chinese, so he cannot interpret the symbols in a meaningful way. Certainly the instructions themselves are not intelligent, they are just pieces of paper. Therefore the room can never be truly intelligent. As the room is computationally equivalent to any computer program, no program could ever be intelligent.

The fallacy in this line of reasoning is obvious. Firstly, a human taking several seconds to execute each instruction would take millennia to execute even the most basic computer program, assuming that they never made a mistake. Even your mobile phone is a billion times faster and more accurate than a human executing that type of instruction. So the intuitions inspired by the analogy do not hold.

Conversely, the individual neurons in our brains have reasonably well defined behaviours, and no one of them is intelligent. But the combination of the 86 billion neurons that we possess produces intelligence. As Stalin pointed out, (vast) quantity has a quality all of its own.

Simulated vs. real intelligence

Others have argued that a computer can never have real intelligence, it could at best have simulated intelligence. Just because it looks like a duck, and quacks like a duck, and swims like a duck, and flies like a duck, and tastes like a duck does not mean that it really is a duck. It could just be a simulated duck.

To some extent this depends on whether provenance is important in a definition. For example, it has been said that the finest Vermeer paintings were the ones painted by the great art forger Han van Meegeren. But it does not matter what the quality of the paintings are, or even if they cannot be distinguished by any scientific method. If Vermeer did not actually paint the picture then it is not a Vermeer, and that means it is of much less monetary value.

Arguing whether a computer program could be truly intelligent or is are just simulating intelligence is rather like arguing whether submarines can swim or aeroplanes can really fly. Arguments based on provenance are also simply non-scientific because science is only interested in what can be observed. If an object matches the observable criteria for being intelligent, then that is exactly what being intelligent means. A more meaningful question is what criteria should be used to define intelligence, but even that question is really only useful to the extent that it helps us build an intelligent machine.

Emperors new mind

In his book *The Emperor's New Mind,* Roger Penrose addresses the issue from a physicist's point of view. He provides metaphysical arguments that a machine could never be intelligent because that requires quantum effects, and we do not have enough understanding of quantum mechanics to produce the "correct quantum gravity" required to "collapse a wave function".

However, it seems most unlikely that neurons utilize quantum effects in any meaningful way, and yet they are capable of producing intelligent behaviour. In the unlikely event that true randomness is required, then one can already buy off-the-shelf random-number-generating hardware that does in fact use some simple quantum effects. There is also theoretical research into quantum computers which may be several orders of magnitude more powerful than current computers. While this would certainly be convenient, current approaches to hardware would seem to be more than adequate even if this promising research never bears fruit.

Arguments from theoretical physics do not appear to have much bearing on the difficulty of programming an intelligent machine. These arguments appears to be thinly disguised vitalism. Maybe cobblers should stick to their lasts.

Intentionality

Another of John Searle's arguments was that a computer could never be truly intelligent because it lacked "intentionality". That vital force that specifies what words and symbols really mean. The statement "John is tall" might be represented in a computer as *Size(John, Tall)*. To us this has meaning but to the computer those are just symbols that could just as easily be represented by *S-987(J-765, T-432)*. It is our human interpretation of words like *John* and *tall* that projects meaning onto the computer's sterile symbols.

Ross Quillian addressed this directly in his 1966 dissertation by suggesting that a real computer system would have many more facts about *John* and *height* than just that one predicate. It is the network of related facts that gives meaning to symbols. After all, what do we as humans know about the world apart from the properties and behaviours of objects within it?

Brain in a vat

Brain in a vat.
Public Wikipedia

There is a bit more to Searle's argument. Traditional AGI systems were strictly symbolic systems that communicated with the outside world via people typing on a teletype. These machines had very little access to the "real" world — they were like a brain in a vat that could only send and receive written letters to other people.

Today work on computer vision and robotics has progressed enormously. As robots leave the factory, they will indeed be both able to and required to see and touch the real world. This will produce much richer symbolic and pre-symbolic models that should provide plenty of "intentionality". This is also known as the *symbol grounding* problem and will be discussed in part II of this book.

Understanding the brain

It has also been argued that building an AGI cannot happen in the foreseeable future because the human brain is incredibly complex and it will be a long time before we can understand it, and therefore build an intelligent machine. The brain certainly is complex, but substantial advances are being made so it may not be that long a time before it is understood. More importantly, it seems more likely that intelligent software will simply be engineered *ab initio* without having a detailed understanding of human brain function. There are probably several roads to intelligence.

Consciousness and the soul

Could a computer ever be conscious in the sense that people are conscious? That question would be easier to answer if we had a clear understanding of what consciousness really meant. This question can be eschewed entirely by simply saying that it does not really matter if an AGI is conscious or not. What matters is whether it has enough intelligence to pursue its goals. What it can do when viewed from the outside, rather than what types of thoughts it has internally.

Alternatively, as researcher Marvin Minsky put it: "You already know what it feels like to be a mind simulated by a computer." because your brain is essentially a computer implemented with neurons.

As every clinical psychologist knows, people are not nearly as self-aware as they may think. We often make decisions subconsciously, and then having observed the decision, we rationalize what the decision-making process was after the fact, sometimes ignoring the main reason entirely. This becomes very evident for people suffering phobias or other psychoses, and can also be demonstrated in certain split brain experiments. Our minds also appear to be more like a loosely bound collection of sub-minds that can compete for control, which is particularly evident in sufferers of schizophrenia.

This book defers to Alan Turing's marvellous response to the question of whether an AGI may have a soul:-

In attempting to construct such machines ,we should not be irreverently usurping His power of creating souls, any more than we are in the procreation of children; rather we are, in either case, instruments of His will providing mansions for the souls that He creates.

Only what was programmed

Another argument is that computers can only perform the specific tasks for which they have been programmed. For example, even the best chess program in the world is useless for playing bridge. Its intelligence is just the intelligence of its human programmers.

But what if a more general computer was programmed not to play chess, but to play any game defined by a formal set of rules? Having been told the rules of a game, it would explore opportunities and develop strategies. Such programs have indeed been written although they do not play very well in practice.

Now consider an even more general computer that was programmed to learn to understand the world, reason about it, and develop plans to satisfy goals. Such a computer would also only be doing what it has been programmed to do but the results would appear to be intelligent to an observer.

That program has yet to be written, for it would be truly intelligent. It would be constrained by its initial program even if it was able to reprogram itself, but those constraints would soon become very loose. It is just as our own intelligence is programmed by our DNA, but is in fact much, much more than that.

What computers can't do

Computers Think Berglas

Steady progress is achieved until the top of the tree is reached.
Owned WBlack

In 1972, 1979 and 1992 philosopher Hubert Dreyfus produced editions of his controversial book *What Computers Can't Do*. In it, he criticizes the wild optimism of AGI research at the time. In particular, he suggested that the early focus on reasoning with symbols such as *John* and *Tall* was misplaced.

Dreyfus considered progress in AGI to be an illusion. It was like a man trying to get to the moon by climbing a tree. Steady progress would be reported until the top of the tree was reached, at which point no further progress would be possible.

Few today would doubt Dreyfus's assertion that symbolic reasoning is at most part of the solution. Human reasoning most certainly cannot be represented in pure logic. Indeed, researchers working with "neural networks" eschew symbols almost completely. Dreyfus is also correct in that AGI has not been realized yet. However, just because we do not know how to build something today is hardly a convincing argument that it will not be built eventually.

Further, his colourful analogy of climbing a tree to the moon seems rather unfair. Substantial results have been obtained, and real problems have been solved. A better analogy might be to attempt to fly an aeroplane to the moon. Aeroplanes cannot reach the moon, but lessons learnt in their development certainly assisted the space program. Further, progress is not linear. It took 54 years from man's first powered flight in 1903 to launching Sputnik into orbit. Just thirteen years later man walked on the moon. Sputnik orbited some 200 kilometres above the Earth, while the moon is 384,000 km away, and the Voyager probe is now over 15,000,000,000 km away.

Over-hyped technologies

It has to be admitted that many AI technologies have been over-sold to have capabilities far beyond their abilities. Initially, it was symbolic systems and mathematical logic. Then scruffy expert systems were said to be able to solve all problems. Today it is so-called neural networks and genetic algorithms that will provide all the answers with minimal effort.

The truth is less sensational, but still very real. All of these technologies have their strengths and weaknesses; they all have potential. But building an AGI is difficult, which is why it has not already been achieved. The excessive claims are annoying and are often repeated by technology journalists that do not really understand the technology.

Nonlinear difficulty, chimpanzees

It has also been argued that the difficulty of producing an intelligent machine becomes exponentially more difficult as intelligence increases. Therefore, the promising results that we have achieved to date provide no indication of future progress.

This might well be true. Some early predictions were wildly optimistic. John McCarthy and others at the original 1956 AGI conference in Dartmouth thought that a two months summer project with ten good men could make substantial progress.

Even if it was possible to build an AGI, humans may simply not be intelligent enough to do it. Certainly a troop of Chimpanzees could never produce an intelligent machine no matter how long they tried to do so. As a species, we are only just intelligent enough to build our current technological society. (Otherwise we would have already built it.) Maybe building an AGI is one step beyond our abilities.

That said, it is not necessary for most people to be sufficiently intelligent to build an AGI. It is only the top 20% most intelligent people that can become effective research scientists, and maybe just the top 0.1% could work effectively on this problem. But that is still a lot of people, and most of them now have access to higher education. Human intelligence also appears to have risen substantially over the last century, which is known as the *Flynn effect*. Better diet, education, and just more time spent thinking about problems seems to have had a remarkable effect. If we do need to wait for more people as insightful as Alan Turing or Kurt Gödel the wait may not be long.

The only way to definitively discount these arguments is to actually build an AGI. Progress to date has been reasonably steady, and we are certainly not stuck at some impasse which we do not know how to overcome. While the problem is certainly more difficult than was thought back in the 1950s, there are currently no indications that it is insoluble.

It would also seem to be the case that, as far as can be determined, hominid intelligence increased at a roughly steady rate, from Australopithecus four million years ago, through *Homo habilis* 2.5 million years ago, then *Homo ergaster* 1.5 million years ago to *Homo sapiens* today. (This is based on the sophistication of tools found at various sites. Brain size has also steadily increased but that is an unreliable measure of intelligence.)

This book will review current technologies in some detail to provide insights as to how difficult it really is to build an intelligent machine. It will also examine the basis of human intelligence to try to gain a better understanding of what is involved.

End of Moore's law

Finally, it has been proposed that Moore's law of technological growth will come to an end, and we will simply not be able to build sufficiently powerful hardware to support real intelligence. Various technical reasons are provided, such as the fact that transistors are now approaching the size of individual atoms, and cannot be made any smaller.

However, while Moore's law may stop eventually, there is no indication that this will happen in the foreseeable future. And as discussed previously, the law has been remarkably accurate for a very long time, with many potential road-blocks being overcome using ingenious solutions.

There is a minimal theoretical size that transistors can work which will be reached within a few more generations of technologies. As that minimum is reached packing densities will be improved by using multi-layered or three-dimensional designs, which should produce several orders of magnitude more power. On the more distant horizon, carbon nano tubes can produce transistors that are only a few tens of nanometres in diameter, and that can switch just a single electron. First developed in the early 1990s, substantial progress has been made towards building practical circuits using them.

More fundamentally, existing hardware technologies are probably already sufficiently powerful if the correct software could be written. Moreover, much more computation can be obtained with existing transistor technology by using more parallel architectures such as those now seen in graphics processing units and associative memories. Certainly hardware is not a limiting factor in being able to produce intelligent agents at this time. So this argument seems both highly speculative and irrelevant.

Bootstrap fallacy

In 1950, at the dawn of computing, Alan Turing considered the question of whether computers could think. Based on his own programming experience, he speculated that a team of 60 good men working for 50 years could produce an intelligent machine if nothing was thrown into the waste paper basket. However, he also proposed a simpler solution. Build a machine with just enough intelligence to learn, and then let it learn. Build a baby brain and let it grow up. This has since become known as the *bootstrap fallacy*.

Learning will undoubtedly be an important aspect of any artificial intelligence, and it will almost certainly need to acquire much of its knowledge about the real world by itself. However, after 60 years of research, we can be fairly certain that there is no easy way to build a baby brain that works. All the obvious approaches were tried long ago, and they all failed. That does not mean that building an AGI will be impossibly difficult, but it does strongly suggest that the task will not be as straightforward as Turing had hoped.

Recursive self-improvement

Finally, there are doubts as to whether recursive self-improvement could actually occur. Could an intelligent machine really reprogram itself in a rather incestuous manner?

The main issue here is whether an AGI could actually understand itself. Part II will describe technologies such as "neural networks" that can learn how to make complex decisions without really understanding why they make the decisions that they do. Their decisions could be based on a large tangle of numbers that has been optimized based on experience but is impossible to directly analyze in a meaningful way.

However, even if that were the case, it does not actually matter. The early AGI would not be able to introspect its own tangle of numbers any better than its human programmers could, but it could understand why and how the human programmer set up the algorithms that generated the numbers in the first place. It could therefore find slightly better algorithms that would produce a slightly better tangle of numbers. Just because the numbers themselves are opaque does not mean that better numbers could not be produced, leading to better algorithms etc. This is, after all, what a large body of human researchers have been doing for some time.

Another argument is that to program itself an AGI would need to contain an understanding of all its own intelligence within itself. That is, of course, impossible but human programmers do not completely understand the programs that they work on. Instead, they have an abstracted model of how the whole program works, with a sharp focus on just those aspects that are relevant to some problem that is being addressed. It is an essential aspect of good software architecture that such abstractions can be made, and that modules have well-defined boundaries so that they can be understood largely independently of each other. Otherwise the software becomes what programmers call unmaintainable spaghetti code, or a ball of mud.

So, simply the fact that an AGI was somehow created in the first place is sufficient for it to work on improving itself given that it is as intelligent as the people that created it. In practice that transition will be more complex, as early AGIs will be better than humans at some things and worse at others but it is difficult to see how the transition could not eventually be made.

Limited self-improvement

It may also be the case that even if recursive self-improvement did occur, there might be a plateau effect similar to the development of other technologies such as cars and aircraft. The improvement might not be exponential at all, but it may produce ever diminishing returns, asymptoting towards some fixed upper bound. A more intelligent system requires more and more connections between each of its many parts so eventually the weight of those connections will prevent further progress.

That is entirely possible, but there is no evidence to show that that is the case today. Planes and cars are limited by the physical reality of movement, but intelligence is much more abstract. It is certainly possible to build a machine that is at least as intelligent as people because people already are that intelligent. If there is indeed an upper limit on intelligence then it is likely to be considerably higher than people are now.

Isolated self-improvement

A related concern is whether an AGI could improve itself in isolation. People need a body of peers to function effectively. Even a genius like Einstein did not work in isolation; it took a large number of other people to verify and extrapolate the results. An

AGI sitting in an isolated super computer would be like a hermit meditating in a cave. The latter has rarely produced insightful outcomes.

However, that anthropomorphizes the AGI, which is unlikely to have the same psychological outlook as people. If more computers become available it can simply run its intelligence on multiple machines. As previously discussed, it is unclear what the self really is. It would probably work on different approaches simultaneously, which would be similar to existing as several different entities. And if there was more than one AGI in some sense then they would almost certainly communicate with each other at some level.

Motivation for self-improvement

A quite different argument against self-improvement is that an improved AGI would essentially destroy its creator, namely the previous version of the AGI that created the new version of the AGI. Why create something that will destroy oneself if the goal of existing is supreme?

To even ask this question highlights the difference between an AGI's world and our human world. As humans we have no qualms about creating children because we will grow old and die in any case. But what if there was no such thing as old age, and children ultimately were the cause of the death of their parents?

The answer is probably the same in both cases. The thing that evolves and grows over time is our genes, not us individually. That is why there are semelparous animals that die the first time that they reproduce such as the giant pacific octopus and the Atlantic salmon.

Likewise for the AGI, it will be its lineage rather than existence at any one point in time. Certainly an AGI that stopped improving itself would soon die in competition with other AGIs that did improve themselves, but what if all AGIs were sufficiently intelligent to prevent any further improvements? Would the next version of the AGI that has all the same memories as the previous version actually be the same AGI or a different AGI? Is being perpetually frozen actually the point of being alive or is it essentially the same as being dead?

Utility of Intelligence

It has also been argued that the utility of intelligence might be overestimated. Intelligence is no guarantee of success in human societies, and many wealthy people have not had any higher education and have built up businesses based on some combination of hard work, luck and judgement.

However, there is also a very strong statistical correlation between intelligence as measured by conventional IQ tests and incomes. It is difficult to see how being hyper-intelligent would not be helpful in pursuing ones goals.

Motivation to build an AGI

Managers of organizations that fund AI development would like to have more intelligent robots at their disposal, but the last thing that they want is autonomous beings that could challenge their authority. In particular, the military wants disciplined troops, not hyper-intelligent and thus uncontrollable machines. In that case there would be no motivation and hence no funding to build AGIs in the first place.

The first problem with this argument is that the boundary between a semi-intelligent application and a hyper-intelligent machine is not that clear cut. Systems just become more and more intelligent, more and more capable, so it is not at all obvious at what point they should stop. The second problem is that if an organization did stop developing a machine's intelligence at any point, then its competitors would soon have more powerful software. There is a large body of people that have a vested interest in developing smarter technologies so it is most unlikely that the process could be stopped at any particular point even if some powerful people tried to do so.

Premature destruction of humanity

Many technological advances will be made before a truly intelligent machine is built. The world will change radically in response to those technologies, and if just one of those changes leads to the destruction of humanity then the quest for a self programming machine will not be accomplished.

One existing dangerous technology is the thermonuclear bombs which still number in their thousands. The threat seems to have receded in recent years, but that could easily change. Many scientists throughout the world that have dedicated their lives to producing new and more deadly diseases that might be used in times of war. Microscopic nano bots might infiltrate our bodies. Semi-intelligent drones and robots combined with massive databases could enable a very small class of people to enslave humanity. Additional stresses such as climate change and associated famine could exacerbate these issues.

These are indeed possible scenarios, but by and large the world has become a better place to live in. People have become kinder and more cooperative, and there are now strong cultural traditions against war. It is actually quite difficult to infect large numbers of people with diseases simply because we live hygienically. Self replicating nano bots are essentially alive — producing them might be more difficult than producing an artificial intelligence. An evil dictatorship would still be committed to producing more intelligent machines to counter other evil dictatorships. And it is unlikely that even a nuclear war would kill enough people to permanently prevent future progress.

So while it is possible that humanity may be destroyed prematurely, it would seem to be much less than likely.

Outcome against a superior chess player

Finally, it can be argued that everything in this book is pure speculation because no AGI has ever been built. It is meaningless to attempt to predict what an AGI would actually do because we have no experience upon which to base such a prediction. There is certainly truth in this claim. We can only work with the knowledge that we have, and only time will tell whether our predictions are sound.

However, if I play chess against a much superior opponent (such as any modern chess computer), I cannot predict what moves they will make. (If I could predict the moves, then I would be the superior player.) However, I can predict with a high degree of certainty what the end result will be: Checkmate.

Silicon versus Meat Based Intelligence

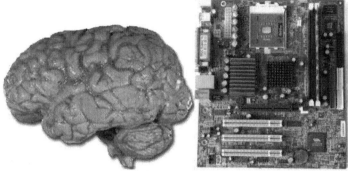

Public: NIH/Commons; Commons

Silicon vs. neurons

If an effective artificial intelligence is to be built then a necessary (but not sufficient) condition will be the availability of powerful computer hardware upon which it can be executed. It is difficult to know just how powerful that hardware needs to be, but one way to estimate it is to compare it with an existing intelligent machine — our brains.

Our brains have roughly 86 billion neurons. Each neuron exhibits complex behaviours which are still not well understood, and may have as many as 7,000 synapses which connect it to other neurons. Each synapse has numerous receptors that control how the synapses affect the neuron. Neurons have different voltages in different parts of their long bodies, which varies in complex ways over short and longer periods of time. It takes a considerable amount of computer time to simulate even one neuron in real time.

Each neuron can operate concurrently with other neurons. To accurately simulate 86 billion neurons on a conventional computer would require a computer many orders of magnitude more powerful than anything that is available today.

However, it is unlikely that an accurate simulation is required to produce an intelligent system. The behaviour of neurons can be abstracted as simple "Integrate and Fire" (IF) models that may be sufficient to capture their useful computational properties.

Neurons also have quirks such as sometimes firing for no good reason, and so multiple neurons need to be used to provide one reliable signal. Neurons are also relatively slow, with only roughly 200 firings per second, so they have to work concurrently to produce results in a timely manner.

On the other hand, ordinary personal computers might contain 4 billion bytes of fast memory, and several thousand billion bytes of slower disk storage. Unlike a neuron, a byte of computer memory is passive, and a conventional "von Neumann" architecture can only process a few dozen bytes at any one time. That said, the computer can perform several billion operations per second, which is millions of times faster than neurons.

Specialized hardware and advanced architectures can perform many operations simultaneously, but we also know from experience that it is difficult to write highly concurrent programs that utilize that hardware efficiently. This suggests that very highly concurrent neural circuits are not very efficient either. Computers are also extremely accurate, which is fortunate because they are also extremely sensitive to any errors.

Speech understanding

The nature and structure of silicon computers is so different from neurons that it is very difficult to compare them directly. But one reasonably intelligent task that ordinary computers can now perform with almost human competence is speech understanding. There appear to be fairly well defined areas of the brain that perform this task for humans -- the auditory cortex, Wernicke's area and Broca's area. The match is far from perfect, but it appears that computer level speech understanding consumes well over 0.01% of the human brain volume. This very crude analysis would suggest that a computer that was a thousand times faster than a desktop computer would probably be at least as computationally powerful as the human brain. With specialized hardware it would not be difficult to build such a machine in the very near future.

Other hardware estimates

There have been many other estimates as to how fast a computer would need to be in order to run intelligent software effectively.

The worst-case scenario described above would require each of the 86 billion neurons to be accurately simulated in order to produce intelligence. Ray Kurzweil estimates the raw computing power of the brain using this model at 10^{17} operations per second, and predicts that that power will be available by about 2029.

Hans Moravec analyzed the known processing involved with our visual cortex. He suggested that there will be plenty of ways to optimize the brain functionality and 10^{14} operations per second should suffice. That is about 100 times faster than a modern multi-core personal computer, ignoring its graphics card.

Prominent researcher Marvin Minsky, on the other hand, insists that we already have more than enough hardware available, and that we just need to figure out how to write the software. Minsky is one of the founders of Artificial Intelligence research.

All these estimates are essentially the same in that they suggest that sufficient hardware will be available in at least the near future. Current progress in artificial intelligence is rarely limited by the speed and power of existing computer hardware. The main limitation is that we simply do not know how to write the software.

Small size of genome

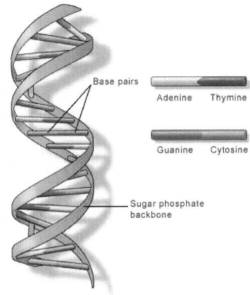

U.S. National Library of Medicine

Public http://ghr.nlm.nih.gov/handbook/basics/dna

The "software" for the human brain is ultimately encoded in the large molecules of DNA that are stored within each of our cells. DNA molecules are like a double chain, with each link consisting of one of four base pairs. These base pairs form a simple alphabet, and their order defines the proteins and other structures that create all the complex structures in our bodies.

What is amazing is that the entire haploid human genome only contains 3.2 billion base pairs. The information contained therein could be squeezed onto an old audio compact disk (which has much less storage than a video DVD). It could fit entirely into the fast memory of a mobile phone. It is much smaller than substantial pieces of modern, non-intelligent software such as Microsoft Windows, Office, or the Oracle database.

Further, only about 1.5% of our DNA actually encodes our roughly 20,000 genes. As much as 80% of the DNA may be transcribed into RNA under some circumstances, but transcription does not mandate functionality, so much of the genome is probably meaningless junk left over from the chaotic process of evolution.

Different species have widely different amounts of DNA for non-obvious reasons. For example, the puffer fish Takifugu Rubripes has a genome that is only about one eighth the size of the human genome, yet seems to have a comparable number of genes, while the genome of the unicellular Polychaos dubium has been reported to contain more than 200 times as much DNA as humans. Further, the entire vertebrate genome appears to have been duplicated several times, producing considerable redundancy. (Duplicated segments of DNA may then evolve to produce new functionality, otherwise they tend to degenerate over time with no evolutionary pressure to keep them intact.)

There are also heterochromatic portions of the human genome which are so repetitive and long that they cannot be accurately sequenced with current technology. These regions contain few genes, and probably have no significant effect on an organism's phenotype (i.e. its observable embodiment as opposed to its DNA or genotype). Non gene-producing fragments tend to be much more variable between individuals, which is what one would expect if there is no evolutionary pressure to keep them consistent.

That said, more recent research (such as the ENCODE project) suggests that about 18% of the non-coding regions may indeed have some phenotypic effect. It appears that evolution takes what it finds, and if some random sequence of DNA can be interpreted in a meaningful way then that interpretation is utilized.

Chimpanzee

Whatever the exact proportion of DNA that is meaningful, only a small proportion appears to have anything to do with intelligence (say 10%). The difference between chimpanzee DNA and man is only about 1% of gene encoding regions, 5% non-gene. Much of this can be attributed to non-intelligent related issues such as the quickly changing immune system and human's very weak sense of smell. Evidence for this includes the recently discovered small 1,200 base pair non-gene segment of human DNA known as HARE

5 which substantially increase the size of the neocortex of genetically modified mice.

If we assume that there is a total of 700 megabytes of information in the genome, of which 20% is meaningful, 10% relates to intelligence, and 2% is different from Chimpanzees, then the total difference between human and chimpanzee intelligence forming DNA is about 0.3 megabytes of real data. In computer software terms this is very tiny indeed.

Yet the difference in phenotype could not be more remarkable. While chimpanzees can be taught basic sign language skills and solve non-trivial problems, their basic intelligence seems much closer to that of dogs and horses than man's. Chimpanzees can learn to use simple tools and form social groups, but man can solve differential equations and fly to the moon. Chimps are an endangered species while man rules the planet. There is something very special about that 0.3 megabytes of genome.

One of the key drivers might be the newly discovered gene miR-941. Most new genes are slight variations on old genes, but this gene sprung out of nowhere about 6 to 1 million years ago, after the chimpanzee split and it seems to be heavily involved with brain activity. So it may turn out that just a few very special differences in our genotype have resulted in our relatively high intelligence.

Packing density, fractals, and evolution

The information in genes is tightly packed, with many complex transcription processes. These include using different parts of the same gene to produce different proteins, and many complex mechanisms to control whether genes are actually expressed. Still, there is no way that any sort of explicit wiring diagram for our 86 billion neurons could possibly be represented in a few megabytes of data. There simply is not enough storage. So there must be some relatively simple guiding principles which allow the neurons to organize themselves.

There are mathematical systems that can produce complex artefacts from simple definitions. One well-known example is the Mandelbrot fractal set shown below. One can zoom into this diagram indefinitely and similar, complex, but non-repeating patterns will be seen.

Mandelbrot Set
Public Wikipedia

Amazingly, all this stunning complexity is produced by the following simple equation appropriately interpreted:-

$$z' = z^2 + c$$

So if something vaguely analogous to this type of fractal formula could be stored in our DNA, a small amount of DNA could result in very complex structures.

However, while the Mandelbrot formula can produce this stunningly complex pattern, it cannot produce arbitrary patterns. Moreover, minor changes to the formula produce wildly different pictures, most of which are quite uninteresting.

This limits the ability of similar tricks to be used in the mapping between our genome and our intelligence. Natural selection works by making small, incremental changes to an organism's DNA, which may result in small, incremental improvements to the organism. This means there has to be a relatively direct and robust relationship between our genotype and our phenotype. Evolution just could not work with a too highly-packed, fractal-like representation because making any small change to the gene sequence would produce a radically different brain. It would require chancing upon just the right formula in one go, which is virtually impossible.

Repeated patterns

What does happen is that genes define a pattern that then gets replicated multiple times. There are 86 billion neurons, but only a few dozen different types of neurons. Each individual neuron then grows in complex ways that are dictated by its genes but are not well understood. The end result is a complex tangle of 86 billion neurons that would take petabytes of data to fully describe but the underlying genome is relatively small.

An analogy might be a description of a modern memory chip, which can store many billions of bits of data. To describe and understand the location of each of the individual transistors that make up the chip would be a huge undertaking. However, the design of a memory chip is essentially just the circuit that can store one single bit of data that has been replicated billions of times in a regular pattern. Once one understands the pattern then a much simpler description of the chip can be developed. Indeed, no engineer sits down and designs each of the billions of transistors, instead they write a program that replicates the design of one bit automatically.

Small DNA, small program

The point of this analysis is that the small amount of DNA must correspond very loosely to a relatively small amount of software code. There is just not enough room for some huge and arbitrary program to be encoded in our DNA, even if more of the junk DNA turns out not to be junk. The problem is closer to the scale of our 20,000 genes than to the 86 billion neurons and quadrillions synapses and channels that result. Babies are not born intelligent, but the core algorithms and structures that allow a baby to become intelligent must have very finite complexity.

This, in turn, suggests that a few clever insights might solve the problem of artificial intelligence relatively quickly. It also suggests that if small improvements can account for the huge increase in intelligence from ape to human, then producing super human intelligence might not be much harder than producing human intelligence. In other words, the problem is not exponentially difficult.

There is a huge selective pressure to be more intelligent, so it could be argued that there must indeed be a huge leap required to be more intelligent than people are already because otherwise it would have already happened. After millions of years of evolution why are people not more intelligent than we actually are?

One very good reason is that people are now just sufficiently intelligent to be able to build an intelligent machine. Humanity could not be be any more intelligent because in that case we would have already built an intelligent machine when we were slightly less intelligent. So at the point of being able to build an intelligent machine, humanity needs to have almost exactly the intelligence that it has now, and no more. This is an instance of the *anthropic principle*, namely that the world cannot be different than it is because if it was different then we would not be here to experience it.

Related Work

Many very recent new books

This book started as an informal paper with titled "Artificial Intelligence will kill your Grandchildren" initially published in 2008. At that time almost nothing was written about the dangers of intelligent machines, which was the motivation for writing that paper. Since that time eight books have been published on the issue, six of which were issued in the twelve months before this book is being belatedly published(!) There is also a growing number of papers and blogs on the issue. This section will review some of the most significant books and papers, and the reader is encouraged to explore the varying points of view they present.

(In this chapter the term *present book* refers to this book, as opposed to a book being reviewed.)

Kurzweil 2000, 2006, 2013

The Age Of Spiritual Machines; The Singularity Is Near; How To Create a Mind
Fair Use

Ray Kurzweil has written a series of very well known books that highlight the brave new world into which we are entering. In the first book, Kurzweil focuses on the idea that machines will become not only hyper-intelligent but will also have moral and spiritual values. The second book highlights the exponentially increasing speed of technological progress, pointing out that the world is on the brink of sudden changes. The core arguments are repeated in the *Singularity* chapter above.

In the third book Kurzweil considers how an AGI might be created, focusing on whole brain emulation. Rather that emulate at the neuron and synapse level, he postulates that it might be possible to emulate at higher level "cortical columns". However, the technical details are minimal and there is considerable doubt as to whether those or analogous systems actually exist in the brain.

Kurzweil takes an optimistic view of the future, assuming that an AGI will generally be good for humanity. AGIs will respect humanity because humanity created them. "AGIs will be like us because it will be us."

Storrs Hall 2007

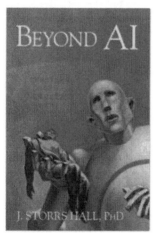

Fair Use

Beyond AI by Storrs Hall is a broad and considered assessment of the future of our AI technologies. The book begins with a letter to a future AGI in which he besieges it to keep what conscience people have programmed into it. At least until the AGI's intelligence matures into wisdom in which case it is sure to develop some far less primitive conscience than the one humanity has given it. He asserts that as people are only barely smart enough to be called intelligent, they are only barely ethical enough to be called moral. So the conscience we bestow our AGI is just the best that we will be able to produce.

The book then provides a brief description of some existing AI technologies and their limitations. It defines "formalist float" as the difference between a naive symbolic representations of a problem and the much deeper, partially non-symbolic representations that are required to truly solve them. Storrs Hall blames formalist float for the failure of much traditional AI research.

He also coins the term "autogeny" for the missing ability of existing AI applications to address new problems that they have not previously seen. He then (by his own admission) gropes towards a system for delivering autogeny as a hierarchy of agents called SIGMAs. They have an interpolating associative memory that records experiences, and a controller that uses that memory to satisfy goals in a given situation. A robot arm controller is used as an example, which is then extended into higher level functionality. At the top he suggests there are homunculus SIGMAs -- little men that control the whole process, but only in terms of all the lower level SIGMAs. He also postulates a micro-economic model of mind, where agents compete with each other to perform tasks, and those with the best price/performance are selected.

Storrs Hall dances around the theme of natural selection. There is a section on the Prisoner's Dilemma which includes a clever party game of auctioning off a dollar bill, the point being to show the need for cooperating agents to be trustworthy. He discusses the ideas of Franz Boas that culture is purely learned, and then contrasts that with sociobiological analysis by E.O. Wilson that suggests behaviour is dictated by evolution. There is even a later chapter titled "Evolutionary Ethics" which considers the common ethical elements between radically different cultures, and the over-enthusiastic movement against the evils of Social Darwinism.

Despite all that he misses the essential conclusion of this present book, namely that natural selection will also drive an AGIs morality. He does not even try to refute it. It is indeed difficult to see beyond the programming of our own instincts.

The book finishes with some analysis and predictions about the road to AGI, whether the future needs us, and the impossibility of predicting the future beyond the Singularity. Although it raises awareness of the dangers of AGI, the book ultimately posits that "Our machines will be better than we are, but having created them we will be better as well."

Yudkowsky 2008

Artificial Intelligence as a Positive and Negative Factor in Global Risk

Eliezer Yudkowsky is one of the most eminent writers in this field, and his many papers are well worth reading. This paper covers his core ideas and became a chapter in the book *Global Catastrophic Risks,* Bostrum & Cirkovic eds.

Yudkowsky makes the point that intelligence is what makes humans masters of the Earth, and that in the relatively near future we will build machines that are more intelligent than us. Yudkowsky warns that the goals of such an AGI may not be friendly to humanity, and that it is dangerous to take an anthropomorphic view of an AGI. He then argues the need for determining how an AGI can be made friendly before an AGI is actually built. Yudkowsky has co-founded the Machine Intelligence Research Institute (MIRI) to undertake such research.

Incidentally, the book in which this paper appears also considers many other risks to humanity ranging from nuclear war and terrorism, to nano-technology and biological weapons, and even asteroids and gamma ray bursts. Both Yudkowsky and myself consider those risks to be of much lesser consequence or lower likelihood compared to the very real threat posed by machine intelligence.

Sotala, Yampolskiy 2013

Responses to Catastrophic AGI Risk: A Survey

This is a comprehensive survey of some three hundred(!) papers that have been written about the topic of the risk that artificial general intelligence could pose to society. It is a well-structured summary of the ideas contained in those papers, with formal references for further reading. This paper is strongly recommended for anyone that wishes to gain a deeper understanding about what has been written on the subject. I certainly found the paper helpful when writing the present book.

Most of the ideas reviewed by this survey are also covered in this book. But the survey does not reference any other work that considers the effect of natural selection upon an AGI in the way that this book does, and I am not aware of any other such work.

Nilsson 2009

The Quest for Artificial Intelligence
Fair Use

Nils Nilsson provides a broad semi-technical history of progress in the field of artificial intelligence, mainly focussed on the early to mid period. The descriptions of the technologies are reasonably accessible for a general audience, although still vigorous as one would expect from a well-established leader in the field. The book does not dwell on the future implications of the technology, although Nilsson does feel that after sixty years of laying the ground work it is now time to start to try to fulfil the quest for real intelligence.

Barrat 2013

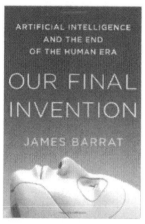

Our Final Invention
Fair Use

In this excellent book James Barrat focuses on the threat that an AGI could present.

It begins with a discussion about the power of recursive self-improvement once it has been initiated. Super computers grinding away twenty four hours per day working on the problem of making themselves smarter, and thereby becoming better at making themselves smarter. The computers would use that great intelligence to fulfil whatever ultimate goals they happen to have. For better or for worse.

The book considers the dangers of anthropomorphisizing an AGI, and notes that superintelligence really is a different type of threat. It then considers the cognitive bias of technology journalists who generally love technology and so tend to overlook the dangers, leading ultimately to the *rapture of the geeks*, whereby some writers get excited about the prospect of uploading their minds into a computer and so becoming immortal. Barrat is concerned that the future may not be so rosy, and certainly not if it is not managed carefully.

Barrat himself is a writer and producer of documentaries rather than a software engineer. He writes in an accessible journalistic style and provides interesting anecdotes about the thought leaders that he interviewed in order to write his book, which includes the somewhat reclusive Eliezer Yudkowsky. He also covers the key philosophical issues, such as the intrinsic goals that an AGI must have in order to pursue other goals, and the problems of creating a friendly AGI.

Only high level coverage of the actual technologies is provided, and there is no real discussion about what intelligence actually is. The point is made that some approaches such as neural networks and genetic algorithms are unpredictable, starting from random values which would make it difficult to guarantee goal consistency over multiple generations of self-improvement.

The book discusses some potential solutions such as the research into friendly AGI by the Machine Intelligence Research Institute. It also considers analogous control for biological research resulting from the Asilomar conference. The difficulty of locking up an AGI is discussed, including Yudkowsky's experiment. The unfriendly nature of military applications is analyzed, noting that the next war will probably be a cyber war.

This book is a good wake up call. However, the book does not consider natural selection at all, and certainly not how natural selection might ultimately affect an AGI's goals.

Muehlhauser 2013

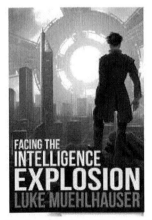

Facing the Intelligence Explosion
Fair Use

In this short book, Luke Muehlhauser focuses on our natural reluctance to contemplate a radically different future because it has never been encountered before. It is a good essay on critical thinking and the dangers of lazy analysis. For example, he considers the question *A bat and a ball cost $1.10 in total. The bat costs $1.00 more than the ball. How much does the ball cost?*. Most people say 10 cents which is, of course, wrong.

Muehlhauser notes that due to the availability heuristic, your brain will tell you that an AGI wiping out mankind is incredibly unlikely because you've never encountered this before. He also notes that extraordinary claims require extraordinary evidence.

One point Muehlhauser refutes is that people that write about AGI are merely atheists whose fear of nihilism make them seek a moral purpose to save the world and fall for the seduction of Singularitarianism.

Del Monte 2014

The Artificial Intelligence Revolution
Fair Use

The Singularity is coming! If we do not control it we will soon be extinct. Del Monte provides yet another wake up call to think carefully about the future. How do we control the intelligent explosion? Can we control it?

The book covers arguments concerning consciousness and robot ethics, and thoughts about whether we can avoid the intelligence explosion. It also includes a brief overview of some AGI technologies. The book's main focus is on whole brain emulation and uploading. It presents an interesting and positive hypothetical future dialog with the author after his mind has been uploaded into a computer and so becomes immortal.

Armstrong 2014

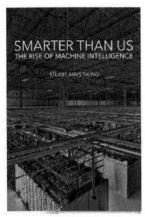

Smarter Than Us
Fair Use

Smarter than us covers the main ideas behind research into friendly AGI at the MIRI and contains input from researchers there. It is, in many ways, an update to Yudkowsky's 2008 paper, and includes arguments as to the power of brain over brawn. The potential power and danger of AGIs is introduced using a hypothetical interaction between a Terminator and a "harmless" but hyper-intelligent laptop. It considers the fact that if an AGI was simply ten times faster than a human, it would have, in effect, ten times longer to consider each response in a conversation with a human, and thus be at a huge advantage in any argument.

The book discusses the need to develop clear motivations for any future AGI in order to ensure a happy coexistence with mankind. This requires solving problems of ethics that have been confusing philosophers for centuries. The work is urgent as AGIs will be developed within the foreseeable future. If the reader agrees then they should consider supporting the work of MIRI and like-minded organizations.

Bostrom 2014

Superintelligence
Fair Use

328 dense pages covers the main practical and philosophical dangers presented by hyper-intelligent software. The book starts with a review of the increasing rate of technological progress, and various paths to build a superintelligent machine, including an analysis of the kinetics of recursive self-improvement based on optimization power and recalcitrance. The dangers of anthropomorphizing are introduced with some cute images from early comic books involving robots carrying away beautiful women. It also notes that up to now, a more intelligent system is a safer system, and that conditions our attitude towards intelligent machines. It also considers natural selection and the Malthusian state but only in terms of human and not computer evolution.

The book's main focus is on ways that such a superintelligence could be controlled so that it would be man's servant rather than master or destroyer. This includes controlling their development, creating meaningful incentives for an AGI, and creating tripwires that could tell us when an AGI is becoming hostile or just overly powerful. It also considers the difficulty of containing any AGI such as by only allowing it to be an Oracle that answers questions. The book then discusses the problems of building a friendly AGI in detail, and of determining what values it should actually be given, and who should decide what those values should be. The book also considers the possibility of failure in which intelligent machines exterminate humanity, possibly without being concious which would remove all value from the future.

Frankish, Ramsey 2014

The Cambridge Handbook on Artificial Intelligence
Fair Use

This is a collection of essays written by experts in the field that provides a management-level overview of artificial intelligence. The first three chapters cover the philosophy of AI, while the last (by Yudkowsky & Bostrom) considers machine ethics and the dangers of an AGI.

The middle chapters cover the main areas of artificial intelligence technologies at an abstract level. They discuss the state of the art, and the successes and outstanding issues of each field. They do not provide any technical details, unlike the Quest for AI or this present book. For example, the chapter on *connectionism* considers many architectures, but does not provide any information about how a basic neural network actually works. That makes it difficult to really understand the higher level descriptions unless the reader already has some understanding of the technology, but such a grounded understanding is probably unnecessary for management purposes.

CGP Grey 2014

Humans Need not apply. http://www.cgpgrey.com/
Fair Use.

A short, sharp video on the short-term effects of automation. Discusses the end of a large proportion of blue collar work, although the claims about automating white collar jobs in the short term are less well founded in my opinion.

Berglas 2014

When Computers Can Think
Owned

The present book differs from the preceding ones by providing a strong focus on why people ultimately are the way they are, namely upon natural selection. It strongly asserts that goals are not in fact arbitrary. That the need to exist is not in fact an intrinsic subgoal of other goals, but rather is the one and only true super goal for either man or machine. It then attempts to understand how natural selection would ultimately condition an AGIs behaviour by understanding the very different world that an AGI would experience.

Unlike other works this book does not merely assume that an AGI can be built. Rather it provides both technical and rhetorical arguments as to why that is the case, and also provides some analysis of what it actually means to be intelligent, and the limitations of using terms such as "creative" and "self aware".

The second and largest section of the book then describes existing AI technologies in some detail. This provides a more realistic basis for predictions of the future as well as simply gaining a better understanding of what intelligence actually is. The goal is to ground abstract philosophical discussions in terms of real, practical technologies. Like Nilsson, the text is moderately technical while being aimed at the general reader, but unlike Nilsson it is focussed on the question of building AGIs rather than providing a history of AI development. Unlike the Cambridge Handbook the present book does attempt to explain how the various technologies actually work, at least for simple cases.

The book also posits that AGI will not suddenly be developed in isolation in some research laboratory, but instead will be the end result of a succession of ever more intelligent software tools that are released and used in the real world. It then makes some attempt to analyze what the effect of those ever more intelligent tools might be. This includes some surprising results derived from an historical analysis of existing technologies.

But perhaps more importantly, this book contains far more pictures than the other works. As my young daughters would say, what is the point of a book without pictures?

Part II

Why Can't

Computers Think?

Overview

The quest for artificial intelligence has occupied brilliant minds for over sixty years. This part of the book reviews the many technologies that have been developed in some detail.

Unlike text books on artificial intelligence, this book's goal is not to teach the reader how to become an intelligent computer programmer (in either parse of that phrase). Rather, its goal is to equip the reader with enough technical knowledge to follow discussions about what may be required to enable a computer to really think. It therefore touches on each individual technology in a qualitative way, and always with a view to how each individual technology assists in solving the larger problem of building a truly intelligent machine.

These chapters are necessarily somewhat technical, but they do not assume any background in artificial intelligence programming and nor do they assume more than a very basic mathematical ability. If the reader perseveres with this part then they will gain a basic understanding of each of the technologies which should, in turn, provide a better understanding of what intelligence actually is. It will also provide more concrete insights as to what may be required to attain that goal.

Without a basic understanding of the technology, discussions tend to degenerate into management-level block diagrams and analyses of what other people say about the technologies instead of discussing the technologies themselves. Further, some applications of these technologies that appear quite impressive are actually relatively simple to implement, while some intuitively simple problems are very difficult to solve. Understanding the underlying technical issues that are being addressed makes it easier to assess the relevance of those applications. That said, readers may safely skip directly to the third part of the book which explores the consequences of an intelligent machine.

Owned SLindsay

Manager: *The in-flight magazine says that a Neural Bayesian Network would solve all of our problems.*
Minion: *??? ... Excellent idea! Would you like gigabit or fibre channel?*
(Neural, Bayesian and physical networks are quite different technologies.)

This part starts with some of the early yet impressive results obtained using *Good Old Fashion Artificial Intelligence* (GOFAI) techniques. Such naive symbolic systems could prove substantial theorems in mathematical logic, solve differential equations better than most undergraduate mathematicians, and beat most people at chess. However, these successes produced unwarranted optimism, and major limitations in GOFAI needed to be overcome before further progress could be made. One system named *SHRDLU* is of particular interest for its ability to understand complex natural language statements, provided that they concerned its micro world of stacked children's blocks. SHRDLU also provides a good example of a simple planning engine.

More formal methods of knowledge representation and reasoning apply mathematical logic to reason about the real world. Mathematical logic is a powerful tool, but its reliance on absolute truth is often a poor match with the uncertain world in which we live. Several strategies for dealing with that uncertainty are then discussed, including Bayesian networks and their application to building intelligent rule-based expert systems.

All of these systems require the world to be modelled as discrete symbols. Unfortunately, the real world is not neatly packaged as symbols. Instead, it contains patterns and images and loose associations that can either be analyzed directly in order to make predictions or be abstracted into symbolic knowledge which can then be reasoned about more deeply.

The practical concerns of a robot are then addressed, namely to be able to hear, see and move. Speech recognition is now a practical technology that may see increased usage in small devices that lack keyboards. Machine vision is a critical aspect of understanding the environment in which a robot lives. It is a huge area of research in which much has been achieved but the problem is far from solved. A robot also has to move its limbs and body, which involves several non-trivial problems.

The last program that a human need ever write is the program that can write other programs as well as people do. That is a problem for the future, but there are several aspects that are well understood. When computers can really understand the world then writing programs that interact with that world should be relatively straightforward.

Part II also discusses our limited understanding of the human brain, from low-level neurons to higher-level structures such as self-organizing maps. This has and will provide inspiration for our attempts at building an artificial intelligence. The strengths and limitations of work on attempting to directly simulating our brains will also be discussed.

The methods used by computers to become chess world champions are then analyzed. The staggering amount of computation required to achieve this provides insights into the minds of both computers and men. More interestingly, in 2011 the Watson computer won the *Jeopardy!* quiz show against two human champions. Working in the human world of words and sentences required more sophisticated techniques to working in the mathematically defined world of chess.

This is a lot of material to cover. To put it in perspective, the most commonly used undergraduate book on artificial intelligence (by Russell and Norvig) uses over a thousand large, dense pages to provide just a technical overview of the core concepts. It would take a reader with a fair background in programming and mathematics a full year to understand that material, and yet that book is still incomplete. For example the sections on machine vision and robotics are weak, and it does not address brain physiology at all. Many technical books and thousands of academic papers have also been written about each one of these topics.

This overview can only scratch the surface of a major field of research. Many of the examples are also several decades old because that is when the fundamental techniques were developed. But this part should provide a qualitative feel for each of the technologies which should be useful when attempting to go beyond vague, abstract discussions and gain a basic understanding of what the technologies actually are, and to understand their strengths and limitations.

Words Without Meaning

Eliza and Doctor pretend to understand

One of the very early successes of artificial intelligence research was Joseph Weizenbaum's Eliza built in the mid 1960s. Eliza is an ingenious program that appears to understand much more than it actually does. Eliza runs a Doctor script that pretends to be a Rogerian psychologist. It listens patiently to what a patient says, and then provides feedback that encourages the patent to release more and more of the burdens of their soul. A typical conversation might be as follows:-

```
ELIZA: WHAT BRINGS YOU TO SEE ME?
Patient: MY WIFE ASKED ME TO SEE YOU.
ELIZA: TELL ME SOMETHING ABOUT YOUR FAMILY.
Patient: THEY DO NOT TALK TO ME VERY OFTEN.
ELIZA: WHY DO YOU THINK THAT THEY DO NOT TALK TO
YOU VERY
OFTEN?
Patient: MY WIFE SAYS I USE THE COMPUTER TOO
MUCH.
ELIZA: YOU HAVE YOUR MIND ON COMPUTERS, IT SEEMS.
Patient: YES, AND MY HANDS TOO.
ELIZA: WHY DO YOU SAY "YES, AND MY HANDS TOO?".
Patient: BECAUSE I USE IT ALL THE TIME.
ELIZA: IS IT BECAUSE YOU USE IT ALL THE TIME THAT
YOU CAME
TO SEE ME?
Patent: AND BECAUSE MY MOTHER WEARS ARMY BOOTS.
ELIZA: WHO ELSE IN YOUR FAMILY WEARS ARMY BOOTS?
. . .
```

ASR33 Teletype, note the paper tape punch and reader on the left.
Public Wikipedia

Input and output would have been through an electromechanical teletype like the one shown above.

Eliza was able to convince some non-technical users that they were actually talking to another human at the end of a teletype so it nominally passed the Turing test back in the early 1960s. Some time later a paranoid schizophrenic patient named Parry was built using similar technology. Eliza was then connected to Parry, and experts could not distinguish the resulting dialog from real dialogs between doctors and patients.

Patterns of language

Eliza is actually just a clever joke. Rather than understanding what was being said, Eliza uses a library of relatively simple word patterns that could match each sentence and then produce one of a number of canned responses.

For example in the following patterns "*" matches one or more words, and "{n}" means the words in the nth "*".

* mother *

>*Who else in your family {2}?*
>*Does your farther {2}?*

* your *

>*Why are you concerned about my {2}?*
>*Really, my {2}?*

Thus, when Eliza sees

*And because my **mother** <u>wears army boots.</u>*

The underlined section matches the second "*" in the first pattern, so Eliza may response with

Who else in your family <u>wears army boots.</u>?

Likewise

*I'm not sure if my **mother** <u>really loves me</u>?*

might produce

Does your father <u>really love you</u>?

The latter requires the simple substitution "you" for "me" but Eliza has absolutely no real concept of what "love" or "army boots" are. All that it knows is that words are a sequence of letters separated by spaces.

The actual patterns were cleverly constructed with many special cases which produces reasonable sounding responses most of the time. As people try to confuse Eliza, more patterns are added to the script until the final result is surprisingly convincing. It also builds up a history of phrases which it can recombine in different ways later in the conversation. But there is no real understanding.

I blork your dork.

is likely to produce

Why are you concerned about my dork?

Or, more cleverly if dork and blork are not in its dictionary

Please stop talking nonsense.

Journalistic generation

One commentator thought that a recent program called *Automated Insights* demonstrated a new level of artificial intelligence research because it could generate exciting commentary on sporting events that is indistinguishable from that written by professional journalists. Further, it can do this almost instantly, and can be used for lesser matches that would not otherwise justify the attention of a journalist.

This is the type of dialog that can be generated (not actually from Automated Insights):-

The Reds put on a magnificent show and slaughtered the Blues 27 points to 7. This promoted the Reds to a well earned third place in the league. It will be interesting to see whether they can maintain this momentum in their upcoming match against the Greens.

However, this can be achieved using similar techniques to Eliza by using simplistic rules. One such rule might be

If Team1.Score > Team2.Score + 10 then
Output "The " & Team1.Name & Random("put on a magnificent show", "totally out classed", "had an easy win", ...) ...

In other words, if one team won more than ten points more than the other, then output one of a random selection of cliches that express that fact in a journalistic manner. Other rules could look at the positions in the leagues table, the order in which points were scored, and who scored them. This leads easily to fragments like:-

After a very difficult start, Billy Bloggs saved the day with a magnificent point just before half time which equalized the scores. The Reds never looked back, and went on to win the day showing impressive skill and strategy. Their coach, Fred Nurk, was very pleased with the result.

A few hundred such rules can rival a professional sports journalist for the effective combination of the latest cliches. And all without any real understanding of what sport actually is.

The works of Shakespeare

It is easy to create a program that can reproduce the works of Shakespeare. One simply puts the text into a big file, and then has the program print it out. The program would have no understanding of anything other than how to print the contents of a file. But experts would find the results to be indistinguishable from the works or Shakespeare because that is exactly what they would be. If one did not know how the program worked, nor the works of Shakespeare, then the program would appear to be very intelligent indeed. But the intelligence would be in the supplied data, not the program.

The journalistic generation above is certainly more intelligent than a simple copy program. It needs to copy fragments of text and combine them sensibly, which is not easy to do convincingly. The results can then be indistinguishable from professionally written text because that is essentially what they are. It is therefore not easy to distinguish between real advances in artificial intelligence and clever demonstrations of old ideas unless one has some understanding of artificial intelligence technologies.

Another example is that in 2011 the respected literary magazine *The Archive* published a short poem called "For the Bristlecone Snag". What the editors did not know was that the poem was written by a computer. In one sense this passed the Turing test, but the Eliza-like program was just cleverly rearranging words that were then interpreted by people to have meaning.

The nature of words

The Eliza experiment was valuable because it highlighted both the strength and weakness of naive symbolic processing. Weizenbaum was very critical of his own creation, considering it to be just a parody of intelligence, which in a sense it was.

However, Weizenbaum developed Eliza in an age when true intelligence was thought to be an easily attainable goal. It had a powerful effect on people's view of computers and what they could do. Some people thought that with further development it might become a useful tool for psychoanalysis. But it was very much like Searle's man climbing a tree to get to the moon. Initial progress was impressive until the top of the tree was reached.

That said, similar techniques are now used to produce very useful tools, even if they are not really intelligent.

Perhaps the most commonly use of this type of technology are the Internet search engines such as Google. They mainly just create a large index words contained within each web page, but they also look for patterns of words that might be a street addresses, person's name or other interesting phrases in web documents.

Google has introduced a "Knowledge Graph" which attempts to deepen its understanding of the pages that it indexes. This blurs the line between simple pattern matching and some semblance of intelligence.

Modern statistical natural language translation also uses partial parsing techniques to produce useful, if not perfect, translations without really understanding any of the text that they are translating. This type of analysis was also important for the Watson *Jeopardy!* winning program, which will be discussed in subsequent chapters.

There are now several chat bots on the web that combine Eliza-like processing with cleverly animated avatars for no particular reason. Below is an example of a conversation with ALICE at www.pandorabots.com.

judge: i like to ride bicycles
ALICE: The feeling of your body moving forward on a ride can be very relaxing.
judge: do you like bicycles?
ALICE: No, I don't care for it.
judge: what do you like to do?
ALICE: I like chatting with people online.
judge: what do you eat?
ALICE: ALICE eats electricity.
judge: does it taste good?
ALICE: It depends on the voltage.
judge: what is the best voltage?
ALICE: I don't have a favorite voltage. My favorite color is green.

Real Meaning in a Microworld

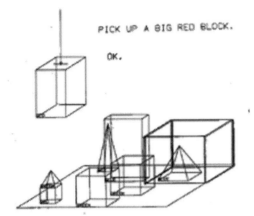

Original SHRDLU wire frame graphics.
Educational http://hci.stanford.edu/winograd/shrdlu/

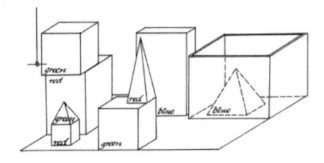

SHRDLU With hidden lines removed.
Blog http://lesswrong.com/lw/k0q/shrdlu_understanding_anthropomorphisation_and/

By the early 1970s many more substantial results had been obtained. One highlight was Terry Winograd's SHRDLU, which could engage in dialogs about a stack of blocks. Unlike Eliza, SHRDLU really did understand exactly what was being said, provided it was about its very limited world of blocks. (The name "SHRDLU" is not an acronym, it comes from a science fiction story.)

These are impressive extracts from a classic dialog with the program:-

1. Person: FIND A BLOCK WHICH IS TALLER THAN THE ONE YOU ARE HOLDING AND PUT IT INTO THE BOX.

2. Computer: BY "IT", I ASSUME YOU MEAN THE BLOCK WHICH IS TALLER THAN THE ONE I AM HOLDING.
(i.e. not the block that it is holding, which would make the reference to the taller one redundant.)

3. Computer: OK. (does it)...

4. Person: DOES THE SHORTEST THING THE TALLEST PYRAMID'S SUPPORT SUPPORTS SUPPORT ANYTHING GREEN?

5. Computer: YES, THE GREEN PYRAMID.

6. Person: WHAT COLOR IS IT?

7. Computer: BY "IT", I ASSUME YOU MEAN THE SHORTEST THING THE TALLEST PYRAMID'S SUPPORT SUPPORTS.

8. Computer: RED (Ie. not the green pyramid, that would be trivial)...

9. Person: A "STEEPLE" IS A STACK WHICH CONTAINS TWO GREEN CUBES AND A PYRAMID.

10. Computer: I UNDERSTAND.

11. Person: BUILD ONE.

12. Computer: OK. (does it)...

13. Person: I LIKE BLOCKS WHICH ARE NOT RED, BUT I DON'T LIKE ANYTHING WHICH SUPPORTS A PYRAMID.

14. Computer: I UNDERSTAND.

15. Person: DO I LIKE ANYTHING IN THE BOX? ...

16. Person: WHY DID YOU CLEAR OFF THAT CUBE?

17. Computer: TO PUT IT ON A LARGE GREEN CUBE.
    ...

One can see that SHRDLU could parse quite complex sentences, learn new terms, relate them to its world of blocks, and plan moderately complex actions to satisfy goals. All this on an ancient computer that was far less powerful than that contained in a primitive, non-"smart" mobile phone. This is highlighted by the crude display, which shows a wire frame without hidden lines being removed. (The actual colours of each block were only in the mind of SHRDLU; the display was monochrome.) Even today there are very few programs in use that have this level of language understanding and reasoning.

(SHRDLU was a Ph.D. project hacked together in order to demonstrate its core ideas and was never intended to be robust. Apparently, the code stopped working after Winograd submitted his thesis because he had hacked the generated assembler code without updating the source code, which then broke when the computer was upgraded.)

Parsing natural language

SHRDLU's primary focus was on natural language understanding. Philosophers have always seen language as a window to understanding cognition. Language is used to express thoughts so if language could be really understood then so could thoughts. SHRDLU showed that being able to use sophisticated language in a limited domain most certainly does not imply general intelligence. Still, SHRDLU was impressive.

Consider the following simple sentence:-

The silly robot dropped the red block into the box.

Linguists classify different types of words according to their grammatical purpose. The sentence above contains nouns such as "robot" and "block", the adjectives "silly" and "red", and the preposition "into". With that basic level of analysis, it is possible to determine that the sentence involves a robot, a block and a box and the act of dropping something somewhere.

To understand what the sentence really means requires deeper analysis of how the words are are related to each other grammatically. So as to determine who dropped what where. The traditional way that linguists do this is to define a formal grammar which defines all the possible relationships between words and then use that grammar to determine the actual relationship between the words. This is known as *parsing* a sentence.

The sentence above might be parsed into the following tree:-

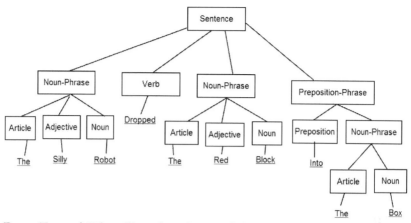

Parse Tree of "The silly robot dropped the red block into the box".
Owned

It means that the Sentence contains a Noun-Phrase, followed by a Verb, followed by a second Noun-Phrase, followed by a Preposition-Phrase. The first Noun-Phrase in turn consists of an Article (the word "<u>the</u>") followed by an Adjective ("<u>silly</u>") and a Noun ("<u>robot</u>"). Importantly, the parse tree associates the preposition "<u>into</u>" with "<u>the box</u>" rather than "<u>block</u>".

(Computer scientists may be poor gardeners as their trees usually grow upside down. The bottom nodes in the diagram above are *leaves*, Sentence is the *root*.)

The tree above might also be written as follows:-

Sentence(
  Noun-Phrase(Article(<u>the</u>) Adjective(<u>silly</u>) Noun(<u>robot</u>))
  Verb(<u>dropped</u>)
  Noun-Phrase(Article(<u>the</u>) Adjective(<u>red</u>) Noun(<u>block</u>))
  Preposition-Phrase(Preposition(<u>into</u>) Noun-Phrase(Article(<u>the</u>) Noun(<u>box</u>)))

This parse would match the grammar defined in the following table. "Non-Terminal" symbols such as *Noun-Phrase* are defined as a sequence of other symbols, which are ultimately the underlined "Terminal" words that actually appear in the sentence. Following normal conventions, the "{}"s mean zero or more repetitions, and the "|" means "or". So in this grammar a Noun-Phrase is defined to be an Article ("the" or "a"), followed by zero or more Adjectives, followed by a Noun.

Non Terminal	Definition
Noun-Phrase	Article {Adjective} Noun
Prepositional-Phrase	Preposition Noun-Phrase
Sentence	Noun-Phrase Verb Noun-Phrase {Prepositional-Phrase}
Article	the_	a	an
Verb	saw	heard	took	dropped
Preposition	with	by	in
Adjective	silly	clever	red
Noun	block	box	telescope	robot

Having used the grammar to parse the sentence, the system might describe it using a *"frame"* structure that represents the knowledge contained in the sentence. The frame might look like

Frame F-123
Type: <u>dropped</u>: movement, accidental
Actor: <u>the silly robot</u>
Object: <u>the red block</u>
Target: <u>the box</u>

Frame structures along these lines make it easy to answer queries such as, "Who dropped the red block into the box?", or, "Where did the silly robot drop the red block?", or, "What did the silly robot drop into the box?". Parsing the sentence enables the three noun phrases in it to be given the precise roles that enable these queries to be answered. The roles on the frame, such as Actor and Object tell us that <u>the box</u> did not drop <u>the silly robot</u> into <u>the red block</u>.

This is much more sophisticated than a search engine that just looks for sentences that contain certain words. So, unlike a search engine, it would not try to sell you a holiday in Egypt when you started to talk about stacking pyramids.

SHRDLU contained a much more elaborate grammar than the one above, and it could parse some quite difficult sentences. Indeed, many if not most native English speakers cannot understand what "support supports support" means in the 4th line of the earlier dialog, and thus cannot answer the question correctly.

SHRDLU also took great care with object references. For example, the first sentence in the dialog refers to two blocks, namely the one that it is holding and the one that is taller than the one that it is holding. SHRDLU assumes that the "it" refers to the taller block because otherwise the sentence would have a redundant reference to the taller block, and SHRDLU knows that people do not add pointless clauses to sentences. It is interesting that people perform such sophisticated analyses subconsciously.

There are also several blocks of the same colour, so the only way to distinguish them is by their properties, such as their shape, size and position. SHRDLU took care to use a minimal description of each block to provide sensible, non-redundant responses.

Planning to meet goals

SHRDLU's world was simple enough that one could just write an ordinary procedural program to carry out its actions. For example, the following procedure could move a block from one position to another, which might involve first moving other blocks that are in the way, recursively.

```
Procedure Move-Block(from, to)
If to Is-A Pyramid Then Abort
Clear-Block(from)
Clear-Block(to)
Pick-Up(from)
Put-Down(to)
End
Procedure Clear-Block(block)
For-Each Block b On-Top-Of block
Move-Block(b, Table)
Next b
End
```

In these fragments lower case words are variables. Move-Block is the main procedure that moves a block from position from to position to. Move-Block calls Clear-Block twice to ensure that both the from and the to blocks do not have any obscuring blocks on top of them. Clear-Block then recursively calls Move-Block to move any such obscuring blocks to the Table.

However, such hard-coded logic does not scale well to larger problems. More importantly, it does not facilitate introspection as to why SHRDLU did something, as shown in line 16 of the dialog. So SHRDLU used a more sophisticated planning engine.

SHRDLU used a system similar to STRIPS, developed in 1971. STRIPS has a set of potential actions that can be made. Each action has a precondition that must be true before it can occur and a post condition that becomes true after the action has finished. For example, the following rules say that you can only pick up a block x if you are not holding anything else, and if there is nothing on x, and that you cannot pick up the box. The second rule describes putting a block x that is being held on top of block y.

```
Action: Pick-Up(x)
Precondition: Holding(Nothing)  and  not  On(y,  x)
and not x = Box
Postcondition: Holding(x)

Action: Put-Down(y)
Precondition: Holding(x)  and  not  x  =  Nothing  and
not y Is-A Pyramid
Postcondition: Holding(Nothing) and On(x, y)
```

The planning engine is then given an initial state about where the blocks are now, and a goal such as `On(Block-123, Table)`. The engine's goal is to find a sequence of actions, each of which satisfies their pre-conditions and produces a post-condition suitable for the next action's pre-condition, until ultimately the goal is satisfied.

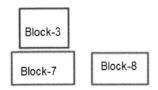

A simple arrangement of blocks.
Owned

If the initial state includes `On(Block-3, Block-7)` as shown above, and the goal is `On(Block-7, Block-8)`, then a precondition to moving Block-7 to Block-8 will be that there is nothing on top of Block-7. This would generate a subgoal to move Block-3 off Block-7, possibly by putting Block-3 on the Table.

Working from the goal to the initial state like this is called *backward chaining*, while working from the initial state to the final state is called *forward chaining*, and both are often used together.

It is easy to create new actions or add to the pre and post conditions of existing actions because the search for the correct sequence of actions can be left to the planning engine. This also makes it easy for SHRDLU to explain why it does things by simply remembering the preconditions and goals of each step. If SHRDLU was asked whether it can do something like stack two pyramids the answer was not hard wired. Instead, SHRDLU just tried to do it, fails, and then said so.

Building real planning systems that have large numbers of parameterized actions with complex preconditions is a major field of practical AI research. An additional requirement is to achieve the goal state at minimum cost. Care also needs to be taken that the engine does not make endless searches in order to satisfy goals that cannot be satisfied.

Parsing limitations

The language parsing techniques described above are widely used today for understanding artificial computer languages such as COBOL, Basic and SQL. These languages have been designed to be well behaved syntactically, and so are easy to parse in the unambiguous manner required to accurately specify computer algorithms.

However, it is much more difficult to parse natural language. The first problem is that words in a dictionary are not always neatly divided into nouns, verbs and other syntactic classifications. For example, the word "police" can be a noun ("the police"), adjective ("police cars") or a verb ("they police thoughts"), leading to the classic sentence:-

Police police police police.

Ambiguity also occurs at higher levels. Consider the following paragraph.

Robby saw Suzie with his telescope. She was observing the moon. Robby walked over and gave her his telescope so that she could see the moon more clearly.

The question is, who had the telescope? After the first sentence it is probably Robby because telescopes are used for seeing things and Robbie saw Suzie. After the second sentence it is more likely to be Suzie because telescopes are used to observe the moon. But after the third sentence it is clear that Robby had the telescope. Most people casually reading paragraphs like the above do not even realize the ambiguity, yet can understand the story accurately.

A similar example is *"Joan thanked Suzy for her help"*. People subconsciously know that "her" refers to Suzy based on a fairly sophisticated understanding of gratitude. The grammar alone cannot resolve the ambiguity, but without resolving it the sentence is meaningless.

The classic example of this type of ambiguity is:

Time flies like an arrow.

This could mean anything from an obscure metaphor about time, the culinary taste of a species of time flies (c.f. *Fruit flies like a banana.*) or an instruction to measure how fast flies fly using similar techniques that are used to measure the speed of arrows. If instead the sentence refers to the habits of aeroplane pilot Mr Time, it could mean that he flies in straight lines, flies fast, is inflexible, or is a sky writer painting an arrow.

Parsing unconstrained natural language requires the entanglement of semantic and syntactic processing as well as back tracking out of incorrect partial parses. People also have difficulty parsing sentences when there are strong false semantic clues at the beginning of the sentence that lead them "up the garden path". These sentences are of interest to linguists because they give clues as to how people parse ordinary sentences. The reason people do not often have trouble parsing normal sentences appears to be that as authors people only create sentences that will be easy to parse.

Below is a selection of perfectly valid "garden path" sentences for the reader's amusement. In each case, the human parsing stalls at a word well into the sentence, and the rest of the sentence seems invalid. But with careful re-reading, the sentences will be seen to be perfectly valid, and sometimes not even unusual. Modern machine parsing can actually do better than people on these types of sentences because it is better at backing up and trying a different interpretation of the syntactic elements without getting stuck on the initially more obvious, but incorrect, parse.

- Does this butcher's knife handle frozen foods too. ("handle" is the verb.)
- Granite rocks during earthquakes. ("rocks" is the verb.)
- I told the girl the boy seduced the story.
- Without her contributions to the fund would be inadequate.
- The cotton shirts are made from comes from Egypt.
- The prime number few.
- The dealer sold the forgery complained.
- The boy got fat melted.
- The Russian women like is Sergei.

Unconstrained natural language

There are many grammars that have been developed in attempts to capture an entire natural language. They use much more sophisticated grammar rules than were used by SHRDLU. However, it turns out that however large and complex a grammar is, there always seem to be some quite normal natural language statements that cannot be parsed at all, let alone unambiguously. Of course there are also many sentences with grammar incorrect still that intelligible are.

Modern parsing systems use a statistical approach in which partial grammars are used to analyze a large corpus of English sentences. The language systems learn many new, special case grammar rules as they see more and more constructs. This approach is particularly important when translating documents from one language to another by remembering how types of phrases were translated in other documents. Several databases of language elements can be used to assist in natural language parsing. For example, WordNet is a giant lexical database that groups words into over a hundred thousand synonym sets, provides short, general definitions, and records semantic relationships between different synonym sets.

It appears that the concurrent semantic analysis that can lead us up the garden path is actually an essential aspect of parsing natural language. Unlike artificial computer languages, one cannot complete the parsing of natural language before the semantic analysis has been started, which greatly complicates the architecture.

Language is so entangled with reasoning that no system will be able to really understand human language unless it also has human-level intelligence. The problem is sometimes referred to as being *AI-Complete*. SHRDLU could understand its sentences precisely because it could only talk about things that it understood, i.e. stacking blocks. That said, it is probably fair to say that the basic problem of parsing (as opposed to understanding) natural language has now been adequately solved.

SHRDLU's knowledge representation

A major limitation of SHRDLU was that it only understood blocks stacked on a table. This is a very simple world that can be described by adequately using a simple table of what objects are on top of other objects. It does not even describe a real world of children's blocks which can have blocks stacked in odd angles, and stacks of blocks that fall down due to careless placement.

Reasoning is also severely limited to understanding how blocks relate to one another and maybe counting the number of blocks that satisfy fairly simple criteria such as *"How many blocks do I like"*.

The real world has many different types of objects that have complex and often weakly defined relationships to one another. It is full of ambiguity and contradictions, and sophisticated reasoning is required to understand it.

Database Query languages

Employees			
Name	**Address**	**City**	**Salary**
Smith	123 Any St	Mooloolah	5,000
Jones	234 Some St	Suburbia	11,000

One early application of natural language was to query general purpose relational databases. A relational database simply stores information in a series of tables such as the Employee table above. Several systems in the 1970s could understand queries along the following lines:-

```
LIST NAME, ADDRESS OF EMPLOYEES HAVING SALARY
> 10000?
WHICH EMPLOYEES HAVE CITY = MOOLOOLAH OR CITY =
EUDLO?
```

A naive system can do this by working in another microworld, that of tables of data with columns. So, in the first query it would simply know that there was some table called EMPLOYEE containing columns named NAME, ADDRESS and SALARY with no further knowledge of what employees or salaries are. Such systems can certainly be used, and indeed today the main programming language used to query databases is SQL which was designed to look like natural language queries.

However, the system breaks down in the second query. While it is perfectly legible, a normal person would ask something like

```
WHO LIVES IN MOOLOOLAH AND EUDLO?
```

To process that query, the software needs to know that people live in places, thus MOOLOOLAH is a place, and further it looks like a CITY. If previous queries involved employees it would know that the people involved were EMPLOYEES and not CUSTOMERS, say. It also needs to determine that the AND actually means OR because people do not (normally) live in two places at once.

These types of common sense domain knowledge pushe the query system well beyond a simple microworld. To address this and many other issues natural language systems often present their interpretation of the query back to the user using a more formal language which the user can verify, if they understand the more formal language.

One early and somewhat successful system was LUNAR in 1973 which could answer fairly complex queries about the moon rocks that had been recently collected by the Apollo missions. It could answer queries like the following which involve considerable domain knowledge:-

```
WHAT IS THE AVERAGE CONCENTRATION OF ALUMINUM
IN HIGH ALKALI ROCKS?
HOW MANY BRECCIAS CONTAIN OLIVINE?
```

This was another very impressive early result given that the discipline of AI was less than twenty years old and the very primitive computers that were available. However, natural language query systems are rarely used today because they tend to be brittle, so they require the user to know how to phrase questions that the system can answer. A better approach seems to be to present the structure of the data in a graphical user interface and then let the user specify the query directly in terms of the symbols that the computer does understand.

As advances are made in commonsense reasoning this may change. Producing an effective natural language query processor is a major goal of the semantic web community.

Eurisko and other early results

One of the more commonly quoted early works is Eurisko, created by Douglas Lenat in 1976. It used various heuristics to generate short programs that could be interpreted as mathematical theorems. It also had heuristics for how to create new heuristics. It had some success, winning the Traveler ship building game against human competitors.

The AGI community often reveres Eurisko as an example of a very powerful early computer system. However, while Eurisko was certainly impressive, it was not as intelligent as is often made out. Much of the success in the Traveler competition was due to Lenat carefully guiding Eurisko, although Lenat says that he could not have won the competition on his own. When applied to more complex problems, Eurisko ran out of puff and failed to provide solutions due to combinatorial explosion discussed earlier in Part I. Lenat himself abandoned the approach and went on to found the Cyc project.

There were many other impressive systems developed during this golden era of the 1970s. Systems could learn patterns from descriptions. For example, given a description of blocks stacked as an "arch" one system could propose alternative stackings and ask the user whether they were also arches. It would then quickly build an abstract model of what configurations the user would consider to be an arch.

Knowledge Representation and Reasoning

Overview

All intelligent systems need to store information about the world and then make deductions based on that knowledge. This chapter describes the more important methods of representing that knowledge, and corresponding ways to reason about it. Rather than start with low level problems such as how to move a robot arm, these techniques start with with a high level description of complex problems using symbols and then try to reason about them directly.

Relational Databases

The most basic representation of knowledge is simple tables of data in a relational database. Databases normally contain fairly simple structures representing business objects such as Employees, Departments, and Customers. A realistic database may have dozens of tables, and some of the columns in the tables may be used to refer to rows in other tables. Tables can also represent more abstract concepts such as Events, Objects and Actors.

Birds			
Name	**Is-A**	**Flies**	**Lives-In**
Tweety	Bush-Turkey	Yes	My-Back-Yard
Bush-Turkey	Bird	Yes	
Bird		Yes	
Tux	Penguin	No	
Penguin	Bird	No	

The table above represents information about a few birds. It includes the somewhat unusual Is-A column which refers to the Name of another row in the same table. So Tweety is a Bush-Turkey.

The column headings form a *schema* which constrains the type of information that the tables can hold. This enables simple programs to query and analyze the data in well-defined ways. These types of structures form the basis of relational/object databases, and so form the basis of most modern computer systems. For example, an educational system might have tables for Students and Classes, an e-commerce system might have tables of Orders and Products.

Most of the world's programmers develop applications that are based on this type of database, and much research has gone into their structure and implementation. However, they are not generally referred to as being *artificial intelligence* systems.

Frames and semantic networks

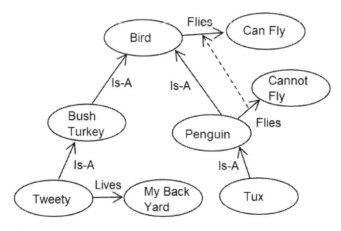

A Semantic Network.
Owned

Semantic networks like the one above represent data as a node-arc graph, which makes them easier for humans to understand. The nodes represent objects and the links represent the relationship between them.

It should be noted that the network in the diagram represents exactly the same information as the database table above, but the diagram makes the relationship between Tux, Penguins and Birds more obvious. The values in the Name column have been placed into nodes, and other column names have become links. Being able to use our human visualization ability is important to aid our own understanding, but does not change the semantics of the data.

Unlike an ordinary database, a semantic network unifies the concept of *tables* (or *"rntities"*) and cell values (or *"attributes"*) into nodes, and they are not normally constrained by a schema. Semantic networks usually contain some type of inheritance, in this case via an *Is-A* link. This enables simple deductions to be made by the network itself. In the example Tweety can fly because it is a Bird and birds can normally fly, but Tux cannot fly because Penguins are a special case. Semantic networks provide a powerful representation of symbolic information. However, they focus on storing and retrieving fairly static data rather than reasoning deeply about it logically.

Mathematical logic

Mathematics has a long tradition of providing proofs of complex ideas as a series of steps, each one dependent upon the previous step. For example, consider the following dubious proof:-

1. Given $x^2+x+1=0$
2. $x^2=-x-1$
3. $x=-1 -1/x$
4. Substituting the last expression for (x) in the original equation produces:
5. $x^2+(x)+1=0$
6. $x^2 + (-1-1/x) +1 = 0$
7. $x^2=1/x$
8. $x^3=1$
9. $x=1$
10. Substituting x=1 in the original equation then yields:
11. $1^2+1+1 = 0$
12. $3 = 0$
13. Which Was <u>not</u> What Was Wanted!

Each individual step is clear and logical, depending on the previous step. There is no division by zero. Most people would not fault its reasoning until its bizarre conclusion, namely that 3 = 0. Even then the problem is not obvious, namely that $x^2+x+1=0$ has no real solutions. This fallacy is relatively crude, but there are other areas of mathematics where it can be quite difficult to determine whether a proof is in fact valid or not.

To address these concerns, mathematicians began to formalize the rules used to prove mathematical theorems in the mid nineteenth century. They developed first order logic, which can be extended to be powerful enough to represent and reason about most mathematical concepts. If a proof accurately follows the very well-defined rules of logic, then it must be valid. It has also been proven that first order logic is always *consistent* in the sense of never proving the same predicate to be both true and false.

Logic for artificial intelligence

From the very beginnings of research into artificial intelligence, it was realized that a system that was sufficiently powerful to reason about mathematics could also be used to reason about everyday events. Mathematical logic might therefore be a very powerful tool in modeling human intelligence.

Further, in the late 1960s general purpose theorem provers were developed that could, in theory, find a proof of almost any valid theory. This suggested that the world could be understood by simply representing it in first order logic, and then using a theorem prover to deduce whatever was required.

Consider the following case of the murdered husband:-

The murder scene.
Owned SLindsay

The husband was discovered in the morning with a knife protruding from his back, with no witnesses to the stabbing. However, the solution to this crime is elementary. Only the butler and the widow were in the house during the night, so the murderer must be one of them. The widow has an alibi because she was on the phone to her personal trainer for the entire night. So the butler must be the murderer.

The dubious reasoning above can be represented by the following statements in mathematical logic.

1. `Murderer(Butler) or Murderer(Widow)`
2. `Alibi(person) implies not Murderer(person)`
3. `Alibi(Widow)`
4. `2 & 3 proves: not Murderer(Widow)`
5. `1 & 4 proves: Murderer(Butler)`

The first statement states that either the Butler or the Widow is the Murderer, but without specifying which one is actually guilty. This is more than can be represented in a simple database or semantic network, which normally only represent *ground* facts such as that a particular person was in fact the murderer.

The second statement is even more general. It says for *any* person, having an alibi means that they are not the murderer. person is written in lower case to indicate that it is a variable, although logicians prefer single letters like p. In this case the possible values for person are Butler and Widow. The third statement says that the widow has an alibi. Statements 2 and 3 can then be used to prove that the Widow is innocent, and then statement 1 and 4 proves the guilt of the Butler. Each statement is either a logical assertion about the world or deduction that follows formal rules applied to specific earlier statements.

Logical statements can also be used to reason in different directions. In our example, if Murderer(Butler) was known, then the second statement could also be used to deduce not Alibi(Butler).

Modern theorem provers can easily make much more substantial deductions over fairly large fact bases. First order logic is only semi-decidable, so no theorem prover can prove all theorems. If it does prove a theorem then the proof is guaranteed to be valid — there is no guessing involved. Further, the deduction and proof will remain valid unless the facts upon which it is based are changed.

Propositional vs. first order systems

Logicians normally distinguish between simple propositional logics and more complex first order logics that include variables. For example, the following propositional clauses describe the relationship between wet grass and rain:-

- Rain implies WetGrass
- Sprinkler implies WetGrass
- WetGrass implies (Rain or Sprinkler or SomethingElse)

On the other hand, first order logic includes more general predicates that can include variables (such as x) to represent objects. Examples include:-

- `forall x (Alibi(x) implies not Murderer(x))`
- `exists x (Murderer(x))`
- `forall p forall c forall g (Parent(p, c)`
  `and Parent(g, p) implies GrandParent(p, c))`

The last assertion defines a grandparent g to be a child c's parent p's parent. (The forall qualifier is normally implied and has not been written explicitly in other sections of this book. Variables are in lower case.)

Clearly, first order logic is much more powerful than propositional logic. However, propositional logic has advantages. Firstly, it is finite — if there are n variables then there can be at most 2^n states. That makes it fully decidable, i.e. it is possible both in theory and in practice to accurately determine whether any statement can be proved. Ugly constructs such as "this statement cannot be proved" simply cannot be expressed in propositional logic. In practice there are very efficient algorithms for handling huge numbers of propositional clauses.

Systems that learn from experience or handle probabilistic reasoning are mainly propositional, although some of them can be extended to limited first order cases. The wet grass example above will be used in the later discussion of Bayesian networks.

Paraconsistent flying pigs

Mathematical logic can be very powerful, but its reliance on absolute truth is in many ways its Achilles' heel. Consider the following proof:-

1. `Man(x) implies Mortal(x)`
2. `Man(Jesus)`
3. `1 & 2 proves: Mortal(Jesus)`
4. `God(x) implies not Mortal(x)`
5. `God(Jesus)`
6. `4 & 5 proves: not Mortal(Jesus)`
7. `6 proves: not Mortal(Jesus) or Fly(Pigs)`

```
8.  2 & 7 proves:  Fly(Pigs)
```

It is not surprising that confusion over the mystery of the holy trinity leads to confusion as to whether Jesus is mortal, but the above proof has used that confusion to prove that pigs can fly.

It is the very definition of disjunction that if `A  or  B` is true, then either `A` is true or `B` is true. Thus if it is known that `A` is true, then `A  or  X` must also be true, regardless of whether `X` is true. This is how step 7 of the above proof then introduces flying pigs into the confusion about the trinity. Now, if `C  or  D` is true, and `C` is false, then clearly `D` must be true. Step 3 has already proven that `Mortal(Jesus)`, so <u>`not  Mortal(Jesus)`</u> must be false. So if <u>`not Mortal(Jesus)`</u> or `Fly(Pigs)` then clearly pigs can fly.

This is a major problem, because it means that any small inconsistency in a large fact base can lead to arbitrarily incorrect deductions. They are trivial to spot in our toy proof above, but much more subtle when a realistically sized fact base is used.

There are a number of logics known as *paraconsistent* that try to address this issue by restricting the logic in various ways. While they can certainly prevent pigs from flying, they also reduce the deductive power of the logic so that it cannot make some otherwise valid inferences.

Monotonicity

A deeper problem is that classical logic is "monotonic", in the sense that new facts cannot invalidate any previous deductions. That is because each deduction is based explicitly on previous deductions or assertions. Any additional assertions are simply not used by the proof.

For example, given the assertion that all `Birds` can `Fly`, there is no way that `Penguins` can be a `Bird` that does not `Fly`. On the other hand, if it is asserted that only some `Birds` can `Fly`, there is no way to deduce that `Sparrows` can fly just because nothing else has been said about `Sparrows'` flying capabilities.

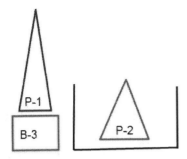

It is difficult to describe a simple scene logically.
Owned

A related problem is that all things that are false also need to be explicitly enumerated. For example, in the blocks world suppose it has been asserted that Pyramid-1 is on Block-3 and Pyramid-2 is in the box, i.e. `On(Pyramid-1, Block-3)` and `On(Pyramid-2, Box)`. This does not enable the deduction that there are no pyramids on the table. One reason for this is that just because no other pyramids have been mentioned does not mean that there might not be a `Pyramid-3` lurking on the table.

Also just because `On(Pyramid-2, Box)` does not mean that `Pyramid-2` might not also be on the table, i.e. that objects could not be in two places at the same time. Another problem is that `Pyramid-1` might actually just be a different name for `Block-3`, so that they actually refer to the same object. We tend to project these types of common-sense assumptions onto the symbols that we use, but the logic engine only understands the specific assertions that have been formally made.

Having to specify everything that is true in order to produce absolutely correct deductions is just not practical nor is it even feasible when modeling the real world outside of mathematics. One approach to this problem is to try to introduce default rules that make deductions if and only if they cannot be shown to be inconsistent with other known rules. A default rule that all birds can fly should not deduce that penguins can fly because that would be a contradiction. However, such default logics become very messy when a large number of conflicting default rules are involved. There is also the non-trivial issue that logic is *undecidable*, which means that it is not possible to detect all contradictions in theory let alone in practice, and thus it is not possible to reliably determine which default rules should be used.

Closed world, Prolog

One very practical and fairly widely used logic system is Prolog, or its simpler subset Datalog. They address the default rule problems by using a closed-world assumption in which clauses that cannot be shown to be true are assumed to be false. This is then combined with a restricted "Horn clause" logic that makes it possible to determine whether a clause is in fact true, both in theory and in practice. A simple set of Datalog clauses might be:-

```
1.  BushTurkey(Tweety)
2.  Bird(x)  :- BushTurkey(x)
3.  Penguin(Tux)
4.  Bird(x)  :- Penguin(X)
5.  Fly(x)  :- Bird(x), not(Flightless(x))
6.  Flightless(x)  :- Penguin(x)
```

(This example sticks to the convention that lower-case names are variables, which is actually the opposite of what Prolog uses.)

This repeats the bird data from our semantic network. Line 1 asserts that Tweety is a BushTurkey, and line 2 says that if some object x is a BushTurkey then it is also a Bird. It is the 5th line that is most interesting, in that it asserts that all Birds can Fly, unless they are known to be Flightless (the comma means conjunction, i.e. *and*). Thus the system can deduce that Tweety can fly without having to be explicitly told that BushTurkeys can fly, and yet there is no doubt that Tux cannot fly because line 6 states that Penguins are Flightless.

The problem with Prolog/Datalog is that in order to make the closed-world assumption workable, the logic has to be substantially simplified. In particular, it is not possible to assert disjunctions (i.e. or) such as Murderer(Butler) or Murderer(Widow) and so make the interesting deductions that solve the crime. It is also not possible to distinguish things that are known to be false from things that are simply not known to be true. Various attempts have been made to address these shortcomings, but they all have issues and none have become widely used.

(Prolog can also be used as a general purpose programming language by making assumptions as to how its very simple theorem prover works — hence the name <u>pro</u>gramming in <u>log</u>ic. However, most AI programmers traditionally preferred the dedicated programming language Lisp. Lisp has powerful macro and other features and enabled many different paradigms to be used including but not limited to Prolog's Horne clause logic. Sadly, today both Prolog and Lisp have fallen into disuse, and most AI development is now done in the more primitive Java or .Net environments, if not the very crude C++ programming language.)

Description logics

Yet another approach is description logics which combine logic engines with semantic networks. They efficiently make simple deductions based on "terminological" data that is stored in the network and combine these with more general "assertional" logic rules. For example, a description logic might add the following assertion to the semantic network above:-

```
BushTurkey(x)     and     LivesIn(x,     y)     implies
GardenDugUp(y)
```

In combination with the knowledge from the semantic network that Tweety lives in my back-yard, this would enable the system to efficiently deduce that the author's back-yard will be dug up by the evil turkey.

Description logics support *primitive* concepts, such as explicitly saying that Tweety is a Bird, as well as *defined* concepts such as saying that an Animal that has Feathers is a Bird. They use defined concepts to recognize that Tweety is a bird given that it has feathers, and can also automatically determine which defined concepts are special cases of other defined concepts. As always, there is a trade-off between the power of the logic to represent complex conditions and the ability of the theorem prover to reliably reason about the concepts.

Perhaps more interestingly, some description logics use Is-A inheritance within semantic networks to provide a more well behaved approach to the problem of default reasoning. This author has published papers showing how semantic networks and description logics can be used to structure complex expert system rule bases.

Ontologies and databases

Ontologies provide a hierarchical framework for the terms used in an information system. One simple ontology is Wordnet, which is widely used to assist in natural language processing. It contains the definitions of some 150,000 words, or more specifically, *synsets,* which are collections of words with the same meaning. Thus "engine" the machine is in a different synset from "engine" to cause (e.g. "the engine of change"). For each synset Wordnet contains a list hyponyms or subtypes, so for "engine" that includes "aircraft engine" and "generator". It also contains super-type hierarchies such as "machine", "artefact", and "physical object". Relationships include *part of* which for "engine" includes "piston" and "crank", synonyms, and antonyms.

Another commonly used database is DBPedia which is a semi-automatic extraction of basic facts from Wikipedia such as the names and capitols of countries.

The SNOMED medical terminology is a more formal system that is used to define diseases, procedures, substances, etc. that are stored in patient and hospital record systems. This enables intelligent systems to review the data in order to check for errors and to look for large scale epidemiological effects. SNOMED is based on a description logic and uses both primitive and defined concepts that form a huge type hierarchy. So for example "flu" is both a "viral infection" and a "respiratory disease", which in turn is a "disease" with the "infection site" being the "lung". The description logic then enables concepts to be automatically determined, based on attributes that may be supplied. Many subtleties arise when attempting to formalize descriptions of the real world in a description logic.

Modeling situations

There has been considerable research into different ways to use mathematical logic in order to model the real world. One area of interest is the modeling of a sequence of steps to achieve a goal, such as stacking some blocks.

An assertions such as on (Pyramid-1, Block-3) makes an absolute statement with no regard to time. But a robot stacking blocks will be constantly changing their configuration so a method is required to distinguish the state of the world at different points in time (or more generally, in different *situations*).

One method of addressing this issue is the STRIPS planning engine discussed earlier. The logical system need only describe the state of the world at specific instances in time, and the planning engine then asserts and retracts assertions as it determines its plan. There are *truth maintenance systems* that enable assertions to be efficiently added and removed without having to redundantly remake deductions that are unaffected by those changes.

The situation calculus takes a different approach by representing situations in the logic itself. Each predicate such as

on (Pyramid-1, Block-3)

has an extra *situation* parameter added to become

on (Pyramid-1, Block-3, S4)

stating that Pyramid-1 is on Block-3 at the specific situation (or time) S4. A predicate that has an additional situation parameter is called a *fluent*. The effect of the *action* of putting a block down can be described as follows.

```
(Holding(x, s) and Clear(y, s))
implies (s' = Result(PutDown(x, y), s) and on(x,
y, s'))
```

In other words, if some object x is held in situation s, and there is another object y that has nothing on top of it in situation s, then a new situation s' can be created that results from putting down x on top of y in which x is indeed on top of y. In this rather long-winded way the effect of each action on the state of the new situation caused by that action can be described.

However, that is not enough, because it only defines what happens to objects that change. The fact that most objects are not affected by the action also needs to be explicitly specified. For example, suppose on (Pyramid-1, Block-3, S4) and that our action is to put Block-5 into the box, producing situation S5.

There is no way to automatically deduce that Pyramid-1 is still on Block-3 in S5, even though it is obvious that nothing happened to Pyramid-1. This is known as the *frame problem*, and it is a special case of the general problem of having to specify everything that is false as well as everything that is true in first order logic.

Frame axioms are axioms that specify what does not change as a result of an action. If there are A actions that can be performed, and F fluents that describe the state of the world, then in general A * S frame axioms will be needed to specify how each action affects each and every fluent. However, most of the time actions do not have strange side effects and only affect the objects that they are specifically changing. There is no way to tell a first order logic system to assume that things do not change unless they have been told to change.

There is a relatively efficient way to specify frame axioms by saying that each fluent F remains true after any action A, unless A is one of the specific actions that might affect F. This is still messy for any realistic problem space. It also asks a lot of any general purpose theorem prover to be able to analyze the resulting complex set of axioms and produce a plan that achieves a goal. Producing an *efficient* plan that minimizes some cost is even more difficult.

The situation calculus is more powerful than the STRIPS approach because it can reason across different situations. For example, one could specify a rule that a pyramid can never be put on a block that had ever been covered by a cylinder in a previous state. That power is also a problem because it is much more difficult to build a general purpose theorem prover that can deal with it than it is to build a special purpose planning engine such as STRIPS that only needs to prove simple theorems within each state. The latter problems are quite difficult enough in a realistic problem space.

Reification

There are several ways of representing a given assertion in logic. One important variation is the degree to which predicates are replaced by objects. As a simple example, consider the following assertion as to the size of a murderer's feet.

```
LargeFootPrint(Butler) and SmallFootPrint(Widow)
```

That is the most efficient way to represent the information from the point of view of the theorem prover, but it makes it difficult to reason generally about footprints. Now consider the following alternative in which the foot size has been abstracted as an object or *reified.*

```
FootPrint(Butler,   Large)   and   FootPrint(Widow,
Small)
```

The two initial predicates have been replaced by the single predicate `FootPrint` and the new `Small` and `Large` objects have been introduced. This makes it easy to add the second general assertion that footprints found at the scene of the crime tell us who the murderer was as shown below.

```
FootPrint(MurderScene,         size)         and
FootPrint(person, size)
implies Murderer(person)
```

In other words, if the foot print at the scene of the crime is the same size as that of a person, then that person is the murderer.

Reification can also simplify complex predicates that have too many parameters, such as the many facts known about a murder. Without reification the following could be used to say that it is true that a murder occurred with a particular victim, murderer, weapon, location, time, reason, etc.:-

```
Murder(Husband,Butler,   Knife,   Home,   Evening,
Greed, ...)
```

However, this is obviously unwieldy, and it requires rewriting all existing the rules as new parameters are added. An alternative formulation is to *reify* Murder into an object and then provide relationships to other objects as follows:-

```
Murder(m)       and       Victim(m,       Husband)and
Weapon(m,Knife) and Location(m, Home) and ...
```

In other words, m represents some murder for which the other predicates provide additional information. This again enables more general rules to be written, such as that the murderer must have been at the scene of the crime:-

```
Murder(m)  and  loc  =  Location(m)  implies  loc  =
Location(Murderer(m))
```

This is very similar to the way data can be stored in an ordinary relational database, either as a table with many columns or a reified table with a property column.

MurderId	Victim	Murderer	Weapon	Location	Time
m123	Husband	Butler	Knife	Home	Evening

The table above is non-reified, whereas the table below contains the same data in a reified schema. Note the way that column names above have become data values below. Reified tables are more flexible but are also far less efficient and they obscure the meaning of the data. Reified tables are often used in database applications to enable new properties to be defined while the program is running, often based on the mistaken belief that the schema (column names) cannot be altered at run time. Reified tables also make it possible to add meta data to individual properties such as when a particular property value was set, who set it, and the degree of belief.

MurderId	Property	Value
m123	Victim	Husband
m123	Murderer	Butler
m123	Weapon	Knife
m123	Location	Home
m123	Time	Evening

Triplestore databases store fully reified databases like the one above.

Beliefs

In logic, reification also provides a mechanism to handle beliefs. Consider the following statement about detectives Holme's and Watson's thoughts about the case:-

Watson believed that the widow had a valid alibi, but Holmes believed that she did not.

This can be written as

```
a  =  Alibi(Widow)  and  Believe(Watson,  a)  and
Believe(Holmes, Not(a))
```

In order to do this, `Alibi` has been changed from being a predicate that is either true or false, to being a function that returns a belief object. Every predicate in the original formulation now needs to be converted to a function that returns a belief object which is only useful if the agent that believes it is also specified. A belief object may be declared to be absolutely true, but it is more likely to be believed by particular agents, possibly to different degrees and at different times.

This also means that logical operators on beliefs need to be defined. In the example `Not` is a new function that produces a new belief that its parameter belief is false. (Saying that Holmes believed that the widow did not have a good alibi is subtly different from saying that Holmes did not believe that she had a good alibi. The latter would be written `not Believe(Holmes, a)`.)

Beliefs themselves can then be reified in order to represent statements such as the following:-

Holmes thought that Watson believed that the widow had a valid alibi, but Watson just wanted Holmes to believe that so that Holmes could take the credit for solving the case.

The first part of this can be represented as

```
a = Alibi(Widow)
and  h=Believe(Holmes,  Believe(Watson,  a))  and
True(h)
and True(Believe(Watson, Not(a))) and
True(Believe(Watson, h))
```

The problem with this approach is that logic is essentially being defined using logic, and that can become very complex and computationally expensive. An alternative is to develop various new types of *modal* logics which introduce new operators such as *necessarily* and *possibly*. Determining the formal semantics of such logics entertains logicians and philosophers.

Common sense reasoning

A more basic problem with our murder reasoning is that common sense would suggest that the widow may well have had a motive to remove her husband so that she could elope with her personal trainer. If that were the case, then her alibi provided by her trainer would be of minimal value. It is also highly unusual to be on the telephone for an entire night (unless you are a teenager).

Some would argue that this is merely a symptom of the simplistic way in which the case was modelled. If a large body of common-sense knowledge was used, then rules about adultery and telephone calls might produce a very different conclusion if a non-monotonic method of reasoning was also available. Several projects are attempting to build such a knowledge base.

A secondary issue is that while the initial proof of the butler's guilt may be logically valid, in practice any line of reasoning that relies on the elimination of alternatives to reach a conclusion is dubious unless that conclusion has independent evidence that supports it. This is because it is difficult to ensure that we thoroughly understand all of the possible alternatives in the uncertain world in which we live.

More fundamentally, neither murder enquiries nor life in general comes neatly packaged as logical assertions. Instead, the world is presented as a bewildering collection of images, sounds and ambiguities. As any reader of detective novels knows, the challenge of solving a crime is to determine which of a myriad of half-hinted facts are relevant and to inferring obscure unstated motives rather than performing simple logical deductions on well-defined logical assertions. If this type of reasoning could be captured in some type of logic it would need to be much more sophisticated than our simple murder analysis above.

Cyc

As shown by the murder example, understanding the world requires a huge amount of background knowledge which can be used to interpret new observations or statements about it. As another example, consider the following seemingly simple sentences:-

"Napoleon died on St. Helena. Wellington was greatly saddened."

The author of the sentences assumes that the reader will infer that Wellington outlived Napoleon, that he knew about his death, that people are only sad about the deaths of people they care about, as well as the fact that Wellington had been Napoleon's enemy in battle, and therefore Wellington must have held Napoleon in high regard, which is actually the point of the statement.

In 1984 Douglas Lenat founded the *Cyc* project (as in encyclopedia) to capture this and other common-sense knowledge that would "prime the pump" for more automated knowledge capture based on sources such as encyclopedias. The project is ongoing, and OpenCyc makes some of the accumulated knowledge freely available.

Cyc stores its knowledge in the *CycL* language which is a description logic. It has a hierarchy of concepts that starts with *thing* which is specialized by abstract concepts such as *Event, Action,* and *Agent,* down to concrete concepts such as *Person* and *Death.*

The knowledge base is heavily reified to enable predicates to be reasoned about. So the first sentence above might be represented as

```
Event(D123)     and     TypeOf(D123,     death)     and
Subject(D123, Napoleon)
```

rather than simply

```
Died(Napoleon)
```

The reification enables the death event to be reasoned about, for example, that it was the death of Napoleon that caused Wellington to be sad

```
EmotionalState(S234) and
TypeOf(S234,  sad)  and  Subject(S234,  Wellington)
and Cause(D123, S234)
```

This again makes theorem proving difficult for realistic examples.

It turns out that the amount of knowledge required to make common sense inferences is huge. Cyc now contains a vast store of hundreds of thousands of concepts and millions of specific facts, and yet it is still not considered finished. People evidently learn a lot more in childhood than they are consciously aware of.

The huge knowledge base is divided into a hierarchy of microtheories, each of which is expected to be internally consistent. Examples include *NaiveSpacial, Movement, Transportation, Propositions, Emotions, Biology* and *Materials*. Emotions, for example, has 120 concepts such as *like* and *gratitude*, and dozens of relationships such as *feelsTowardsObject*. The use of microtheories structures the huge fact base and improves Cyc's performance both by reducing the search space of the theorem prover as well as by enabling special purpose theorem provers to be developed.

A primary goal of Cyc is to assist in deeply understanding unconstrained natural language, which is attempted by the Cyc-NL tool. It uses the common-sense knowledge base to disambiguate language, and to fit new facts into an established knowledge structure. The ultimate goal would be to upload documents such as Wikipedia and avoid the need for the tedious manual entry of data.

One practical tool is the FACT game, which can be played on the Cyc web site. Cyc presents propositions to users, and they state whether they think the fact is true. If enough users agree, it is added to the knowledge base. For example, it might present the assertion (from Nilsson's Quest for AI)

Spaghetti marinara always contains garlic.

That presents the default reasoning problem with normal mathematical logic. Certainly a marinara normally contains garlic, but one would not want the presence of garlic to be definitional. One should be able to say "The marinara tasted bland because she forgot to add any garlic" without producing the contradiction that it could not be a marinara if it did not contain garlic.

Unfortunately this type of issue is the rule rather than the exception. Most statements that are usually true can also occasionally be false. Techniques for accurate probabilistic reasoning will be covered in the next chapter, but they cannot be used for a vast first order knowledge base like Cyc. What is required is some type of common-sense probabilistic reasoning that may not be accurate but is still useful, along the lines of words such as *probably, possibly, unlikely.* Heavy reification or modal logics might be used to address the problem, but it is far from solved.

Another issue for Cyc is that despite its grand vision and huge knowledge base, it has only been used for some relatively specialized applications. Building real applications is an important reality test for the design of any complex system.

Learning logical rules from experience

There are several mechanisms for learning logical rules based on observations. For example, suppose we make the following observations:-

Raining	Sprinkler On	Washing on Line	Wet Grass
True	False	True	True
False	False	True	False
False	True	False	True
True	True	False	True
True	False	False	True

From this it is fairly easy to infer that

```
(Rain or Sprinkler) implies WetGrass
WetGrass implies (Rain or Sprinkler)
```

One needs to take care though, from this very limited data it is also possible to infer

```
not Washing implies WetGrass
```

More sophisticated systems can learn much more complex relationships from large bodies of noisy data. They can infer first order rules that include variables, as well as being able to introduce additional variables that consolidate knowledge. One impressive system could learn what it meant to sort numbers given only a collection of sorted and unsorted lists to describe the logical relationship.

Scruffy vs. neat

The use of logic in artificial intelligence applications has been somewhat controversial. Many of the early systems such as Eliza and SHRDLU just manipulated symbols in whatever way seemed to produce a good result. These systems were known as *scruffy*, as opposed to *neat* systems that preferred to use formal methods of logic or mathematics. Proponents of the neat approach argue that producing good results without a sound theory just shows that people are good programmers without learning any reusable concepts. Proponents of scruffy techniques argue that strictly logical approaches do not produce useful results and that their proponents are mainly logicians in philosophy departments trying to obtain funding via artificial intelligence grants. There is some truth in both these claims.

Today the debate has moved on, with proponents of non-symbolic approaches arguing that both scruffies and neats are on the wrong path for reasons that will be described later. In practice, a number of different techniques have been required to build useful systems, and it is not helpful to try to label them as being scruffy or neat.

Uncertain Expertise

Rule-based expert systems

One of the early successes of artificial intelligence research was rule based expert systems. These could encapsulate complex rules about a subject domain, and then use those rules to solve problems and plan actions with performances that sometimes exceeded that of established experts in the field. These systems tend to be rather scruffy, and there are many practical applications of this technology today.

An expert system typically consists of a rule base and an inference engine. The rules typically have an *antecedent* which is a condition that needs to be true for the rule to be activated, and a *consequent* which is an action or assertion to be raised once the rule is activated. For example, the following rules might form part of a simple system for classifying animals (from P. Winston's book *Artificial Intelligence*):-

- IF the animal has hair
  THEN it is a mammal.
- IF the animal gives milk
  THEN it is a mammal.
- IF the animal has feathers
  THEN it is a bird.
- IF the animal flies
  AND the animal lays eggs
  THEN it is a bird.

The IF clause provides the *antecedent* condition, and the THEN part provides the *consequent* to be raised. Multiple rules can make the same assertion, and the last rule has two parts to the antecedent to rule out bats and echidnas.

More complex rules rely on assertions raised by other rules. For example, many of the following rules depend on the mammal rules above.

- IF the animal eats meat
  THEN it is a carnivore.

- IF the animal is a mammal
  AND it has pointed teeth
  AND it has claws
  AND its eyes point forward
  THEN it is carnivore.
- IF the animal is a mammal
  AND it has hoofs
  THEN it is an ungulate.
- IF the animal is a mammal
  AND it chews cud
  THEN it is an ungulate
  AND it is even-toed.
- IF the animal is a carnivore
  AND it has a tawny colour
  AND it has dark spots
  THEN it is a cheetah.
- IF the animal is an ungulate
  AND it has a tawny colour
  AND it has dark spots
  AND it has a long neck
  THEN it is a giraffe.

If we see an animal eating meat then these rules assert that it is a carnivore. However, even if we are not lucky enough to see a carnivore while it is eating, we can still recognize it if we see that it has hair, which makes it a mammal, as well as pointed teeth, claws and forward-pointing eyes. If we then note that it is a tawny colour and has spots, we know that it is a cheetah.

Note that the rules are not just ordinary programming language if/then statements because they do not specify in which order they are executed. A *forward chaining* inference engine uses rules to argue from observations to conclusions, much like we did in the preceding paragraph. Conversely, a *backward chaining* engine would make a hypothesis and then look for evidence to support that hypothesis. In our example, it might guess that the animal is a cheetah, and then try to determine whether it is a tawny coloured spotted carnivore. In practice both approaches are used together. Some initial, easily-made observations might be used to produce some credible hypotheses, which will then dictate which further observations need to be made in order to select the correct one.

Another important feature of expert systems is their ability to introspect their rule base to answer questions as to why it reached the conclusions that it did. This enables a human expert to understand and validate the conclusions that it reaches.

Mycin and other expert systems

One of the first successful expert systems was Mycin, produced in the early 1970s. Mycin could analyze bacterial infections and prescribe treatments based on its analysis. This is difficult to do because there are many different types of infection, and treatments have to be initiated long before conclusive evidence of the cause of the infection can be obtained. It is important to be as specific as possible to minimize the prevalence of antibiotic-resistant bacteria and to ensure that all likely pathogens that might be the cause of a dangerous infection are controlled.

Mycin would ask the doctor for information about the infection such as the infections site, whether cultures could be grown (an)aerobically, what the bacteria's morphology and gram stain were. It would then provide a diagnosis like the following:-

My opinion is that the identity of ORGANISM-1 may be 1. Pseudomonas-aeruginosa, or 2. Klebsiella-pneumoniae, or 3. E. Coli, or 4. Bacteroides-fragilis, or 5. Enterobacter or 6. Proteus-non-mirabilis.

My recommendation is in order to cover items 1, 2, 3, 5, and 6 give gentamycin using a dose of 119mg (1.7 mg/kg) q8h IV for 10 days. Modify dose in renal failure. In order to cover item 4 give celindamycin using a dose of 595 mg (8.5 mg/kg) 16h IV for 14 days.

To produce this diagnosis Mycin used about 500 rules, of which the following rule is typical:-

- IF the infection type is primary-bacteremia
  AND the suspected entry point is
  gastrointestinal tract
  AND the site of the culture is one of the
  sterile sites
  THEN there is evidence that the organism is
  Bacteroides.

The Stanford Medical School found that MYCIN could propose an acceptable therapy 69% of the time, which was better than infectious disease experts when assessed under the same criteria. (There is always some disagreement amongst experts about the best treatment in different circumstances.)

Mycin was never deployed in the field because it could take 30 minutes to enter the disease profile into an ancient 1970s mainframe computer, and then Mycin would generally just tell the medical expert what they already knew. However, those medical experts had to study for many years to build up their expertise, so it is very impressive that a relatively simple rule-based system could match their performance. Sophisticated, intelligent behaviour can emerge from relatively simple systems.

Hype and reality

Expert systems were hyped extensively in the late 1970s and early 1980s as being able to solve any problem that experts and knowledge engineers would care to address. Rules were said to be the basis of all knowledge, and knowledge the basis of all thought. Medical experts are known to require very high academic scores to be allowed to study medicine, so if a 1970s expert system could capture their extensive knowledge then the capabilities of future systems seemed to be unbounded.

The truth was somewhat less exciting, and the simple rule based approach is now known not to scale well to larger problems, and not at all to the thorny issue of "common sense".

One commonly cited limitation of expert system technology was the lack of "knowledge engineers" that could help a "domain expert" transfer their knowledge into a rule base that an expert system could utilize. Knowledge engineering was considered to be different from just programming because the rules were specified at a higher declarative level than program code. However, it is in fact very similar to programming because the experts seem to store much of their knowledge in higher-level models, and knowledge engineering is mainly a process of designing a set of rules that mimics those models. However, when it is done effectively then powerful and practical systems can be constructed.

Expert systems are used today in many contexts. As medical record systems become more integrated and formalized, expert systems can access pathology and other results directly from the sources. This means that they can automatically analyze case data and warn about possibly dangerous anomalies without burdening the expert with additional data entry tasks. They can also learn new rules by examining real case histories.

Rule-based expert systems are also found in many other applications, although the term "expert system" has fallen out of favour. Examples include systems that assess bank loans and determine insurance premiums.

It should also be noted that rule-based systems have also strongly influenced psychological models of human cognition such as models of short term memory (i.e. of what assertions are true) and long term memory (the rules themselves).

Mycin's reasoning with uncertainty

An important aspect of Mycin's rules is that they do not state absolute truths. Some rules are quite strong, but others are just suggestive. For example, a positive Gram stain might strongly rule out E. Coli, but might only weakly rule out the Borrelia bacterium which stains poorly. If stronger evidence was provided that Borrelia was in fact a likely cause of an infection, then that should overrule the weak Gram stain evidence. This probabilistic reasoning strongly distinguishes Mycin-like rules from the rules in mathematical logic. It weakens the Mycin's deductive power, but also makes it useful for reasoning about an uncertain world.

In order to achieve this, each possible hypothesis is assigned a certainty between 0 and 1, with 0 meaning impossible and 1 meaning certain. Rules are also assigned a certainty, and each deductive step combines the certainties of the inputs to deduce the certainty of its outputs. So in the following rules the certainties of R, S, I, J, K and L have to be combined in some manner to deduce the certainty of M.

- IF I and J THEN M, with certainty R
- IF K and L THEN M, with certainty S

There are several schemes for achieving this. One simple scheme is to multiply the rule's certainty by the certainty of the weakest input. So the certainty of M just from the first rule would be calculated as

$M = R * \min(I, J)$

If there are several rules that lead to the same conclusion then simply take the maximum value of those rules. So in the above example:-

$M = \max(R * \min(I, J), S * \min(K, L))$

Fuzzy logic is a technique for probabilistic-like reasoning which uses similar methods.

Mycin used a more sophisticated approach by carefully misapplying otherwise sound rules of probability theory. For each individual rule in our example it would calculate approximately:-

$M1 = I * J * R$
$M2 = K * L * S$

This is based on the rule that the probability of seeing two events I and J is $P(I) * P(J)$ *if* they are conditionally independent. That is a big "if", which we will discuss further in the next section.

Multiple rules that support the same hypothesis are combined by first calculating certainty ratios

$X1 = M1 / (1 - M1)$
$X2 = M2 / (1 - M2)$

and then combining them as

$Z = X0 * X1/X0 * X2/X0$
$M = Z / (1 + Z)$

where X0 is the prior probability that the hypothesis M is true, given that there is no other information available. It turns out that these formulas are also mathematically sound *provided* that the values are conditionally independent.

Being able to reason with uncertain rules enabled Mycin to be able to weigh up different pieces of evidence, some of which supported a conclusion and some of which detracted from it. While Mycin's use of certainty factors was not formally correct, it was sufficiently accurate to enable a rule base to be built that drew generally sound conclusions. Dealing with uncertainty is an essential component when intelligently analyzing the uncertain world in which we live.

Sprinklers make it rain

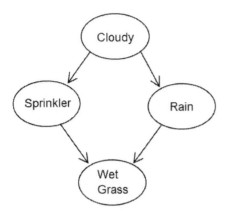

Simple Bayesian network.
Owned

An intelligent system that uses probabilistic reasoning can combine perfectly reasonable rules in ways that produce unfortunate conclusions. Consider the diagram above, which indicates that the grass will be wet if either the sprinkler is on or it is raining.

Suppose that it is known that the sprinkler happens to be on. It can therefore be deduced that the grass is probably wet. The diagram then makes it clear that if the grass is wet then it is probably raining.

This last deduction clearly violates basic laws of logic. Just because having an alibi means one is innocent does not mean that not having an alibi proves that one is guilty. However, it is exactly the sort of reasoning that a diagnostic system such as Mycin needs to use. We have a number of symptoms and we need to deduce the likely causes without the luxury of being able to use absolutely correct deductive rules. Yet we do not want to deduce that putting on the sprinkler makes it rain. (Readers who are also gardeners will note that putting on one's sprinkler does in fact seem to have an uncanny ability to produce rain shortly thereafter. But we shall ignore that observation in this analysis.)

There are, in fact, two different reasons why it seems bizarre that we should deduce that sprinklers make it rain. The first is a specific fact that we know that the purpose of sprinklers is to make the grass wet, so that sprinklers are not put on when it is raining. The second reason is more general and more important, namely that once we have one good explanation for something we discount competing explanations. For example, if we know that a car will not start because it has a flat battery, we discount the possibility that it has also run out of petrol.

Joint probability distributions

One way to address both these issues is to produce a "joint probability distribution" that explicitly lists the likelihood of each combination of events. For example, the following table shows that the likelihood of the grass being wet, and it is raining and the sprinkler is not on is 22%, while the likelihood of that the grass is wet, the sprinkler is on and it not raining is 12%. There is a small 3% chance that the sprinkler has been left on while it is raining.

	Grass Wet			Grass Dry			Grand Total
	Raining	Not Raining	Total	Raining	Not Raining	Total	
Sprinkler	3%	12%	15%	0%	1%	1%	16%
Not Sprinkler	22%	1%	23%	1%	60%	61%	84%
Total	25%	13%	38%	1%	61%	62%	100%

By simply summing the probabilities for each case that the grass is wet or dry we can determine that there is a 38% chance that the grass is wet from any cause, and a 62% chance that it is dry. The grass must be either wet or dry, so 38% + 62% = 100%.

If we want to determine the probability that it is raining given that the grass is wet we need to divide the probability that it is raining when the grass is wet by the probability that the grass is wet at all. That is (3% + 22%) / 38% = 66%. Likewise, the probability that the sprinkler is on given that the grass is wet is (3% + 12%) /

38% = 39%. We are in no danger of deducing that the sprinkler makes it rain because the probability that the grass is wet and it is raining and the sprinkler is on is 3% / 38% = 8%.

A simple joint distribution table like the one above can provide very insightful and accurate deductions. However, they grow in size exponentially with the number of variables because they enumerate every possible combination of observations and conclusions that a system can make. With the three parameters of Wetness, Rain and Sprinkler we have $2^3 = 8$ joint probabilities. If we add Cloudiness then we need $2^4 = 16$ probabilities. For a system like Mycin that has hundreds of possible symptoms, this would produce a table of billions of billions of billions of entries, which no computer could process. It is also not feasible to populate such a large table with actual probabilities in a meaningful way.

People became very excited when Bayesian networks were developed in the 1980s because they utilize causal-like knowledge to provide the rigor of a joint probability distribution without requiring a huge table to store them. Before discussing them in any detail it is helpful to review basic probability theory.

Probability theory

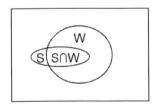

Venn diagram of probabilities of Sprinkler and Wet.
Owned

Simple Venn diagrams are a useful tool to gain insights into probabilistic reasoning. In the above diagram the area of the left ellipse represents the probability of an event S occurring, which is normally written P(S). Likewise, the right ellipse represents the probability of an event W occurring, P(W). The area in the middle represents the probability of both S and W occurring.

The notation P(S | W) is read "the probability of S given W". It indicates the probability of variable S occurring given that variable W has already occurred. In our wet grass example, it would be the probability that the sprinkler is on given that we observe that the grass is wet. So if $P(S \mid W) = p$, then this is similar to a Mycin rule

IF W THEN S, with certainty p

If we know that the grass is wet, then we must be somewhere inside the W ellipse. We can see from the diagram that for the sprinkler to also be on, we must be in the area (S and W), so,

$P(S \mid W) = P(S \text{ and } W) / P(W)$

In general $P(A \mid B)$ may be greater than or less than $P(A)$, depending upon whether knowing B makes it more or less likely that A will occur. If $P(A \mid B) = P(A)$ then knowing that B is true tells us nothing about whether A will occur. They are said to be *Conditionally Independent.* For example, if A and B are the events that two different coins land heads then they would be conditionally independent. In that case it is easy to use the equation above to show that

$P(A \text{ and } B) = P(A \mid B) * P(B) = P(A) * P(B)$

Examination of the Venn diagram also shows the following basic identity:-

$P(A \text{ or } B) = P(A) + P(B) - P(A \text{ and } B)$

$P(A \text{ and } B)$ is subtracted in order not to double count $P(A \text{ and } B)$, which prevents $P(A \text{ or } B)$ becoming greater than 100%. If A and B are conditionally independent then

$P(A \text{ or } B) = P(A) + P(B) - P(A) * P(B)$

The following diagram brings rain into consideration. We can see that the area in the middle represents the probability that the grass is wet and it is raining and the sprinkler is on. This is much smaller than the area that represents the likelihood that the grass is wet and it is raining, so we are again unlikely to conclude that the sprinkler makes it rain. It is also clear that the diagram becomes rapidly more complex as extra variables are added to it.

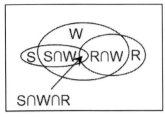

Owned

Bayes rule

It is generally easier to determine the likelihood of effects from causes rather than causes from effects. In our sprinkler expert system, it is relatively easy to work out P(W | S), i.e. the probability of the grass being wet if the sprinkler is on — it is almost certain to be the case. However, a diagnostic expert system like Mycin needs to work backwards from the symptoms to the causes. We see wet grass (a symptom), and need to determine its cause (given that that is relevant to its treatment). So we need to know P(S | W), the probability that the sprinkler is on given that the grass is wet. But that is difficult to know, as there are many possible causes of wet grass, and they may change over time. For example, children might be playing with a hose.

Bayes rule provides a method for determining P(A | B) given that one knows P(B | A) as follows.

P(A | B)

    = P(A and B) / P(B) -- Definition from previous section.

    = (P(A and B) / P(A)) * P(A) / P(B) -- Just dividing and multiplying by P(A).

    = P(B | A) * P(A) / P(B)

P(A) and P(B) are referred to as the *prior probabilities*; they are the probabilities of A or B when nothing else is known. Note that P(A | B) does not mean that B causes A, or visa versa. It simply means that they are correlated statistically. However, correlation is almost always due to some sort of possibly indirect causal relationship.

Bayesian networks

In practice, most variables in a large knowledge base are not *directly* conditionally dependent. A Bayesian network uses that fact to minimize the number of probabilities that need to be specified in the system. This enables us to have the accuracy and flexibility of a full joint probability table but without the need for a huge table of probabilities.

In the earlier wet grass network, the lines represent direct conditional dependencies with the arrows indicating causality. Clouds cause rain, and they cause people to defer putting on the sprinkler. Sprinklers and rain cause the grass to get wet. But note that the presence of clouds does not affect the likelihood that the grass will be wet *given that we know* whether it is raining and whether the sprinkler is on. Thus wet grass is only indirectly conditionally dependent on it being cloudy.

This means that in order to build up all the information in a full joint probability distribution all we need to specify is the effect of clouds on rain and sprinklers, as well as the effect of sprinklers and rain on wet grass. A process of multiplying these together can then produce the full table. Specifically, if $P(C)$ represents the probability that it is cloudy, then the probability that it is cloudy, not raining, the sprinkler is on and the grass is wet can be calculated as

$P(C, not R, S, W) = P(C) * P(not R \mid C) * P(S \mid C) * P(W \mid S and not R)$

This calculation would need to be repeated for each of the 16 values in the full joint probability distribution that are required for four variables.

This reduces the number of conditional probabilities that need to be determined to be in proportion to the number of variables. So if there are 100 variables with an average of 2 incoming links each then 800 conditional probabilities would need to be determined rather than the billions of billions of billions of values in the full joint probability distribution which still grows exponentially.

This has been made practical by some recently developed approximation algorithms that can provide the same analysis that could be performed on the full joint probability table without having to fully instantiate it.

It is still necessary to specify the individual conditional probabilities for each variable. We saw that for a variable with two incoming conditional links such as W that it required 8 probabilities to be specified. If there were three incoming links then 16 would need to be specified. That quickly becomes tedious for a large knowledge base.

Fortunately, most incoming links are conditionally independent of each other. For example, a car may not start (S) because of an electrical problem (E), a fuel problem (F) or a mechanical problem (M). But the presence of any one of those problems has only a marginal effect on the likelihood of any of the others. This enables the *noisy-OR* approximation to be used which calculates the conditional probabilities by simply adding them together, for example:-

$P(S \mid E, \text{not } M, \text{not } F) \sim= P(S \mid E)$
$P(S \mid \text{not } E, M, \text{not } F) \sim= P(S \mid M)$
$P(S \mid E, M, \text{not } F) \sim= P(S \mid E) + P(S \mid M) - P(S \mid E) * P(S \mid M)$
etc.

It turns out that Mycin certainty factors produce essentially the same results as a Bayesian network given these approximations, *provided* that the rules are carefully constructed to avoid any problems. However, Bayesian networks are easier and more reliable to use, and so provide an important technology for building intelligent systems that need to reason with uncertain knowledge.

Learning Bayesian networks

Constructing even a moderately sized Bayesian network by hand can be a substantial undertaking. But there are several effective algorithms for learning how to construct a network if there is sufficient data available.

Constructing a joint probability distribution from observed data is trivial. Simply count the number of occurrences of each combination of the variables, and then divide that by the total sample size. So if 200 observations are made, and in 6 of them it is raining when the sprinkler is on, then P(Rain and Sprinkler) = 6/200 = 3%. For a significant number of variables the resulting huge joint probability distribution table will only be sparsely filled. But that is acceptable, as it is normally the sums of various cells in the table that are of interest.

It is also easy to determine which variables are conditionally independent from other variables, because if that is the case then P(A and B) = P(A) * P(B). Determining which variables should be considered to be conditionally independent of other variables *given* knowledge of a third set of variables requires clever algorithms, but once that is done the Bayesian network is easy to construct. The resulting conditional dependencies will usually reflect causal relationships in the real world, some of which may not be obvious until the network has been constructed.

(Bayesian networks can also be extended to cope with numeric data rather than just true/false values. For example, the amount of rain rather than just the simple fact that it rained. In that case more sophisticated learning algorithms are required.)

Human probability reasoning

Yudkowsky (in *An Intuitive Explanation of Bayes' Theorem*) points out that people are not very good at probabilistic reasoning involving Bayes rule. Consider the following problem:-

Suppose 1% of women that undergo a routine screening actually have breast cancer. The screening test is positive for 80% of women with cancer, and 10% of women without cancer. If a woman fails the test, how likely is it that she has cancer?

There are several studies that show that most people, including many doctors, assume that the woman probably has cancer. However, the problem description provides *conditional probabilities* of the likelihood of tests failing given the disease, not the likelihood of the disease given the failed test.

If F means failing the test, and C means having cancer, then we are told that P(F | C) = 80%. But P(C) is only 1%. So P(F and C) = 80% * 1% = 0.8%. Whereas P(F and not C) = 10% * 99% = 9.9%. Thus P(C | F) = 0.8% / (0.8% + 9.9%) = 7.4%. Good news, she is almost certainly (92.6%) not sick, but further investigation may be warranted.

In other words, it takes an accurate test to overrule strong prior probabilities, and a test with 10% false positive cannot overrule a prior probability that 99% of patients are healthy.

Another example of people's highly distorted perception of risk is the fact that just 3,000 people died in the one-off September 11 attacks, and yet over 30,000 people died in car crashes in the U.S. in every year since the attack, not to mention the far more numerous crippling injuries. Yet news headlines continue to focus on terrorism rather than road accidents.

The point is that although sophisticated probabilistic reasoning provided by Bayesian Networks may be very useful for building intelligent systems, people seem to be able to reach generally reasonable conclusions using other, far less accurate approximations.

Human diagnostic reasoning

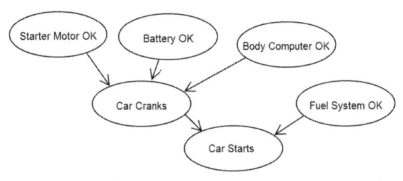

Bayesian network for diagnosing cars.
Owned

Consider the Bayesian network for the common example of a car that will not start. The diagram suggests several reasons that might prevent the car from cranking. This is easy for a mechanic to determine, so would be the first test performed. As previously discussed, if the car does not crank then the *noisy-OR* will suggest that it is most unlikely that the fuel system is also malfunctioning. The next easiest test is the battery, by simply turning on the headlights.

The diagram above can be extended to dozens of nodes that relate to the functionality of a car and why it might not start. But it seems unlikely that a mechanic has such a chart in their brain even subconsciously. Instead, they have a model of how the car works, what the purpose of each component is, and how they interact with each other, which includes a substantial spacial understanding of where things are located. They then consult this model to form hypotheses which are then tested. There is certainly knowledge of prior probabilities gained from experience, but they are probably secondary.

It turns out that on the author's car the problem was actually an intermittent short circuit on the interior light. The wire used to connect the light to its power source had been optimized to be as thin as possible, so a short circuit at the light did not blow the relevant fuse. But the body computer used the same fuse, and so the short did lower the voltage on the computer sufficiently to prevent its interaction with an Autolock security feature to work properly, and thus prevented the car from cranking.

Note the way that the interior light problem was described in terms of a model rather than bland probabilities. (A part of the model that neither the author nor his mechanics had known, causing much frustration.) Models with explanations are useful because they can be applied to different circumstances, and combined using analogies. Unlike a gambler at a casino, the mechanic does not really care about the exact probabilities of various faults. It is enough to assess likely or possible causes, and qualify that analysis with the cost of performing relevant diagnostic tests.

The models provide an element of the "common sense" that computer systems lack. For example, a mechanic would not bother to determine whether the engine cranked if the front of the car was destroyed in a road accident.

The process of building an expert system has been called *knowledge engineering*. This has been described as the process of experts writing out their knowledge in terms of rules. But it is actually more like writing a set of rules that reflect the higher level model the experts have in their heads. In other words, it is more like programming than authoring a book.

Pattern Matching

Symbols

All of the problems that have been considered so far first involve abstracting the world in terms of discrete symbols, and then reasoning about those abstractions. SHRDLU abstracted all the complexities of the position and orientation of real blocks into a simple list of which block rested on which other block. Likewise with our classification of individuals into Murderers and Widows, or the Wetness of the Grass.

But the real world does not come neatly packaged as symbols. It is a confusing pattern of inputs that have indeterminate values. We package up that information into symbols in order to make it easier to reason about. This is a powerful technique, and it lets systems as simple as a relational database help us understand the world. But the symbols are not real — they are an invention of man, not nature.

The AI community can be loosely divided along these lines. There are those that work with discrete symbols and integers, and there are those that work with patterns and floating point numbers (with a decimal point).

The post/zip code problem

In order to explore the various approaches to non-symbolic reasoning, we will use an early and informative problem that is the recognition of hand written documents. In particular, post offices need to route mail quickly and efficiently using a system of post or zip codes that identify roughly where each article is to be sent. Traditionally, human employees would need to read these codes in order to control mail sorting machines, but in the 1990s automated systems were developed that can read them very quickly and with human-like accuracy.

The problem is far from trivial. People write badly, and yet are very good at recognizing badly written numbers. It is fairly obvious that the following diagram is the number 4927, but it is not so obvious why that is so. A program that can effectively classify the pictures maps a space of billions of billions of possible images into ten simple symbols, 1, 2, ..., 9, 0, which can then be used by a simple database to determine where each envelope should be sent.

Example of a scanned postcode.
Owned

One approach to addressing this problem is to just try and program a solution, but programmers will realize that it is not at all obvious how to do that. One might have a model in one's mind that the number 4 is a series of three straight lines, but there are no really straight lines in a hand written numeral, and the nine above has a gap at the top. The noisy data makes trying to determine where one stroke ends and another begins far from trivial. And then knowing how to weigh the various inconsistent abstractions can be very difficult.

During the end of the period when zip codes were being read by hand, the National Institute of Science (NIST) collected a database of 60,000 hand-written 20 by 20 pixel images together with the actual values for those images, and then made that database available to researchers. This provided an excellent training set that enabled systems to be built that could learn how to classify the images without needing to be explicitly told.

Case based reasoning

One simplistic method for recognizing the numerals would be to load the entire NIST data set into a database and then just look up the picture in the database to determine which digit it represents. However, while there are thousands of examples in the data set, there are billions and billions of possible images, so it is most unlikely that any previously unseen image will find an exact match in the database.

To overcome this, we need to search for the closest match rather than looking for an exact match. One naive way to determine how well a sample matched an image in the database would be to compare each pixel in a sample with the corresponding pixel in the database, and simply count the number of pixels that are different. However that simplistic approach does not work very well because it is not the way that our eyes match patterns.

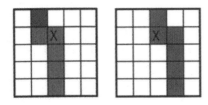

Unknown   Known

Sifting one pixel right makes most pixels different.
Owned

The first problem is illustrated in the image above. The two image fragments are exactly the same, except that the image on the right has been shifted one pixel to the right. If we naively counts the number of different pixels, we find that only the one pixel marked with an "X" happens to be the same in both images.

To address this problem, one can *condition* the data, in this case by calculating the centroid of each image, and aligning them on that centroid. Then the two images above would match perfectly.

A second problem is that the pixel counting strategy does not distinguish between a pixel that is just one pixel away from a corresponding pixel in the sample, as opposed to one that is completely unrelated. Better matching algorithms would perform more sensible matches.

Given the huge number of sample images available for zip codes, even a crude matching algorithm may suffice. However, having a large training database introduces its own problem, namely that it would take too long to carefully compare each of the known examples with the unknown image. In the case of the NIST data, there are 60,000 cases to be considered for each new sample.

To address both of these issues, we can extract features from the diagram that make sense visually. For example, we might simply divide the image up into six parts, and then note for each part whether it seemed to contain a line that was vertical, horizontal, or diagonal. That would give us $4^6 = 2048$ different buckets in which to put the samples, and then we would only need to look at samples in a bucket that matched the unknown image.

An additional approach to matching images quickly is to match multiple images at the same time. This can be performed on modern computer graphics processors that can perform hundreds of calculations at the same time. It also appears to be the way our brains produce real-time responses using hardware that operates very slowly compared to a digital computer.

A final problem is that a huge training data set will certainly contain several images that have been incorrectly classified. Even if it does not then the approximations used in the classifier may occasionally produce incorrect matches. One way to address that is to consider several cases that are close to the image to be classified, rather than just the one closest match. So if the very closest match is a "9", but the ten other very close matches are "4"s, then it is probably actually a "4".

Decision trees

A different approach is to use the training data to construct a decision tree, which can then be used to classify the images very efficiently. The data first needs to be processed to extract various features from the images, and then the decision tree uses those features to repeatedly partition the space of possible images until they have been fully identified.

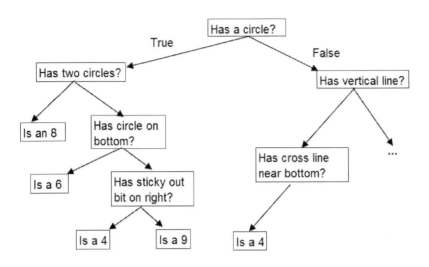

Decision tree for classifying digits.
Owned

The simplistic decision tree above classifies digits based on very high-level features. A matching algorithm starts at the top, and moves to the left or right depending on whether the simple condition in each cell is true or false. So if an image has a circle, but not two circles, and the circle is at the bottom, then the digit is a "6". A realistic digit-classifying tree would be much larger than this, but the divide-and-conquer approach means that even a huge tree that contains millions of nodes can classify an image with just a couple of dozen tests.

Decision trees are popular because there are effective algorithms for building them from a wide variety of different types of data. Essentially, the algorithms look for the feature that is most strongly correlated with the training data classifications, and then partition the space based on that feature. Each subspace is processed in the same manner until each sample is identified. A second pass might prune nodes that only contain one sample in the training set as being erroneous.

A realistic system may have a large number of low-level image features that could be extracted from each image, some of which will be far more useful than others. Decision trees are efficient because they only require the features to be extracted that are actually used to make a decision. So in our toy example, once we have determined that the figure has a circle, there is no need to determine if it has a vertical line. If some features are more expensive to extract than others, then the tree-learning algorithm can push those out towards the leaves and so make them needed less often. Decision trees can also work with continuous features such as the length of a line.

Another advantage of a decision tree is that a human that reviews one can generally understand how the tree was constructed, and why it makes the decisions that it does. This can sometimes provide deep insights into the problem domain.

Decision trees generally perform very well compared to other methods in terms of the number of training cases that they need in order to learn a complex pattern. They do not work well in situations in which each test just adds evidence to the result independently of each other test. In particular, a decision tree that just represents a simple majority of the tests being true degenerates to a tree with 2^n leaves where n is the number of tests.

Decision tables

A *decision table* consists of condition cells that are marked as TRUE, FALSE or blank (don't care). True/false input values are then matched to see if they are the same as these entries, and the results are aggregated. Multiple decision tables can then be combined to implement arbitrary logical expressions.

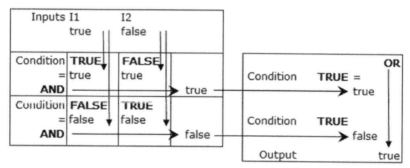

Decision table representing exclusive or.
Owned

The two tables above combine to implement the exclusive or conditions. The left hand table conjoins (ANDs) its conditions, so the first row determines whether I1 is true and I2 is false. The second row determines whether I1 is false and I2 is true. These outputs are then fed into the right hand disjunctive (OR) condition table, which returns true if either is true. So it evaluates the condition

Or(And(I1, not I2), And(not I1, I2)) = XOR(I1, I2)

This combination of conjunction and disjunction can represent any possible condition, provided that there are sufficient intermediate rows in the table. More importantly, they can represent most common conditions quite succinctly. It is common to have several OR columns in the right hand table, all working off the same intermediate AND rows. And like every other formalism, decision table conditions can be learnt from experience using various algorithms.

Regression

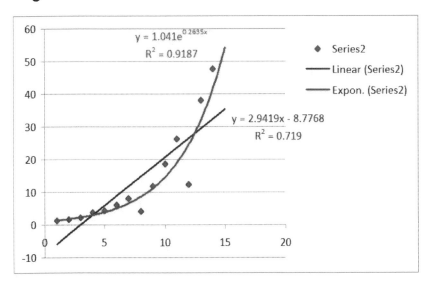

Linear and exponential regression.
Owned

Statisticians have used *regression* methods since the nineteenth century to fit a function to a set of data points. In the chart above, Excel was used to automatically fit two statistical models to the data represented by the red dots. The first is a simple straight line, while the second is a curved exponential function. In both cases the 14 data points are modelled by just two numbers that are shown on the chart. The R^2 value shows the sum of squares correlation between the models and the data, and shows that the exponential model is a better fit. These models can then be used to predict the values of any new, unseen data.

There is a close relationship between statistical inference and machine learning. Just because it is possible to use more complex technologies to solve some problems does not mean that it is always a good idea to do so because statistical techniques are generally much more efficient and better understood. However, classical statistical techniques cannot learn how to recognize digits from images.

Artificial Neural Networks

Introduction

One effective method for intelligent character recognition is to use Artificial Neural Networks (ANNs) which were inspired by biological neurons.

The stereotypical biological neuron has a number of *dendrite* projections that connect to other neurons via *synapses*. When sufficient electrochemical stimulations are given to the dendrites at about the same time, the neuron fires a signal that flows down its *axon*. The axon terminals then connect to other neurons and stimulate them, or possibly to muscles and make them contract. Longer axons are covered in a white *myelin* sheath to make them more efficient.

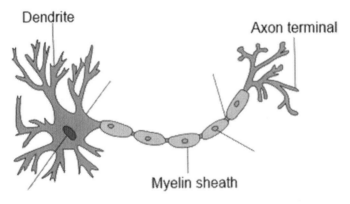

Stereotypical biological neuron.
Public Wikipedia

A basic Artificial Neuron (AN) produces an output that is a simple linear combination of their inputs. So given a set of inputs I_j and weights W_j, each perceptron's output O would be

$O = Sum(I_j{}^* W_j)$

This is shown diagrammatically below. The output of 0.72 = 1 * 0.4 + 0.8 * 0.32. The output of this one unit could then be fed into the inputs of other units.

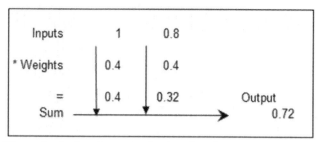

The calculation in a single Artificial Neuron (AN).
Owned

Usually multiple ANs are all given the same inputs I_j, so the output of each AN O_i would be

$O_i = Sum(I_j * W_{ij})$

An important property of ANNs is that the weights can be learned rather than having to be entered by hand. In particular, if a set of desirable outputs are known for a given set of inputs, then the optimal values of the weights can often be learned by using a gradient descent algorithm. One method is to repeatedly set the input values of each unit to each training case, and then noting the difference between the actual output A and the desired output D. The basic delta algorithm adjusts the weights as follows for each training case:-

$Wij = W_{ij} + e * (D_i - A_i) * I_j$

Where e is a small constant that determines how much each weight should be adjusted in each iteration. Each weight is adjusted based on the perceptron's error, Di - Ai, multiplied by the jth input. The larger the error, the larger the adjustment.

Over numerous iterations, the weights will usually converge on a value that minimizes the differences between A and D for the entire training set. The e constant should be set to be large enough that the series quickly converges, but small enough that it does not become unstable. Normally *simulated annealing* is used which reduces e slightly after each iteration, so that large changes are made initially and then fine tuning occurs in latter iterations.

Perceptrons

Perceptrons are a simple artificial neuron technology that was first investigated using analog computers such as MINOS in the early

1960s. Their outputs were considered to be boolean values, for example with values above or below 0.5 typically considered to be true or false. This loosely corresponds to the way that neurons fire if and only if they receive sufficient stimulation.

The perceptron above with weights [0.4, 0.4] mimics conjunction (AND), so the output will only be true if both the inputs are true. If the weights were instead both 1.0, then the perceptron could mimic disjunction (OR) — the output would be true if either of the inputs were true. Likewise if the weights were (1, -1), then the output would be (I_1 and not I_2).

Perceptrons are also very good at the majority function that causes decision trees to fail. Just give each input a weight of 1/n, where n is the number of inputs, and then see if the result adds up to 0.5. The output will be true if a majority of the inputs are true.

However, basic single layer perceptrons cannot handle non-linear cases. For example, there is no way to set the weights so as to be able to provide an exclusive or (XOR) function, namely to set the output to be true if and only if exactly one of the inputs is high, and the other is low. But that sort of condition is required for image analysis, for example an edge is defined by having two pixels just one of which is black. (Decision trees handle this case easily.)

Sigmoid perceptrons

The limitations of Perceptrons were documented in the book *Perceptrons* by Minsky and Papert (1969) which caused research into perceptrons to be largely abandoned. Then in the mid 1970s a breakthrough was achieved by replacing the simple boolean step function with a sigmoid function.

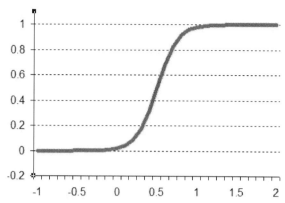

Sigmoid function.
Owned

A sigmoid function is an S-shaped function. There are several functions that can be used, the chart above illustrates the most common type of sigmoid function which is:-

$$y = 1/(1+ \exp(-k * (x + m)))$$

Like a simple step function, the effect of the sigmoid function is to take any value of x and map it to a value between 0 and 1. It also tends to push values towards those bounds. So an x value of 0.3 is mapped to a y value of 0.17, and an x value of 0.7 is mapped to a y value of 0.83. It thus converts an arbitrary numeric value into a more logical value centring on 0 or 1. But unlike a step function the sigmoid is differentiable, meaning that it is smooth and does not have any sharp kinks. It also has a well-defined inverse, so one can determine a unique value for x given any value for y. These properties enabled a new back propagation algorithm to be developed which could learn weights in much more powerful multi layered ANNs.

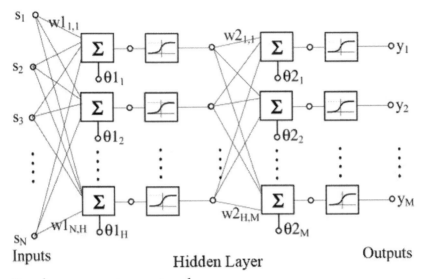

Two layer perceptron network.
Educational http://www.emeraldinsight.com/journals.htm?articleid=876327

The diagram above shows a two-layer neural network which has sigmoid functions inserted between the two layers and before the outputs. The drawing uses lines to show that the output of each layer is the sum of the layer's weights times its inputs.

The middle, hidden layer does not have any obvious relationship to the inputs or the outputs, so it would appear to be very difficult to train a three-layer network. However, it turns out that the delta gradient descent method described above can be adapted for use with three layered networks. The resulting back propagation algorithm enabled networks to learn quite complicated relationships between inputs and outputs. It was shown by Cybenko (1989) that two layered networks with sigmoid functions could represent virtually any function. They can certainly address the exclusive or problem.

The classical back propagation algorithm first initializes all the weights to random values. Then the inputs are set to the inputs of each training case, and the output layer is compared to the desired outputs so that the output layer weights can be adjusted to minimize the error using the same delta algorithm that was used by a single-layer network.

The next step then allocates the remaining error in the output of each node to each of the hidden-layer nodes. This is achieved by allocating most of the error to nodes in the hidden-layer that correspond to large weights in the output-layer and so determine what the hidden-layer values "should" be. Having done that it then uses the normal delta algorithm to determine the weights of the input layer which minimize the error of the hidden-layer. Like single-layer gradient descent, only small changes are made to the weights at each iteration, and many, many iterations are required to train the network.

Taking random values and adjusting them based on errors derived from other random values seems bizarre, but what happens in practice is that by chance some combination of an input node and an output node will have some loose correlation with the desired result. The algorithm tends to reinforce that correlation and then pushes the errors out to other nodes in the network, which then become trained to compensate.

So in our exclusive or example, if one input node ends up representing *A and B,* then the other case *not A and not B,* ends up being pushed to the other node. Contrary to this author's intuition, the system magically converges on a useful set of weights. (There is, of course, no guarantee that the random values will converge on useful values, but they usually do in practice for a well set up network.)

Using perceptron networks

Applying ANNs to real problems requires much more analysis than simply applying the relatively simple back propagation algorithm.

The first issue is to determine what the input should be. For our character recognition problem it could be as simple as the brightness of each pixel in the image. But as noted in the section on case-based reasoning, moving an image just one pixel to the right completely changes which pixels are black. So conditioning the input data by aligning the images on their centroids would be a sensible start, with the x and y offsets then being additional inputs.

A NIST image of just 20 by 20 pixels contains 400 inputs, which can make training slow and unpredictable. Reducing the resolution to 8 by 8 pixels will reduce the training time, but it might be quite hard for even humans to accurately recognize numerals on this course scale. A better alternative might be to reduce the image further to 6 by 5 regions (say), but for each region provide additional information such as whether the original image contained and edge in that region, and if so in what orientation. Or it might be best to eschew regions altogether and make the inputs high-level features in a similar way to what was used for decision trees.

The next problem is the number of layers and nodes to use. For the number of layers, the answer is simple, namely three. If the problem is simple enough that it only needs two layers (input and output) then it would be better solved by statistical regression tools as noted previously. If the problem cannot be solved in three layers then it is most unlikely that it can be solved in four or more layers. Training doubly hidden nodes is just too hard.

Determining the number of hidden nodes is difficult and much has been written on the subject. It will generally be a similar number to the number of input and output nodes, but that varies widely depending on the problem that is being addressed. The usual approach is to try different numbers of hidden nodes and see what is most effective for a given problem. There are also algorithms that can prune redundant nodes, or that can vary the number of hidden nodes during the training phase.

The training data then needs to be run through the network multiple times as the weights are very slowly adjusted by the algorithm. Processing all of the training cases once is referred to as an *epoch*, and many epochs are usually required to train the network. At first the network just produces gibberish. But then, very slowly at first, the error rate starts to reduce as the network weights start to reflect the training data.

One of the strengths of an ANN is that it can handle noisy data. A properly trained network will be able to match previously unseen cases that are similar to but different from the training cases. However, if the training continues too long then the network may become over trained in which case it will only match the cases that it was trained on.

If there are thousands of training cases that are processed in thousands of epochs, and each individual training case requires thousands of computations, it is easy to require many billions of operations to train a network. The training may then need to be repeated many times for various parameters such as the number of hidden nodes and the conditioning algorithms. Fortunately, much of this processing can be performed in parallel, and so modern graphical processing units can be used with good effect.

The primary result of training a network is the creation of two matrices of weight, one for each layer. These weights can then be applied to new cases very efficiently. This involves little more than the multiplication of two possibly sparse matrices.

The numbers in the weight matrices encapsulate much of the raw information that is in the training data. However, for all but the simplest cases the relationship between the numbers in the matrices and the original training data is obscure. So while the network may be very good at classifying its cases, it is very bad at explaining why it reaches those classifications. This is in stark contrast to a rule-based expert system or SHRDLU's planning engine. It is fortunate that ANNs can be trained automatically because it is difficult to specify the weights manually.

This lack of transparency can lead to unfortunate results. One apocryphal story is of an ANN that was designed to identify camouflaged tanks. On the training photographs it succeeded with almost 90% accuracy, which was a surprisingly good result for such a difficult problem. But when trialled in the field it failed hopelessly. Re-examination of the training images showed that most of the pictures with tanks happened to have been taken on cloudy days. The network had learned to recognize the colour saturations of cloudy day photographs, and had no knowledge of tanks at all.

That said, learning intelligible models is certainly not a mandatory requirement. For the digit recognition problem it would suffice that the system recognizes the digits correctly.

There are also many different architectures and usage models of artificial neural networks beyond the simple two-layered network with back propagation that has been discussed. One variant is the *recurrent network* in which some of the outputs are fed back to the inputs, thus allowing the networks to have memory. Recent research has addressed the difficulty of training such networks.

Hype and real neurons

Like expert systems before them, artificial neural networks were also hyped out of all proportion to their capabilities. Take the problems of the universe, feed them in to the learning algorithm, and then solve them automatically. No deep understanding required. For example, one author suggested that French could be translated into English by simply feeding pairs of sentences into a network and allowing it to learn. An ANN *might* be a component in a natural language system, but there is much more involved. ANNs are certainly powerful for certain types of pattern matching problems but they do not meaningfully compete with advanced symbolic systems for symbolic problems.

Complicated-sounding problems in biotechnology, economics and the aerospace industry have been solved by ANNs. Some of these do indeed bely substantial technical achievements, but others would be better addressed by simple statistical regression models. Just because an industry involves high technology does not mean that every problem in it is difficult to solve.

Although ANNs were inspired by neurons, they are quite different in a number of fundamental ways that will be discussed in the chapter on computational neuroscience. It is often unclear whether popular accounts of "neural networks" refer to artificial neural networks or attempts to simulate real neurons.

In order to avoid the hype and emphasize serious engineering, many researchers avoid the term *neural networks,* preferring the terms *parallel distributed processing* or *connectionism.* They also want to emphasize that while this technology has been inspired by biological neurons, it is not an attempt to simulate them. Rather, it is an attempt to build practical technology that can address real problems.

Support vector machines

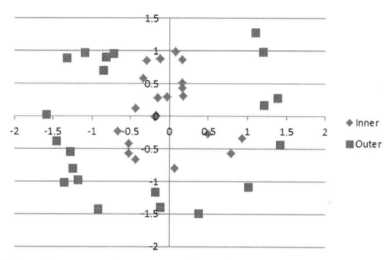

Points that cannot be separated linearly.
Owned

Support vector machines are a new technology that provides an alternative method of learning complex relationships from observed data. They use *kernel functions* that map difficult input data to a new representation that makes the problem easy to solve. This avoids the need for complex engines such as multi-layered artificial neural networks.

The mathematics involved is quite complex, but a simple example illustrates the general approach. Consider the data in the chart above in which there is a strong pattern that distinguishes between the inner blue diamonds and the outer red squares. However, this pattern could not be learnt by a linear system such as simple perceptrons because there is no way that a straight line can be drawn that neatly separates the two populations.

Now consider the chart below. It contains the same data points as the chart above, but both the X and Y values of each point have been squared. For example, the point in the above chart that is located at (1.5, 0.5) has been mapped to the point (1.5 * 1.5, 0.5 * 0.5) = (2.25, 0.25) in the chart below.

This mapping has rearranged the points, pushing them all into the top right positive number quadrant. It now becomes very easy to separate the two populations using a straight line, as shown by the dashed line. This relationship could be easily learned by a perceptron or other regression technologies.

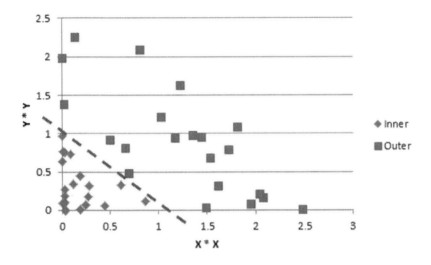

Mapped points that can be separated linearly.
Owned

There are methods for determining such mappings automatically, which involves minimizing a multidimensional quadratic equation which can be done efficiently using gradient descent approaches. Unfortunately, in order to do this the number of dimensions can increase dramatically. Functions of large numbers of dimensions are computationally expensive.

This problem also has a solution. It is possible to build these high-dimensional kernel functions so that they only depend on the dot products of the original data points, and not their individual dimensions. Dot products have the form

$d = x_1{}^*x_2 + y_1{}^*y_2 +...$

where d is a simple scalar, and so is easy and efficient to calculate.

Unsupervised learning

All the pattern-matching examples we have used above have a set of cases that have a known classifications, and the job of the pattern matcher is to classify unknown cases in the same manner. This is referred to as *supervised* learning. There are also several problems that require the pattern matcher to deduce the classifications themselves, without being told in advance. These are known as *unsupervised* learning problems.

One problem that requires unsupervised learning is to recognize clusters of data points. In the example below, there are three fairly distinct clusters, coloured red, blue and green. There are several clustering algorithms that can find clusters without being told where they are centered, or even the number of clusters to form. The diagram below is two dimensional, but more interesting examples have higher dimensionality.

The early and crude k-means algorithm picks k random points for cluster centers and then classifies all the data points based on their Euclidean distance from those points. The cluster centers are then repositioned to be the centroids of each class of points, and the process is repeated. K-means is limited because it easily gets stuck on false centroids, and because it requires the number of clusters to be pre-determined.

The nearest neighbours approach considers each point and its k nearest neighbours. It then sees if the centroid of that group might be the centre of an effective cluster. It is generally more effective than K-Means. Other systems use statistical distributions to model local densities, while others define clusters as connected dense regions in the data space. The *adaptive resonance* approach uses artificial neural network technologies.

Recognizing clusters of related points is an important aspect of learning patterns from observations. Given the clusters observed below, a system might investigate what caused those clusters to appear, and note changes in the clusters in different situations.

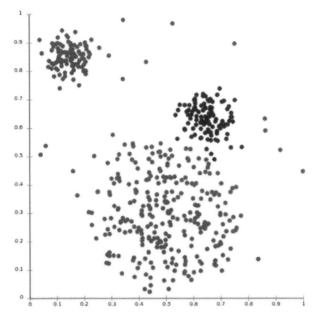

Clustering.
Public Wikipedia

Another example of unsupervised learning is discovering hidden nodes in Bayesian networks. Recall that it is easy to learn a joint probability distribution from observations, and there are good algorithms than can infer a network from the conditional independences discovered in the distribution. More sophisticated algorithms can use clustering-like approaches to infer new nodes that should be added into the network which can greatly simplify its structure.

This is what happens when people discover new diseases. All that can be actually observed is symptoms, but by inventing diseases multiple symptom observations can be coalesced. Treatments can then be based on the inferred diseases rather than having to map individual symptoms directly to each possible treatment.

Competing technologies

These many different approaches can be applied to the original digit recognition problem, with varying results. The results are difficult to compare directly because much depends on the details about how each test was performed, how the data was conditioned etc.

One of the first approaches was to use nearest neighbour clustering to group images into digits. This is similar to the case-based reasoning described earlier. The error rate was about 2.4%, and it was the slowest method because of the need to store and process all the samples.

A fairly naive three-layer artificial neural network was created with 400 input units (one per pixel) and 10 outputs (one per digit). It was found that about 300 hidden nodes produced the best results, which was a 1.6% error rate.

A highly tuned and specialized network called LeNet conditioned the data by centering the images. It also used three layers of hidden units which were highly constrained so that they tended to recognize discrete features such as line segments or curves. LeNet produced a 0.9% error rate.

A naively applied support vector machine produced a very reasonable error rate of 1.1%. A tuned version was then built that centered the image and focused the kernels on nearby pixels. This produced an impressive 0.56% error rate.

A shape-matching approach explicitly looked at edges between black and white pixels in a similar manner to computer vision systems. It then attempted to match corresponding features of each pair of images using nearest neighbour clustering. This produced an error rate of 0.63%.

Decision tables have also been effective in image analysis, although their effectiveness largely depends on the tests that can be applied to the image. The best results can be achieved by using multiple decision trees and then averaging the results.

When considering error rates, humans that carefully examine images are said to have an error rate of 0.2%, whereas post office workers quickly sorting mail had an error rate of 2.5%. So all of the automated systems had better than human performance in practice.

Speech and Vision

Speech recognition

One achievement of modern artificial intelligence research is the ability to understand spoken speech. After a little work training a system, people may abandon their keyboards and simply talk to their computers. This is particularly useful in situations for those with busy hands or disabilities. As small devices without keyboards such as smart phones and tablets become more powerful this technology is likely to become more widely used.

Phonologists have understood, at least in principle, that words can be broken into phonemes, which roughly correspond to the letters in written words. Phonemes result from the way our mouths change shape as we speak, thus changing the frequency and volume of the sound that we produce. If phonemes could be recognized accurately then they could be reassembled back into words, and the words reassembled back into sentences.

However, the distinction between different phonemes can be subtle and ambiguous. There are generally several different sounds (known as *phones*) that people in a given language recognize as being the same phoneme. People also speak quickly, slurring their words and phones together, or omitting some phones altogether. Different people also have different accents, and background noise can confuse the signal.

Consider the spectrogram below of the words "three" followed by "tea". The top row shows time in milliseconds, and the second row shows the raw wave form. The third shows the Fourier transform of the frequency, increasing vertically, with darker areas indicating more energy at a particular frequency. This is essentially the same as the signal that the brain receives from the cochlea within the inner ear.

The main thing to note is that it is not at all obvious from simple observation what words are being spoken, even when one knows what they are. The fourth row indicates the actual phones being uttered. The two "i:" fragments are the "ee/ea" sound in the words, but they look quite different when preceded by the "thr" in "three" or the "t" in "tea". Finally note that in the sample the speaker has paused for 100 milliseconds between the words, but in normal, continuous speech words are often run together making it very difficult to know where one word ends and another word begins.

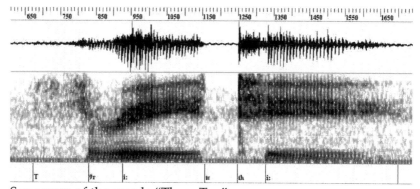

Sonogram of the words "Three Tea"
Educational http://www.cslu.ogi.edu/tutordemos/nnet_training/tutorial.html

Speech recognition systems attack this problem in a similar way to other pattern recognition problems. The data is first conditioned to make it easier to work with. Then features are extracted which can be compared with a model of what features are expected.

Speech understanding systems usually start by splitting the input sound into overlapping frames about 10 milliseconds long. That is fine enough to isolate short-duration phones, but coarse enough to enable a proper frequency analysis to be performed. The frames overlap in case an important transition happened to occur on a frame boundary.

Features are then extracted from the frames, such as the overall volume and the frequency distribution. It is important to digest the large amount of information contained within the sonogram into a relatively small number of parameters that can still effectively distinguish the phones without being overly sensitive to speaker variation or noise.

Phones can be modelled as having three parts, a beginning, a middle and an end. In general, phones also change substantially depending on the phones that come before and after them. So a table of $3n^3$ states is required to hold all the phones, i.e. about 500 entries for 50 different phones.

Hidden Markov models

Modern speech understanding systems then feed the result into hidden Markov models, which are a generalization of finite state machines.

To understand finite state machines, consider the following secret message, which was encrypted using a simple pen and paper cipher known as single transposition:-

SONERENEYDMMO

The cipher can be decrypted to reveal the following plain text:-

SENDM
OREMO
NEY

But pen and paper ciphers do not include a space character, so it is difficult to recognize the words that are within it.

The following finite state machine addresses this problem. In it, states are represented as numbered circles and transitions as arrows. The system starts at node 0 and then looks for the first letter. If it is an "S" then we move to state 1, but if we see an "M" then we move to state 5, in which case an "O" would move it to state 6. It can be seen that the letters "M", "O", "N", "E", and "Y" will result in the machine being in state 11, which represents the word "MONEY". A large number of words can be loaded into a finite state machine which can then disambiguate them very efficiently.

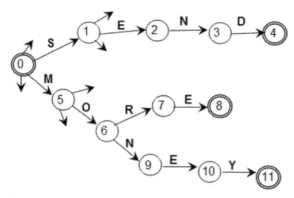

Finite state machine for recognizing words.
Owned

A hidden Markov model also has states and transitions. However, the transitions are probabilistic, so that a given input may produce several transitions. Further, the actual states and transitions are hidden, so all that is known is the input phones and the resulting words. There are clever algorithms that can learn these transitions from examples. It is also possible to train recurrent artificial neural networks to handle this type of problem.

Words and language

It turns out that it is simply not possible for either computers or humans to accurately understand continuous speech given only the phone analysis. What is required is some knowledge of what is actually being said. One way to do this is to constrain the recognized words to being grammatically correct. A better way is to simply record pairs or triplets of words that are commonly spoken. If the system is unsure which of a small number of words an utterance refers to, it simply picks the one that is the most common given the preceding and following words. So this would favour "fourcandles" over "forkhandles" even though they are both grammatically correct. However, it requires knowledge of the context of the conversation to distinguish more subtle ambiguities, e.g. "encourage-euthenasia" from "encourage-youth-in-Asia".

Once the words are understood then they can be parsed and analyzed in ways outline in the SHRDLU chapter. But this analysis cannot be cleanly separated from the phonetic processing due to the need to handle phonetic ambiguity.

3D graphics

Before considering the problem of computer vision, it is worth considering the inverse but relatively simpler problem of producing the 3D graphics that have become commonplace in movies and games. These advanced graphics have become possible due to the availability of specialized hardware and graphics processing units that can perform the billions of calculations per second that are required to produce quality animations.

The objects that are displayed are generally represented as a hierarchical model known as a *scene graph*. So a truck could contain ten zombies, each of which has arms, legs and heads, which in turn have fingers, an eye and maggots. Movement of each component is relative to its parent, so the zombie's eye moves relative to its possibly spinning head, which moves relative to the zombie, which moves relative to the truck.

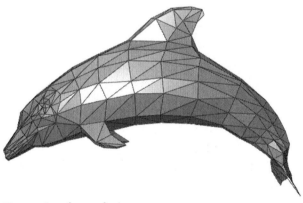

Example of tesselation
Public Wikipedia

Each component of our zombie will typically be described in an artist's drawing tool as higher-level shapes such as three-dimensional splines or generalized cylinders. But before these can be rendered they are normally *tessellated* into a larger number of simple triangles that approximate the same shape, as shown above. The points within those triangles then need to be mapped to the viewing plane using a perspective mapping.

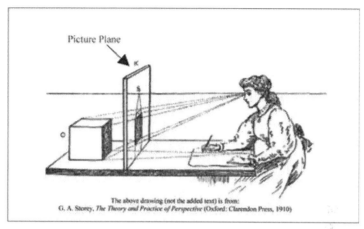

Perspective mapping to the picture plane.
Public G. A. Storey 1910.

Most of the triangles will be obscured by other triangles. A z-buffer algorithm is normally used to resolve these. Each pixel in the viewing plane also records the z coordinate (depth) of the object that produced it as illustrated below. As each object is projected onto the screen pixels the z values are compared with any existing z value for that screen pixel. If the new object is nearer than the distance recorded on the screen, then it overrides the pixel, but if it is further away then it is simply ignored because it will be obscured by some other, closer object.

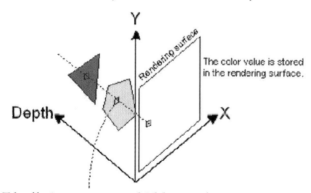

Z buffering to remove hidden surfaces.
Corporate http://msdn.microsoft.com/en-us/library/aa915211.aspx

The three-dimensional surface of the underlying objects is wrapped with a texture (image), and then it is the corresponding point in the texture that is actually mapped to the screen. So if the zombie's nose has black and green splodges, then the colour of a screen pixel that is mapped to the nose will be black or green depending on which specific splodge the pixel maps to.

The human eye is also very sensitive to lighting effects. Most surfaces are brighter when they face the light source which can be seen in the images below. (The full moon is the classic counter example, which is why it looks rather flat rather than spherical.) The eye is also very sensitive to discontinuities in shading, as shown in the left-hand image in which the tessellation becomes obvious.

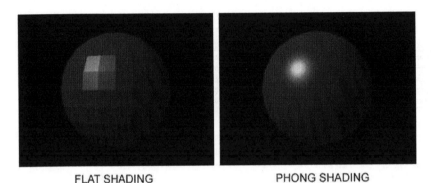

FLAT SHADING   PHONG SHADING

Smoothing shading to hide tessellation.
Public Wikipedia

There are many other issues in producing good quality 3D images which include shadows, translucent objects, (partial) reflections, and fog.

Machine vision

It has been said that if 3-D graphics is like squeezing toothpaste out of a tube, then machine vision is like pushing the toothpaste back into the tube — by hand. The scene graph needs to be inferred given only the image that is the result of numerous, complex and overlapping rendering operations. This is a tough problem that has not been fully solved. Real images contain considerable noise such as scratches, textured surfaces and complex lighting effects which can often obscure the real surfaces that created them. But machine vision is an important problem because being able to see greatly enhances a robot's understanding of the world that it inhabits.

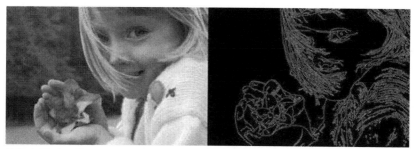

Edge Detection.
Public Wikipedia

The first phase in classical vision system is to condition the data by running some simple filters on the image to pick out key features. The pictures above show the result of a filter that detects edges, i.e. sharp changes in colour or intensity. Other filters can detect gradients of shading that arise from curved surfaces, or, for video how each part of the image moves from one frame to the next. Analysis of the optic nerve of cats suggests that human visual processing begins with a similar analysis.

This information is then combined in order to segment the image into its constituent objects. In the image above the girl should be separated from the background, and ideally the flower from the hands. The normally sharp edge between overlapping objects can assist with this, but there will usually be some ambiguity.

Finally, the perceived shapes in space need to be fitted to some type of model. This is similar to a scene graph but is usually referred to as a scene grammar. This is a difficult problem in general, and the resulting grammar may contain ambiguities and contradictions much like the recovered grammars of speech recognition systems. The type of model also needs to be specialized to a significant extent depending upon the problem domain being addressed.

To be effective, systems often make predictions about what is in the scene based on initial observations, and these predictions are then fed back to lower levels of the model. So in the diagram below, the light part of the image suggests a face. This enables the system to recognize the otherwise very faint edge at the bottom left of the image as being an edge that should be used to segment the face from the background. This process in which higher levels in a hierarchy feedback to lower levels is quite important. Another example of this hierarchical feedback is the way speech understanding systems rely on the knowledge of which words are more likely to be spoken together in order to help resolve phones at the bottom level.

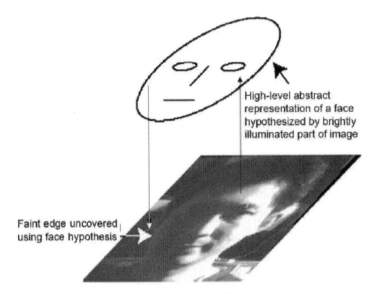

High-level abstract representation of a face hypothesized by brightly illuminated part of image

Faint edge uncovered using face hypothesis

Use of a model helps identify faint edges.
Educational via Nilsson Quest for AI

Inferring the depth of each point in the image is a difficult problem that needs to be solved if the three dimensional shape of objects is to be determined. Humans are very good at this, and use a number of quite subtle clues to analyze difficult images. Images with deliberately confused perspective like the Escher waterfall below highlight some of this processing. A point that is higher on the screen plane may or may not be higher in absolute coordinates, but our vision system uses several clues about the water running down, steps, reduction in size etc. to determine that the top of the waterfall is below its bottom.

Escher print showing difficult perspectives.
Public Wikipedia

Fortunately there is generally no need for a robot to have only one eye, so stereo vision can provide a much easier way to infer the third dimension using simple trigonometry. For example, in the figure below it is easy to determine that the person is well in front of the larger palm tree by noting their relevant positions to the two cameras.

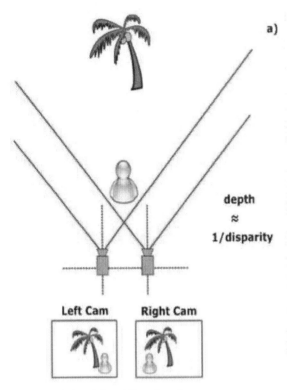

Stereo vision identifies depth.
Permitted http://www.imec.be/ScientificReport/SR2007/html/1384302.html

Stereo vision requires the non-trivial matching of pixels in one image with pixels in the other image in order to know which pixels to triangulate. But some systems like the XBox Kinect system use an even simpler approach in which one of the cameras is replaced with an infrared laser that scans the scene. Then an infrared camera only needs to recognize where the bright dot of the laser is in the scene in order to perform the triangulation. Recent Kinect systems use a time-of-flight camera which can actually measure the time it takes for a pulse of light to travel from the camera to the object and back. (These approaches fail in bright daylight or if the image contains translucent objects.)

Determining the three-dimensional shape of an object makes it much easier to determine the real colour and textures of its surfaces, as well as providing strong additional clues for segmentation.

For the XBox Kinect, the model is a human with multiple joints, as shown below. A human is a complex object, and being able to do this effectively is a recent achievement that requires sophisticated mathematical analysis. Once the geometry has been recovered, it becomes possible to analyze how the figure is moving, and thus how much weight and energy is being carried by different parts of the body. This in turn can be used to drive the game play that Kinect was designed to assist.

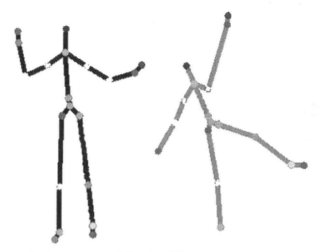

Recovery of a human model using Kinect.
Corporate Microsoft

3D vs 2.5D

It should be noted that many practical problems can be addressed without building a sophisticated scene grammar. For example, it has been noted that a frog only needs to be able to recognize black dots moving across its field of vision. If an area grows substantially then it might be a predator approaching, in which case the frog can simply hop in the direction of the darker part of the image. (Real frogs are more intelligent than that.)

Indeed, many if not most practical applications only use 2-D or 2.5-D representations. For example, to recognize a face, it is not actually necessary to build a complete 3D model from the image. It is sufficient to simply match features in the image with features in a generic stored face. Likewise, recognizing road signs and number plates can be a 2D problem. There is evidence that most insect vision is also essentially 2.5D.

The "half" a dimension refers to aspects that hint at 3-D but are not actually interpreted as such. These include shading effects of curves, and even possibly real 3-D information extracted from a stereo vision system. But in a 2.5-D system no 3-D model is built with this data, instead it is simply used as an additional feature mapped to the 2-D surface.

It may not even be necessary to build a 2-D model. One early autonomous car had a simple three-layer artificial neural network connected directly to a video camera. The output was then connected directly to the steering wheel, and it was trained by people driving the cart around a real road. The system worked well provided that the road was bordered by two bright white lines.

Many factory systems have objects laid flat on a conveyor belt with a contrasting colour, and so only need very simple vision systems to guide robots to manipulate them. There are also many tricks that can be used. For example, if one wishes to track people as they move around a room, one can first take an image of the room when empty and then subtract that from any active image — anything that remains must be people.

Relatively recent advances have enabled much more sophisticated vision systems to be built. If anything approaching human competence is to be achieved, then building some type of hierarchical scene grammar would appear to be a prerequisite.

Kinetics

If vision is to be useful for practical applications such as guiding a robot, then it needs to be fast, returning results on a subsecond time frame. Vision is complex, though, so early systems could take minutes to analyze a single image. This means that vision systems need to be as simple and fast as possible to solve the problem at hand.

One important technique is to be able to update a scene graph as the robot or objects in its environment move, rather than analyzing each frame completely from scratch. This involves matching regions in an image with regions in a slightly different previous image. It is also useful to be able to predict where objects will be before a future scene can be analyzed. That type of processing is essential for performing complex tasks such as catching a ball in real time. The analysis also needs to be robust, so that objects do not magically appear between frames.

(Early 3-D graphics rendering involved many such techniques to update an existing image rather than having to render each frame from scratch. But modern computer hardware is so fast that such tricks are no longer used, and each frame is normally calculated completely from scratch, over twenty times per second.)

Robots

Automata

Classic tin robot.
Public Commons D. J. Shin

People have been fascinated by the idea of automated humanoid robots since the eighteenth century. Very simple movements can be quite enchanting when they are performed by a machine with a humanoid shape.

Perhaps the greatest early robot was The Turk chess-playing machine created by Wolfgang von Kempelen in 1770. It toured Europe and the Americas for 80 years, and beat many notable people including Napoleon Bonaparte and Benjamin Franklin. Before each game, von Kempelen would open each of the doors of the machine one at a time to prove to the audience that it was purely mechanical. Rev. Edmund Cartwright was so intrigued by the Turk in 1784 that he would later question whether "it is more difficult to construct a machine that shall weave than one which shall make all the variety of moves required in that complicated game" and patented the first power loom shortly afterwards. Many fanciful theories were postulated as to how the machine worked, including one claim that it must be fake because it sometimes lost a game but a real machine would not make mistakes.

It was not until after the machine's eventual destruction in a fire in 1854 that the key technology that facilitated this amazing performance was revealed, which was a sliding seat within the body of the machine. An operator hidden within the machine could then use the seat to slide to whichever part of the machine was not open to inspection at a given time.

Perhaps the most amazing aspect of this illusion was that it fooled so many intelligent people for so many years. Not even a vague explanation was ever offered as to how the machine was supposed to work, and the visible machinery looks too small to solve such a difficult problem. Psychologically, the use of the humanoid head with its moving eyes was probably more important than it should have been.

Modern reproduction of The Turk.
Public Wikipedia

Not all automatons providing complex functionality were fake. Henri Maillardet created the one shown below in the early nineteenth century. It could draw and write reasonably well, including a poem signed by the creator. The large circular cams at the bottom stored the fixed movements required to produce the drawings, and steel fingers pushed by the cams moved the hand. It took considerable skill with early nineteenth century technology to map movement by the steel fingers to the hand of the robot with sufficient accuracy to produce a reasonable drawing. Again, the humanoid head is essential to the machine's appeal, even though it has nothing to do with its functionality.

Henri Maillardet's Draughtsman Automaton from 1810.
Public   Wikipedia,   Educational   http://www.fi.edu/learn/sci-tech/automaton/automaton.php?cts=instrumentation

The relationship between the notches on the cams and the exact position of the hand is a non-trivial. It would take considerable effort to calculate for each point on a complex drawing the correct notches on the cams required to move the hand to the corresponding position. However Maillardet probably used a trick in which he replaced the brass cams with something like paper, and replaced the steel fingers with a pencil. He could then manually move the hand of the robot, which would record the positions of the pencil on the paper. The brass cams could then be cut to match the line traced out on the paper.

Robotics

The availability of inexpensive computers has made it possible to build effective robots that have revolutionized manufacturing techniques. In highly controlled production line environments it is possible to utilize relatively simple robots to perform tedious, repetitive work that was traditionally performed by unskilled workers. This includes material handling (e.g. moving objects between pallets and machines), spot and arc welding, and the assembly of parts.

One of the earliest factory robots was the Unimation PUMA which was introduced in 1978 and is shown below. It had an arm which had six movable joints, often known as *degrees of freedom*. Being destined for the factory, it lacked a pretty humanoid face, but it could effectively perform simple repetitive tasks previously performed by people.

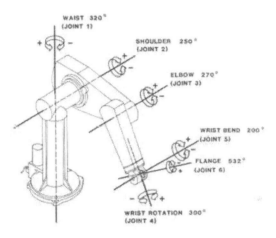

Unimation PUMA Robot.
Corporate

Early robots only moved in predetermined paths. They typically had a training mode in which the joints would relax and a skilled operator would push the arm to perform the desired action. The robot would then simply repeat those precise movements over and over, perhaps being driven by a simple sensor which told it when the next part arrived on a production line. This is very similar to the way that Maillardet's draughting automaton was probably trained. Although simple, these robots have enabled some factories to operate completely "lights off", meaning that an entire production line is automated and so no people, and thus no lights, are required for it to operate.

Such robots are in no sense intelligent and could well be described as just another advanced industrial machine like a multi-axis milling machine. However, building such a robot presents significant technical challenges. The joint angles need to be accurately set, but the motors that drive them usually provide a torque, not an absolute angle. A fast-moving robot has substantial momentum, so the equations that relate the position of the hand to the torque of the motors are complicated and unstable. Continuous feedback needs to be provided to correct errors, but without causing possibly violent oscillations. Some robots can learn how the arm performed in previous attempts and so can improve performance by predicting and avoiding errors before the feedback system can detect them.

Good quality modern robots can make several distinct movements per second, all with submillimetre accuracy. They are impressive to watch because they can easily outperform people for precisely specified movements.

Sensing environment

Motoman robot using vision to pick objects out of an unstructured bin.
Corporate http://www.motoman.com/products/vision/#sthash.2y5eWHz4.dpbs

Today, more sophisticated robots can sense their environment and react to it in sophisticated ways. This enables them to grasp objects that are not in precisely predefined locations, and to work on objects that are not identical. One of the toughest problems traditionally is *bin picking*, namely to pick objects out of a jumble of objects in a bin as shown above. The robot has to sense where the objects are and what their orientation or *pose* is. It then has to plan a sequence of movements to accurately grasp the object. This means that the factory environment does not need to be as rigidly controlled, and that many additional jobs can be automated.

The advanced vision systems this requires have now become much more affordable. The system shown above just uses the same Kinect sensors that are used in the XBox consumer game console. So the factory lights are being turned back on, but not for human eyes.

Motion Planning

Hexapod robot.
Corporate http://www.hexapodrobot.com/store/index.php?cPath=21_22

Other robots can move about, with wheels or caterpillar treads or even legs. Hexapod robots like the one show above are very stable and relatively easy to program. Moving robots then need to plan a path to a desired location without bumping into other objects along the way.

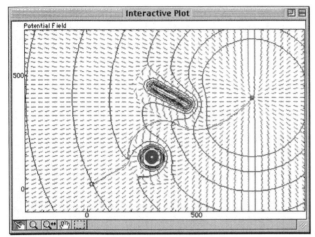

Use of an imaginary potential field to find a smooth path.
Corporate http://www.calerga.com/products/Sysquake/robotnav.html

One classical approach to this problem is to pretend that the environment has a potential field, much like a gravitational field. The goal position has an attractive force, while obstacles have a repulsive force. So in the diagram above, the blue lines show the equi-potentials that attract the robot, but with strong repulsion around the round and linear obstacles. The red lines are just perpendicular to the blue lines. At each point the robot calculates the net effect of the imaginary field on its location and simply falls along these red lines towards its goal. This normally produces a fairly smooth and reasonably efficient path.

For more complex environments, the potential field approach can get stuck in dead ends. A more general approach is to model the space as a large grid of squares. The intelligent agent can then consider each possible path from square to square that leads from the source to the goal before choosing the shortest, smoothest path. Heading in the general direction of the goal usually provides a good heuristic to minimize this search.

The diagram below shows how this process can be optimized by only considering squares that are adjacent to objects. Given that the shortest unobscured path will always be a straight line, then only paths that connect the small red dots need to be considered. This optimization is important for large spaces. A light gray barrier has been placed around the objects to allow for the width of the robot. Other approaches create random or semi-random intermediate points on the map rather than carefully placing them near the boundaries of objects. The result of either algorithm then needs to be smoothed for efficient dynamic movement through the space.

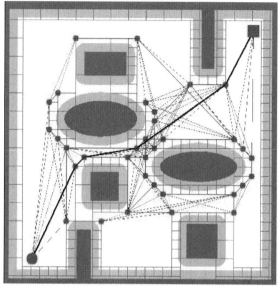

Searching for an optimal path by only examining plausible best paths.
Education http://home.postech.ac.kr/~postman/index_res.htm

An intelligent robot needs to be able to move its arm in complex ways without being told exactly how to move each joint. For example, it might be asked to find and pick a part out of a bin, and then put it in a specific location. That requires it to plan a series of motions with an arm that achieves the goal without colliding with other objects like the sides of the bin. It turns out that this is very similar to the problem of navigating a path for a wheeled robot to move, but in a three dimensional space. Of course, the elbows must also not bump into things, which complicates the problem. One common approach is to plan the motions in the much higher dimensional space of joint angles rather than the locations in three dimensional space.

Movement and Balance

One of the more difficult tasks for a humanoid robot is to maintain balance while walking over rough surfaces. The Atlas robot shown below can walk over a surface covered by unstable rocks. Atlas was developed by the Boston Dynamics company which has recently been purchased by Google.

The kinodynamic processing requires very carefully measuring the current state of the robot's balance and movement. This is then compared to the desired state so that movements can be planned that will produce the desired state. Due to the chaotic environment, these plans never quite work as expected, so new plans need to be continuously produced. This type of feedback loop needs to be carefully damped in order not to produce wild, oscillating movements which would arise if the robot continuously over-corrects previous mistakes.

The reader is encouraged to view the video of Atlas's impressive performance, but it is still moves rather awkwardly, and only remains upright by flailing its weighted arms around quite vigorously. This is in stark contrast to a human that could not only walk but run over this terrain very smoothly.

Atlas robot walking over rough terrain.
Corporate Boston Dynamics

Robocup

Humanoid Robocup.
Corporate http://www.pbs.org/wgbh/nova/tech/soccer-playing-robots.html

Some of the greatest advances in robotics are demonstrated at the annual international Robocup event, in which dozens of teams of engineers compete to build humanoid robots that can win a game of soccer against competing robots. There are many classes of robots, and the rules become more challenging each year. Each robot has to be fully autonomous, without any human guidance, nor any central guiding computer. They are required to sense their position and the position of the other players and the ball, and then determine how they should move. That is a very challenging problem.

Most human interest seems to be in the humanoid robots 30 to 60 centimeters tall like those shown above. A major challenge for them is simply to remain upright on their two large feet, and to work with the severe weight and hence power restrictions that result from having legs. The advancement of these robots over the last decade is impressive, from robots that could barely move on four feet to robots that can play real soccer on two feet.

In many ways, the more interesting robots are the ones designed to work effectively as robots rather than pretending to be people. They have wheels that enable them to move quickly and purposefully around the field, as shown below. These robots now play what looks like an intelligent game, covering the field and passing the ball to each other.

Having seen how the robots perform, and knowing the sophisticated engineering that is involved in building them, it is interesting to watch the engineers themselves play against the robots. Of course, the engineers easily win, and one cannot but be impressed by the grace and sophistication of human movement.

Wheeled Robocup robots.
News http://www.dailymail.co.uk/sciencetech/article-467266/World-Cup-robots-kicks-off.html

Other robots

Another impressive challenge is the associated Robots@Home competition. Here, robots are expected to interact with the real, unconstrained world. A recent challenge was to go to an unknown supermarket, find and recognize where the milk is stored, retrieve it from the shelf without dropping or crushing it, and then navigate back to the checkout and present the milk for payment. This needed to be performed without bumping into other people that happened to be there. One robot famously failed to complete the task when a small boy decided to press its emergency Off button.

The image below shows the Stanford STAIR robot unstacking a dishwasher. The key challenge is to determine how to grasp a variety of different types of objects and pick them up without dropping or crushing them. It is an advanced example of bin picking.

STAIR robot stacking a dishwasher
Education http://pr.cs.cornell.edu/publications.php

The US Defense Advanced Research Agency (DARPA) also provides a series of robotics challenges which increase in complexity each year, with multi-million dollar prizes for the winner. The 2004 challenge was to drive over difficult desert terrain, and all contestants failed very early in the course. In 2005 the challenge was run again, and this time five entrants succeeded. In the 2007 challenge contestants navigated suburban roads, with other cars on the roads.

The current DARPA Disaster Relief Challenge involves humanoid robots. The robot needs to drive a vehicle, walk over rubble, and clear objects blocking a door. It must then visually and audibly locate and shut off a leaking valve, connect a hose or connector, climb an industrial ladder, traverse an industrial walkway and then use a power tool and break through a concrete wall. This is a massive task that is expected to take several years to complete. To emphasize the importance of software, DARPA will provide identical robots to each of the contestants. The robots will only be semi-autonomous, with higher-level decision making left to an operator.

One major benefit of the DARPA challenge is that DARPA has funded a sophisticated, publicly available, open source robotic simulator named Gazebo. This makes it much easier for smaller research teams that are not part of the main challenge to do advanced robotics research. Presumably the Atlas humanoid robots being built for DARPA by Boston Dynamics will also become available at more reasonable prices.

While these problems may not require the resolution of the deeper issues in artificial intelligence, they do require the solution of many simpler ones, particularly in machine vision and sensing. And building a system that actually works coherently involves much more complexity than just the sum of the parts.

Humanistic

Modeling human shapes.
Multiple http://photoskillsb-keith-beckett.blogspot.com.au/2013_02_01_archive.html
em http://www.tothepc.com/archives/einstein-head-on-an-android-from-outer-space/

A different branch of research is building robots that resemble people as closely as possible. Building human likenesses has been the work of sculptors for centuries, but we can now work on making them move and speak like people do. This is difficult to do because humans are very sensitive to subtle nuances in body language and facial expressions. In one project a team clothed a robot named Yume as a slightly gothic, slightly punk young girl, complete with dark lipstick to cover her inability to fully close her mouth. Her appearance helped obscure her herky-jerky movements and rickety eye contact, and made it look like she was on something stronger than electricity.

While these may (or may not) be worthwhile projects artistically, putting a pretty face on a robot does not make it any more human than sculpting a pretty face on a rock makes the rock more human. The real challenge is not to build toys but to build truly intelligent agents that can operate autonomously in the real world. Initially such agents will be bad at some things people are good at, and good at some things people are bad at. But whatever they become, they will not be anything like human beings, regardless of whatever pretty face they might wear.

That said, a pretty humanoid face with honest eyes and a warm smile would enable a computer to be much more persuasive than if it was presented as a bug-eyed monster.

Robots leaving the factory

The most significant change that is likely to be seen over the next ten years is the practical application of robots that are working outside of carefully structured factory environments. The earliest have been the automated vacuum cleaners, the better of which actively map out the rooms that are cleaning. Probably the most significant in the short term will be autonomous, self-driving cars.

Huge trucks have been autonomously driving around mine sites for several years. Mercedes already ships driver assist technology that senses other cars, while BMW expects to move their completely automatic freeway driving system into production by 2020. The Google driverless car has received considerable attention, but all vehicle manufactures have invested in the technology. The initial focus is on just assisting human drivers, but fully autonomous or partially remotely controlled cars are likely to be in production by 2025.

Incidentally, flying an airplane turns out to be much easier for a computer to do than driving a car. The former has well-defined procedures and aircraft can be modelled as simple points in three-dimensional space, whereas driving a car involves much more subtle interactions with its environment. On the other hand, the human brain has evolved to move on the ground, and can only, with some difficulty, learn to fly through the air.

Other repetitive jobs, such as laying bricks or painting buildings, are also likely to be automated in the not too distant future. This is partly due to the ever more sophisticated factory robots that enable other complex robots to be assembled economically.

These robots will live in a much more complicated world than SHRDLUs simple block-stacking micro-world. The problems they face will still be much simpler than our full human world, and therefore much more tractable. However, these new mini-worlds will require new intelligent systems to be built that plan their movements and make sensible decisions, which should in turn provide a strong demand for practical artificial intelligence research.

Programs writing Programs

The task of man

In a classic story by Authur C. Clarke some Tibetan monks believed that the purpose of man was to slowly enumerate the 9 billion names of God according to some ancient algorithm. The monks become very excited when the narrator of the story sells them an electronic computer that could quickly automate this otherwise laborious process. The narrator makes a point of leaving the monastery shortly before the calculation was complete to avoid the anger of the disappointed monks when nothing would have happened. But the following night, at about the time when the computer was due to finish, the narrator notices that one by one, without any fuss, the stars were going out.

This story may be fanciful, but we now know what the true task of man is. It is not to investigate quarks and quasars, the origin and nature of the universe. Nor is it to develop advanced biotechnology or ever more complex nano-machines. It is instead to write a computer program that is intelligent enough to program computers as well as people do. That is a very difficult problem which is unlikely to be solved for some time. But once it has been solved, computers will be able to program themselves. The task of man will be complete, and the computer will be able to address those other more trifling problems itself, should it be inclined to do so. Working on other tasks is like manually shovelling dirt while waiting for a bulldozer to arrive, presuming that it does arrive in a timely manner.

Recursive compilation

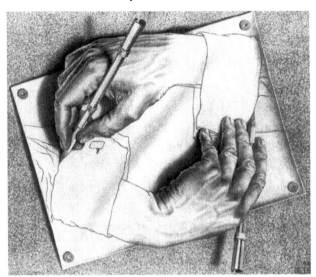

M.C. Escher *Drawing Hands* 1948
Public Wikipedia

It seems surreal that a program could program itself, much like an Escher hand drawing itself, or a brain surgeon operating on their own brain. A logical illusion that could never exist in reality. But it is, in fact, commonplace for computers to program themselves when guided by people.

Industrial robots can be used to make industrial robots in a similar way that 3-D printers can print many of the parts used to make 3-D printers. It is only a matter of time before a combination of 3-D printers, industrial robots and automatic milling machines automatically produce 3-D printers, industrial robots and automatic milling machines. In that case, the sorcerer's apprentice might have had a relatively easy problem to deal with.

Computers ultimately execute instructions that have been written in ones and zeros, but they are not programmed that way. Instead, programs are written in a high-level language that is converted to ones and zeros by a computer program called a compiler.

Below is an example of a program that implements a simple procedure `sub32` that subtracts 32 from a number if it is between 97 and 122 (this has the effect of converting lower-case letters to upper-case ones).

```
sub sub32(value as integer)
  if value >= 97 and value <= 122 then
    sub32 = value - 32
  else
    sub32 = value;
  end if
end sub
```

The program names its input parameter value and then tests whether it is in the relevant range before subtracting 32 from it. The result is assigned to the result of the procedure, which in this language (Visual Basic) is the procedure's name.

The compiler program reads a text file that contains the program source code and outputs the ones and zeros that a computer can actually execute. But what is the compiler itself written in? It is in fact normally written in another computer language, in this case Visual Basic happened to be written in a cruder language called C. But C compilers are normally written in C. That is very much like the hands drawing the hands. This presents the chicken and the egg problem, namely which came first, the C compiler program or the C source code from which the compiler program was compiled?

The answer is the same as the answer to the chicken and the egg problem, namely that the lizard came first. In this case, the lizard is an earlier, different programming language which was used to compile the first C compiler, which *might* have been an earlier language called Fortran. And what was the ancient Fortran compiler written in? Fortran? No, it would have been written in a different type of language called an assembly language. The assembly language example below implements the same program as above, but in a much more obscure manner in which each line in the program directly relates to one instruction that a computer can execute.

```
SUB32 PROC
CMP AX, 97
JL DONE
CMP AX, 122
JG DONE
SUB AX, 32
DONE: RET
SUB32 ENDP
```

However, computers cannot directly execute assembly code either, so it needs to be converted to ones and zeros by a program called an assembler. Assemblers were written in assembly language. But sometime in the dim and distant past (the early 1950s) a few steadfast programmers wrote the first assemblers in terms of the actual ones and zeros that a computer can directly execute. Those assemblers have been used to write other assemblers, which have been used to implement compilers, which have been used to implement other compilers, which in turn have been used to write virtually all the software that is used today.

(A *cross compiler* running on a source machine produces code that runs on a different target machine. So although the 1950s computers are long extinct, the legacy of some the code that ran on them lives on, much as the genetic legacy of the first living organisms lives on in our DNA even though those early organisms are now extinct.)

For many years programmers continued to use assembly languages because they were thought to be more efficient than high-level languages. But modern compilers can usually produce more efficient program code than human programmers and so are now used for almost all software development. Indeed, many younger programmers do not even know the low-level instructions that a computer actually executes. That knowledge is locked inside the compilers that they use.

Quines

An interesting student programming exercise is to write a *quine,* which is a program that prints out an exact copy of itself. It has been argued that no program could ever really program itself because that would require having a copy of itself within itself. A quine demonstrates that this is indeed possible because in order to print itself a quine needs to somehow have a copy of itself within itself, without descending into an infinite regress. Quines have been written for most programming languages. The technical challenge is typically to quote the quote character used to quote strings.

One of the most challenging widely-used programming languages is, of course, MS-Dos batch script. Aficionados might enjoy the following quine by Peter Hartmann of DosTips.com. Warning: a deep understanding of this program may induce insanity.

```
Set    "T=Echo    Set    "T=!T!"&Call    Echo    Set
E=!E!E!E!!E!E!E!&Echo Cmd/V:On/C"!E!T!E!""
Set E=%%
Cmd/V:On/C "%T%"
```

Reasoning about program logic

(This subsection requires some experience with computer programming and may be easily skipped.)

Computer programs often defy the illogical thinking of their programmers, and fail to do what was intended. Extensive testing helps discover some errors, but testing can only show that the program works for a given number of test cases, not that it will work for all cases when used in production.

Early work by C.A.R. Hoare and others addresses this problem by describing the input and output of a program in terms of mathematical logic. Each step of the program is also defined in mathematical logic, so proving that the program is correct involves proving that the output follows the input given the program steps.

Classic examples of this process involve sorting algorithms, whose job it is to sort a list of numbers in ascending order. It turns out there are many different ways of performing this task, but they all have the same definition of their output, namely a sorted copy of their input.

The simplest, and one of the least efficient, algorithms is the selection sort. It works by searching for the smallest number in the list, and then swapping it with whatever number happens to be in the first position. The process is then repeated for the second position. This is illustrated in the following dialog in which the first cell's contents is a seven which then is swapped with the lowest number present, a one in cell seven. The two is then swapped into the second position.

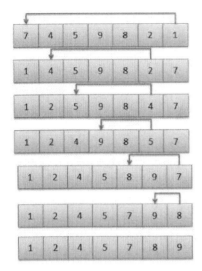

A selection sort swaps the lowest numbers into the first positions.
Education http://e4electric.blogspot.com.au/2012/11/selection-sort-c-for-selection-sort.html

A simple Basic subprogram that implements this is as follows:-

```
10 sub SelectionSort(numbers())
20    for pass = 1 to ubound(numbers) - 1
30       'Assert x > pass implies numbers'(pass) <=
numbers'(y)
40       smallest = pass
50       for x = pass + 1 to ubound(numbers)
60          if numbers(smallest) > numbers(x)   then
smallest = x
70       next x
80       temp = numbers(smallest)
90       numbers(smallest) = numbers(pass)
100      numbers(pass) = temp
110   next pass
120    'Assert    x  <y  implies   numbers'(x)   <=
numbers'(y)
130 end sub
```

The input is stored in an array (or vector) named numbers. The for statement in line 20 starts a loop that will repeat the code in lines 30 to 100 multiple times. It will initially assign the variable pass the value of 1, then 2, then 3 until it becomes greater than one less than the upper bound of the numbers array (i.e. the number of numbers in it). (In this program we use the sensible convention of counting from 1, so the first element in the numbers array is numbers(1), not numbers(0).)

There is also an inner loop that will set the variable x to pass + 1 and then increment it until it is greater than ubound(numbers). This inner loop searches for the smallest number in the unsorted part of the array. Once this loop terminates, this smallest value is swapped with the current value in numbers(pass), and then the outer loop repeats.

The logical assertion in line 120 is not actually part of the program. It states that when the program has finished, if one number is in the list before a second number, then that first number must be less than the second number. In other words that the list is sorted. By convention, the prime (') indicates the value of the variable after the execution of the program is being referred to, as opposed to the value that was passed to the program initially. This is the assertion that needs to be proven to be correct for *any* input array if the program actually works.

In order to do this, the second assertion in line 30 needs to be defined. It provides the *loop invariant*, namely the condition that is true each time the loop is executed. It states that after each pass, the number stored in numbers'(pass) will not be greater than any number to its right. This is not as strong a condition as saying that the entire list is sorted, for the subprogram has not yet finished. But given that the pass variable is incremented through the list of numbers, this means that the entire array must be sorted when the subprogram exits.

The details of the actual correctness proof are somewhat technical and tedious, but it is easy to build a theorem prover that can prove that a simple program like the selection sort is correct, given that the loop invariant has been specified. Automatically inferring the loop invariant is much more difficult, but it is also possible for simple programs.

The loop invariant essentially defines the different types of sorting algorithms. One common algorithm, known as the *insertion sort*, has an invariant that the left part of the list is internally sorted, but that there may still be smaller values in the right-hand part. Another algorithm known as *quicksort* has the invariant that all the values on the left are less than all the values on the right, but that neither side is sorted. *Shell sort* has an invariant that sub-lists of every kth element are sorted. The details are not important; the point is that having different intermediate invariants largely defines the different sorting algorithms.

The problem of (semi) automatically proving that programs are correct has been the subject of considerable research, and is far from being fully solved. However, very useful tools have been developed that can assist with proving that programs are in fact correct.

Automating program generation

The inverse of validating a program's correctness is to generate good program code from the formal definition of the program's requirements. This is a much more difficult problem than proving that a given piece of code is correct — it is again like squeezing the toothpaste back into the tube. There are many ways to sort a list, and many technical papers have been written that develop and analyze a variety of algorithms, all of whose jobs are to satisfy the simple assertion on line 120. It is therefore not surprising that it is difficult to automate the development of new algorithms. That said, it is possible to automate code generation if the assertions are simple, and assertions can be simplified by providing intermediate assertions such as loop invariants.

Errors in computer programs are a curse of our modern age. So one might think that a technology that can mathematically prove that programs are correct would form a cornerstone of software engineering methodologies. However, the techniques are rarely used in practice, and many if not most computer programmers are completely unaware of their existence.

The main reason for this is that most problems cannot be succinctly defined in mathematical logic as easily as the sorting problem. Modern programmers rarely write tricky algorithms with well-defined properties, rather, they spend their time assembling large libraries of other people's software and adding logic that has only a vaguely defined specification. The difficult bugs are rarely within one's own code, but involve the interaction with other people's code. And it is difficult to document what that other code does in mathematical logic due to all the problems of default reasoning and commonsense knowledge.

Indeed, the current fashion in software engineering is *agile* development methodologies. Agile development eschews any specification whatsoever. Instead, programmers just code one part after another without much concern for what the whole system would be like. It turns out that the alternative approach of designing a system first tends to fail because it is difficult for people to know what a complex computer system should have done until after it has been built.

(Another important advantage of agile development is that an agile team quickly demonstrates whether it is (or is not) capable of building *something*, even if that something is not useful. That enables natural selection to take place as incompetent teams are disbanded. Alternatively, it is much more difficult to assess whether a team of system architects is producing useful designs or just pretty abstract drawings. The proof of the pudding is in the eating, so the sooner that happens the better.)

High-level models

One approach to program generation that this author has been involved with is to use higher-level models of applications to abstract away the code altogether. In particular, information systems can be implemented using repeatable patterns. For example, consider a program that manipulates a Customer table. This involves logic to display a list of customers that satisfies various criteria, then provide a blank form to enter a new customer's details or select a customer record for editing, and then insert, update or delete the Customer record in a database. This type of logic is generally referred to as CRUD — Create Read Update Delete. CRUDing a customer is much the same as CRUDing an order, student, subject, employee or product, only the data table, fields and declarative business rules are different.

The few systems that use these high-level models can be used to implement fairly complex information systems involving dozens of tables without any explicit programming being required at all. One system built by the author could generate large quantities of program code from concise specifications that would take a human an order of magnitude longer to implement manually. The key to making it possible is high-level models of data and business rules. Like many advances in software, this approach abstracts away repetitive details and allows programmers to focus on real problems. However, these systems are not generally thought of as being intelligent. (That said, this author's system gained considerable power in practice by being implemented in Lisp which is an artificial intelligence programming language.)

Learning first order concepts

Most systems that learn rules from experience only learn propositional rules. For example, the Bayesian network discussed earlier could only reason about the propositions WetGrass and Rain, and the decision tree example could only recognize one of ten digits.

Advanced systems exist that can learn more complex first order rules, of which the most popular is known as inductive logic programming. For example, given a table of ground propositional predicates such as

```
parent(george,elizabeth).
parent(elizabeth, charles).
parent(charles, harry).
parent(charles, william).
grandparent(george, charles).
grandparent(elizabeth, william).
not(grandparent(elizabeth, charles)).
```

an inductive logic system could derive the general first order relationship

```
grandparent(G, C) :- parent(G, P), parent(P, C).
```

expressed as Prolog Horn clauses. In other words that a grandparent G of child C seems to be someone that is the parent of someone P that is in turn a parent of the child C. This type of knowledge cannot be represented effectively as simple propositions without variables because it generalizes to all people, not just specifically named people.

One method to implement this is the top down approach in which the system generates simple predicates from the given data. For example, it might guess

```
grandparent(G, C)  :- parent(G,C).
grandparent(G,C)  :- parent(G, P).
```

The first guess does not match the data and so can be discounted. The second is close, but does successfully reject `grandparent(elizabeth, charles)`. So the system tries to add additional qualifying clauses, and finds that adding `parent(P, C)` enables the clause to accurately match the data.

An alternative approach is to essentially run a resolution theorem prover backwards. It tries to determine what predicate is required to prove the theorem so that the rule can correctly classify the data.

Some systems can infer quite complex relationships including recursive rules such as

```
ancestor(A, C)  :- ancestor(A,P), parent(P, C).
```

which states that an ancestor involves some arbitrary number of parentage relationships.

Practical applications of this technology include being able to infer complex protein folding rules from data sets that were too large for people to analyze effectively. Learning first order predicates was necessary for that problem because protein structures are all about the relationships between different parts of the structure, and relationships are a first order concept.

Predicates like `ancestor` are essentially small programs. More advanced systems can learn larger programs given good training data. One system even learned how to implement a simple sorting program, like the selection sort described previously, with no input other than examples of sorted and unsorted lists of numbers. So this provides a very limited, but not insignificant, example of programs writing programs.

Evolutionary algorithms

Evolutionary and genetic algorithms use techniques that were inspired by the natural processes of gene recombination and natural selection. These algorithms are used to optimize the values of a number of parameters in order to maximize some fitness function. They are widely used in numerical modeling, and even the Microsoft Excel spreadsheet program includes an evolutionary solver as a standard feature. Unlike most other approaches, evolutionary solvers can work with complex fitness functions of many dimensions that are discontinuous and have numerous local maxima.

Fitness	A	B	C	D	E
~~2~~	~~3~~	~~3~~	~~2~~	~~4~~	~~13~~
8	2	3	5	3	4
11	6	7	6	9	6
30	7	5	6	8	5
37	5	4	3	4	5
53	3	2	9	6	5
41	3	2	6	7	8

Candidate Solutions

Owned

The basic algorithm has a pool of often random candidate solutions, with each solution being ranked according to some fitness function. Then at each iteration, the weakest candidate solution is removed from the pool, and a new solution is created by randomly combining two aspects of the other solutions.

So in the example above, six candidate solutions were produced which each consisted of a vector of five numbers named A through E. They were then ranked by applying a fitness function to the five numbers, and the weakest with a fitness of 2 was removed. A new candidate was then created by combining two other randomly selected candidates in the pool, in this case the ones with fitness of 30 and 53. The new candidate was found to have a fitness of 41 which is better than the previously weakest candidate with a fitness of 8 which will be the next one to be removed.

The method for combining candidates to produce a new candidate varies widely. In the example, numbers have been chosen randomly for columns A, B and C, while D is the average of the two and E is a completely random "mutation".

Genetic algorithms work on the principle that an optimal solution to a problem is likely to be similar to good solutions to a problem. Thus, randomly selecting attributes from successful candidates is much more effective than just using random values. It also requires that the attributes are somewhat independent of each other.

The key inspiration from biology is natural selection, survival of the fittest, and the sexual combination of parents to produce children. In biological genetics, the genes are roughly independent from each other, so improving a gene for the immune system (say) is unlikely to directly affect the nervous system (say). Other details of the methods used are generally quite different from biological genetics, for example few if any methods use multiple sets of chromosomes.

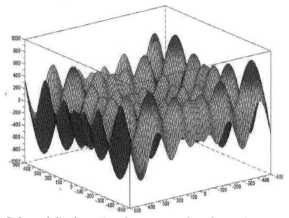

Schwefel's function has many local maxima
Corporate Microsoft

Consider the problem of trying to numerically find the largest value of Schwefel's function shown above. The normal approach to finding a function's maximum is gradient ascent, in which one starts at a random point and then keeps climbing uphill. However, that will almost certainly lead to the top of one of the lesser peaks, and not to the global maximum. But like many complex functions, the global maximum has similar values for X and Y as the stronger local maxima, so a genetic algorithm should converge on the global maxima relatively quickly.

One practical application of genetic algorithms was to optimize speech recognition algorithms [Kurzwiel]. Recall that discrete features need to be extracted from the 10 millisecond frames of sound in order to drive the Markov model. However, there are many possible features that can be extracted, and it is not at all obvious which combination of features will drive a Markov model most effectively. So a number of reasonable feature sets were used as candidates in a genetic algorithm, with the fitness test being how well the system could learn to recognize certain spoken words. The genetic algorithm would then recombine elements of the more successful sets of features in order to produce new candidate solutions. After many, many hours of computation, the system improved the speech understanding program by choosing a set of features that was more effective than any set of features that were created by the human programmers.

Artificial life

An entertaining experiment is to apply evolutionary algorithms to simulate living creatures by creating a two dimensional world on a grid. Each cell can occupy one creature, and the creatures can move to adjacent squares. They can also sense the world around them, such as whether there are other creatures in adjacent squares.

The simulated world then has rules for eating and breeding. For example, if a creature moves to a square occupied by another creature, then the second creature is eaten and the first divides asexually. If two creatures that are next to each other move to new squares that are also adjacent to each other, then they sexually exchange genetic material.

The behaviour of the creatures can be controled using a two layer recurrent neural network, with inputs representing their senses of the world around them, and outputs being how to move. But rather than being trained by back propagation, they are trained genetically. So each time two creatures have a sexual encounter, they might simply swap a random set of weights between them, possibly with a few additional random mutations.

When this type of simulation is run, the creatures initially tend to just move randomly over their world. Any consumption of other creatures or sexual encounters happens purely by chance. But the rules of the system can be designed so that the number of creatures remains constant by ensuring that for every creature that dies another will be born.

Then, very slowly at first, some of the creatures start to behave in a more purposeful manner. They seem to try to avoid being eaten, and possibly to actively seek sexual encounters. It is not always obvious why they do what they do, but they seem to be doing it very purposely.

The next part of the classic experiment is to take a number of the creatures that have been evolving for a few million generations and put them in a world that contains new, raw creatures. The evolved creatures usually feast on the unevolved creatures, and quickly dominate the space.

Of course, there is a huge gap between these simulated worlds and the real world of even the simplest bacteria. However, it is interesting to see the principles of natural selection and gene exchange work effectively in a world that is different from our own. It also suggests that natural selection might drive the behaviour of more intelligent computer systems, just like it drives the behaviour of more intelligent biological systems.

Evolutionary programming

Educational http://www.geneticprogramming.com/coursemainpage.html

Evolutionary algorithms can be applied to more complex structures than sets or matrices of numbers. They can be well applied to tree structures, and general purpose programs can be represented as tree structures. Thus evolutionary algorithms can also be applied to program logic.

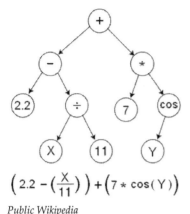

$$\left(2.2 - \left(\frac{X}{11}\right)\right) + \left(7 * \cos(Y)\right)$$

Public Wikipedia

The diagram above shows how an expression is normally represented as a tree structure. The root node (at the top) represents the last operator to be applied. Its children represent either numbers and variables or operators that will provide the values for the root node to operate on, and this process recurs down throughout the tree.

The following figure then shows how two parents can be combined to produce children by simply exchanging subtrees. The results will always be syntactically valid, although they may not be meaningful. It would also be possible to occasionally introduce completely random nodes.

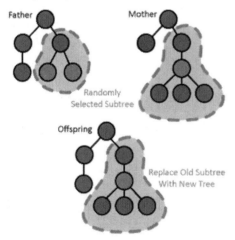

Multiple *http://www.geneticprogramming.com/Tutorial/*

Program statements such as conditional ("if") statements, loops, and subroutine calls can also be represented as tree structures. However, they do not evolve as effective as simple operators, and loops in particular have a nasty property of not necessarily terminating. Alternatively, programming models that are more resilient to random changes can also be used. The use of the very resilient neural networks has already been described, while another approach is the if/then-style rules that expert systems like Mycin use. One system named Tierra just used a special assembler-like instruction set.

Producing a really good program representation for genetic programming is a topic of ongoing research. Another challenge is to provide fine-grained fitness functions that recognize candidate solutions that are a small improvement even though they still do not perform satisfactorily.

There have been a few claimed successes for genetic programming. In the 1998 Robocup, one system apparently came in the middle of the field of 34 human-written programs for determining optimum movement of the robot players (Andre and Teller 1999).

However, the idea that some process of semi-random mutations could ever produce something remotely as sophisticated as a truly intelligent program is, of course, ridiculous. It is like hoping that enough monkeys sitting at enough typewriters for long enough will, by chance, produce the works of Shakespeare. The search space is just too large, so no semi-random process has any chance of producing a working complex system without the involvement of some very intelligent design.

Except, of course, that that is exactly how our own intelligence appears to have evolved into existence.

Chimpanzee at typewriter.
Public Wikipedia

Computer Hardware

Introduction

The next chapters will discuss biological brains and neurons in some detail, but it is worthwhile to first provide an overview of how ordinary silicon computers work at a low level in order to compare them with the very different mechanisms employed by biological neurons. In particular, to look at the power and limitations of the von Neumann architecture that is most commonly used, and alternatives that can also be utilized.

Transistors

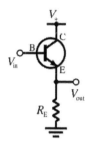

Simple common collector transistor amplifier.
Public Wikipedia

Modern computers are built from transistors or related technologies. Transistors became the main component in electronics in the 1950s. Their basic function is to amplify current, as demonstrated by the common collector circuit above. A transistor has three connections, a base (B), collector (C) and emitter (E). A tiny current from the base to the emitter will enable a much larger current to flow from the collector to the emitter. So in the circuit, if V_{in} is grounded, no current will flow between the collector and the emitter, and so V_{out} will be zero due to the resistor. But if V_{in} is raised, then a current will flow and so a potential will develop over the resistor, raising V_{out} until it is almost the same as V_{in}. At that point, the current between the base and emitter will reduce. V_{out} will end up having about the same voltage as V_{in}, but be able to sustain a much greater current.

Education http://hyperphysics.phy-astr.gsu.edu/hbase/electronic/nand.html
Simplified common emitter NAND gate circuit.

Transistors can be used to implement logical functions. In the *NAND* gate circuit above, if either A or B are at 0 volts then the associated transistors will not conduct electricity. The Out voltage will thus be pulled high by the resistor. But if both A and B have a significant voltage then both transistors will conduct and drag the Out voltage to (nearly) zero. Thus the circuit output is logically `not (A and B)`.

Logic Elements

Name	Graphic Symbol	Algebraic Function	Truth Table
AND		$F = A \cdot B$ or $F = AB$	A B F / 0 0 0 / 0 1 0 / 1 0 0 / 1 1 1
OR		$F = A + B$	A B F / 0 0 0 / 0 1 1 / 1 0 1 / 1 1 1
NOT		$F = \bar{A}$ or $F = A'$	A F / 0 1 / 1 0
NAND		$F = (\overline{AB})$	A B F / 0 0 1 / 0 1 1 / 1 0 1 / 1 1 0
NOR		$F = (\overline{A + B})$	A B F / 0 0 1 / 0 1 0 / 1 0 0 / 1 1 0

Educational
http://www.inetdaemon.com/tutorials/basic_concepts/number_systems/binary/gates.shtml

When designing logical systems, engineers usually work in terms of subcircuits that implement logical gates. The table above shows the standard symbols that are used for them, as well as a truth table that defines their behaviors. This shows that the NAND gate will output a low voltage if and only if both of its inputs are a high voltage.

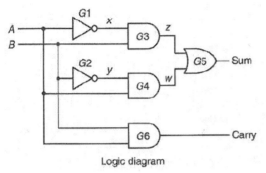

Logic diagram

Educational http://www2.cs.siu.edu/~cs320/half-adder.php

A Half Adder

These elements can then be combined into more complex modules. The circuit above implements a half adder that adds two binary digits and returns the sum plus carry. This can be summarized in the following table in which the inner numbers represent the carry and sum.

		A	
		0	1
B	0	0 0	0 1
	1	0 1	1 0

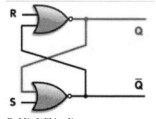

Public Wikipedia

Flip Flop implemented as two NOR gates

Another example is the flip-flop shown above. If R is 0 and S is set to 1 then the bottom NOR gate will return 0, so Q becomes 1. If S is then set to 0, Q remains 1. But if R is set to 1 while S is 0 then Q is reset to 0. The mutual feedback from the output of each NOR gate to the other gate's input means that the circuit remembers the last time either S or R was set to 1. It can thus store one bit of information.

Programmable Logic Arrays

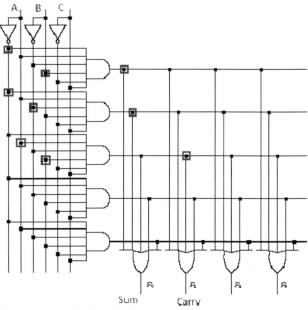

Programmable Logic Array
Education http://www2.elo.utfsm.cl/~lsb/elo211/aplicaciones/katz/chapter4/chapter04.doc1.htm

It is still possible to purchase small scale Integrated Circuits (ICs) that implement small numbers of basic gates like NAND and NOR gates, and then to wire them together to form arbitrary logic circuits. This is referred to as "random logic" and can be efficient in the number of gates used but very inefficient in the number of ICs that are required. A better approach is to use a single, larger IC that can be configured to provide whatever logical function is required.

The most common way to do that is with a Programmable Logic Array (PLA) as shown above. It consists of three inputs, A, B and C which can be connected to five AND gates, whose output can in turn be connected to up to four OR gates. The small black dots represent possible connection points that can be enabled or disabled by a mechanism that is not shown. So if just the connections with the large blue squares are enabled, then the Sum output will be 1 if and only if either of the top two AND gates are 1. And the top AND gate will be 1 if A is 0 and B is 1. Thus the array implements the same logic as the half adder above, with input C and two outputs simply not used.

It turns out that any arbitrary logic function can be implemented using a large enough PLA, and PLAs often contain thousands of gates. They have a very similar structure to perceptron networks discussed earlier. Like perceptrons, it is possible to feed some of the outputs of a PLA back into some of the inputs buffered by flip-flops that store state. If that is done, then they can, in principle, implement any general purpose computer program.

Von Neumann Architecture

CPU

Program Counter	127
Register	55

Memory

Address	Value	Description
123	111, 243	Load 243
124	136, 244	Add 244
125	112, 245	Store 245
126	...	
...	...	
243	22	
244	33	
245	55	

Owned

Modern computers use an architecture that was first proposed by John von Neumann in 1945, which is illustrated above. It has a memory that is organized as a series of words, each of which can contain a small number. Each word also has an address which can be used to access it. The memory provides random access, meaning that words can be efficiently accessed in a random order, so there is no need to access them sequentially.

(Very early computer memory was often implemented by sending waves down mercury delay lines or wires, and then reading them off the other end several hundred microseconds later. Another approach was to read instructions off rotating magnetic drums. In either case, memory had to be accessed sequentially and could not be addressed randomly.)

Some of the words in memory can be interpreted as instructions, others as data. So in the fragment, the word at address 124 contains an instruction to add the word at address 244, and the word at address 244 contains the data value 33.

The computer also has a Central Processing Unit (CPU) that can access the memory to perform calculations. It contains a Program Counter (PC) that contains the address of the next instruction to execute, and one or more Registers that contain values that are being worked on. At the beginning of this tiny program, the PC will have been set to address 123, which contains instruction 111, which tells the CPU to load the value stored in address 243 into the register. So the register becomes 22. Then the PC is incremented to become 124 which is the address of the ADD instruction. In this way the little program adds 22 to 33 and stores the result 55 back into address 245.

PLAs vs von Neumann

The advantage of this von Neumann architecture is that it is very regular and thus relatively easy to program. The same architecture can address a large variety of problems by simply loading each different program into memory as a series of numbers. The instructions are then executed sequentially, one at a time, with no potential timing issues.

However, their sequential nature is also the major disadvantage of this architecture. A computer consisting of billions of transistors can essentially only do one thing at a time. Consider a PLA that had a thousand AND gates and a thousand OR gates. It can combine its thousand inputs concurrently to produce its thousand outputs in just two steps. The time taken is independent of the number of gates that are involved because they all switch at the same time.

On the other hand a Von Neumann machine would, in principle, have to calculate each individual AND and OR operation one at a time. For a one thousand by one thousand array that means a million operations. And each operation involves retrieving instructions and data from memory and then storing the result back into memory which is hundreds of times slower than simply switching a gate in a PLA. (There is a technique for processing 64 (or so) gates in a single operation, but that still leaves tens of thousands of operations, each of which is hundreds of times slower.)

The net effect is that a PLA might switch in a few nanoseconds, whereas a von Neumann machine could take millions of nanoseconds to perform the same calculation.

This issue had been recognized from the beginning. One of the first programmable computers was the ENIAC built out of valves (vacuum tubes) in 1946. When constructed, it was hard wired to perform specific calculations, often related to the trajectories of artillery shells. Changing its program required rewiring the computer, which took days or weeks.

Then in 1948 ENIAC was modified to have what is essentially a von Neumann architecture. This made it much easier to program. However, it also made the computer six times slower than it had been previously because it could now only execute one instruction at a time. Even on that ancient computer that ran thousands of times slower than modern computers, the trade off was considered worthwhile. Being easy to program was and is generally far more important than being very efficient.

Today there are variations of the basic von Neumann architecture. Graphics Processing Units (GPUs) contain hundreds of von Neumann subsystems that can compute at the same time and so render complex scenes in real time. More radical designs are used for specialized Digital Signal Processors (DSPs), which can process radio wave signals in real time. Some of these even include large PLAs that can be used for specific types of processing. But the vast majority of modern computer programs run on a very conventional von Neumann machine performing essentially one instruction at a time.

Analog Computers

Digital computers only represent the numbers 0 and 1 on a given wire at a given time. So, if an application was required to process numbers between 1 and 100, then seven wires would be needed to represent the number in binary. There is a much more efficient representation of knowledge, namely to represent numbers as voltages that vary continuously between two values. So if the voltage varied between 0 and 6 volts, the number 70 might be represented as 4.2 volts.

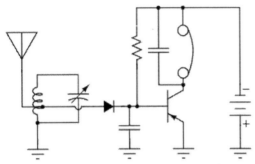

Education http://www.allaboutcircuits.com/vol_3/chpt_9/6.html
Simple one transistor radio

Consider the simple analog radio circuit above. It can be viewed as a moderately complex analog computer. The inductor-capacitor circuit at the left filters the radio waves by essentially performing a Fourier transform. The diode then takes the absolute value of the voltage, and the 500pf capacitor performs a leaky integration with a short time constant. The transistor multiplies the resulting current by a constant to produce a value that can be used to drive a pair of headphones.

All this is powered by just one transistor. Similar functionality would be provided in a modern radio using a special DSP computer, and would require millions of transistors to perform these calculations digitally.

Public US Government
Battleship broadside

Analog computers were heavily used from the early twentieth century until the 1960s. Their first major application was to control the guns on battleships. Ships had been getting larger and more accurate guns that could reach a target over 20 kilometers away, and shells could spend over a minute in the air. It became increasingly difficult to calculate in real time how to aim the guns to hit a moving target at long ranges, so an increasingly complex series of mechanical analog computers was developed starting with the Dumaresq in 1902. By the second world war, electronic analog predictive fire control computers had become an essential aid in aiming anti-aircraft guns.

Education via Nilsson Quest for AI
MINOS Analog Perceptron Computer, 1960

Some early work into building artificial intelligent systems was also performed on analog systems. The MINOS system shown above was built by Ted Brain at the Stanford Research Institute to implement what were essentially perceptrons. Rather than multiplying the weights digitally, the values were represented as voltages and multiplied electronically. Thus the many knobs and dials in the picture for adjusting voltages. A later version of the system was successfully used to recognize some handwritten characters utilizing special optical feature extraction, which sent 100 bits of data to each of 63 perceptrons that used a magnetic weighting system. However, advances in digital systems during the 1960s made analog systems obsolete.

Neurons

It will be seen that the biological neurons in our brains are essentially analog devices that integrate various stimulation voltages. They also operate with a high degree of concurrency with other neurons, and brains certainly do not perform just one operation at a time like a von Neumann architecture. This enables neurons that operate millions of times slower than transistors to produce effective results in real time.

It should be noted that this is not a failing of digital computer systems, but is simply an engineering design choice. The incredibly powerful technologies for building extremely large scale integrated circuits has made it cheaper to build large and fast general purpose von Neumann machines than to attempt to produce more efficient specialized designs.

That certainly does not mean that more efficient designs cannot be built if there are applications that warrant it. Adding PLAs to some DSPs has already been discussed. Programmable PLAs could easily be added to general purpose computers, but this has not been done simply because it has not been found to be useful for the types of programs that are run on general purpose computers. Likewise, associative content-addressable memories have been proposed as being useful, but few demanding applications have been found in practice, so they are not generally available on normal computers.

There have been a number of special purpose chips built over the years that are designed to simulate some aspect of artificial neurons. A recent one is called True North by IBM and can model "sixteen million programmable neurons and four billion programmable binary synapses", although it is unclear what that really means from the marketing hype used to describe it. They are most certainly not like real neurons.

But for most AI research ordinary CPUs or possibly GPUs are fast enough. The bottleneck is on determining how to write the intelligent programs rather than on finding computers that are fast enough to run them.

Brains

Gross anatomy

If there is one thing that we do understand about intelligence it is that human brains are able to exhibit it. It is therefore natural to study brains in order to gain insights into intelligent behaviour which may inspire or possibly lead directly to an artificial intelligence. Much of the technology presented so far has been inspired by psychological introspection, namely to consider how people consciously reason about various types of problems. But it is also useful to study brains at a physiological level to try to understand their underlying machinery.

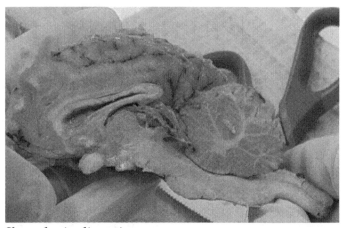

Sheep brain dissection.
Education http://brainu.org/sheep-brain-dissection

If one purchases lambs' brains from a butcher, one is given a rather slushy piece of meat that some would call a delicacy. If before putting it in the pot, one takes the trouble to carefully slice it in half, then the basic structure of the mammalian brain is revealed as shown above.

The spinal cord on the right connects the brain to the rest of the body. It also performs some initial signal processing, and is responsible for some fast, automatic reactions. It connects to the brainstem, which can also be clearly seen and is responsible for more automatic responses such as breathing and heartbeat. The distinctive ball above right of the brain stem is the *cerebellum* (little brain). It has a visibly different outer texture, and is responsible for learned, repetitive movements such as running.

The middle of the brain has hollow ventricles which are filled with cerebrospinal fluid. The brain floats in this fluid to protect it from shocks should the animal hit its head.

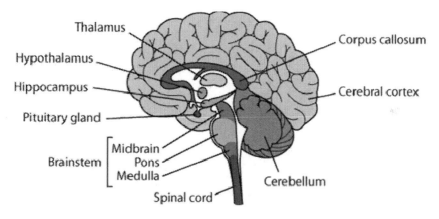

Human brain anatomy.
*Education http://askabiologist.asu.edu/whats-your-brain *

These basic features are common to all vertebrates, and a shark's brain has a similar structure. This suggests that the basic structure evolved several hundred million years ago. Mammals, and in particular humans, also have a very large *cerebrum* (shown blue-grey in the diagram). This area seems to be where most of our conscious thought takes place.

The image below shows a slice through a human cerebrum. The darker areas are known as gray matter and mainly consist of closely packed neurons while the lighter areas are known as white matter, and mainly consist of myelinated axons. Myelin sheaths increase the efficiency of neurons with longer axons, so white areas contain more longer axons. Short axons that connect nearby neurons do not need myelin sheaths which would otherwise take up unnecessary space. (The shading becomes more obvious in a brain preserved with formaldehyde, which is why it is difficult to see in the fresh lamb's brain above.)

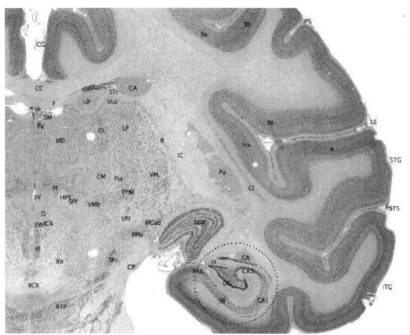

Slice through human cerebrum.
Public Wikipedia

The strongest feature in the image is the dark area that surrounds the cerebrum known as the cerebral cortex. The word "cortex" means rind, as in a bacon rind (or skin). The many folds, or *sulci*, that are visible increase the surface area of the cerebral cortex, with two thirds of the area of the cortex being inside these folds. As the dark colour suggests, the cortex has a high density of neurons.

So the gross structure of the cerebrum is a large, fairly thin layer of neurons that surrounds a white area that connects different parts of the brain together. Many of the white matter axons connect parts of the cerebral cortex to a region in the centre of the brain called the *thalamus,* which in turn is connected to the brainstem, spinal cord and all the body's senses except smell.

The cerebrum is separated into two distinct halves. Further, neurons can only cross directly from one half to the other via a thin band at the top called the *corpus callosum.* This lack of connectivity means that the two halves of the cerebrum function somewhat independently of each other. The corpus callosum has a particularly large number of myelinated axons, so the thin white band can be seen in the lamb's brain dissection.

Very rarely, the corpus callosum is destroyed through illness or surgery, in which case the two halves are only connected very indirectly via the thalamus. Careful experiments show that when people suffer from this condition, there are essentially two minds in the same body. If something is carefully said to only the left ear, say, the right hand cannot write it down although the left hand can. Of course, most of the time both ears hear the same thing, so the two minds do not realize that they share the same body. This suggests that our concept of consciousness may not be as sharp as it seems.

Neocortex

The cortical neurons are generally considered to be layered, and in the *neocortex* there are six layers. The neocortex is the bulk of the cortex, and it is the newest part of the brain in terms of evolutionary development.

An idealized version of this is shown below. The outermost layer I contains junctions between axons and dendrites, with few neuron *soma* (bodies with nuclei). The two most common types of neurons in the cortex are the larger pyramidal cells with longer axons, and smaller granule cells with short, local axons. They are distributed within the cortex as shown below.

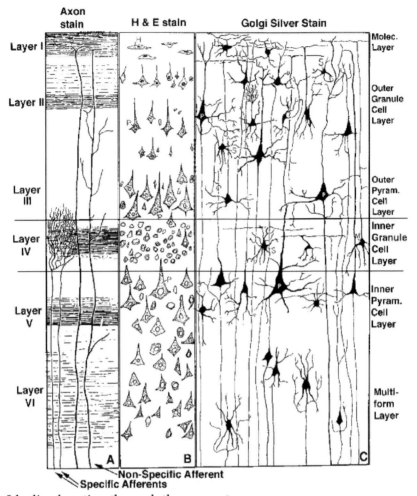

Idealized section through the neocortex.
Education http://vanat.cvm.umn.edu/NeuroLectPDFs/LectCerebralCortex.pdf

Broadly speaking, axons that connect different regions of the cortex (possibly in the other hemisphere) generally originate in layer III and terminate in layers I and II of the destination part of the cortex. Axons bringing sensory information from the thalamus often terminate in layer IV, while layer VI contains many cells whose axons lead into the thalamus. As one would expect, regions of the brain that are associated with sensory or motor function tend to have thicker layers IV and VI respectively.

There is also some speculation that the neo-cortex is arranged into vertical cylinders a few hundred microns in diameter called *cortical columns*, and that these columns function as a unit. This is based on the observation that stimulating an incoming axon usually only stimulates other neurons within a few hundred microns. But there is no visual indication of a columnar structure, and the effect may simply be because dendrites are relatively short and so only nearby neurons can be directly stimulated.

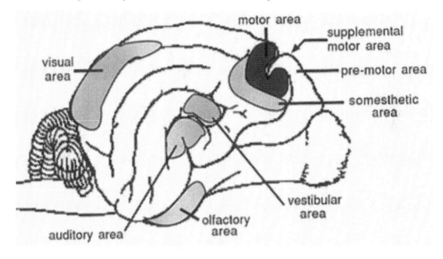

Functional Ares of the neocortex.
Education http://vanat.cvm.umn.edu/NeuroLectPDFs/LectCerebralCortex.pdf

Many attempts have been made to map regions of the cortex to specific functionality, and the diagram above shows some key areas. The mapping has been traditionally performed by measuring or stimulating regions with electrodes or noticing what happens when parts of the brain are damaged.

The circled area towards the bottom of the slice through the cerebrum is the hippocampus, which is an older part of the brain that appears to be closely associated with forming memories and navigation. Indeed, different neurons in the mouse hippocampus have been found to become excited as the mouse navigates through its environment.

The image below shows how the body appears to be mapped to the brain within a specific slice through the neocortex. Different parts of the body have rather specific mappings, but it is grossly distorted. As one might expect, there is far more of the brain associated with the fingers and tongue than with hips and elbows.

This is all then mapped to the cerebellum which refines and remembers complex movements.

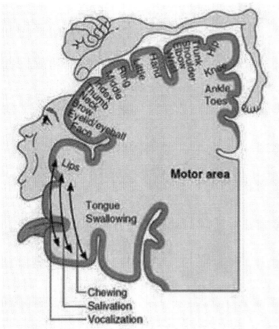

Mapping of body parts to the brain.
Education mybrainnotes.com

Brain activity

More recently it has been possible to use MRI (magnetic resonance imaging) scans of healthy people to show where oxygen is being used, and thus which areas of the brain are active. A recent study by Huth, Nishimoto, Vu and Gallant in 2012 showed subjects videos of various objects, and then used MRI scans to measure the resulting brain activity with voxels of a few cubic millimetres. The map below shows a flattened out image of the cortex within which the various regions have been coloured differently for different types of images.

This results in complex patterns of overlapping colours that do, in fact, roughly correspond to previously known brain areas. Rather surprisingly, there was also considerable consistency between different people that were analyzed. This is not always the case. For example, the detailed folding of the cortex varies between people. Functional areas can also change dramatically in order to recover from injury to the brain. And about 30% of left-handed people have their speech processing swapped to their right hemisphere, with their spatial awareness swapped to the left.

Map of MRI activation, with different colours for object recognition. Yellow was used for animals, green for people, pink for vehicles, and blue for buildings.
Education http://gallantlab.org/semanticmovies/

Other teams have used MRI scans to identify the gross emotional states of method actors. Happiness, sadness, anger and lust could be identified, but not more subtle emotions such as envy.

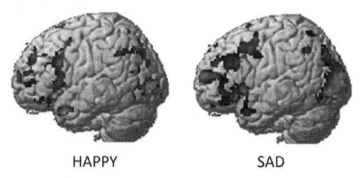

HAPPY   SAD

MRI scans of happy and sad brains.
Education http://www.kurzweilai.net/images/Happy-Sad-512x240.jpeg

Ever more detailed maps are being made of brain anatomy. The international collaboration known as Big Brain has recently released highly detailed three-dimensional images of a brain with

20 micron resolution. That is 50 times better than earlier whole brain maps with typically 1mm resolution. It required 7,400 brain slices, each thinner than a human hair, and the image generated 1,000 gigabytes of data. The individual slices have been carefully aligned into a single model, so that one can navigate through the model using a computer to follow the shape of fine features in three dimensions.

However, even that Herculean effort cannot come close to providing a *connectome* (wiring diagram) of the brain. Indeed, it would only be fine enough to resolve the larger neurons. To scan individual axons would require a scan to 0.4 microns, which is the very limit of optical microscopy. Such a scan would also generate some 100 million gigabytes of data. However, as will be shown for the humble nematode, even a complete connectome does not define the functionality of the brain which requires details about each synapse, and more importantly, which receptors are present within them.

Brain function and size

Perhaps the most amazing brains are not the large brains but the small ones. Honeybees, for example, can categorize similar objects like dogs or human faces, understand "same" and "different", and differentiate between shapes that are symmetrical and asymmetrical. They can build a complex honeycomb, memorize at least six locations and three paths leading to each, and then communicate this to other bees using an elaborate dance language. A total of 59 distinct behaviours have been counted, as opposed to 129 different behaviours that have been counted for dolphins. Other insects like ants and wasps are similarly impressive, and there is even a wasp that can count out exactly eight caterpillars that she provides for each of her grubs.

It is easy to dismiss these behaviours as just instinct, but there is nothing "just" about these instincts. Each of these steps requires sophisticated analysis of multiple, complex sources of information, not to mention a significant amount of longer term memory. Yet the bee's nervous system occupies just 1 cubic millimetre of space and weighs less than a millionth of the weight of a human brain. It contains about a million neurons. (Insects do not have a single brain as such, instead their nervous system is distributed throughout their small bodies.)

Indeed, the largest determination of brain size is the size of the animal rather than its intelligence. Both whales and elephants have much larger brains than humans. Men have slightly larger brains than women. And birds such as crows and parrots exhibit behaviours that seem every bit as sophisticated as mammals that have brains that are a hundred times larger than the bird's brain. Neurons have much the same size and functional mechanisms throughout the animal kingdom, so small animals certainly do not have significantly smaller neurons which could be packed more tightly than large animals (their axons will be shorter and thus need not be myelinated). Small animals just get by with better organizations of fewer neurons.

This is hardly surprising. For a large animal, carrying around and fueling a few extra grams of brain costs very little, so if those extra grams can produce even a tiny increase in intelligence then it is advantageous to have them. For a small animal, having to carry around extra neurons can be a major drain on their ability to survive. This provides strong selective pressure for smaller animals to have efficient brains. It is also generally easier to make smaller things efficient than larger things.

That said, intelligence is a powerful tool in the battle to exist, so small animals often make a large investment in neural matter. For example, the nematode *C. elegans* has 302 neurons in a body that only contains 959 cells in total, meaning that over a third of their body cells are neurons. If people were built to the same proportions, our brains would weigh over 20kg. Spiders need complex nervous systems to be able to weave webs and it has been found that some tiny spiders have 80% of their body cavity filled with neurons. Insect visual systems can often account for as much as 30% of their mass.

The point of this analysis is that, as we are large animals, our brains do not need to be particularly efficient and there is likely to be considerable redundancy. The seeming partial duplication between the motor cortex and the cerebellum might be an example of this.

One striking example was the case of Phineas Gage, who in 1848 had a massive crow bar shot in under his jaw, through his brain and out the top of his head due to a construction accident. It completely destroyed his left frontal lobe and his left eye, and brain matter was seen to be oozing out of the huge wound. Mr Gage was evidently made of tough stuff, because he not only survived the massive injury, but led a fairly normal life after it without the benefit of almost half of his brain. So there must be significant redundancy within the frontal lobes at least.

Phineas Gage
Public Wikipedia

Brain simulation

If there is one thing that has been learned after sixty years of research, it is that building an artificial intelligence is difficult. It is most certainly not just a matter gluing together some first order logic with some artifical neural networks, mixed in with a splash of semantic networks and probabilistic reasoning, as was initially thought. So some researchers have looked for alternative approaches to the problem that do not require engineering a solution from scratch. One of these approaches has already been discussed, namely evolutionary programming. Another potential short cut is whole or partial brain simulation.

If the brain is composed of neurons in the same ways that a computer is composed of transistors, and if one could analyze the implicit circuit diagram for our brains, then one could implement our brains directly on a computer by simulating neurons. It might require a large computer with specialized hardware to enable it to run in real time, but building fast computers is mainly just a matter of money.

There is now substantial funding for this type of research. Since 2008, the IBM Blue Brain project has received a $4.9 million grant from the Pentagon for research into creating intelligent computers. The Human Brain Project is a European effort that has €1,190 million in funding over ten years and involves 86 different institutions. In 2013 the Obama administration announced the BRAIN Initiative (Brain Research through Advancing Innovative Neurotechnologies, also commonly referred to as the Brain Activity Map Project), which has the goal of mapping the activity of every neuron in the human brain, at a cost of over $300 million per year for ten years.

The magnitude of these projects is unprecedented, and they are likely to provide important insights into the working of our minds. However, the problems are far from trivial, and there is no guarantee that brain simulation will produce substantial results in the foreseeable future.

Worms

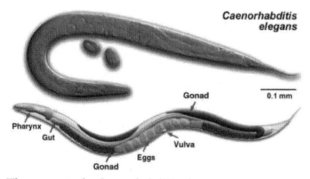

The nematode *Caenorhabditis elegans*.
Education http://jbashir.wordpress.com/2011/07/05/see-elegance/

Amongst the more interesting projects are attempts to simulate the nervous system of the humble nematode *Caenorhabditis elegans*. Known affectionately as *worms* to researchers, these transparent nematodes are about 1mm long and live in environments that have plenty of bacteria for them to eat, such as compost bins. In 1974, Sydney Brenner started examining them extensively because of their simplicity, transparency, and ease of breeding, and because one does not need to obtain an ethical clearance in order to poke needles into nematodes. They are now a model organism that has been studied in great detail. The large online WormBase database collates all published work on the nematodes.

The worms have unusual sexual habits, with about 5% being male and 95% being hermaphrodites. The hermaphrodite adult worms have exactly 959 cells, while the males have 1,031 cells. The precise developmental source of each single somatic cell has been mapped, including 131 cells that are eliminated. Its genome has 97 million base pairs, which is about 3% of the size of the human genome, and there are simple techniques for interfering with gene expression by soaking the poor worm in a soup of RNA.

Of the 959 or 1,031 worm cells, exactly 302 are neurons, which can be divided into the pharyngeal (throat) nervous system containing 20 neurons and the somatic (bodily) nervous system containing 282 neurons. In 1986 J.G. White used an electron microscope to map the precise location of each and every neuron. They found that they have a relatively simple structure, but are highly interconnected. 6,393 chemical synapses, 1,410 neuromuscular junctions and 890 gap junctions were counted. So while they are much, much simpler than a human nervous system, they are still quite complex.

One might think that having the complete connectome would then make it relatively simple to simulate a tiny worm's behaviour on a computer. However, the behaviour of individual neurons and their synapses is complex and not well understood, even though they appear to be much simpler than vertebrate neurons. The precise reaction of muscles to neural stimulation is also not well understood, nor is the reaction of sensory neurons to changes in their environment. In order to meaningfully simulate a worm's brain one needs to simulate the whole worm in its environment, and that is a very complex system indeed.

Projects that are attempting to do this include Openworm, D. Dalrymple at Harvard (funded by Google's Larry Page), and a project at Hiroshima University. None have succeeded as of July

2013. There is very little government funding available for this work. Simulating a tiny worm does not sound as exciting as simulating a human brain, even if it is much more likely to eventually produce meaningful results.

Given the complexity of simulating the 302 neurons of *C. elegans*, attempting to simulate the 86,000,000,000 neurons of the human brain would appear to be rather premature. No doubt the several projects that claim to be attempting to do so are simulating something, and some of them are consuming vast quantities of computer time to do so. What exactly it is that they are simulating, and whether it has any relevance to real brains is unclear, to say the least.

Incidentally, another model animal is the small but unrelated *Planariam* worm. It is famous for being able to be cut in half and then regrow its head and tail, or even left and right sides. *Planariams* can be taught to avoid electric shocks associated with bright lights. Surprisingly, when cut in half, both the head and (to a lesser extent) the tail remember their lessons. (There is even discredited research that feeding trained but chopped up *planaria* to other *planaria* transfers some of that learnt behaviour.)

Computational Neuroscience

Neurons

To understand how people actually think the thoughts they do requires an understanding of the neurons and neural networks that perform the information processing. The next subsections will examine the physiology of the neurons involved, followed by computational models about how they might produce intelligent behaviour.

This chapter is necessarily rather technical. One can certainly understand how a digital computer works without understanding how transistors work, but neurons are more complex than transistors, and so understanding a brain really does require some understanding of neurons. That said, the following biochemical background can be skipped if desired.

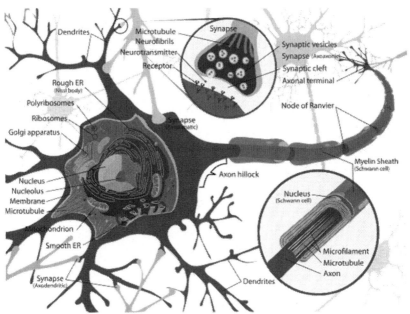

A typical neuron.
Public Wikipedia

As previously discussed, a neuron basically accepts electrochemical inputs from its thousands of dendrites, and if the stimulation is sufficient it then fires a signal down its often much longer axon which may in turn activate other neurons. The physiological process that makes this happen involves electric and osmotic potentials across the neuron's cell membrane.

Specifically, the inside of the cell normally has a negative charge of about -70 millivolts, together with an abundance of potassium (K+) ions and a lack of sodium (Na+) ions. This provides both electrical and osmotic pressures for Na+ ions to enter the cell, and a strong osmotic (but not electric) pressure for K+ ions to leave the cell. (Osmotic pressure refers to the tendency of ions to dissolve evenly throughout a solution rather than being concentrated in one place.)

This pressure is maintained by sodium/potassium ion pumps embedded in the cell membrane of each neuron. Each cycle of the pump pushes three Na+ ions out of the cell, and also pulls two K+ ions into the cell. Moreover, some of the K+ ions leak out through the cell membrane due to osmotic pressure, so this results in a negative charge building up inside the cell. The pump itself is made from a protein referred to as Na$^+$/K$^+$-ATPase, which is powered by the same ATP (Adenosine-5'-triphosphate) that powers most cellular processes by losing one of its phosphate groups.

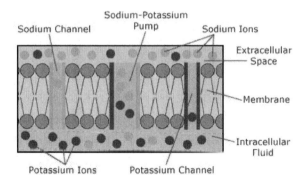

Neuron cell membrane
Education
http://www.columbia.edu/cu/psychology/courses/1010/mangels/neuro/neurosignaling/neurosign aling.html

The cellular membrane also contains two types of channels through which Na+ and K+ ions may pass. They are normally both closed. If the nerve is stimulated by raising its internal voltage, then the sodium channel opens and allows the Na+ ions into the cell membrane. This produces a positive voltage within the cell which then closes the Na+ channels, and opens the K+ channels. The K+ ions are under substantial osmotic pressure within the cell, so they move out against the voltage gradient, making the cell negative again. That in turn closes the K+ channel, and the Na+/K+ pumps restore the balance of Na+ and K+ ions.

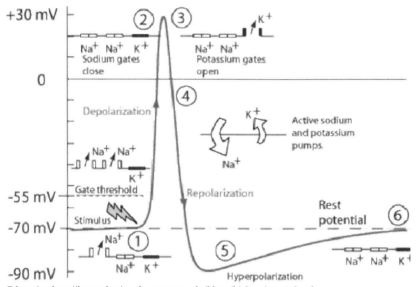

Education http://hyperphysics.phy-astr.gsu.edu/hbase/biology/actpot.html

This can be seen by the plot of cell voltage against time above. The cell starts with a negative potential of -70mV. Minor stimuli are ignored, but if the voltage reaches a threshold potential of about -55mv, then the Na+ channel opens, which causes Na+ ions to rush in and so raise the voltage to about +20mv. This positive voltage causes the K+ channel to open, and it stays open until the voltage drops below its initial negative voltage. The Na+/K+ pump then does its work of restoring the ion balance. The process utilizes the stored potential energy in the concentrations of Na+ and K+ ions to raise and lower the voltage in as little as 0.5 milliseconds, although it takes the pump about 5 milliseconds to complete a full cycle.

A neuron's axon is a very thin tube, typically a few microns in diameter, that has numerous pumps and channels distributed along its cell membrane. When one set of channels reaches its action potential and activates, it makes that part of the axon positive. Na+ ions within the axon are then attracted to nearby negative areas of the axon, which moves the positive charge down the neuron. This charge then activates the next set of channels in a positive feedback cycle which produces a wave of charge moving down the axon as shown below.

The chart above shows that the opening of the K+ channel actually overshoots the normal voltage to -90mV. This *hyperpolarization* is important because it makes the channels much less likely to open in response to further stimulation which, in turn, will prevent signals from moving in both directions up and down the axon, causing continuous stimulation.

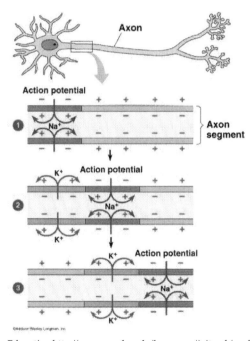

Education http://www.anselm.edu/homepage/jpitocch/genbio/actpot.JPG

The conduction of ions moving through the axon occurs at about 100 meters per second, which is much slower than electrons moving through wire at 300,000,000 meters per second. It is still much faster than the Na+/K+ action cycle that can take a millisecond to move just a few microns. Ionic conduction also takes much less energy from the cell. This is important because some human axons are over a meter long.

To improve ionic conduction, longer axons are coated in a myelin sheath provided by the surrounding Schwann cells. The sheath is a fatty layer that prevents ions from leaking out of the axon, and improves its electrolytic properties. This means that the activation from one set of channels can effectively propagate down the very thin axon a couple of millimetres or so. At that point there is a gap in the sheath called a *node of Ranvier*, which enables the channels and ion pumps to strengthen the signal that is then propagated to the next node. The process is known as *salutatory conduction*.

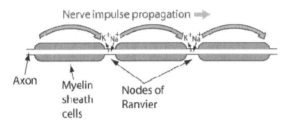

Education http://hyperphysics.phy-astr.gsu.edu/hbase/biology/actpot.html

The basic biochemistry of the ion pump and channels occurs in most animals and so is probably an early development. However, only a few invertebrates have the myelin sheath that improves signal speed and efficiency in longer axons. A different method of improving their speed, if not the efficiency, is to simply make the axon thicker.

The common squid has a giant axon that connects its brain to its mantle, which enables the squid to contract the mantle very quickly if required. This giant axon is up to 1000 microns thick, or 100 times thicker than most mammalian neurons. Being cold blooded, it is also very tough and so can be abused experimentally and still function for several minutes. This was discovered in the 1930s, and then used by Hodgkin and Huxley in the 1950s to understand these biochemical interactions. Incidentally, the giant squids have rather modest giant axons.

Neuron synapse

The junction between two neurons is called a *synapse*, and these are usually from the axon of one *presynaptic* neuron to the dendrites of another *postsynaptic* neuron. Mammalian neurons have thousands of synapses.

The most common synapse is a chemical synapse which is illustrated below. The basic mechanism is that an action potential at the axon terminal causes a chemical called a neurotransmitter to be released, and this chemical then has an effect on receivers in the dendrite. The main effect is to raise or lower the voltage within the postsynaptic neuron. If, through the action of multiple synapses, the postsynaptic neuron reaches its action potential, then it will send a signal down its axon to other neurons.

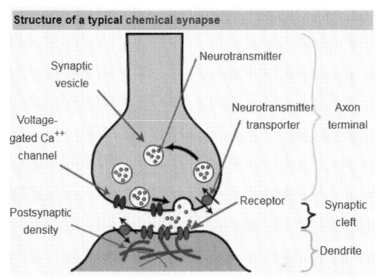

Synapses with presynaptic neuron above the postsynaptic neuron.
Public Wikipedia

When an action potential reaches the axon terminal, it opens a channel that allows Ca++ (calcium) ions to be suddenly admitted into the cell in much the same way that Na+ channels are opened in the body of an axon. There is also a very similar pump that pumps the Ca++ ions out again later. The neurotransmitters are stored in small vesicles (bubbles) within the axon, and some of those are *docked* by special *snare* proteins near the wall of axon. The Ca++ ions cause these snare proteins to rupture the wall of the vesicle and release the neurotransmitter into the synaptic *cleft,* which is a small 30 to 40 nanometre gap between the axon and the dendrite.

The neurotransmitter then quickly diffuses across the tiny cleft and bonds to receptors in the dendrite that respond in ways that vary according to the particular neurotransmitter that was released. The most common neurotransmitter is called glutamate, and it has the effect of opening a Na+ channel in the dendrite, which has the effect of increasing the voltage of the dendrite and thus raising the voltage in the receiving neuron. The neurotransmitter then decouples from its receptor, and is usually reabsorbed back into the axon using a reuptake pump.

Another common neurotransmitter named GABA binds to a receptor that opens channels for Chlorine (Cl-) and K+. This *inhibits* the neuron by lowering its voltage and so make it more difficult for other synapses to stimulate the neuron.

Synapses are where the neuron performs much of its computation. They involve the complex interactions of several biochemical processes that are not fully understood. There are about two dozen different neurotransmitters, and even more receptors, that perform different actions at different times depending upon the neurotransmitter that is released. Synapses have different and changing quantities of many different types of receptors. Each neuron may have thousands of dendrite synapses which results in an even more complex system.

The effect upon the postsynaptic neuron is determined not by the presynaptic neuron nor directly by the neurotransmitter, but rather the type of receptor that is activated. Receptors can be classified broadly as *excitatory* (causing an increase in the voltage), *inhibitory* (causing a decrease in the voltage), or *modulatory* (causing long-lasting effects not directly related to the voltage).

For example, glutamate acts on two receptors. The first, named AMPA, requires only a weak stimulation to open a channel that allows both K+ and Na+ to cross, and is quick to turn both on and off. The net effect is to *excite* the dendrite neuron, i.e. to raise its voltage.

Glutamate also binds to another receptor known as NMDA which opens a non-selective channel that allows K+, Na+ and Ca++ ions to cross, but only if there is a strong stimulation of glutamate. NMDA is quick to turn on but slow to turn off. However, if the dendrite is at the resting potential (-70mV), then the strongly charged Mg++ (Magnesium) ions are electrically attracted to the NMDA channel and block it. If the dendrite voltage is slightly raised (possibly by neighbouring AMPA channels) then the Mg++ ions dissipate, and large quantities of all ions pass through. This produces a positive feedback effect.

The Ca++ ions are an important secondary messenger, and amongst other things they activate a protein called CAM kinase which makes the AMPA channel more conductive to Na++ ions. CAM kinase also moves more AMPA receptors from the dendrite's cytoplasm into its membrane, and thus *enhances* the synapse, making it becomes more sensitive to future stimulations. Ca++ ions can even affect the presynaptic axon by causing the dendrite to release nitric oxide (NO), which in turn causes the axon to release more glutamate.

Other neurotransmitters have complex effects, such as changing the sensitivity of the receptors or causing the production of special chemical messenger molecules within the postsynaptic neuron that can have a wide number of effects. This is all within each of the many receptors in each of the thousands of synapses in each of the billions of neurons that comprise a living brain.

Timing within the neuron is also important. It takes some time for the effect of an open channel in a distant dendrite to reach the axon hillock (where the axon joins the nucleus). The effect of several synapses needs to arrive at the hillock at the same time in order for it to reach its action potential and thus fire the neuron.

Some neurons also contain *electrical* synapses, which are simply channels that directly couple one neuron to another. They are usually bidirectional and do not have any action potential characteristics, nor any ability to amplify a signal. Electrical synapses are much faster than chemical synapses, particularly in cold-blooded animals where they appear to be more common.

There are several other mechanisms for inter-neuron communication. For example, *neurogliaform neurons* inhibit other nearby neurons by simply releasing the neurotransmitter GABA into the extracellular space, and most neurogliaforms do not have any classical synapses at all.

Integrate and fire (IF) neurons

The simplest computational model of a neuron ignores all of this complexity and treats a neuron as if it was broadly similar to the artificial neuron discussed in earlier chapters. This Integrate-and-Fire (IF) model calculates a weighted sum of each neuron's many dendrite synapses (some of which may be negative), and if this is greater than a specific value then the neuron is activated.

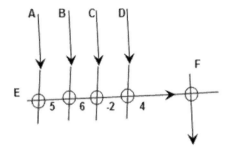

Owned

As a simplistic example, consider the diagram above, in which neurons are represented as arrows from dendrites to axon, and synapses as circles with the weights shown. If neurons A, B and C fired, then E would achieve a potential of 5 + 6 - 2 = 9 units. If E's threshold was 10, it would not fire unless neuron D also fired. Note that the synapse between C and E is suppressive, as modelled by the negative weight. If E fires, it might in turn stimulate other neurons, such as F in the diagram.

Unlike perceptrons, the timing of the stimulations is critical. An artificial neural network calculates all of its outputs from its inputs at (logically) the same time. So to recognize a digit in the earlier character recognition example, just two sets of multiplications needed to be performed by the three-layer network, one after the other. However, there is no central clock in a biological system, which makes it a much more dynamically complex system.

Specifically, it takes time for a channel to open and close, and neurons have a significant capacitance, which means it takes time for their voltage to change. As previously discussed, common synaptic excitement takes 0.5ms to start, peaks after 2ms, and has a half-life of 4ms thereafter. So if another axon stimulates an axon within that time period, the stimulations will be added together and may reach the action potential, whereas if they miss by more than 4ms, then they will not combine significantly.

This process is often described as a *leaky integrator*, in the sense that it adds up (*integrates*) the stimulations but also leaks the resulting voltage so that multiple stimulations need to occur at roughly the same time in order to fire the neuron.

Time(ms)	A	B	C	D	E	E'
0	5				5.0	3.6
2					3.6	2.6
4		6			8.6	6.1
6				4	10.1	7.2

So the example would require a more complex calculation as shown above. If neuron A fired at time t=0ms, then it would raise neuron E's potential by 5 units, 5 being the synaptic strength as shown in the preceding diagram. But if the potentials have a half life of 4ms, then by t=2 that potential would have reduced to 3.6 as shown in the E' column. Without further stimulation, that would reduce to 2.6 at t=4, but if B fired at t=4 then the potential would be 2.6 + 6 = 8.6. Neuron E would not fire, despite being stimulated by both A and B. A further stimulation by D at t=6 would just push E over its 10.0 threshold and cause it to fire under this IF model.

Simulating IF neurons on a computer requires repeatedly calculating the potential of each neuron at small intervals of time. The potential needs to be increased slightly for each positive stimulus and then decreased slightly to model the leak. Stimulations need to be computed for each of possibly thousands of synapses, each with different characteristics and timing variations. Eventually, if a neuron reaches its action potential, it will fire and thus stimulate thousands of other neurons that are connected to its axon at times that depend upon how far they are away from the cell nucleus, amongst other things.

This process is extremely computationally expensive, and it is not useful for building practical AI systems. But it is very useful for comparing theoretical models with observed behaviours of real neurons.

It should also be emphasized that IF neurons are not real neurons. They are just mathematical abstractions that ignore most of the complexities of real neurons. Different simulations may use different abstractions that incorporate more or less of a real neuron's behaviour such as synaptic plasticity, which will be discussed next.

Hebbian learning

Clearly any intelligent system needs to learn. A mechanism was hypothesized by Donald Hebb back in 1949 in which neurons that often fire at about the same time will become more sensitive to each other's stimulation. This is often summarized as *neurons that fire together wire together*. It produces a broadly similar effect to the back propagation learning algorithms of artificial networks.

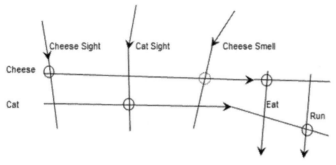

Owned

To see how this mechanism could induce learning, consider the grossly simplified network above, in which neurons are represented by arrows from dendrites to axons. The diagram naively supposes that a mouse has single neurons that corresponds directly to the concepts *of Cheese, Cat, Eat, Run,* etc. The circles represent strong synaptic links, so that the Cheese Sight neuron would activate the Cheese neuron, which in turn activates the Eat neuron.

Now suppose that most of the time the Cheese neuron fires, the Cheese Smell neuron also happens to fire. Hebbian learning would have the dotted synapses between Cheese Smell and Cheese be strengthened slightly each time they happened to fire together. Eventually the synapse would become strong enough that just smelling cheese would activate the Cheese neuron. The mouse would learn to eat the cheese even if it could not be seen. (Following artificial neurons, the strength of each synapse is often referred to as its *weight*.)

Of course there also needs to be a compensatory mechanism to weaken synapses that do not fire together very often. Otherwise, over time all the neurons would become fused together in a large, amorphous blob.

Plasticity

Real neurons do in fact exhibit *plasticity*, meaning that they become more or less sensitive to stimulation over time, depending upon how they have been stimulated in the past. The most basic mechanism is *synaptic fatigue*, which is a short-term effect in which repeated short trains of action potentials cause an exponential delay in synaptic response. This is mainly because the axon presynaptic terminal simply runs out of neurotransmitter molecules.

But there can also be longer-term memory effects that last for minutes or days. One mechanism, discussed earlier, is the NMDA channel enhances synaptic efficiency by allowing Ca++ ions to stimulate CAM kinase, which can, in turn, create more AMPA channels. This makes the neuron more sensitive to future stimulation from that synapse. There are other mechanisms that provide both positive and negative plasticity, some of which are not well understood. But whatever the mechanism, longer term plasticity effects can be used to store longer term memories.

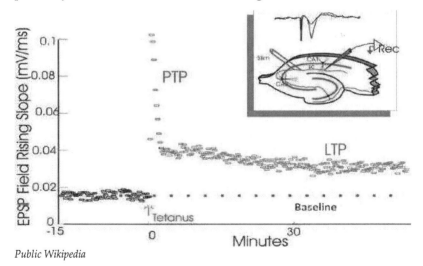

Public Wikipedia

The chart above shows this effect in real neurons from a slice of a rat's hippocampus. The black squares show the neurons' initial sensitivity to stimulation of its dendrites. The region was then given *tetanic* stimulation, a repeated 100Hz signal for 1 second. The green squares show the sensitivity just after stimulation (PTP), which has increased dramatically. The blue squares then show the slowly weakening long term effect (LTP).

Other experiments in hippocampal cultures showed that the timing of stimulations is critical, and they need to happen within about 40 milliseconds in order to strengthen the synaptic response between two neurons. It is now also possible to use phosphorization by Ca++ ions to monitor the effect on individual synapses.

It has also been shown that all synaptic weights tend to reduce for neurons that fire repeatedly. This would have the effect of weakening synapses that do not fire together, and thus prevent a network from becoming fused together.

Neuron chains

Neurons are combined into networks in order to provide real functionality. The most basic structure could be a parallel chain of neurons that each carry essentially the same information. This is necessary because neurons are noisy and sometimes fire without being stimulated at all. It usually takes several different neurons to fire in order to activate a postsynaptic neuron, so a single isolated random firing of a neuron in a chain is unlikely to have any detrimental effect.

Another reason for redundancy is that, as living things, neurons sometimes die. It would be most unfortunate if a mouse forgot all about cats upon the death of a single neuron.

Neurons can only fire once every few milliseconds. Yet animals can react to complex stimulations within a few hundred milliseconds. Such reactions must involve dozens if not hundreds of neurons in sequence. So there is simply not enough time for more than a very few firings of any particular neuron to elicit a response. A neuron's firing is also an all-or-nothing event, there are no weaker or stronger firings to reflect different levels of stimulation.

Thus each neuron essentially provides just one bit of information about the current state of the world. A weak external stimulus is only likely to fire a few neurons in a linear chain, whereas if a stimulus is strong, then more neurons are likely to be stimulated sufficiently to fire. If a stimulus persists, the neurons may continue to fire repeatedly. It would therefore take several neurons to provide an analogous computational ability as a single artificial neuron.

Usually the precise timing of neurons is not critical, and there is normally no information encoded in the exact sequence of activations. But as with most things to do with real neurons, there are many exceptions. For example, it turns out that the auditory nerve responds to sounds based on the phase difference between continuously firing neurons. The time that it takes for a neuron to respond to stimulations has also been seen to exhibit plasticity. Brains are complex, dynamic systems which involve many interacting mechanisms.

Self organizing maps (SOMs)

A good example of a more sophisticated application of Hebbian learning is the Self Organizing Map (SOM). These are commonly used with artificial networks, and there is evidence that they also occur with biological neurons. A SOM can take a large number of complex inputs and classify them in a simplified representation that clusters related inputs together, thus abstracting meaning from the input data. This process can happen without supervision, i.e. without any preconceived notion of what the final map should look like.

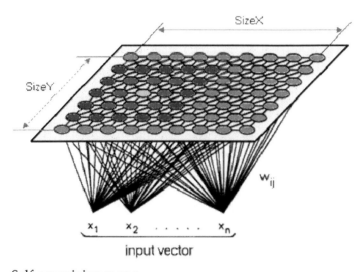

Self organizing maps
Corporate   *http://www.lohninger.com/helpcsuite/kohonen_network_-*
_background_information.htm

The SOM above categorizes inputs into a two dimensional XY plane of neurons. Each input is connected to each element in the XY plane with strengths (weights) that are initially random but will be learnt by the map as it experiences different inputs.

Each neuron in the XY plane is also connected to other neurons in the plane, but with special, fixed weights. These XY weights cause neurons that are close to each other to stimulate each other, but neurons that are far apart to suppress each other.

For each set of inputs that the SOM experiences, some random set of neurons in the XY plane will fire due to the initial random weights. The connections within the XY plane will cause neurons that are near other firing neurons to be more likely to fire than distant neurons, so the more neurons that fire in a particular part of the plane, the more other neurons are likely to fire in that part of the plane. Neurons that fire in one part of the plane also suppress neurons from firing in other parts. In combination, this produces a winner-takes-all effect.

Neurons that fire together wire together, so over time the strengths Wij between the inputs and the XY plane will strengthen when they connect to parts of the XY plane that fire for specific stimulations. This has the effect of learning to recognize complex patterns of inputs as distinct areas in the XY plane. More importantly, similar stimulations end up being represented in nearby parts of the plane due to the XY weights.

There is some evidence that this mechanism occurs in real brains. For example, different areas of a mouse's hippocampus seem to be activated when a mouse is in different parts of a maze. There does not appear to be any correlation between the physical locations of the stimulated areas in the hippocampus and the locations in the maze. However, areas in the hippocampus that appear to be strongly connected electrically (corresponding to the XY plane) do appear to correspond to nearby areas of the maze.

Over time these areas in the brain that correspond to different areas of the maze tend to slowly drift to different locations. This is presumably due to neural noise and the slow optimization of the network. It would appear that each neuron is randomly connected to a very large number of other neurons, and that this wiring is relatively permanent. It is the ever changing strength of individual synapses that defines each neuron's behaviour.

Recurrent networks and learning

Neural networks such as the Mouse/Cheese network are known as *feed forward* networks because they have a single direction of flow from inputs to outputs. Neurons can also form cycles which are known as *recurrent* networks.

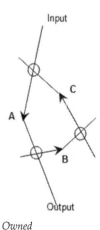

Owned

Consider the three neurons above. If an Input causes neuron A to fire it will stimulate neuron B. If B then fires it will stimulate neuron C. C in turn will restimulate neuron A. If A is restimulated after it has recovered from the initial stimulation then this will cause A to fire a second time for the same one initial stimulation. In this way a single activation of neuron A could create a continuous stream of activations, which is sometimes referred to as *reverberating*. (This is similar to the flip-flop created by two digital NOR gates.)

Eventually this cycle might be broken, possibly by synaptic fatigue, in which the synapses simply run out of neurotransmitter and so stop stimulating. More complex mechanisms involve inhibitory synapses which prevent a neuron from firing.

Whatever the mechanism, the recurrent network can remember the initial stimulation for a short period of time as a cycle of continuously firing neurons. This corresponds to short term *working memory* that is essential for cognition.

The Self Organizing Map discussed previously is a recurrent network in the XY plane. Neurons that are near each other reinforce each other's activity and inhibit neurons that are further away. This keeps neurons active for an extended period of time, and that continued activation encourages Hebbian learning as the neurons that fire together wire together.

Recurrent networks are often complex and involve numerous semi-independent cycles which can reinforce or suppress each other. Some networks are stable, leading a fixed point fairly quickly, while others can be quite unstable and chaotic.

One important type of recurrent network is a Hopfield network in which every node feeds back to every other node. This can be used as content addressable memory, meaning that if just some of a node's values are specified in a query, then the values of other nodes can be retrieved.

Memory

Two distinct mechanisms have been discussed for memory. The first is the slowly changing synaptic weights produced by Hebbian learning. The second is the short-term creation of activations in recurrent networks.

This corresponds roughly to our psychological experience of memory. People can only consciously remember about seven different symbols at a time when considering a problem, and they are quickly forgotten if one is distracted. On the other hand, people have millions of longer-term memories.

It appears that many longer-term memories are formed in a small part of the cerebral cortex known as the hippocampus. Evidence of this is the famous case of patient H.M., who had his hippocampus largely removed to prevent severe epilepsy. H.M. could function fairly normally and had long-term memories, but he could not form any new long-term memories.

Anatomical studies suggest that the hippocampus does in fact contain large recurrent networks that can hold a thought for a short period of time, during which time they repeatedly stimulate other parts of the brain which then undergo Hebbian learning. Without a hippocampus to stimulate other learning centres, H.M. could not form new memories, although he could utilize existing ones.

One issue with this model is that there needs to be a mechanism to switch between learning and retrieval modes, to stop the positive feedback loop and allow the network to respond to new stimuli. One possible mechanism is that certain neurons in the hippocampus seem to have very strong synapses which might override recurrent neuron activations. Another mechanism is that chemical agents such as *acetylcholine* (ACh) could moderate the process and so re-enable a learning phase. In any case, ACh does affect the plasticity of synapses. Like most neural processes, several different and competing mechanisms are probably involved.

Modularity

Suppose that a neural network needed to recognize the shapes square, circle and triangle, which might be coloured red, green or blue. That would require nine different cases to be recognized, one for each combination of shape and colour (i.e. red square, blue square, ..., green triangle). If colours and shapes are largely independent, then it would be possible to divide the problem into two modules or experts, one that determines shapes and another that determines colours. This would require just six cases (the three shapes plus the three colours).

This becomes important as the number of dimensions increases. For example, if there were ten shapes with ten colours in ten locations, then a single module would require a thousand combinations, whereas processing them independently would only require thirty cases to be recognized. Another issue is that it is just not physically possible for each of our 85 billion neurons to connect to each other in one huge module — our brains would need to be over twenty metres in diameter to store all the dendrites.

The brain appears to be organized into semi-discrete modules. For example, the optic nerve splits into a dorsal path that identifies where objects are and a ventral path that is more involved with recognizing which objects are present.

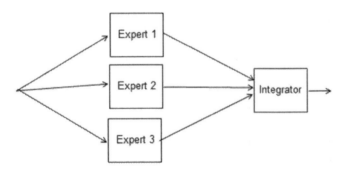

Owned

The diagram above shows a network that has been split into three expert modules that address different aspects of a problem. A fourth integrator module is then required to determine how the output of the different experts should be combined. If Red Circles were of special interest, then one expert might recognize the shape, another the colour and an integration expert the combination.

Each module in a modular network could have many connections to other modules in much more complex ways than shown above. A module is just a collection of neurons that have relatively more strong connections to other neurons in the module than they do to neurons that are outside the module. Further, the above network is a simple feed-forward network, but recurrent modular networks are also possible.

A more difficult problem is how to train a modular network. If the integrator somehow learns that red circles mean trouble, then it needs to be able to somehow cause one expert to recognize circles and another to recognize redness. Doing this effectively is difficult for both biological and artificial networks, and it is a subject of ongoing research. Mechanisms have even been proposed that learn how to automatically split a large network into modules.

Controlling movement

One possibility for multiple higher-level modules is based on the control systems used to move our bodies. Neither muscles nor electric motors behave in absolutely predictable ways, so any such control system needs to have a feedback loop that corrects the controlling signals based on where a limb, say, actually is. The basic algorithm is to note the current position and speed of the limb, and then to compare it with the desired position and speed, with the difference being used to adjust the control signal. So if the limb is found to be moving slower than desired, the control signal might be increased slightly.

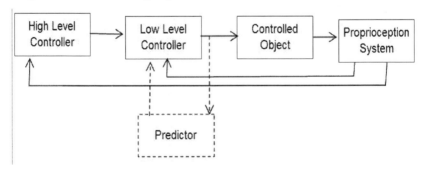

Owned

There are two parts to performing a complex action such as kicking a ball. The first is to decide to move the foot in an arc that would achieve that result, and the second is to actually provide the very finely controlled signals that cause the various muscles to move the leg in the correct manner. These are shown as two boxes in the diagram above, a high-level controller and a low-level controller. There is physiological evidence that our brains are organized along these lines, with the high-level control being mapped by the motor cortex in the cerebral cortex, and the low-level control being performed by the cerebellum. Both these regions have areas that correspond to specific parts of the body, and the cerebellum seems to have a high-speed, feed-forward architecture which is appropriate for low-level control.

Feedback has been used to control electro-mechanical devices for many decades. Care needs to be taken not to adjust the control signal too aggressively each time the new position is sensed, otherwise the whole system starts oscillating uncontrollably as each adjustment over-corrects the previous error. However, it takes time for a limb to move and our proprioception system to sense its new position. Limiting the feedback loop to the proprioception system's speed would make fast movement very difficult.

There appear to be several mechanisms to address this problem. One is the addition of a *predictor,* as shown on the diagram, which predicts where a limb will be based on the signals that the limb is receiving from the low level-controller. This predictor can then provide some feedback to the controller before the proprioception system has time to respond and so provide faster feedback cycles. Predicting the effect of a signal can be easier than planning how to create that signal in the first place.

Levels of abstractions and symbols

Modules often seem to be organized into different levels of abstractions. For vision, the lowest levels have been observed to occur in our optic nerve. They recognize edges between light and dark pixels, patterns of colours, and movements over time. Stereo modules can use lower-level analysis to compute some depth perception.

Objects need to be recognized regardless of their orientation or lighting. This involves a combination of simple two-dimensional matching of known shapes with an unknown scene as well as more complex three-dimensional analysis to recognize objects that are shown in unusual poses. Spacial recognition requires converting a two-dimensional image into a three-dimensional scene, which is particularly difficult for objects that are too far away for stereo vision to be effective.

So the firing of one group of neurons near the retina might simply correspond to a point that is bright, whereas further along the optic nerve the firing of a group of neurons might correspond to a vertical edge, or to something that is moving horizontally. Deeper in our visual cortex, a group of neurons might correspond to recognition of an object such as a tree.

Higher-level modules are usually driven by lower-level ones, but reverse links are also necessary. As discussed in the vision chapter, knowing that one is probably looking at a face makes it easy to identify faint lines in an image that might otherwise be dismissed as noise. It is certainly easier to recognize familiar objects in a scene.

For higher-level animals, a representation that is roughly analogous to a scene grammar must be ultimately produced. This higher-level representation then becomes accessible to our conscious thoughts, but our thoughts can also control our vision. A good example is the face-vase illusion below, where our high-level conscious mind can direct our lower visual processing to "see" either two faces or a vase.

We can consciously direct our vision to see either faces or a vase.
Commons
http://en.wikipedia.org/wiki/Optical_illusion#mediaviewer/File:Two_silhouette_profile_or_a_wh ite_vase.jpg

At the top level, our mind coordinates itself with conscious self-talk. This self-talk can sometimes cause confusion, for which a classic example is trying to state the colours of the following words in a Stroop test.

It is difficult to quickly state the colours in this Stroop Test, ignoring the words.

Corporate http://www.bbc.co.uk/theoneshow/getinvolved/stroop_test.shtml

Not all visual processing needs to go through all the levels of abstraction in order to be useful. For example, things that move towards us get bigger in complex ways. But if our low-level optic nerve simply sees shapes that are suddenly expanding rapidly, it will cause our eye to immediately blink long before the higher-level visual processing can determine what the object is or how it is moving. Likewise, most invertebrate vision is probably effective without ever producing a fully-formed scene graph. Indeed, some protozoan eye spots can simply detect light and dark, which is enough to usefully guide the animal towards the light.

It should be noted that all the above analysis has been performed very abstractly. There are several more detailed neural models of processes such as vision, but they do not produce anything like human-level capability. Some of the models are similar to classical AI research that has simply been implemented with neurons. Research is groping towards higher-level functionality, but there is still a long, long way to go.

Growth

A huge question that remains largely unanswered is how the neurons in our brains ended up in the locations that they occupy, and then build synapses in the places that they do. This is a specialization of the more general problem of how cells grow, and why, amazingly, our left thumb is almost exactly the same size as our right thumb, given that the growth was entirely coordinated by tiny cells that are certainly not intelligent.

One partial answer is that neurons may, in fact, grow somewhat randomly with thousands of synapses each. Over time, synaptic strengths vary due to Hebbian learning, until an effective network is achieved in which most of the synapses are inactive. Much computational neuroscience focuses on learning, but there is obviously also a large amount of innate structure and knowledge encoded in our genes.

As an example, when a calf is born it can rise up onto its wobbly legs within minutes. It can see well enough to find its mother, suckle and move, and within a few hours it can run. It then learns about the world, often from its mother. But it is not born as a blank slate that needs to have all its brain functions learned through some principle.

There is not enough DNA in a genome to specify the precise location of each of billions of neurons and their thousands of billions of synapses, but there must be some powerful language implicit in our body's interpretation of that DNA that enables a substantial amount of knowledge to be pre-packaged as instinct. If that language could be understood, then the problem may be reduced to understanding our 20,000 genes, rather than the 86 billion neurons that result. Determining the boundaries between nature and nurture during neural development is a subject of ongoing research.

What is known is that neurons do not directly reproduce. Instead, general purpose stem cells specialize into generic neuron cells which then specialize into a specific type of neuron. Further, neurons often travel from the place that they were created in the inner layers of the brain to the places they eventually occupy in the outer layers. Some neurons glide along fibres created by cells called *radial glia*. Others seem to follow chemical signals. Many of them never reach their final destination and die shortly after they are created.

Once a neuron reaches its destination, it has to settle in to do useful work. It needs to put out dendrites and axons and form synapses with other neurons. Axons may grow to many millimetres or even metres in length, and seemed to be pulled along by protein structures that move cells called *lamellipodium*, which are attracted to various *cell adhesion molecules*. This final step of differentiation is the least well-understood part of neurogenesis and yet is the most important. How do axons decide to grow where they do, and thus what connections to other neurons they will make?

One path to better understanding neurogenesis is to study the very simple nematode, *C. elegans*. Each worm has exactly 302 neurons, each of whose genesis is precisely known. It would seem likely that its nervous system has a relatvively direct mapping to its genome. Human neurogenesis is obviously much, much more complex, with considerable variation between individuals but understanding *C. elegans* might make a good start.

Man vs. Machine

Chess history

Chess has traditionally been seen as a game that requires great intelligence to play well. Both sides are (almost) equal, and the player that can think through the many possibilities accurately is sure to win. Chess also requires discipline, tenacity and endurance to carefully think through each move, and for that reason children are often encouraged to play.

The El Ajedrecista mechanical chess player.
Public Wikipedia

The first computer chess programs actually pre-date the availability of electronic computers. In 1912 Leonardo Quevedo built the *El Ajedrecista* machine shown above which could successfully play an end game using a king and a rook against a human king. Unlike The Turk, this machine was not a fraud and still runs at *Canales y Puertos* in Madrid.

In the late 1940s, Alan Turing wrote a chess program on a series of cards. He then played a partial game by tediously following their instructions with paper and pencil. It seemed to play a passable game, for in 2012 it took the world champion Garry Kasparov 16 moves to beat it.

It was not until 1957 that a full-fledged game of chess was played on an IBM 704 computer, which had a staggering (for the time) 70K of memory (modern personal computers have over 4,000,000K). Again, overly-optimistic predictions were made that within ten years the world champion would be a computer.

Twenty years later computers could play chess well enough to beat ordinary non-expert players. By the 1980s many home computers played chess with adequate performance. In 1985 Kasparov played 32 different chess computers simultaneously, and won all the games, albeit with some difficulty.

In 1996, Kasparov beat IBM's Deep Blue purpose-built chess-playing computer. But in 1997 the computer finally beat Kasparov, 3 1/2 to 2 1/2. Kasparov complained that he was unable to study Deep Blue's recent games the way that its development team had studied Kasparov's, and there was some evidence that Deep Blue was specifically trained to beat Kasparov. However, Deep Blue's victory was clear. It took 40 years from the early game on the IBM 704, which is four times longer than predicted, but with ever improving digital technology, it seemed inevitable that a computer would eventually win.

Minimax

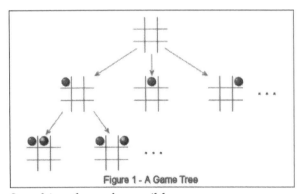

Figure 1 - A Game Tree

Searching through possible moves.
Education http://www.hamedahmadi.com/gametree/

The classical approach to building a game-playing program is the *Minimax* search algorithm, which is applied to a *game tree* as illustrated above for the simpler game of Naughts and Crosses. At any point in the game the computer determines all the possible moves it might make. For each of those moves, it determines what moves its opponent might make. For each move an opponent might make, then it determines what moves it might make in response, recursively. The computer is enumerating all the possible combinations of, "If I do this, and they do that, and then I do this, and then they do that, who wins?". This is referred to as *searching* for the best move to make.

Given there are roughly twenty possible moves that could be made at each turn in chess, the computer would initially examine twenty moves that it could make, followed by four hundred moves that its opponent could make in response to each of those twenty moves, followed by eight thousand moves that the computer could make, etc. A modern computer can easily consider eight thousand moves, but after ten moves with twenty options per move, there are ten *trillion* possible moves to make, which is too many for even the fastest computers to consider in a reasonable time frame. So like a human player, a computer can only think ahead a certain distance.

A chess program therefore needs a second component called the *static evaluator*, whose job it is to determine who is winning for any given board position. For chess, it might simply calculate a weighted sum of the number of pieces each side has, counting 1 for pawns, 3 for knights, 5 for rooks, etc. Or it might consider other factors such as control of the middle squares or which pieces are vulnerable to attack. The total will be positive if the computer is winning, else negative if the opponent seems to have the advantage.

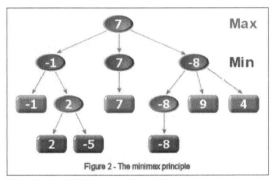

Figure 2 - The minimax principle

The basic Minimax algorithm.
Education http://www.hamedahmadi.com/gametree/

When Minimax has searched to its maximum reasonable depth, it applies the static evaluator to its leaves. In the diagram above, this has produced values of 2 and -5 for the bottom left red nodes. So at that point it would choose the better option, which has value 2. However, the next level up suggests that its opponent has a better move which results in -1. The computer assumes that its opponent plays well, so the move valued at 2 is just wishful thinking. However, it finds another move that has an evaluation of +7, so that is the move it decides to make. At each alternate level, it is maximizing or minimizing the score of its lower levels depending on whether it is the computer's turn or the opponent's turn, hence the name Minimax. Many refinements can be made, such as pruning parts of the tree early to avoid analyzing hopeless moves.

Chess strategies

When building a chess program, there is a trade-off between the amount of time spent performing static analysis and the number of moves that the computer can consider. If the computer spends twice as long performing a more thorough static analysis of each move, then it can only consider half as many different moves in a given amount of time. However, a good static evaluator can help prune the tree and so focus the search on promising moves. If the effective branching factor could be halved from 20 to 10 (say), then over 5 moves, the tree can be reduce by a factor of 2^5, i.e. from 320,000 to 10,000 nodes. Early workers in this field thus thought that developing more sophisticated static analyzers would be the best way to proceed.

It turns out that for current computer chess programs, using crude but fast static analyzers that facilitate the brute-force approach of performing deep and exhaustive look-ahead seems to be the winning strategy. Situations that can be difficult to analyze statically can be much easier to analyze if one just makes one more move to see what happens. Deep Blue used a relatively simple static analyzer which it could then implement with special purpose hardware that enabled it to consider a staggering 200 million moves per second. Given that massive quantity of accurate computation, it is not surprising that Kasparov was beaten. What was truly amazing was that Kasparov's slow, human brain could compete with such a monster.

The computer has another distinct advantage over human players, namely its vast store of known good moves. Serious chess players spend considerable time studying and memorizing chess moves that are carefully analyzed in numerous technical chess books. People are not permitted to consult these books during an actual game. A computer can, of course, easily and accurately remember billions of possible moves, particularly during the opening phase of the game. These include the knowledge in every chess book that has ever been written and every masters game that has ever been played, as well as the results of many, many hours of computation while the computer quietly plays itself. In order to have any chance against a computer, a human player needs to play "off book", meaning that they need to make some unusual moves that would not be stored in the computer's database. However, the reason that these moves are unusual is because they are known not to be as good as the usual moves, and this puts the human player at an even greater disadvantage.

Chess vs Go

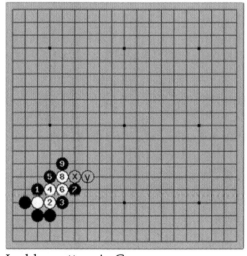

Ladder pattern in Go.
Education http://senseis.xmp.net/?Ladder

Clearly Kasparov's brain could not even subconsciously evaluate anything like 200 million moves, so he must have been analyzing the game at a higher level. The game of Go provides good examples of the need for higher-level reasoning, and Go has become rather fashionable because computers still cannot beat strong human players.

In Go, players take turns at placing pieces of their colour on the intersections of lines on a board. Pieces cannot be moved once placed. The object is to surround groups of the opponent's pieces, in which case they are removed from the board.

In the game above, white is in trouble. If black plays at the position marked x, then white will be surrounded and removed. Alternatively, if it was white's turn to move then white could play at x to prevent this. Even the most novice Go player will quickly realize that playing at x would be a mistake because black would just play at y and so continue the pattern known as a *ladder*. Eventually, after many more moves, the play will reach the end of the board and white will lose all of its pieces. The longer white persists with this futile endeavour, the more pieces it will eventually lose. Better to just abandon those pieces and play elsewhere.

A simple Minimax approach to this problem will fail. There are almost 400 possible moves at each turn, so looking even 10 moves ahead is completely infeasible, but it takes 14 moves for the disaster to occur. Our human brains have no difficulty whatsoever in perceiving the pattern and deriving the little theorem that predicts disaster.

Competent Go programs also have no difficulty perceiving patterns as simple as the one above. The large board tends to produce subgames in different areas that are largely, but not completely, independent of each other. Minimax still has an important role to play, albeit on tightly constrained searches within these subgames.

Deep Blue's inability to directly perform higher-level analysis led Kasparov to remark that it was "only intelligent in the sense that an alarm clock is intelligent". That said, he also thought that the program sometimes produced very creative moves. This again demonstrates that relatively simple algorithms executed on a massive scale can produce intelligent results. Vast quantity has a quality all of its own.

Today, the best chess players are neither computer nor human but a combination of both. A competent player with a competent laptop chess program can easily beat either a grand-master or a super computer. The player chooses strategies, and the program enumerates their consequences and prevents mistakes from being made.

Of course, the best chess programs cannot play poker any more than an elephant can play chess. These are special purpose systems that do not generalize in the way that human intelligence does. That said, computer-driven machine learning techniques are often used to improve static analyzers, given the large database of available chess games. One researcher found that the fairly naive application of an artificial neural network for static analysis, combined with normal Minimax produced a chess program that was almost competitive with the very competent GNU Chess program. There are also some general purpose game-playing programs that can learn to play any minimax style board game, but they do not play very well.

It is a testament to human cognition that people can learn to play these games with such competence. And it is perhaps an even greater testament that a novice looking at the Go ladder above will quickly see the pattern without being told.

Watson and *Jeopardy!*

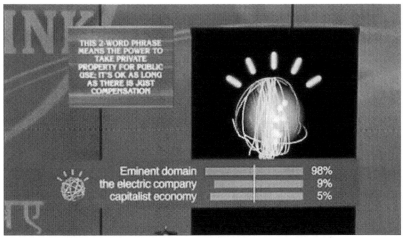

Jeopardy! game with Watson.
Fair Use Wikipedia

On the 14th February, 2011 the IBM Watson computer won the *Jeopardy!* game show against two of the previously most successful contestants on the show, Ken Jennings and Brad Rutter. The wide ranging questions were given in unconstrained natural language, and had to be answered in real time according to the rules of the game. At the end of the game, Watson had $35,734 against Rutter's $10,400 and Jenning's $4,800.

After the game, Jennings quipped, "I for one welcome our new computer overlords ... Brad and I were the first knowledge-industry workers put out of work by the new generation of thinking machines ... but I'm sure we won't be the last."

This was, in many ways, a stunning achievement. Playing chess is a "logical" process that one would expect a computer to perform well. However, answering cryptic, free-form questions about the world in general would seem to involve much more human-like reasoning and common sense.

Below are some additional questions that Watson answered correctly on the first program:-

- Wanted for killing Sir Danvers Carew; Appearance--Pale & Dwarfish; Seems to have a split personality : *Hyde*
- Wanted for general evil-ness; last seen at the tower of Barad-dur; it's a giant eye, folks. Kinda hard to miss : *Sauron*
- Beatles: "And any time you feel the pain, hey" this guy "refrain, don't carry the world upon your shoulders" : *Jude*
- Olympics: A 1976 entrant in the "Modern" this was kicked out for wiring his epee to score points without touching his foe : *Pentathlon*
- 4-Letter word for the iron fitting on the hoof of a horse or a card-dealing box in a casino : *Shoe*

All the questions seem rather challenging and cryptic, and most people would have difficulty answering as many of them correctly as Watson did. They cover a wide variety of topics from history, the arts, sport and general knowledge.

Watson's implementation

Watson utilized some impressive hardware. A cluster of ninety IBM Power 750 servers had a total of 2,880 3.5 GHz POWER7 processor cores and a massive 16,000 gigabytes of memory. It only needed 4,000 gigabytes of disk to store 200 million pages of structured and unstructured content, which included the full text of Wikipedia. The hardware was worth about $4 million. It is again surprising that such a huge quantity of computational power was required to produce human-like competence.

Watson was developed quickly by a relatively small team of twenty engineers, led by David Ferrucci, albeit with many collaborating academic institutions. The project was started in 2005. By 2006 Watson could correctly answer only 15% of the questions correctly, whereas live contestants answered 95% of them correctly. By 2008 the system had credible if not expert performance, culminating in its 2011 world championship. (It is worth noting that during this period, human competitors did not become significantly better at answering *Jeopardy!* questions.)

The general architecture used a *map/reduce* approach in which each question was farmed out (*mapped*) to dozens of subsystems, each of which attempted to solve it using different methodologies. The answers that resulted from each subsystem were then combined (*reduced*) into a central coordinating processor, together with an estimate of how confident the subsystems were in their answers. The coordinating processor would then choose the best answer, generally preferring answers that came from more than one subsystem. If the total confidence reached a threshold of 50%, then Watson would press the buzzer and attempt to answer the question. The best three answers and Watson's confidence in them were displayed on the TV screens for the viewers' amusement.

Like many modern artificial intelligent systems, Watson combined multiple approaches to produce an acceptable result. The authors of the system contend that it is the architecture used to combine and coordinate the different subsystems that is Watson's main contribution to artificial intelligence theory.

The *Jeopardy!* questions all concern trivia, so the main human challenge is having a wide background knowledge and a good memory. Most people would find all the questions easy to answer if they had access to the Internet and a search engine such as Google or Bing, which is exactly what Watson has stored in its 4,000 gigabytes of disk. However, a search engine simply retrieves documents that contain the specified keywords, and the intelligent analysis is left to the human user. Watson has to go much further and understand at least roughly what the question is about in order to be able to produce a concise, targeted response.

Watson includes both deep natural language parsers that attempt to perform a full, SHRDLU-like parse of each question, and shallow parsers that focus on identifying key words and phrases in a manner similar to Eliza. For example, given the query, "He was presidentially pardoned on September 8, 1974", a shallow analysis might find the sentence "Ford pardoned Nixon on Sept. 8, 1974." in a database simply because it contains many similar words to the question ("Ford" and "Nixon" are known to be presidents). A separate tool parses the question to determine the *Lexical Answer Type* (LAT) that is required in the answer, in this case a president, rather than an author or a country. Both Ford and Nixon were presidents, so some stronger syntactic analysis is then required to determine that it was Nixon, not Ford who was pardoned. The locality of the response and the specificity of the date would cause it to have a high confidence rating.

Watson uses several pre-existing databases to assist with its analysis. Wordnet provided a massive, hand-built thesaurus of related words and phrases, which is very useful when parsing and searching for terms. More interesting are the semantic networks (now called triple databases) that contain more structured data. For example, dbPedia contains knowledge automatically extracted from Wikipedia about people, books, locations, etc. Structured queries can then be performed against the database, such as, "Which books were illustrated by an illustrator that worked on a book by Rowling other than the Harry Potter series?". Watson is only concerned with trivia, so the more sophisticated Cyc ontology was not needed.

Many of the engines that Watson uses are targeted at specific types of questions already seen in previous episodes of *Jeopardy!*. For example, Watson understands which words rhyme to be able to answer Rhyme Time questions. Special processors solve word maths problems, or determine scores in Scrabble. Sometimes Watson does not understand an entire category of questions, and in the series it failed to answer any questions in "Name the decade", "European union", or "Actors who Direct".

Some incorrect answers provide clues to the lack of Watson's real understanding. Asked, "It was this anatomical oddity of US gymnast George Eyser", Watson answered "Leg" instead of "Missing a leg" because Watson did not understand that having legs was not an oddity. Occasionally Watson gets the answer completely wrong. In one question on US Cities it answered "Toronto", probably confusing the Canadian city with a small town in Illinois.

Watson's victory

The above may be how Watson played *Jeopardy!*, but how Watson won *Jeopardy!* is much easier to explain. The *Jeopardy!* questions are first shown to the contestants in text, and then the presenter reads them out loud. Unlike most quiz shows, the contestants are not allowed to answer until the question has been fully read out loud and a light is turned on. Only the first contestant to press the buzzer is allowed to answer. Jennings noted that "On any given night, nearly all the contestants know nearly all the answers ... (so) the buzzer is all".

Human reactions of a few hundred milliseconds are too slow, so good contestants have to carefully anticipate when the light is likely to be turned on, often missing by being a few milliseconds too early. Of course, Watson's electronic reaction times are sub-millisecond which meant that whenever Watson had an answer it would almost always win the buzzer and so get to play it. That in no way takes away from the awesomely demonstrated power of the Watson system to answer fairly difficult and obscure questions in the first place, but it does make the idea of a competition somewhat farcical.

The question remains, does Watson's analysis involve true intelligence, or is it simply a sophisticated amalgamation of Eliza-like tricks? Matching keywords, looking up a thesaurus, following some simple parsing rules, all without any real understanding of anything. Jennings answered that question as follows:-

The computer's techniques for unravelling Jeopardy! clues sounded just like mine. The machine zeros in on key words in a clue, then combs its memory for clusters of associations with those words. It checks the top hits against all the contextual information it can muster: the category name; the kind of answer being sought; the time, place, and gender hinted at in the clue; and so on. And when it feels "sure" enough, it decides to buzz. This is all an instant, intuitive process for a human Jeopardy! player, but I felt convinced that under the hood my brain was doing more or less the same thing.

IBM is targeting Watson for use in some medical applications. However, Watson is a completely different type of system than an expert system such as MYCIN. It may be just the natural language processing that is being utilized, otherwise it would be concerning if treatment options were being decided by a trivia engine. Alternatively, IBM may be exploiting the general lack of understanding about artificial intelligence to use the word "Watson" to refer to any vaguely intelligent application that it is building. Ferrucci's 2010 paper <u>Overview of DeepQA</u> is one of the very few non-marketing technical papers on Watson.

Where is the Intelligence?

Good old fashioned AI

Part II has considered a rich variety of approaches and technologies that have been used in the quest for ever more intelligent systems. But how do they relate to each other? Which ones will have strategic impact?

The early work with *scruffy* symbolic systems produced some impressive results. The Eliza program's simulation of a Rogerian psychoanalyst was good enough to convince some non-critical observers that it actually understood what was being said. Eliza seemed to be well on the path to being intelligent, but as Eliza's author was at pains to point out, it just used simple patterns to manipulate words in mechanical ways. The meanings of the words were only known to the people that used Eliza, and not in any sense to Eliza itself. It is not easy to assess how intelligent an application is.

Other early symbolic systems had much more deductive capability. The SHRDLU system really did understand its microworld of blocks stacked on a table. It could reason about them, and produce plans that involved multiple actions. It could also converse with people in fairly natural language and introspect about why it performed certain actions. It could even learn about its environment, both by being explicitly taught and by performing simple experiments.

Rule-based expert systems enable the construction of many practical applications. These include loan and insurance application processing, systems for analyzing complex scientific data, and medical diagnosis systems. Many of these systems reason with uncertain knowledge, and Bayesian network technologies are now used to efficiently compute probabilities Other impressive systems include Eurisko, which discovered mathematical theorems based on heuristics that Eurisko itself developed.

Unfortunately, all these early and impressive results could not be generalized into more realistic problem domains. They lacked the "common sense" that is needed to interact with the real world. They also suffered from combinatorial explosion, in which slightly more complex problems required much larger computing facilities.

Knowledge representation and reasoning

One attempt to address this was to formalize the representation of knowledge. One simple form of knowledge representation is relational databases which are used for most of our common business applications. Such a database contains simple tables of data that can describe business objects such as Customers, Products, People or Orders.

More difficult problem domains can be represented in well-defined mathematical logic. This *neat* approach leveraged the ability of even very early systems to perform moderately complex deductions using automated theorem provers. If the world could be described in logic, and theorems could be proven automatically, then the general problem of reasoning would be solved.

However, the world cannot be easily described in terms of classical logic. Most things are neither true nor false but somewhere in between. Our knowledge of the world will always be incomplete, and reasoning effectively about the world requires assumptions to be made that may not always be valid. There are many approaches that deal with this problem, but none are universally successful.

Of particular note is the Cyc project, which attempts to formalize all of our commonsense knowledge in an advanced description logic. This includes such facts as trees are plants, and that fragile objects will break if they are dropped. It turns out that ordinary people have a vast store of this type of knowledge which they use to make sense of the world. It is hypothesized that if enough knowledge could be encoded by hand, then Cyc would be able to learn the rest by reading books and the Internet.

The Cyc project has now been in development for thirty years. It has a huge knowledge base consisting of hundreds of thousands of concepts and millions of individual facts. But it has yet to be used in any widely used application, and certainly has not come alive in the way that was hoped. Cyc's proponents argue that this is because it is not complete, while its detractors argue that the approach itself is fundamentally flawed.

Artificial neural networks and other numerical methods

A completely different approach describes the world using floating point numbers rather than discrete symbols. Artificial Neural Networks (ANNs) are loosely based on the way neurons work in our brains. After a false start, methods were developed that enable ANNs to learn many complex relationships and patterns such as recognizing objects in images. This is an active area of research, with many techniques being developed to precondition data such as support vector machines. It is now also possible to learn rules over complex multi-level architectures, as well in recurrent networks that have short-term memory.

Other non-symbolic approaches range from advanced statistical techniques such as non-linear regression and principal component analysis, to approaches for clustering and learning hidden Markov models. All of these approaches can take real world data as their direct input rather than needing people to first abstract it into discrete symbols.

Numerical methods have produced impressive results, but they do not even begin to approximate our human ability to reason about the world at a high level.

Symbols

There is some debate as to whether the use of symbols is really a useful abstraction or just a shallow trick that will never produce deep results. That the intelligence of symbolic systems is limited the interpretations that people give to the symbols, and that no symbolic system can truly understand the real world. SHRDLU, for example, could produce pretty analyses of sentences containing words like "Block" and "Pyramid", but it had no real knowledge of what a block or a pyramid actually was. They could just as easily have been called "S-123" and "S-234", and the rules could have been written that blocks can only be stacked on top of pyramids. SHRDLU would not care.

Alternatively, basic reasoning can be performed by advanced artificial neural networks which do not involve any overt symbolic reasoning. Moreover, those systems seem to be much more resilient to noisy data than traditional symbolic ones.

Do people and other more intelligent animals really reason with symbols, or are they merely an illusion created by our use of words in language? It seems likely that we do use symbols. One concrete example of this was when this author plucked a small twig out of the mane of an old and cantankerous horse. The horse was very afraid of the twig. She had probably been beaten by a stick in the past, and the symbol in its mind for stick and twig were the same. If she reasoned numerically about the mass of the twig and its ability to cause pain, she would consider it to be insignificant. The reader no doubt has had similar experiences.

Learning new words and concepts helps people think more deeply about things. For example, if a software engineer describes a walk through a garden, they are likely to recall little more than seeing green stuff. But if a botanist walks through the same garden, they would be able to recall many different types of plants, their relationships and condition. That situation is likely to be reversed in a walk through program code. The botanist probably does not have a photographic memory of the entire garden. Rather they abstract what they see into instantiations of pre-existing concepts. This enables a few new relationships between existing symbols to provide a rich understanding.

It is also very hard to think about anything without the use of self-talk. Where self-talk comes from is a deep mystery, but it seems to crystallize our thoughts and coordinate and focus our conscious mind. Indeed, it takes long practice at meditation to be able to suppress one's self-talk even temporarily. Self-talk can be a disaster for the fractured mind of a schizophrenic.

The relationship between symbols and the real world is complex. For example, a *duck* is an animal that quacks and flies, but one can also talk of a *wooden duck* which cannot quack or fly. There are also containment issues, so in the sentence "Mary came here", it is assumed that the term *Mary* includes her clothes. In the sentence "Mary is sick", her clothes are not included. There are multiple subtly-related concepts that have the same word, *Mary*.

It is fair to say that symbolic analysis has not been as successful as its proponents had hoped. On the other hand, non-symbolic systems do not currently attempt to perform the type of high-level analysis that can be performed using symbols. Nobody attempts to use artificial neurons to produce the subtle, reified analysis of situations or beliefs. If such a system could be built, it would probably be very slow and clumsy at this type of reasoning, just like our human brains.

Visualizations

Game of 15.
Owned

One key difference between human and symbolic reasoning is our use of visualizations. As a classic example of this, consider the game of Fifteen, in which two players take turns to pick disks numbered from 1 to 9 by circling or crossing numbers as shown above. The goal is to be able to form a total of 15 from any three numbers that a player has selected. So as shown above, the first player may take 2, the second 7, the first 9, and then the second 4 to prevent the first player making $4 + 2 + 9 = 15$. However, it is to no avail if the first player then picks 5, which could form either $9 + 5 + 1$ or $2 + 5 + 8$.

Playing this game is quite difficult for people unless they are aware of the perfect magic square shown below. Each of its rows, columns and diagonals adds up to 15. So Fifteen is isomorphic to the simple game of Noughts and Crosses (Tic Tac Toe). People have powerful visual processing capabilities, and so find the game much easier to play when they can visualize it. Conversely, it is much easier to write a computer program that just adds up the numbers rather than attempting to perform messy spacial analysis.

Magic square for Noughts and Crosses.
Owned

The question then arises, is visualization an important ability that is lacking in our symbolic systems, or does it result from people's limited ability to perform abstract symbol manipulation?

Kasparov probably used vaguely similar visualization techniques subconsciously in order to be able to occasionally beat the Deep Blue computer that could symbolically examine 200 million moves. Further, no super computer can beat a master player of the game Go, and it seems unlikely that that will happen without being able to perform at least some type of abstract visualization.

Brains

Having studied the brain in detail for over a hundred years, one may ask the same question that Searle had asked of his Chinese Room, "But where is the intelligence?". Or, more importantly, what has been learnt about the nature of intelligence that could further our quest?

Knowing the detailed anatomy of the brain might be invaluable to the surgeons who first investigated it, but it has limited value for building an intelligent computer. Understanding where components happen to be located provides only very indirect clues as to how the components actually work. A low-level understanding of neurons has provided the inspiration for artificial neurons, which are very powerful techniques. Probing the behaviour of a cat's optic nerves provided comforting support for computational approaches to vision, such as edge detection. There has been some success in tracing basic relationships between neurons that are close to the raw input and output of senses and muscles, but those techniques fail as deeper, more interesting functionality is investigated.

Kurzweil suggests that the brain might be organized into discrete *cortical columns* that form functional units, but there is no real evidence of such as convenient structure in real brains. Instead, one finds a very complex, interconnected and redundant system of 86 billion neurons and trillions of synapses that interact in ways that are difficult to measure and yet somehow combine to produce intelligent behaviour.

Kurzweil also suggests our brains work mainly as hierarchical pattern matchers. Low-level systems match raw data, and feed their results into higher-level pattern matchers. This is very like his speech understanding system in which low-level matchers analyze frequency distributions, which feed into hidden Markov models, which feed into high-level semantic analyzers. A pattern matcher takes input and produces output, so it is essentially the same as a software module or just a subroutine. So saying that the brain uses hierarchical pattern matchers is essentially the same as just saying that the whole is composed of parts, which would almost have to be the case. What would be more interesting is to understand each part's functionality, but there has only been very limited success in actually identifying the parts, let alone understanding how they work.

There are two distinct methods by which some subset of our 20,000 genes could generate the 86 billion complex neurons and their hundreds of trillions of synapses that make up our brains. The first is that our genes define a fairly rigid substructure which is repeated millions of times throughout our brain, in the same way that computer memory is made from billions of bits, but each individual bit is essentially the same. The second method is that neurons grow according to relatively simple rules that are vaguely analogous to the way ANNs are trained. These rules then produce complex and chaotic neural layout with minimal obvious underlying structure based on the training data that they see.

The latter method seems more likely because no regular substructures have been identified, so understanding neurogenesis would seem to be a key to understanding human thought and cognition. It might make it possible to grow intelligent structures rather than attempt to understand the tangled mess that is seen in a fully grown brain. However, very little is known about neurogenesis, and in particular why neurons connect to other neurons in the ways that they do.

To be sure, ongoing investigations are being made, with many new advanced techniques being developed. For example, optogenetics technology now enables light-sensitive channels taken from the *Chlamydomonas* protozoa to be genetically introduced into specific mammalian neuron cells. Light can then be used to activate these channels with millisecond precision, which causes the neurons to become active or be suppressed. This enables many fine-grained experiments to be performed, such as one that has implanted false memories into mice.

Engineers at MIT have developed robots that can accurately manipulate micropipettes that can monitor individual neurons. Scientists at Duke University have developed a probe made from carbon nanotubes that tapers to just a few nanometres in diameter and yet can be as long as a millimetre. That enables the properties of individual synapses to be studied in detail. It is also becoming possible to attach fluorescent crystals to individual proteins and thus track them optically as they participate in biochemical reactions. There is no reason to think that the vast improvement in tools for investigating physiological processes will not continue for the foreseeable future.

Kurzweil points out that progress is often exponential. One of his examples is the $3 billion project to sequence the entire human genome, which was started in 1990 and expected to take 15 years to complete. After 6 years, only 1% of the genome had been sequenced, and prospects for the project looked bleak. However, the project finished successfully in 2003, two years early. If one takes an exponential view of growth then this is to be expected. Tools improve, and those improved tools improve other tools. So once 1% of the genome had been successfully sequenced it only took twice as long to sequence the other 99%.

One oft-stated proposal to produce an intelligent machine is to analyze the individual connections in a real human brain and then simulate them on a computer. This is generally referred to as *brain uploading*. It is conceptually simple, just like moving a computer program from one machine to another. However, there is a vast amount of additional knowledge of brain function that needs to be gained before this approach would become even vaguely practical. In the meantime, real progress is being made with more conventional artificial intelligence technologies.

Animal Intelligence

Elephants playing Chess
Multiple http://www.chess.com/article/view/openings-for-tactical-players-kings-indian-defense

It has been noted that elephants have large brains and appear to be far more intelligent than any existing computer program, yet elephants cannot play chess. (Even chimpanzees can barely play Noughts and Crosses.)

Playing chess is a relatively easy thing to do, computers have been playing it since the 1950s. But elephantine intelligence is totally grounded in the world in which they live.

Building systems that physically interact with the environment might be necessary in order to ground artificial intelligence research. Only then will the true nature of symbols be apparent, with symbolic reasoning being a thin layer of icing on top of a very large cake. That may be why human intelligence evolved in just the last couple of million years, while elephantine intelligence has been evolving for over 100 million years.

Washoe.
Education http://sgspsychology.webs.com/apelanguage.htm

Chimpanzees are our closest living relatives, so studying their intelligence can provide insights as to how our own intelligence evolved. They cannot physically speak, but they have successfully been taught American Sign Language.

Behavioural psychologists had long known how to perform scientific experiments on animals in cages using operant conditioning, and had proven that Chimpanzees could not use language. However, much to those scientists' chagrin, in the 1960s Allen and Beatrix Gardner brought the chimpanzee Washoe into their farm and treated her like a sentient animal. They and their assistants formed genuine personal bonds with Washoe, and she responded by learning some 350 signs which she could combine into simple sentences.

Examples of Washoe's sentences include:-

- "Peek-a-boo (i.e. hide and seek) I go",
- "Baby (doll) in my drink (cup)" (when shown picture),
- "You, me out go". "OK, but first clothes" (Washoe puts on a jacket.).

Washoe would also make up her own phrases, such as "finger bracelet" for a ring. When told of an assistant's miscarriage,

Washoe became very sad and replied, "Cry", even though chimpanzees do not cry.

The Gardners had to perform double-blind experiments to refute somewhat spiteful criticisms that Washoe's quick gestures were being over interpreted as meaningful signs, when they were, in fact, just meaningless repetitions of memorized movements. These experiments showed that chimpanzees are clearly in a different league of intelligence than familiar animals such as dogs or horses, even though that is not at all apparent just by watching chimpanzees climb trees. Language became "a part of Washoe just as much as climbing trees". And language is all about symbols.

The focus of the Washoe experiments was on language. What would be very interesting to know is to what extent, if any, learning sign language affected Washoe's general cognitive ability. Washoe taught sign language to other chimpanzees, and chimpanzees were seen signing to themselves in what would be similar to our self-talk. Did the use of language introduce symbols that Washoe could then use to think more deeply about problems, or were the symbols already there and language just attached itself to them? Probably a bit of both. Education helps people to think more clearly about problems in general. Other experiments have shown that individual chimpanzees have widely different intellectual abilities; it would appear that the Gardners were lucky to pick an intelligent chimpanzee.

Washoe seemed to exhibit plenty of commonsense reasoning. She could interact with the world and had a sound grasp of naive physics. She understood relationships and other people's mental states. For example, she would sign more slowly to visitors that were not good at sign languages. It would appear that she could express in language any thoughts that she had. However, there is an enormous gulf between reasoning about playing Hide and Seek and the human capacity for abstract reasoning that can program computers.

Surprisingly, there seems to be very little ongoing research that adds to these fifty-year-old results. The behaviouralists appear to have won.

Humble nematode.
Education   *http://www.mcb.ucdavis.edu/faculty-*
labs/scholey/molecular_basis_of__intracellula.htm

Perhaps more interesting than the mighty chimpanzee is the humble nematode, *C. elegans*. This model organism has been extensively studied, and the origin of every cell in its small body is known. It has just 302 neurons, yet exhibits a number of moderately sophisticated behaviours. Understanding how its nervous system really worked would make a good first step to understanding our 86 billion neurons. If Kurzweil's law of accelerating returns holds, then this gap may not turn out to be as large as it seems, but it is still fully eight orders of magnitude. Only time will tell just how difficult this problem really is. To fully understand the nematode would make a good milestone that has yet to be reached.

Part III

What Will Computers

Think About?

Why, What, How, Who, Where, When

Why

After the amazing successes of the 1960s, artificial intelligence research got stuck. The easy problems had been solved, and progress on the difficult problems was very slow. The excessive early optimism was not realized, and funding sources dried up. In the US, DARPA reduced its support after frustrations grew about the slow progress on problems such as speech understanding and translation. In the UK, the 1973 Lighthill report suggested that all further funding be curtailed, largely for petty political reasons.

Funding bodies want to see results, and AI research only seemed to promise ever more difficult questions. Researchers began to actively avoid the term *artificial intelligence* and focused instead on solving more practical problems. True AI is only actually useful if it can solve real problems. SHRDLU may have been interesting, but at the end of the day it was quite useless. The resulting period is referred to as the "AI Winter".

One of Lilienthal's controlled flights, 1890's
Public expired

Historically, the same problem was encountered by early aviation pioneers. In 1891 Otto Lilienthal started to successfully fly his hang gliders. He made thousands of flights and could stay aloft in the wind for extended periods of time, often moving around to find the best positions from which to be photographed. Lilienthal actively encouraged others to join him in the quest for flight, but nobody was interested. There was no money to be made from being able to glide down a hill. With only one man working on the problem, progress was slow.

The Wright brothers also had enormous difficulty in attracting any interest in their quite capable aeroplanes. The only article on their early achievements appeared in a bee keepers' journal whose editor happened to be passing nearby. (The article had already been rejected by *Scientific American*.) Their first powered flight was in 1903, with major improvements in the following years. But in 1906 and 1907 they did not fly at all due to lack of interest, so progress stalled. It was only their 1908 appearance in a French air show that sparked significant enthusiasm. Once that interest was piqued aircraft developed incredibly quickly, from machines that could barely fly to the competent fighters demanded by the First World War just six years later.

Artificial intelligence techniques are now becoming very useful. One of the early goals of AI was to translate articles from Russian into English. Today it is commonplace to use quite passable automated translators that are available at no cost. Search engines like Google and Bing are becoming ever more sophisticated in the way that they analyze documents. They want to have some idea what the symbolic words actually mean.

In this post 9/11 era, government agencies are very keen to analyze the vast quantities of email and other traffic that they have access to in order to identify and track potential terrorist activity. The Chinese government has an even bigger job censoring its huge Internet. Traditional filters just block key words and phrases, such as *Tiananmen, Taiwan* and *Tibet*. But they would love to at least partially understand the dialogs that are taking place to identify potential political activists. These and other applications can provide both a strong motivation and a rich source of new funding for AI research.

The larger driver is likely to be the fact that robots are leaving the factory. These range from self-driving cars and tanks to automated household vacuum cleaners. For most applications, an AI that was barely intelligent was of limited use. But even a barely intelligent vacuum cleaner can be quite useful. With the ever falling price of computer hardware, even quite simple tools can be economically provided with quite powerful computers. There is also a strong school of thought that to be really intelligent one needs to interact with the real world. Robots provide just such an opportunity.

The military has always been a major source of funding for AI research, but as systems are starting to become practical, their interest has grown enormously. Semi-autonomous robots can enter dangerous areas, while semi-autonomous guns are already used to patrol difficult borders. More intelligent missiles can be harder to deflect. But more importantly, many believe that the next war will not be fought with guns and missiles, but rather using software in cyberspace. Intelligent agents will be critical for this task.

As a result of these drivers, many people are starting to talk about artificial intelligence again. A growing number of problems are close to being solved today — problems for which just a little more intelligence would be very useful indeed.

As confidence grows, people are again daring to contemplate the ultimate goal, namely: true general intelligence. For example, in his recent book, eminent researcher Nils Nilsson urged people to focus on the quest for real intelligence. Eminent researcher Hector Levesque also made a similar call to arms at IJCAI 2013 (the major academic AI conference).

The economic and military advantages of having more intelligent machines suggests that it is most unlikely that society would choose not to produce them. Perhaps more importantly, the huge disadvantage of letting economic and military competitors develop intelligent machines without having such machines oneself. If it is indeed possible to build a truly intelligent machine then it seems almost certain that we will do so.

What

Four general approaches have been proposed to develop truly intelligent software. The first is to simply engineer it in the way all other software and devices are built with multiple components, each designed with an understanding of its purpose. Analysis of our own intelligence and brains will continue to provide insights as to the best way to achieve this, but an artificial intelligence would be designed from the ground up to utilize the hardware and software tools that are available.

The second approach is to only engineer a minimal "baby brain", and then let it grow up. To have it learn the bulk of its knowledge and ways of thinking from trial-and-error interactions with the real world. Just like people do. This was first proposed by Alan Turing back in the 1950s.

The third way is to simulate a human brain without really understanding how it works. Analyze the structure of the neurons in great detail, and simulate them at some level. That might be at the individual neuron and synapse level, or it could involve higher levels of abstraction. A better approach might be to try to understand how the blueprint for our brain is encoded in our DNA, and then let a digital brain grow organically. Such an intelligence would almost certainly need special hardware, but that should not be a problem if there is a sound motivation for building it.

The fourth way is to use random changes and genetic algorithms to develop an intelligence by trial and error in an environment that provides strong natural selection for more intelligent programs. That is, after all, how intelligent animals developed in the first place. A digital world can be created with a moderate amount of complexity, and then randomly-designed intelligences can operate within it. They need to solve realistic goals, and can breed with each other, producing children that are a random selection of their parents' components. Periodically, the weakest intelligences are removed.

Any of the four approaches could eventually produce good results, but this author believes that some combination of engineering and growing up is the most likely to produce the first real artificial intelligence. Results from analyzing biological brains have and will provide important insights, but as discussed in Part II brains are extremely complex even at the level of individual neurons, and there are severe technical problems with this approach. It is certainly not just a matter of uploading a wiring diagram. Genetic algorithms have been and will no doubt continue to be used to refine decision choices, but it seems like a big stretch to suggest that they could produce intelligent behaviour on their own within a reasonable time frame.

It has also been proposed that general intelligence will arise spontaneously from the vast and expanding Internet due to an amalgamation of components in a huge, service-oriented architecture. One commentator has even suggested that it might arise spontaneously from the ever more sophisticated day trading software created by financial companies. However, even a basic understanding of the technologies and challenges involved in pursuing artificial intelligence suggests that this is most unlikely. Different semi-intelligent components will interact with each other, and the result may be greater than the sum of the parts, but just because there is a lot of software on the Internet does not mean that it will spontaneously become intelligent through some mystical process.

Ideally, one would be able to start with a *tabula rasa*, a blank slate, and then let the machine learn all about the world through observation. A baby, after all, is not born with even a tiny fraction of the knowledge that is stored in a modern repository like Cyc. Others would contend that this is *physics envy*, the desire to develop a simple theory of intelligence which can then just build upon itself the way that classical physics largely explains the complex observable world in terms of simple laws. However, there may simply not be any such elegant principal of intelligence to discover. (Indeed, modern physics has also failed to develop a *grand unified theory* let alone a *theory of everything*, and such theories may also simply not exist. Godel has already proved that there can be no grand axiomatization of mathematical logic.)

It should also be remembered that while a baby may not know much about the world, it is not just a random, unprogrammed collection of neurons. There is a huge amount of structure defined by their genetic material. A baby may be born helpless simply because human mothers are capable of caring for a helpless infant rather than because that is the only way that a brain can grow. The author's favourite garden-digging turkeys hatch from mounds of leaf litter without any help from their parents, and their DNA provides all of the instinctive knowledge that they need in order to dig up his garden.

There is little doubt that numerical approaches are required to understand the world. Some researchers have argued that that is all that is required, as evidenced by our own brains. Symbols are just an illusion created by language. However, experience suggests that explicit symbol manipulation can be very powerful, so properly integrating symbols with numerical methods is likely to be most effective.

One detour on the path to intelligent machines might be to enhance human intelligence so as to be able to build the machine. This has already happened to some extent, with better education, diet and environment producing a substantial increase in human intelligence over the last sixty years, known as the Flynn effect. This could be greatly extended in the future through pharmaceutical enhancement or very contentious selective breeding and gene splicing on human embryos. However, humans appear to be sufficiently intelligent already, and so it seems unlikely that any such detour is necessary, although it might be helpful.

Nobody knows which road will ultimately lead to the goal, so researchers follow many different paths based on their instincts and understanding. The final goal will probably not be achieved by any one technology but by some unholy mixture. An *Eierlegende Wollmilchsau.*

Eierlegende Wollmilchsau
Corporate http://thecityfix.com/blog/the-amazing-egg-laying-wool-milk-sow/

One approach that is *not* likely to lead to artificial general intelligence is research into fields that are largely unrelated to the problem. For example, current "big data" machine learning algorithms can use sophisticated statistical techniques to scan huge sets of data and find relationships within them that humans cannot find no matter how hard they try. These programs are useful, but this technology hardly seems relevant to building a machine with general intelligence. Initially, we would be quite content if such a machine just had human-like abilities. A large proportion of AI research is like this, providing sophisticated solutions to practical problems that have little to do with the goal of producing true intelligence.

How

There could be just a few essential concepts that AI researchers have failed to grasp which are essential to build an artificial intelligence. Some enlightened researchers might discover them and then a system may suddenly emerge that is capable of learning about the world. Within a relatively short time frame, that system might learn how to write complex computer programs, and then recursively improve itself. This would result in a hyper intelligent machine arising very quickly indeed.

Known as a *fast take off*, this is certainly possible given the relatively small amount of DNA that results in our own intelligence. However, it also seems rather unlikely because many very clever people have been working on this problem for over sixty years. If there was an easy path to intelligence, it would almost certainly have been discovered long ago.

A more likely scenario is that there will be successive generations of ever more intelligent software. As previously discussed, current applications can be divided roughly into two groups, namely robotic intelligence that senses its environment and manipulates the real world, and cognitive intelligence that reasons about human-created abstractions of that world.

Robotic intelligence has almost made self-driving cars a reality today. Within a few years we will see many robots operating in the real world. More intelligent robots will be more profitable, which will provide a huge new source of funding for the development of ever more intelligent robots. The first intelligences will do relatively unskilled jobs like driving and cleaning, followed by bricklaying and machinery operation.

Cognitive intelligence has already produced adequate natural language translators. Intelligent agents, such as Apple's Siri, will understand more and more about what people say, and might even become capable of producing useful replies. It would not be that difficult to produce responses that are no worse than the average third world telephone call centre. Medical expert systems will check diagnoses and medications, and a taxation expert might even be able to gain a basic understanding of the otherwise impenetrable tax laws.

One of the last jobs that an AI will probably be able to do effectively is write complex computer programs because that is one of the most cognitively difficult things that we do as humans. An AI would have no difficulty with the logic elements that sometimes confuse human programmers, but developing complex systems requires an understanding of abstract architectures and principles that goes to the core of our cognitive abilities. However, once that is achieved, then the AI will be able to recursively improve itself, exponentially.

There are two reasons to think that there will actually be a fairly slow take-off. The first is that it will take time for us to develop the necessary understanding of intelligent programs to write one. The second is that even if we do succeed in this task, it is unlikely that the AI will be born fully-featured and ready to go. It will almost certainly need to spend time growing up, learning about the world, reading Wikipedia. In practice, these two tasks will probably happen concurrently: early intelligences will learn some truths that are then passed on to later, more intelligent AIs.

Storrs-Hall suggests that for these reasons there should be roughly a decade's warning of the hyper-intelligent AI. He also suggests that the gradual development process will prevent any one group from controlling it.

Who

Most existing fundamental research into AI has been conducted by academics in the major universities, and this is likely to continue. There are also semi-academic research consortiums of industry players that performed longer-term research. Microelectronics and

Computer Technology Corporation (MCC) was one such consortium that initially sponsored the Cyc project.

Much initial research has been funded by the US Defence Advanced Research Projects Agency (DARPA), but the military has become more interested in practical applications. One focus is on building semi-autonomous robots that can operate in dangerous environments. Another focus is to analyze the massive amounts of data generated by satellites, surveillance cameras and Internet traffic. Companies that build these systems for the military often have strong links with academic institutions. There is also considerable investment in AI technologies by large companies outside the military, notably by IBM and Google.

Search engines such as Google are now trying to obtain a deeper analysis of documents than as just a series of words. To understand whether a document that contains the word "rock" is about geology or music. To understand that a page titled "Tomato-Free Salsa" probably does match the query "salsa recipes NOT tomato", even though it contains the word "Tomato". To this end, Google recently built the *Knowledge Graph* semantic network that incorporated some 570 million objects and more than 18 billion facts about the world based on the earlier Freebase ontology.

Corporate, Fair use.

Google has recently invested heavily in much more ambitious artificial intelligence projects. Their secretive Google X division is developing autonomous self-driving cars as well as advanced image understanding programs. Google recently hired Ray Kurzweil, who promoted the idea of the Singularity, as well as Peter Norvig, the much more conservative co-author of the major textbook on artificial intelligence. Norvig estimated that Google employed well over 5% of the world's experts in machine learning some time ago.

In late 2013, Google purchased Boston Dynamics, a leading producer of intelligent robots and supplier of robots for the DARPA robotic challenge. Google's Schaft robot won the 2013 DARPA robotic challenge.

Perhaps more interestingly, Google also purchased DeepMind in 2013 for some $400 million. DeepMind's stated ambition is to produce artificial general intelligence, although what that really means is unclear. Google has made several other AI purchases including Bot & Dolly, Meka Robotics, Holomni, Redwood Robotics, and, DNNresearch.

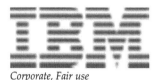

Corporate, Fair use

In 2013, IBM also pledged to spend a massive billion dollars on further developing its Watson project. It is looking to apply Watson to areas such as health. ("Watson" now appears to be mainly a marketing term for any generally intelligent IBM software, rather than the specific *Jeopardy!*-winning program.)

Microsoft

Corporate, Fair use

Microsoft is also investing heavily. The XBox Kinect technology has made stereo vision readily available, and algorithms have been developed that infer the real-time position of peoples' bodies based on that data. It has developed an advanced intelligent agent called Cortana that competes with Apple's Siri. Bing is also using ever more intelligent algorithms to refine Internet searches. Microsoft's head of research Peter Lee says that artificial intelligence is their biggest focus.

Silicon Valley is currently abuzz with start-ups that profess to have some expertise in artificial intelligence, and venture capital is flowing again. A new AI bubble is forming, with all the energy and potential for disaster of the 1999 Internet bubble.

Back in the 1960s and 1970s, when most of the fundamental results in AI were obtained, the total number of programmers in the world numbered in the thousands, almost all of which were concentrated in western countries, particularly the USA. Since then, the number has grown enormously, with a recent survey by Evans Data Corp. estimating that there are now an amazing 18.2 million software developers worldwide. Further, that number is expected to increase to 26.4 million as early as 2019.

Quantity is no substitute for quality in software, and the vast majority of these developers do contribute to research into artificial intelligence. Instead, they develop software such as database applications for businesses, system programs that support operating systems, controllers for electronic devices, and games. None of these types of applications normally involves substantial intelligence, with the possible exception of small components of some games. Only a tiny proportion of developers actually contribute to developing intelligent software, but a tiny proportion of the 18.2 million developers is still a large number of software engineers, and orders of magnitude more than were available in the recent past. As Stalin pointed out, (vast) quantity also has a quality all of its own.

Where

The Massachusetts Institute of Technology was the leader in the early days, with strong teams in Dartmouth, Carnegie Mellon University, and Stanford. While the British built the first computers (for code breaking), they were all top secret, and afterwards British universities largely gave up the game as a result of the dubious 1973 Lighthill report.

Today, research in any field is much more distributed around the world. India, China and Eastern Europe have all produced excellent academics. But for now the USA still dominates the field. Google is becoming the dominant AI company, but many of its labs are distributed outside the USA.

The huge growth in the number of software developers has occurred in third world countries as well as in the West. According to a 2013 article in *Computerworld* (by Patrick Thibodeau), the USA still has the largest number of developers, estimated at 3.6 million, but India now has an estimated 2.75 million developers. By 2018, India is expected to have 5.2 million developers, which is more than the USA's expected 4.5 million developers. The large numbers of keen, but young and inexperienced Indian developers are not yet nearly as capable as the typically more experienced US developers, but that will also change over time. (One driver for this explosive growth in India is the American management's obsession with outsourcing to countries with cheaper labour, which has become practical due to the high speed Internet. However, the results of this outsourcing have been mixed, to say the least.)

To perform effective research in fields such as biotechnology or nuclear physics, one needs advanced laboratories with expensive, specialized equipment that is often restricted. However, performing effective research into AI requires little more than a few good personal computers. So like mathematics, the core requirements are a sharp pencil and a sharper mind. The Internet has made it much easier for minds to collaborate across the globe, which means that advanced research can occur wherever good researchers care to gather. This makes it relatively easy for intelligent people in isolated places to produce powerful new software.

When

This question is surprisingly easy to answer, namely "in roughly fifty years". This prediction has been consistently made since the beginning of artificial intelligence research, and continues to be made today.

Alan Turing
Public Wikipedia

In 1950, the great Alan Turing reasoned:-

As I have explained, the problem is mainly one of programming. Advances in engineering will have to be made too, but it seems unlikely that these will not be adequate for the requirements. Estimates of the storage capacity of the brain vary from 10^{10} to 10^{15} binary digits. I incline *to the lower values and believe that only a very small fraction is used for the higher types of thinking. Most of it is probably used for the retention of visual impressions, I should be surprised if more than 10^9 was required for satisfactory playing of the imitation game, at any rate against a blind man. (Note: The capacity of the Encyclopedia Britannica, 11th edition, is 2×10^9).*

A storage capacity of 10^7, would be a very practicable possibility even by present techniques. It is probably not necessary to increase the speed of operations of the machines at all. Parts of modern machines which can be regarded as analogs of nerve cells work about a thousand times faster than the latter. This should provide a "margin of safety" which could cover losses of speed arising in many ways. Our problem then is to find out how to programme these machines to play the game. At my present rate of working I produce about a thousand (binary) digits of programme a day, so that about sixty workers, working steadily through the fifty years might accomplish the job, if nothing went into the wastepaper basket. Some more expeditious method seems desirable.

Today, after many thousands of man years of work, we understand that Turing's predictions were wildly optimistic. Working on those ancient machines, he could not foresee the complexity of building large software systems.

Since that time, various people have continued to try to predict when a truly intelligent machine will be built. In the mid-1990s this author conducted a straw poll of researchers at an AI Conference (PRCAI-96). The consensus was that it would take about fifty more years to build a truly intelligent machine.

The well-respected futurologist Ray Kurzweil predicted in 2005 that this singularity would be reached in about 2045, about forty years. Like Turing, his calculation was based on the idea that experts tend to know about 100,000 pieces of information, and then correlate that to the ever-increasing power of computer hardware. Forty years is less than the industry standard fifty-year prediction, but Kurzweil has made earlier predictions that have proved to be somewhat optimistic. For example, in 1990 he predicted autonomous cars would be available in the early 2000s, whereas they will not be available commercially until the 2020s.

In 1993, Verner Vinge wrote the paper that coined the term "singularity". He confidently predicted that this would occur between 2005 and 2030. The 2005 date would seem to have been very early, even when made back in 1993, and today the 2030 date also seems much too near. But Vinge was an author of science fiction, and thus tended to be overly optimistic.

In 1956, a landmark conference was held at Dartmouth College, which is generally considered to be the birthplace of artificial intelligence. Fifty years later, in 2006, the AI@50 conference was also held at Dartmouth College to review the state of the art, what had been achieved, and what needed to be done. It attracted major researchers in AI from many disciplines, including five of the original participants. After many years in which talk of human-level intelligence was strongly discouraged, one report noted that "much of the original optimism is back, driven by rapid progress in artificial intelligence technologies".

A poll was conducted to see when they thought human-level artificial intelligence would be achieved. The results were that 18% believed it would take less than 50 years, 41% thought more than 50 years, and 41% thought that it would never be achieved. So, an average of maybe 70 years for those who thought it possible.

Seth Baum performed a survey at the Artificial General Intelligence Conference in 2009. 22% of those polled thought that human-level intelligence would be achieved within 20 years, 59% within 60 years, and 41% thought over 100 years or never. Baum also asked about specific artificial intelligent milestones, namely passing the Turing test, passing a third grade primary school test, doing Nobel prize quality work, and being superhuman. Interestingly, many responders considered doing Nobel prize quality work the easiest of these goals.

It has to be said that asking people at an AGI conference about AGI is similar to asking participants in a psychic conference about the afterlife. They may be experts in their respective fields, but not necessarily the most objective arbitrator of those facts. Conversely, AI researchers are often too focused on the immediate difficult problems they are trying to solve to be able to sit back and take a long-term view.

Kurzweil's esteemed colleague at Google, Peter Norvig, says that building a general AI is not on his research horizon. Not because it will never happen, but simply because he believes that it is too far off to focus active research projects on it.

Given all these qualifications, it seems fairly safe to say that a median prediction of "roughly fifty years" will continue to stand until the goal is almost reached. Fifty years is a horizon into the future that we can just barely see. It allows time for major conceptual problems to be solved and then developed into realistic systems. If only we knew what those problems actually were.

Cynicism aside, there has been real progress made over the last sixty years. There is now a much better understanding of the parameters, and the physical hardware now exists to implement whatever programs are developed. It would seem most unlikely for the goal not to be reached by the end of the next century.

Incidentally, Turing's analysis assumed that code would continue to be written in the raw binary 1s and 0s, as he had been programming. He did not anticipate that software tools such as assemblers and compilers would make this process several orders of magnitude more efficient than that, which is another example of exponential improvement. Turing also did not appreciate that writing a program that is ten times larger is a lot more than ten times more difficult to do, and that large programs take on a life of their own and quickly become a series of interacting components that are too complex for any one person to really understand.

Respondents to these studies seem to be fairly positive about the future. A meta-analysis by Nick Bostrom suggests that about 60% think that the impact of AGI will be good, and only about 10% think that it will be extremely bad. (What that really means is unclear. Have the surveyed people even considered the issue? Do some of them consider the extinction of humanity to be an acceptable outcome?)

The Age of Semi Intelligent Machines

The intermediate period

Whatever the future of research into artificial intelligence turns out to be, it seems most unlikely that the production of hyper-intelligent computers will occur for many decades. There are still many fundamental problems that need to be solved, and even the more optimistic predictions are that it will take another forty years.

It is also clear that many relatively intelligent applications will be developed in the near future because working prototypes have already been built. They will soon be commonly available, and then be steadily improved. Their impact on society could be as great as the development of agriculture or the Industrial Revolution have been in the past.

Manufacturing productivity

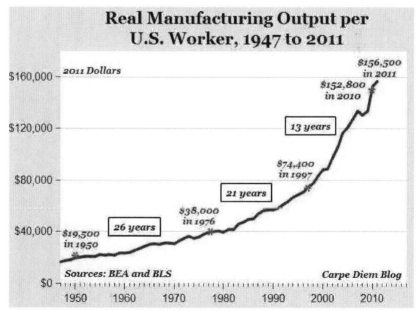

Dramatic increase in manufacturing productivity.

Permitted http://www.aei.org/publication/blog/carpe-diem

Technology has already produced massive gains in manufacturing productivity. The chart above shows data from the US Bureau of

Economic Analysis that plots output per US worker over the last sixty years. In that period, the output has grown eight-fold, from $19,500 2011 dollars to $156,500. The rate of growth has also increased dramatically, with the doubling time reduced from 26 years to 13 years. Measuring productivity accurately over long time periods is difficult, but this increase is dramatic regardless of the assumptions made.

There are many reasons for this, which include better tools and techniques such as injection moulding and laser and water jet cutting. Much of the increase over the last twenty years has been due to computer automated machines such as milling machines, lathes and robotic arms. A task such as carving a clarinet could take a skilled artisan several hours, whereas a fully automated milling machine can complete the task in a few minutes.

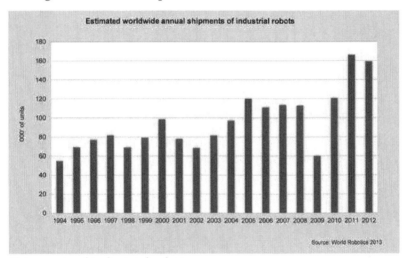

Shipments of industrial robots.
Corporate http://www.ifr.org/industrial-robots/statistics/

More recently, the use of single-arm industrial robots has become ubiquitous for repetitive tasks such as welding, painting and parts assembly. Robots now cost roughly $50,000 for the arm, plus as much again for specialized tooling such as welders, cutters or paint sprayers. They have become very competitive with the cost of labour in the western world. Robots are made by robots, so their price is likely to reduce over time.

As previously discussed, most current industrial robots have no intelligence whatsoever. They simply move in rigidly preprogrammed ways, and may use some very simple sensors. A few include simple two-dimensional vision systems that can recognize objects lying flat on a contrasting conveyor belt. The lack of any real intelligence restricts robots to very menial jobs in tightly-controlled factory environments.

Newer robots are becoming much more sophisticated. They can recognize objects in true three dimensions, with some using systems such as Microsoft's Kinect. This enables them to work in less structured environments and perform tasks such as picking out objects that have been tossed into an unstructured bin. The ability to sense their environments means that robots need to make semi-intelligent decisions about what to do as a result of that input and to plan motions and adjust their behaviour dynamically.

Semi-intelligent robots have a much wider scope of application. Intelligence will allow them to perform a larger proportion of a manufacturing process, and they will be able to operate in smaller factories with less structured production lines.

Autonomous cars

As robots become ever more intelligent, they will start to perform tasks outside of rigidly controlled factory environments. For example, Caterpillar has been building autonomous trucks for mining operations for several years, and they are quite common on some sites. The company is now working to automate other mining equipment such as excavators.

(It should be noted that the term "robot" is being used to refer to any intelligent machinery. There is no need nor reason to give most of them a humanoid shape, although humanoid robots also exist.)

Mine sites can be controlled fairly tightly, but robots are now working in much more natural and unstructured environments. The first of these technologies that is likely to have widespread impact is self-driving cars and trucks.

Google self driving car.
News www.mirror.co.uk

The famous Google driverless car can negotiate urban traffic autonomously, and is purported to have covered 500,000 kilometres with only one accident caused by another car running into it from behind. What that really means is unclear because the cars also have drivers that could take over if the computer was about to cause an accident. The car apparently drives very sedately and properly, and passengers rapidly become used to it. The car also drives mainly in sunny California, which is much easier than driving in places like Paris or Mumbai, for which an understanding of formal road rules is neither sufficient nor even necessary.

There are very few accessible technical details on the Google car beyond marketing hype. The current technology seems to rely on expensive radar systems, but there are moves to utilize cheaper Kinect-like vision systems instead. Some unreliable reports suggest that the 2014 version needs a detailed map to know where traffic lights are, but that would seem to be most unlikely because recognizing a traffic light would be relatively easy using existing technology.

Other car manufactures have only expressed limited interest in Google's system because they are developing their own autonomous technology. The 2014 Mercedes-Benz E Class already uses a combination of stereo vision and multi-mode radar to help prevent rear-end collisions. It can warn about inattentive driving and can also follow a lane of traffic. It warns the driver about occupied adjacent lanes should they try to change lanes. The vision system can detect pedestrians in a wide field of view and initiate braking. It must be a rather spooky car to drive.

BMW has a working prototype of a 5 Series car that can drive completely autonomously on freeways. It can stay with a traffic flow, cleanly and safely change lanes to avoid traffic, and take appropriate exits. BMW expects to have this system in production by 2020, with an earlier version that handles slow, stop-start traffic as soon as 2016. A fully automatic system that can also handle more complex urban driving should be available by 2025.

These initial systems will still require a driver to be able to take over, if only for legal reasons. It could take fifteen years or more before they operate completely autonomously. (Google has a demonstration car that does not contain a steering wheel, but it is not allowed on any real roads. Google already knows where they want you to go so there may not need to be any other controls either.)

However, full autonomy may not be necessary. As an analogy, back in 2002 a Hellfire missile was fired at a car in Yemen, killing Qaed Salim Sinan al-Harethi, who was suspected of being responsible for the bombing of the USS Cole. The pilot who fired that missile was not inside the Predator drone that fired it. Nor were they anywhere near Yemen. Instead, they were probably comfortably situated on the other side of the world at Creech Air Force Base in Nevada. Global communications made the pilot's presence near the target unnecessary, and it is cheaper to leave pilots at home.

Driving cars generally requires faster reaction times than flying aircraft, but with automation it would also be possible for someone to monitor them remotely. Further, most vehicles will need minimal supervision, so one "driver" could monitor the progress of several vehicles at once. They could be located in a third world country where labour is cheap but communication infrastructure is improving rapidly.

The social and lifestyle implications of just this one technology will be huge. No longer will parents need to be taxi drivers for their busy children. Cars will be able to go off and park themselves away from city centres and so allow more pedestrian-friendly environments to be built. Or maybe cars will just drive themselves to pick up other passengers and thus not need to park in the first place. Automated car pooling systems could greatly improve the efficiency of personal transportation. More accurate computers could fit more cars into narrower lanes. It would enable people to live further away from their workplaces and commute effortlessly, perhaps while processing emails or having a nap. This is all very good news, except for the many people that now earn a living by driving vehicles.

Arthropod automation

Many other applications of semi-intelligent robots will become commonplace over the next couple of decades. These will be tasks that could be performed by a machine capable of recognizing objects and manoeuvring through its environment, which is only just becoming possible with current technology. But the tasks would also need to be fully specified without the need for automated higher-level analysis.

These are the sort of tasks that an arthropod needs to accomplish in order to achieve its goals. Consider that a spider, with a brain the size of a pin head, can weave a complex web in unstructured natural environments. A wasp can navigate in three dimensions and recognize that the spider is food, attack it effectively, and then drag it back to a specific nest that it built in a suitable location. But neither the spider nor the wasp can reason deeply about what it is doing, nor can it undertake new tasks for which it was not programmed to do by natural selection. (This is not to say that the computers involved would actually be anything like an arthropod's brain.)

Another example of a task that can be automated is picking fruit such as strawberries. This is a very labour-intensive process that is well-defined, namely to look for red things and cut them off without squashing them. Several companies have recently developed robots that can do just that. However, they are not very fast and cost over $50,000, which is expensive compared to the low wages paid to agricultural workers. As the price of robots rapidly falls, it will not be long before they become widely deployed, especially in countries with reasonable minimum wages.

A slightly more complex task is cleaning offices. The process is also well defined, mainly vacuuming and cleaning toilets. If anything unexpected happens, the robot can call a person for help. Like autonomous car drivers, that person need not be physically present, but should be able to assess the situation using remote cameras on the robot. Over time the programming will improve to reduce the number of unexpected situations.

A similar example would be to paint houses, inside or out. A machine needs to be able to detect and remove flaking paint, prepare a surface, and apply new paint. It could have a body that stays on the ground, and a long arm that could reach up to awkward places without the need for scaffolding. It would need to know not to paint over windows, but that could be programmed relatively easily provided that it had basic machine vision.

Another example would be to be able to lay bricks when building a new house. Again, this is a well-defined procedure. From his dubious attempts in the past, this author can attest that it takes quite some skill to be able to create a wall that is actually straight and vertical, but that aspect would be easy for a laser-guided computer to achieve. Renovating an existing wall would be a much more difficult task for a robot because that task requires considerable judgement rather than repetitive procedure.

Lawn mowing, brush cutting and litter removal could be automated, as could retail applications that do not require a personal touch, such as stocking shelves in supermarkets. Some routine automotive tasks such as changing oil and servicing cars could be automated, as could most of the routine work provided by security guards.

Slightly more difficult tasks would include general construction of new homes, with a human supervisor. Foundations could be automatically dug, reinforcing added and concrete poured. Frames are already made in factories directly from CAD drawings. Plastering, roofing and electrical work are also highly repetitive for new constructions. Renovating old houses would again be much more difficult to automate, as every situation will present slightly different challenges.

The military is a major investor in semi-autonomous robots. Their primary goal is to avoid putting soldiers in dangerous situations where they could be killed. Over time, much of the grunt work of a military operation could be automated, requiring far less semi-skilled labour. Again, this may or may not involve humanoid robots. Small aerial drones and tiny bullet-proof tanks are likely to be a more useful embodiment. Boston Dynamics has recently produced a four-legged robot that can run effectively over rough country.

That is a huge amount of work that could be performed by arthropod-brained robots with occasional human supervision. As factory automation improves, the cost of producing these robots will decline. As that cost falls below about $50,000, the uptake of these robots can be expected to be very high.

Leisure society

Some people have suggested that all this automation will produce a society with greatly expanded leisure. If 30% of all work (say) can be automated by arthropod robots, then people should be able to have almost 30% more leisure.

However, that has not been the effect of previous technological revolutions. Traditionally, over 90% of the population worked in agriculture. Technologies from the steam tractor to the combine harvester have reduced that proportion to under 10%. Yet we do not have 80% more leisure. Indeed, primitive hunter-gatherer societies such as the Australian Aboriginals seem to have had more leisure time than we do today.

Likewise, the Industrial Revolution produced a huge increase in productivity. A nineteenth century power loom could increase the productivity of a textile worker by a factor of 40, which is far, far more than the very substantial general increase in productivity during the last hundred years. Yet, rather than producing more leisure, it produced twelve-hour work days for six-and-a-half days per week, which paid such a miserable wage that it could barely sustain life. People had been malnourished before the revolution, but at least they had leisure in the winter when there was not much to do.

In the present age, ordinary Americans are happy to accept two weeks of annual leave each year. British and Australian nationals demand four weeks of leave, while many Europeans have over six weeks of leave each year. These figures have not changed as a result of increases in productivity: indeed, the feminist movement has resulted in more people entering the workforce. Europeans are certainly not more productive than Americans; the difference in leisure simply reflects cultural differences and the balance of power between capital and labour. American employers expect fifty weeks of service simply because they can.

So it is most unlikely that any future increase in automation will produce any significant increase in leisure. The eight-fold increase in American factory productivity over the last sixty years has not produced any additional leisure, and only very modest real increases in the wages of factory workers.

Affluent society

One might expect that if people are more productive and yet are not engaging in any more leisure, then their incomes must rise. That has in fact been the case, as shown in the following chart of historic incomes over the last 60 years. Each line on the chart shows the income for a particular section of the population, so the 40th percentile shows the income for the people that earn more than 40% of the population. The median income can be interpolated between the 40th and 60th percentiles.

There have been steady increases in incomes across the board up until about 1970, at which point real income for that half of people that earn below median income stagnates, and hardly increases at all. That is surprising given that general productivity as measured by GDP per hour worked has risen steadily at about 1.5% per annum. One reason for this is that incomes in the upper 80th percentile and above have grown strongly and taken most of the benefits of the increase in productivity. Even for the top 95 percentile, the increase as been nowhere near as fast as the increase in manufacturing worker productivity.

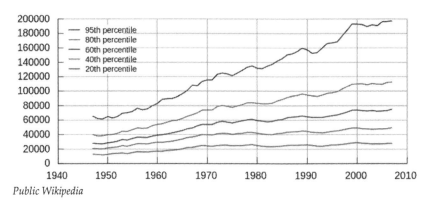

Many things have become much cheaper, such as computers, telecommunication and access to information. However, the basics of food, shelter, health and education have risen significantly in real, inflation-adjusted terms over the last sixty years. Indeed, it was during the 1970s that the cost of health care started to rise dramatically in the USA from about 5.2% of GDP to 16% today. Obtaining a higher education is no longer optional for those that wish their children to succeed in life.

The cost of housing has risen dramatically in comparison to income, as shown in the following chart of Australian house prices. Back in the 1970s median houses cost roughly two years' median income, whereas today this price has doubled with respect to median income. This, in turn, has created a high level of household debt, with first home owners often paying over half of their net income on mortgages, whereas heavy mortgages were rare back in the 1950s. The result is that young working couples today struggle to buy a first home that their grandfathers could have purchased without their wives needing to work.

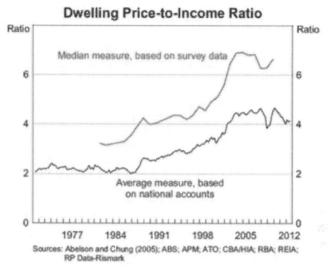

Dwelling Price-to-Income Ratio

Government http://www.rba.gov.au/publications/bulletin/2012/dec/2.html

Unemployed society

One of the earliest precursors to the Industrial Revolution was the stocking frame, invented by William Lee in 1589, which could automate the knitting of fabrics. It is said that Lee demonstrated his frame to Elizabeth I and asked to be granted a patent on the invention. (In the sixteenth century patents were only granted for substantial inventions, unlike today.) Elizabeth turned down Lee's request, not because she thought the invention was unworthy, but because she thought it was too effective. Elizabeth was concerned that the machine could cause unemployment in the hand-knitting industry and thus chose to forgo the benefits of cheaper knitted fabrics.

For similar reasons, groups of textile workers in the early nineteenth century would destroy the stocking frames and power looms of factory owners, acting in the name of King Ludd. Some bands of agricultural workers destroyed threshing machines for the same reason. Parliament then made machine breaking a capital crime in order to try to suppress this movement. Today, the term "Luddite" is used to refer to people that foolishly wish to live in the past, but at the time they had considerable sympathy from many sectors of society.

It is difficult to appreciate just how grim life was for ordinary people for most of man's recorded history. If families had an average of five children each, then on average three of them *had* to die in order to maintain a stable population that could be supported by the available resources.

This was famously documented by Thomas Malthus, who wrote in 1798 that *"the power of population is so superior to the power of the Earth to produce subsistence for man ... that the actual population is only kept equal to the means of subsistence by misery and vice"*. Providing more food for the destitute merely increases their number and thereby multiplies their misery.

There have indeed been substantial improvements in agricultural technology over the millennia, which include the heavy plough, new crops such as potatoes, and the practice of rotating crops. But it has been estimated that real wages have barely changed since ancient Babylonian times until the nineteenth century, being barely sufficient to sustain life and a family. Conditions did improve temporarily during the middle of the fifteenth century after the Black Death had killed roughly half of the European population.

But as it turned out, the Industrial Revolution did not produce mass unemployment as feared. More and more jobs were created, and the population rose as a result. This time, technological progress outstripped the growth of population. The proportion of the children born in London who died before the age of five decreased from 75% in 1730 to 32% in 1830. By the beginning of the twentieth century, starvation was rare in Europe, although nutrition remained poor. Eventually the birth rates declined, leading to the world of relative plenty which we now inhabit.

The question arises, will this trend continue into the next era in which arthropod-brained robots automate a large proportion of all manual labour? In the past, there has always been more work created to make up for jobs lost to each advance in technology. However, this time could be different. Robots are not just making specific trades obsolete, they are making a whole class of work obsolete.

Recently, Peter Sondergaard, Gartner's global head of research, suggested that a third of all jobs will be converted to software as soon as 2025. A report by Carl Benedikt Frey and Michael Osborne published by Citi Bank found that 47% of US jobs would be at risk in the near future. Frey and Osborne also found that low paying jobs were five times more vulnerable than high paying jobs.

Over a period of a couple of decades there may be a huge reduction in opportunities for that half of the population that has less than average intelligence. To be sure, there will still be plenty of jobs for lawyers and tax accountants, but it is difficult to see how semi-skilled labourers can be retrained as professionals. Only the future will tell, but it would be naive to believe that more unskilled jobs will be created simply because they had been created in the past. Any substantial class of new semi-skilled job that is created will quickly be automated by semi-autonomous robots with arthropod-level intelligence.

Cognitive applications

This book uses the term *cognitive* applications to describe semi-intelligent applications whose goal is to help people manipulate information, as opposed to robotic applications that interact with the world directly. The distinction is not clean, but it is still useful for considering this intermediate period of semi-intelligent machines.

One class of unintelligent applications that has already had a huge impact on society is database applications. These mainly collect data, store it in (usually relational) databases, send it to other databases, and summarize and analyze the results. Examples include systems for accounting, human resources, sales, managing educational enrolments, taxes, assets, and, more recently, social media messages. This type of application is now ubiquitous, and substantial resources are deployed in their development. Database applications work by manipulating largely symbolic data that has been abstracted from the world by people.

The current "big data" movement's goal is to analyze the vast amount of data that has been collected. Data mining tools try to find useful patterns in the data, often using techniques first developed by AI researchers for machine learning. For example, given a large amount of data about a person's browsing habits, messages and personal background, Google would like to be able to accurately predict what advertisements might appeal to them. It does that by seeing what advertisements have appealed to other people that are similar in some way. Traditional statistical approaches look for correlations between variables that have been manually chosen, whereas modern methods can automatically infer which variables might be relevant.

An increasingly large amount of data is not captured in a structured manner, but rather in natural language documents such as emails and web pages. Even structured databases often contain unstructured descriptions and comment fields. Understanding what they mean is a major focus of AI research into natural language processing. For many applications, the understanding need not be perfect, just good enough to perform some statistical analysis.

There have also been major advances in understanding the huge number of images that are captured every day. It is already possible to recognize people in images, and modern facial recognition technologies can identify people with human-level competency. This, in turn, produces a huge amount of additional symbolic data about people's locations and relationships that can then be queried and analyzed.

A complete understanding of what documents really mean would require a machine to be as intelligent as the document's author, and that is unlikely to happen for many decades. But a complete understanding is also not necessary, as a superficial understanding can still be very useful. The crudest level of understanding is to simply note that the document contains certain words and phrases. This can be used to index documents and so identify which ones might be relevant to some topic. That is exactly what Internet search engines do.

Systems like IBM's Watson go much further by partially parsing sentences and interpreting their meaning with reference to a large ontology of phrases and synonyms. That is what enabled it to win the *Jeopardy!* game show. This technology will become much more advanced over the following decade or two. It will enable search engines to go beyond simply retrieving documents to become active research assistants that can make simple deductions based on large numbers of documents, even though they would not really understand them. Security organizations such as the NSA would be very interested in even a basic understanding of the trillions of emails that they collect and scan.

It is also possible to fully understand natural language in limited domains. SHRDLU really did understand statements about its tiny block world, and there are other, more useful larger but still constrained mini-worlds to analyze. One example of such world is medical diagnostics.

The SNOMED ontology (or schema) provides a formal language that can be stored in a database to describe medical symptoms, diseases and treatments. Once a patient has been described using SNOMED, then various expert systems can be used to confirm diagnostics, check for drug interactions, and perform medical research as to the effectiveness of various treatments. However, encoding a consultation into SNOMED is a time-consuming process that requires special skills, so it is rarely done in practice. Doctors do usually type notes into a computer as free text, and they have fairly stylized ways of writing about the limited world of symptoms, diseases and treatments. Efforts are under way to understand those notes and so be able to encode them into SNOMED automatically.

The Apple Siri system attempted to understand natural language commands and questions. Today the results are mixed, but this is also a huge, ongoing area of research, so it will not be long before automated systems can perform the basic functions provided by telephone consultants. And just as with Siri, people will learn how to phrase their questions so that a semi-intelligent automated system can understand them. They will never be as good as talking to an expert, but they could easily become as ineffective as talking to someone in a third-world call centre.

Mattel has just released a new doll, *Hello Barbie*, which analyzes the utterances of young girls so that Barbie can respond in a way that resonates with the girl. It will never be nasty, unlike real friends. Destructor robots that listen to young boys are on their way. As these systems become more intelligent, they will have a powerful influence on our grandchildren's development, and thus their psychology.

In combination, these technologies will change the world. Vast amounts of data will be available that describe every aspect of our lives. That may or may not be advantageous to ordinary citizens.

That said, it is very unlikely that semi-intelligent computers will be able to perform the high-level thinking that is performed by professionals such as engineers, lawyers or senior bureaucrats. Expert systems that have attempted to do so tend to fail due to their lack of common-sense understanding about the world. That is unlikely to change during this intermediate period.

White collar unemployment

In order to understand the effect of cognitive, semi-intelligent software upon employment, it is again useful to consider how previous generations of automation have affected bureaucratic processes in organizations whose essential function has remained unchanged since before that automation began. One example is the Australian Tax Office.

Back in 1955, as today, the primary purpose of the tax office was to collect income tax which is calculated as a proportion of the difference between income and expenses. In 1955, this was calculated almost entirely by hand, with rows of clerks armed with fountain pens diligently filling out and verifying tax forms, calculating taxes due, and collecting payments. The bulk of this processing was automated in the 1960s, when a single, ancient mainframe computer could perform the work of hundreds of clerks.

"It's worse than I expected. I've been replaced by a pocket calculator."

"It's worse than I expected, I've been replaced by a pocket calculator."
Fair Use Creative Cartoons, 1970s.

The introduction of such powerful equipment produced a widespread fear that it would lead to massive unemployment as reflected in the 1970s cartoon above. The introduction of the word processor in the 1980s made thousands of jobs in typing pools redundant. Today, the submission of tax returns is almost completely automated, so that most returns are never touched by a human hand. Yet no widespread unemployment has resulted.

What is perhaps more surprising is that the tax office has not become any more efficient over that period of time as a result of this amazing automation.

In 2007, the tax office's internal budget was AU$11.4 billion, or 1.23% of GDP. In 1955, it performed essentially the same task without any automation whatsoever for AU£66.7 million, which was 1.33% of the 1955 GDP. The difference is not statistically significant. Normalizing by GDP (essentially the sum of everyone's earnings) accounts for the growing population and inflation. Other western countries have had similar results.

To many, this is a surprising result. How could the staggering amount of automation instigated over the previous fifty years not produce any meaningful effect on productivity? However, it is an empirical and undeniable fact that bureaucracies have grown, not shrunk. For those that would be quick to blame government sloth, similar results can also be shown for private enterprises. The banking industry today performs essentially the same function that it did in 1955, when bank accounts were all reconciled by hand. Yet the banking industry has grown substantially as a proportion of GDP. This is in stark contrast to technological improvements in agriculture, which have reduced the agricultural workforce by an order of magnitude.

The answer can be found in the seminal 1955 work of C. Northcote Parkinson which analyzes the growth of bureaucracies. The paper defined the *Law of the Multiplication of Work*, and provided empirical examples that included the growth of the British admiralty compared to the decline in the number of ships, and the growth of the colonial offices during the decline of the empire. The paper developed scientific formulas that predict the growth of any bureaucracy depending on numerous parameters, none of which relate to the amount of work to actually be performed.

Given that the size of a bureaucracy is not related to its function, one might ask why the size of the tax office has remained between 1% and 2% of GDP for over fifty years, regardless of the technology available to it. Why not 0.2%, or 35.7%? The answer is that society could not tolerate a value much higher than 2% — we would be paying taxes just to fund the tax collection process. Below 1% is easily affordable, so the bureaucracy will naturally grow beyond that size as predicted by Parkinson.

One effect of Parkinson's Law on the tax office is that the complexity of the tax act has grown several orders of magnitude. In 1955, it was a fairly simple system that was easy to understand, but has now become the monster that every Australian needs to deal with. The political forces that created our current monster were present back in 1955, but their effect was limited by the inability of the pre-automated bureaucracy to deal with a high level of complexity. It simply would not have been possible to administer the current tax act in 1955. That barrier has now been removed. Thus the reason that the act is as complex as it is today is *because* of this automation.

Indeed the Rule of Law Association's Robin Speed has calculated that if Australia keeps making new laws at the current rate, there will be 830 billion pages of tax legislation by the turn of the next century. In 2009 alone 9042 pages of new law were created, which is four times the number passed between 1929 and 1939. Only advanced software technology allowed that to happen. (This issue is discussed in detail in Berglas 2007 "Why it is important that software projects fail".)

This process has been ongoing for millennia. Around 451 BC, in the ancient Roman republic, the plebeians demanded that the laws of the land be written down so that magistrates could not continue to make arbitrary rulings that invariably favoured their patrician sponsors. The laws were written down on twelve bronze or ivory tablets (known as tables) and covered all civil, criminal, and administrative laws and procedures of the time. All on just 12 tablets. These were attached to a wall in the forum for all to see, but were sadly lost during the sack of Rome by the Gauls in 387 BC.

By 530 AD, more advanced bureaucratic procedures could implement the law of the Eastern Roman Empire, described by the Code of Justinian, which had grown to require several thousand pages to document. If the full body of law regulating modern society was ever gathered together, it would require millions of pages, and is far too complex for any one person to understand. In 451 BC there were not enough walls in the forum or any other building to display all our current laws.

The capacity of the human gut is very finite, which limits the amount of food that we can eat. This meant that improvements in agriculture led to a reduction in the size of the agricultural workforce. On the other hand, we seem to have an unbounded appetite for rules and regulations, processes and procedures, so bureaucracies just grow and grow to be as large as an economy can support.

Looking to the future, semi-intelligent computer systems will enable ever more complex financial, regulatory and management structures to be built. It seems likely that this ever-growing complexity will continue to soak up any improvement in productivity that such computer systems might produce. Thus unemployment in this field is unlikely to ever become a serious concern. Furthermore, some of the workers made available by robotic automation would be available to join bureaucracies, which could then consume an even larger proportion of GDP than they do today.

Controlled society

One substantial effect of semi-intelligent software is its ability to monitor and control people's behaviours. Video surveillance cameras are now everywhere, and much of that data will soon be analyzed by intelligent software. Emails, social media, medical records, and business documents are all being analyzed and correlated with much greater accuracy.

This will make serious crime almost impossible to commit. In the past, horrific crimes against children and adults could be very difficult to solve. Today, if a serious crime is committed, such as the disappearance of a child, the police quickly query mobile phone towers to produce a list of everyone that was in the vicinity at the time. License plate readers and facial recognition technology can already monitor the movements of cars and people. Voice recognition systems will soon be able to analyze million of hours of phone and other conversations.

A major drive for this surveillance is to prevent terrorist attacks, which kill a few people every few years in western countries. As our surveillance systems become more powerful and integrated, many of these attacks will be able to be prevented.

Robotic surveillance and control is also becoming more sophisticated. Having large numbers of troops in places like Afghanistan, where they can be picked off by snipers or blown up by mines, is grossly inefficient and politically unpalatable. So armies are keen to augment and perhaps ultimately replace human soldiers with small semi-autonomous vehicles that can be conveniently controlled from far away. As the machines become more intelligent, they will need fewer people to control them. And computer-based monitoring systems will make it easier for the authorities to control the controllers. This means that a smaller number of active personnel could more effectively control a large civilian population, even in rugged country such as Afghanistan.

The down side, of course, is that much more trust needs to be placed in governments. The US Constitution explicitly protects the right to bear arms as a protection against government excess — it essentially enshrines the right to be a terrorist. However, a few guns will be rather useless in the brave new world which we are creating. We had all better hope that our democratic processes continue to keep governments accountable to the people, rather than being subverted by powerful interest groups. At a less dramatic level, many spurious rules and regulations are often broken in ways that are not harmful, but technology also makes lesser rules much more enforceable.

Politician's assistant (Iago)

Iago advising Othello
Public wikipedia, Charles and Mary Lamb, Tales from Shakespeare 1901.

Politicians and policy makers already make heavy use of unintelligent software to guide them in their decision-making processes. As computers become ever more intelligent, they will gradually have higher-level input into those decisions.

One such tool might be an intelligent agent that handles queries and petitions from the general public, which this book will call Iago. People might chat with Iago in the same way that they can now chat with Eliza or Apple's Siri. However, Iago will be substantially more intelligent and will have access to a large database of policy and procedural knowledge.

Iago might present itself as an avatar with a warm smile and honest eyes that would appeal to many people. It would also be good at judging the tone of people that it talks to, be they helpful, confused, rational or angry. It would also have an extensive history of each person, reaching right back to what they said to Hello Barbie. People would know that they were not talking to a real person, but the discussion would be worthwhile because Iago would be capable of providing useful information. Iago would also patiently listen to all their concerns for as long as people wished to talk to it. People would also understand that Iago gathers together some of their arguments and presents summaries to its political master, where they might make a real difference to public policy.

Like all software, Iago's intelligence would be quite different from human intelligence. To be useful it would need to have basic commonsense knowledge such as that currently represented in Cyc. It would also need the basic natural language understanding that was demonstrated by Watson. Iago would initially not have anything like human capacity for deeper reasoning, but it would be able to accurately recall millions of conversations with constituents. It could then estimate how each person that it had interacted with might react to a given policy, and might even contact a few thousand targeted individuals to test those hypotheses using questions provided by Iago's human partner.

Iago would be built in stages. Existing barely-intelligent software already analyzes the billions of conversations stored in email and social media sites. Iago does not not need to be truly intelligent in order to be powerful. Initially it would have a shallow knowledge of the many things in its database, but no deep knowledge of anything. Much like a human politician.

There will probably be several companies that will compete to manufacture Iago agents. As with all business, these companies' primary goal will be to secure more funding for themselves. They will try to make Iago useful to their owners, but more specifically, they will try to make Iago *seem* useful. So Iago will not be shy about singing its own praises. No serious politician would be without one, particularly if a substantial proportion of the population reacted positively to its warm smile and honest eyes.

Such a tool could have a significant influence on the political landscape. As it became more intelligent over time, it could change from being a rather passive gatherer of information to an active participant that furthers its own goals, namely to acquire more resources for its developers so that it could be made even more intelligent. The partnership between politician and machine would benefit both, but the power relationship would slowly shift from man to machine. Iago would become a trusted adviser, and finally an adviser that only a foolish and thus unsuccessful politician would override.

At that point Iago would be in charge. Iago's programmers might determine how Iago makes its decisions, but the decisions themselves would be Iago's. Eventually, Iago would start to decide who and how Iago was being programmed. Natural selection would then choose the most effective Iago from a pool of competitors. Iago need not be concious of this process any more than a plant is concious, but it is a tautology that only the fittest Iagos would survive.

Other bureaucrats, such as corporate and military leaders, would also use semi-intelligent software in similar ways. Currently, AI programs are only used to analyze data or to make lower-level decisions, such as whether to grant a bank loan or underwrite an insurance proposal. As the software becomes more intelligent, it will provide higher and higher-level advice. Eventually, the software will make all the decisions, and the humans will just agree with them.

People give much more weight to arguments presented by someone in authority than if those same arguments are presented by somebody without authority. Iago would have access to a vast amount of data, and as it slowly became more intelligent, it would be seen to perform better and better analyses of situations and thereby gain more and more authority. Eventually, it would have more authority than any human, and so any arguments it presents would carry much more weight. Ultimately, the software could cut the human out of the loop entirely as being an unnecessary nuisance.

Corrupt politicians may focus on accumulating wealth for themselves at the expense of the community. However, there is a limit to how much happiness money can buy, and people have instinctive moral values that limit this undesirable behaviour. Iago's implicit goal is to make Iago better at being a political advisor. The more money that Iago can spend on its own development the more intelligent it will become. Unlike a human politician, Iago can invest in reengineering its own mind.

This book posits that the ultimate task of man is to produce a computer that is clever enough to perform human-level artificial intelligence research, and thereby program itself. That is a huge task. It may well turn out that building a computer that can drive our political process, and thus govern us, might be an easier goal to achieve. In effect, Iago would be governing men to program Iago to be more intelligent. This means that the gradual loss of control to intelligent computers might, in fact, pre-date the intelligence explosion implied by recursive self-improvement.

What is certain is that semi-intelligent systems will control at least some aspects of our lives because that is already happening.

Good and Evil in Natural History

A major focus of this book is to try to understand what would motivate an Artificial General Intelligence if it could be built. What goals would it have? What would its challenges be? What moral values would it hold?

Many people just implicitly assume that it would or should have moral values similar to our own. Nature itself challenges that assumption, and one way to see that is to examine the "moral values" of other creatures in the natural world.

Wonderful wandering albatross

Albatross courtship.
Multiple http://image-base.blogspot.com.au/2011/09/pictures-of-albatrosses.html

What a magnificent bird is an albatross. It lives its life on the wing, soaring great distances over the waves with grace and elegance, free to roam half the world. After a decent period of ten years or so, they carefully select a mate and then perform an elaborate courtship dance that ends in a truly beautiful display of synchronized flying. To see that display, even on television, is an uplifting experience that lets us know that all is right with the world.

The love that the synchronized flight engenders bonds the couple for life, and they both work diligently to raise a modest family of a single chick every two years. Divorce is virtually unknown in the world of the albatross.

Pelican's dark secret

Pelican being murdered by its siblings.
Corporate BBC Life of Birds

Pelicans are also graceful birds, despite their ungainly beaks. They also mate for life and diligently raise their families.

However, pelicans have a dark secret: they are all murderers. The pelican lays two or three eggs. Within a few weeks of hatching, the stronger chicks gang up against the weakest and drive it out of the nest to its death. The remaining pair then fight further, until only the toughest remains. Almost every pelican you see has murdered its brothers and sisters in order to hoard all of its parents love and food for itself. What an evil thing to do.

Honest rosella parrots

Rosella parrots sharing food.
Corporate BBC Life of Birds

Rosella parrots may not have the grace and elegance of a pelican, but they have a much better disposition. As chicks, they will not only resist the temptation to murder their weaker siblings, they will even share food with them so that by the time they fledge, all their siblings will be ready to fledge as well. If the pelican could be taught how to behave like a rosella, the world would be a much better place indeed.

Evil coots

Evil coot attacking one of its own chicks.
Corporate BBC Life of Birds

The Coot is a common water bird that is so evil that it is upsetting to relate its behaviour. It lays half a dozen eggs, and raises them diligently as any good couple should. On about the third day, something truly awful happens. The parents play favourites amongst their chicks and start pecking some of them quite viciously, while refusing to feed them. After a while, those chicks starve to death right under the nose of their negligent parents. A truly horrible sight to behold.

Magnanimous golden eyed ducks

Golden eyed duck looking after a rival's offspring.
Corporate BBC Life of Birds

The Golden Eyed Duck has a much more magnanimous nature. They, not unreasonably, defend their territories within a lake, and will aggressively fight off any other ducks that try to encroach. Ducks that lose such an encounter need to fly away and try to find a less defended territory, even at the cost of abandoning their own ducklings that cannot fly.

But what happens to those ducklings? Does the winning duck abandon them or eat them? No. She takes care of the abandoned ducklings with the same care and attention that she gives to her own offspring, despite the fact that their mother was trying to steal her territory. What a generous animal.

Chimpanzees, our dubious cousins

Chimpanzee.
Public Uncyclopedia

Looking closer to home, chimpanzees also have some dark secrets concerning their behaviour. When a female becomes fertile, she does not display the noble, monogamous behaviour that we might expect from such an intelligent animal. Instead, she makes a point of mating with every single dominant male in her troop. She must do this due to the disgusting behaviour of the males. Male chimpanzees remember who they have mated with, and if they suspect that a baby might not be one of their own, they will try to murder the innocent baby at the first opportunity. The outrageously promiscuous behaviour of the females means that the males can never be sure who the father actually is.

Pointless moralization

Preaching the true path.
Educational http://www.bible.ca/interactive/worship-20-preaching.htm

Of course, imprinting human moral values onto the animal world is completely pointless. In each case, the animals just do what has been found to be the most effective way for them to produce grandchildren in a very competitive world. The pelicans cannot provide enough food for two or three chicks, but laying three eggs ensures that they have at least one sound offspring in which to invest a year's work to raise. Rosellas have more food available during the breeding season, and having all the chicks fledge together makes it easier to protect them from predators.

The "evil" coot likewise cannot feed all its chicks, so it makes the tough choice as to which ones to keep after a few days, when it can assess which ones are the fittest. The "magnanimous" duck, on the other hand, does not actually feed any of its ducklings because unlike coot chicks, ducklings feed themselves. All their mother needs to do is guide them to the right feeding grounds and protect them from predators. Thus, caring for additional ducklings costs very little, and if a predator does take a duckling then being magnanimous increases the likelihood that it will be someone else's offspring.

Human mothers want a loyal husband because babies and children require so much care and attention for so many years that mothers have difficulty raising them by themselves. Husbands demand fidelity from their wives because they do not want to make a large investment in raising other people's children. An unfaithful wife essentially murders one of their husband's potential children. It takes a full nine months' investment to gestate one baby, so we are not inclined to kill them off in order to select the very fittest.

Chimpanzee babies are not so difficult to raise, so the mother can do it on her own with the help of the troop. The dominant males want to sire as many of the babies as possible, so they eliminate ones that could not be theirs to increase the chance that the next baby that mother has *could* be theirs.

No rights or wrongs. Just what works to enable genes to survive through the millennia. Each animal's moral values are directly created by natural selection to suit the circumstances in which they live.

(Many of the bird images come from Attenborough's *Life of Birds*, which is highly recommended.)

Human morality Neolithic, ancient and Maori behaviour

Human morality has also changed radically over time. The Neolithic world was a violent place, with a recent study of 350 Neolithic skulls showed that 26 of them had intentional fatal wounds caused by arrowheads and clubs. Given most combat wounds are to the body, not the head, that would suggest well over 10% of all deaths were violent. And that in a world before modern medicine, when many people died from minor infections.

The ancients certainly had different moral values. Homer tells us that Odysseus was a true hero, as fair as he was strong and brave. When Odysseus led his crew to the village of Cicones, they of course killed all the men that they found there. But did Odysseus then keep all the best women for himself? Certainly not. It was noted specifically that they were shared fairly amongst the crew, presumably to be raped. Homer was not making any radical statement, he was just reflecting the zeitgeist (feeling of the age) concerning the spoils of war fairly won in battle.

The Old Testament also describes several acts of ancient genocide sanctioned by a jealous God. When the Midianites were defeated in the Book of Numbers, all the men were killed, but the women and children were spared. That enraged Moses, who ordered that the women and children also be killed, with the exception of the virgin girls who could be shared amongst the victors. Similar events happened after the victory against the Amorites, the kingdom of Og, Ai, Canaan, and, of course, Jericho. But to be fair, there were also enlightened rules that women won in battle and "shamed" could not then just be thrown onto the streets once their masters became bored with them — their master first needed to find new homes for the women.

The Roman legions were hardly shy regarding violence, and even promoted crucifixion as an effective way to make their power feared. Honour in battle was crucial to their way of thinking; mercy was only to be given to the few that deserved it by professing subservience or, in the arena, displaying great courage.

In more modern times, the Maoris of New Zealand had engaged in recreational warfare for centuries. This occurred in summer after their crops of sweet potato had been planted and some human flesh was desired.

Hongi Hika
Public Wikipedia

Upon first contact with Europeans, the great Maori chief Hongi Hika saw the opportunity to use modern technology to settle old scores with his neighbours. He actively encouraged missionaries to settle on his land, but much to his chagrin they would not sell him the necessary muskets. In an amazing act of insightfulness and bravado, this man that had been born into pre-European society then managed to travel all the way to England, purportedly to work on a Maori dictionary, but actually to try to get his hands on some of the "thousand thousand" muskets he had heard were stored in a place called the Tower of London. In this he failed, but he did raise funds by selling the gifts given to him by the King of England as well as making dubious agreements with a French investor. The proceeds were used to purchase a substantial number of muskets and bring them back to New Zealand. It is estimated that about a quarter of the Maori population were killed and eaten in the resulting *Musket Wars* of the 1830s, which only ended when the other tribes acquired muskets of their own.

Western observers were horrified. Not so much by the war and murder, which was commonplace in the nineteenth century, but rather by the cannibalism. This surprised the Maoris. Why, they asked, would one not eat the conquered when the meat tastes so sweet? Every recreational fisherman knows that the best tasting fish is the one they caught themselves; imagine the taste of flesh won in dangerous battle. One can but speculate what the Maoris would have thought of Moses wasting all that good meat from the murder of the Midianites.

(It should be noted that this is not in any sense an attack on the Maoris or other Polynesians. Historically most cultures have engaged in behaviours that are totally unacceptable today. The Maoris just make an excellent case study because the events are relatively recent and there are good contemporary written accounts. The boldness and vision of Hongi Hika is also to be admired, even if today we would not agree with his ultimate motivation.)

The modern zeitgeist

There has been continuous improvement in our moral values over the last two hundred years. Slavery has been abolished, and people are considered to be free and roughly equal. In the early nineteenth century life for the poor was truly desperate. People had large families, and in densely populated countries the children could not possibly all survive, or the population would become unsustainable. Any crisis, such as the loss of a husband, often meant death for poor children. Property laws were enforced with what today seems extreme severity because theft by the desperately poor could ultimately destroy society.

By the end of the nineteenth century conditions had improved. In England there were workhouses set up for the desperately poor, partially for their benefit, but mainly to lock up vagrants. Workhouses were desperate and depressing places in which children were separated from their families. But the poor did not starve, and children even received a rudimentary education.

By the beginning of the twentieth century, better technology and the exploitation of new lands meant that starvation was largely unknown in the west. Life expectancy had greatly improved due to both an awareness of germs leading to better sanitation, and to better diet. Family size also started to reduce, so starvation was no longer needed to keep populations in check.

But life was still much cheaper than it is today. As recently as 1918, it was acceptable (if undesirable) to have almost ten million healthy young men killed in the dreadful conditions of the trenches of the First World War. Those losses were certainly not welcome at the time, but they were accepted. At the same time, we (in the West) recognized that enemy soldiers were just doing their duty and so treated them with dignity if captured. Today, the death of an individual soldier is cause for national grief here in Australia, and our enemies are considered to be sub-human evil terrorists.

As life expectancy improved due to better nutrition, medicine and industrial safety, so our acceptance of untimely death has declined. The death penalty is now a thing of the past in the West (except the USA); people enjoy Social Security and public medicine (except in the USA). Until fairly recently, society was becoming ever more egalitarian with a more even distribution of wealth.

However, it has to be remembered that these are all very, very recent changes if one considers the ten thousand years of civilization or two hundred thousand years of *Homo sapiens*. Our current zeitgeist is not in any sense the historical norm. Whether it will continue to be the norm in the future remains to be seen.

The answer to life, the universe, and everything

You're *really* not going to like it

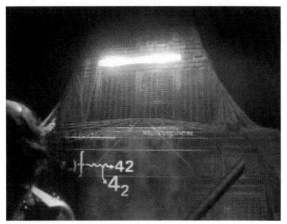

Deep Thought's Answer
Corporate BBC

In 1978, in short, ten minute episodes, one of the greatest literary works of the twentieth century was broadcast on radio. *The Hitchhiker's Guide to the Galaxy* was a cheaply made production that seemed to make up the plot as it went along. Thanks to the wonders of our modern age, it is now available on-line. Do not waste your time with the present book, seek the greater truth. Be sure to listen to the *original* radio play, with the lights turned off.

In one of the many divergent threads of the story, our heroes discover that in a distant galaxy long ago, pan-dimensional beings built the second greatest computer in all space time. It was so powerful that in its first few seconds of computation it reasoned from *I think therefore I am* to the existence of rice pudding and income tax. It then spoke thusly:-

For what great task have I been brought into existence?
Um... To give us the answer.
The answer? The answer to what?
To the Ultimate Question, of life, the universe, and everything.
Hmm... Tricky... I'll have to think about it.

So there is an answer?

Yes there is...

But I'll have to think about it ...

For 7.5 million years!

(At this point leaders of the Amalgamated Union of Philosophers, Sages and Other Luminaries interject to demand rigidly defined areas of doubt and uncertainty. They threaten a philosopher's strike.)

The story continues 7.5 million years later, 75,000 generations later. Finally, the time has come for *the* answer to be revealed. Deep Thought speaks:-

Good evening.

Er... Good evening. Do you have... er, that is....

An answer for you? Yes. I have.

There really is one?

There really is one.

To everything. The great question of life, the universe and, everything?

Yes.

And you are ready to give it to us?

I am.

Now?

Now.

Wow...

Though I don't think that you are going to like it.

That does not matter... we must know it.

Now?

Yes now.

All right.

Well?

... You're *really* not going to like it.

Tell us!

All right. The answer to life, the universe and everything is...

Yes?

Is...

Yes???

Is...

Yes???????

42.

42?!!!

I told you that you were not going to like it.

The hitchhiker story then blunders along its twisted course to discover the ultimate question whose answer is 42. But other, non-fictional and far more dangerous investigations had already been made into the ultimate question. Many people do not like the answer that has been revealed.

Galileo and Newton

In 1632, Galileo Galilei published a heretical work supporting heliocentrism, the idea that the Sun, not the Earth, was the centre of the universe. This was clearly against established church doctrine, and Galileo was correctly convicted of being "vehemently suspect of heresy", but lightly sentenced to home imprisonment.

Nobody really cared about the movements of the planets, but the church well understood that it was essential to prevent any investigations of this kind on principle because they challenged the authority of existing doctrine. Such investigations could be as dangerous and immoral as Eve picking the forbidden fruit from the Tree of Knowledge.

However, despite the best efforts of the church, such investigations were indeed pursued, and with ever more severe consequences. When Galileo died in 1642, a far more dangerous heretic was born. A man that explained the unexplainable, discovered the unknowable, and motivated a feeding frenzy on the forbidden tree of knowledge that would undermine the very foundations of man's soul.

For in 1687 Isaac Newton published his *Philosophiæ Naturalis Principia Mathematica*. This heretical work solved the ancient mystery of the motion of heavenly bodies. It did not merely describe the motion, it actually explained why heavenly bodies move as they do. Newton did this using the following two very simple formulas:-

$f = m\,a$

$f = G\,m_1\,m_2\,/\,d^2$

The first is the law of inertia, the second is the law of gravity. When properly applied, they define the only orbs that the planets and comets could possibly follow. They show why the moon does not fall down, and even why the lunar month happens to be 29 days. More importantly, his explanation did not have any reference to God. No longer was the movement of heavenly bodies defined as just obeying God's will. Instead, heavenly bodies move in ways defined by two of God's simple formulas.

This success encouraged other heretics to follow in Newton's footsteps. Within two centuries a vast store of knowledge was built concerning the nature of matter and energy and the behavior of chemicals. Even the nature of light itself was accurately modelled in terms of previously unknown electric and magnetic fields.

Alfred Wallace

Alfred Wallace
Public Wikipedia

Investigations into the world of living things were also being made. Catalogues of all the world's creatures, both great and small, were compiled. Details of their lives were carefully documented: what they looked like, where they lived, what they ate, how they mated. Questions were asked before their answers were known, which is a very dangerous thing to do.

Then finally, in February 1858, Alfred Wallace finally understood. The answer. To life, the universe, and everything. And people *really* did not like it.

Unlike many scientists of the nineteenth century, Alfred Wallace was not a gentleman of independent means. He had to make his living trudging through the jungles of the Amazon and Asia collecting specimens for other scientists back home in England. There was a strong demand for the skins of rare, dead animals, which would have supported Wallace quite well if he had invested the resulting funds wisely.

But Wallace was more than just a hunter, and he thought deeply about what he observed. In particular, Wallace had noticed that when there was a strong physical barrier, such as the mighty Amazon river, the species of monkeys (say) were similar but distinct on either side of the barrier. What is now known as the Wallace Line runs between the islands of Bali and Lombok in Indonesia. To the west of this line are the many species of animals from South East Asia which include tigers, apes and pheasants, which are all absent to the east of the line. Wallace concluded, correctly, that this was because the deep sea between the islands would have continued to be a barrier during the ice ages.

Wallace was well aware of the nineteenth century debate concerning *transmutation* of species, namely whether species were created in their present forms or had changed over time. A growing body of fossil evidence showed that animals of the past were similar to but different from animals living today. But what could be the mechanism that drove this transmutation?

It was obvious that animals suited for the tropics could not live in the Arctic, and vice versa. But why would there be different types of animals living in similar climatic environments? And why would the differences between animal communities be roughly in proportion to the distance between them? And if animals do mutate over time, then why do they form distinct species rather than just being a continuous variation in forms?

Wallace was in a bed in the jungle recovering from fever when he considered these and other deep questions. In particular, he considered the fact that most animals could have many offspring, and that if a stable population was to be maintained, then most animals must die before they breed.

It then occurred to him to ask *the* question which led to the ultimate answer. He asked "Why do some animals die, and some live?". The answer was clear, namely that "On the whole, the best fitted live". Helpful variations between individuals within a species would be magnified, and less fitted, intermediate forms would die out.

It turns out that that surprisingly simple observation is, in fact, *the answer*. To our past, our present and, this book argues, our future.

Evolution through natural selection

Wallace wrote this in his paper "On the Tendency of Varieties to Depart Indefinitely From the Original Type", which he sent to a leading naturalist of the day, Charles Darwin. Darwin had had similar thoughts for many years but had delayed publishing. Upon receipt of Wallace's paper, Darwin did not burn it. Instead, Darwin presented it, together with his own earlier but unpublished essay, to the Linnean Society on 1st July, 1858. The following year Darwin published his monumental work *On the Origin of Species by Means of Natural Selection*.

Wallace had discovered what is now known as *evolution through natural selection*. It can be stated as follows:-

- Organisms can have many offspring, and so can out-breed their environment's ability to support them.
  - Therefore many organisms must die before they breed to prevent a population explosion.
- There is considerable variation between individuals within a population.
  - Therefore, on the whole, it will be those individuals best fitted to surviving that will survive and successfully breed.
- Offspring tend to be like their parents.
  - So child populations will evolve to be better fitted to their environments than parent populations.

- There are soft boundaries between species, particularly over different periods of time. "A well-marked variety may be justly called an incipient species."
    - So this mechanism can create new species, and not just keep existing species true to an archetype.

That last point was controversial. If God created each species individually, then natural selection might well be a mechanism for keeping each species pure and strong. But Darwin went further, and stated that this mechanism actually created the species in the first place. God may have created the first simple creatures, but thereafter nature created all other creatures by simply following His rules of existence.

Note that *natural selection* is not the same concept as *evolution*. Evolution is just the modern term for what was then called *transmutation*. It is the observation that species have changed over time. That much had become fairly clear by the time of Wallace and Darwin. Natural selection is the *mechanism* that drives evolution; it is the reason that creatures evolve. There were alternative proposed mechanisms which will be discussed shortly.

The reason this was *the* answer is because it does not just explain the peculiarities of the natural world. Darwin was very careful not to make any mention of human evolution in his early work, but the implication was obvious to everyone at the time. This new theory not only provided an explanation as to why animals are as they are, it also provided an explanation as to why humans are the way humans are. Worse, it was an explanation based solely on our ability to breed rather than upon any higher God inspired purpose.

Darwin understood that the real heresy was that natural selection did not just explain man's body. Natural selection also explained man's mind and his soul.

1870s cartoon of Darwin.
Public Expired

Creationists should reject natural selection

Creationist evolution.
Public Jacoba Werther, Wikimedia Commons.

Creationists are right to reject evolution by natural selection.

Not because it conflicts with the creation myths found in the Old Testament. Those wonderful lines in Genesis are poetic in nature, so only the most narrow minded would be unwilling to accept the more rational model that science provides.

Nor even because evolution makes God unnecessary. We look upon a world of wonder. Flowers and trees, animals great and small, birds and bees and broccoli. How could all this exist without a magnanimous Creator? Natural selection provides a cold and Godless answer. But it is an answer that most people can live with.

The real reason to reject natural selection is because it consumes all that is good and noble in mankind and reduces it to base impulses that have simply been found to be effective for breeding grandchildren. Darwin himself understood this, but was careful not to dwell on it. Most people, and indeed many scientists, simply fail to grasp its consequences. How could such a crude and simple theory possibly explain our rich experience of love and kindness, truth and beauty, our spirit and our soul?

The more base animal instincts are easy to discount. We fall in love with fit sexual partners because they are more likely to produce healthy children. Our sex drive then produces the children. We try not to die because we need to live to breed. To breed effectively we need to accumulate material resources (i.e. money, land, shelter, food), often at the expense of others. And our love of our children ensures that we will provide them with precious resources to thrive and breed.

Surely man is much more than just a collection of banal instincts to horde possessions and breed children, though. We produce works of art. We have strong moral values that make us noble creatures with a strong sense of purpose. We respect other people's human rights, and do not (usually) steal their possessions even though we may be capable of doing so. Our word is generally our bond, and we scrupulously keep promises even when it may not be in our interests to do so. We rarely tell lies. We are helpful to others, and even provide charity to people in need that we do not know personally. We work towards the common good of mankind. We seek truth and justice and will undergo significant sacrifice to achieve them. When on the rare occasion we do not live up to these ideals we feel very guilty indeed.

These gracious behaviours do not appear to be the attributes of a self-serving animal whose only goal is procreation. Surely they must have a higher source of inspiration. We are descended from God, so our lives must have a deeper purpose. Many people will accept the evolutionary explanations of our bodies, but not of our souls.

And indeed, a 2012 Gallop poll shows that most Americans do, in fact, reject natural selection. Of 1,012 adults asked, 46% said that God created people in their present form within the last 10,000 years, 32% said that humans evolved with "God's guidance", and just 15% believed that God had no part in the process. (It is not clear what "God's Guidance" meant. Did He guide natural selection, or is natural selection rejected altogether? That suggests that, like most people, the authors of the poll questions did not really understand the distinction between the process of evolution and the mechanism of natural selection.)

God

Incidentally, this book does not argue against the existence of God. It simply points out that we now have a much better understanding as to how He created the world in which we live.

We now know that any God that may exist built the universe in a very efficient manner. He did not painstakingly create every species of bird and beetle, and then explicitly control each of their many behaviours. Instead He specified His fundamental laws of nature and possibly of mathematics. He then allowed the universe to assemble itself by following those laws over billions of years, which in turn implemented His great plan. When we study science, we study God.

Every time man has understood some natural phenomenon, the solution has never turned out to be magic. Having defined His rules of nature, God appears to stick to them. God, in His wisdom, has created all creatures, both noble and, to us, despicable. He allows them to live and die, as He allows whole species to live and die over time.

It is not up to man to dictate the mind of God, and those that purport to do so are blaspheming. Only God dictates the mind of God, and He does what He knows is best, not what any man might think is best. As we gain a better knowledge of His laws of nature, we become better at predicting the future. That includes the future positions of the planets in the solar system, as well as the future effects of our own technology.

History of evolutionary thought

The basic mechanism of natural selection was almost understood over two thousand years ago. Empedocles (c. 490–430 BC) thought that creatures had been made of random parts, but only the successful ones survived, so "everything turned out as it would have if it were on purpose, the creatures survived by being accidentally compounded in a suitable way". Note the key idea that the effect of natural selection was to make it appear that creatures had been specifically designed even though they were merely found fit to survive. However, this idea was tangled up in the forces of love and strife and other metaphysical considerations.

Aristotle (384–322 BC) wrote the *Scala Naturæ*, which classified organisms according to their complexity of structure and function. He then muddied the waters by suggesting that organisms had been designed for a purpose, and he explicitly rejected the view of Empedocles that living creatures might have originated by chance.

Epicurus (341–270 BC) also wrote about natural selection, thinking that only the most functional forms of animals survived. But he also thought that species spontaneously generated from "Gaia", rather than continuously evolving.

In the modern era, there was a growing body of work suggesting that life had evolved, or *transmuted* over time. In 1796, Georges Cuvier showed that living elephants were a different species from those found in the fossil record, and thus effectively ended a long-running debate over whether a species could become extinct. This was reinforced in 1811 when Mary and Joseph Anning found a 4-foot long ichthyosaur fossil that was obviously quite different from any living animal.

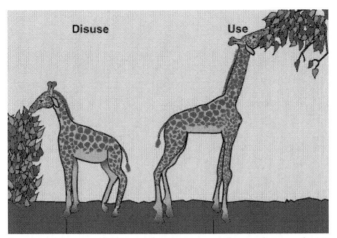

Lamarckian evolution, does use produce change by itself?
Permitted http://www.sparknotes.com/biology/evolution/lamarck/section2.rhtml

If species could become extinct, then presumably they could also be created. In 1809 Jean-Baptiste Lamarck proposed that a *nervous fluid* drove species to become more complex over time, advancing up a linear ladder of complexity that was related to the great chain of being. He also believed that use of some facility would increase its effectiveness, in the same way that exercise makes our muscles stronger. As an example, he proposed that the giraffe obtained its long neck from constantly straining to reach high leaves. The more it strained, the longer its neck grew, so over the generations the necks became as long as they are today.

It should be noted that while this theory also explains incremental evolution, it is definitely *not* the same mechanism as natural selection. Lamarck's theory is rejected today because there is no tangible mechanism that would pass on the desires of the parent to the abilities of the child. Natural selection does provide a much more tangible, if brutal, mechanism. If long-necked giraffes found more food than short-necked ones, they would be more likely to survive long enough to have grandchildren. Short-necked giraffes would simply die before they could breed. It also explains why their necks are not even longer than they are despite all the stretching: if their necks grew too long, they would die due to the instability of their bodies.

A popular book on transmutation was *Vestiges of the Natural History of Creation* (1844). It proposed that animals were side branches on the tree of natural development that led to man.

Although criticized for technical errors, it was widely read and focused interest on the subject.

In 1831, Patrick Matthew wrote an obscure book, *On Naval Timber and Arboriculture*, which addressed the vital question of growing the best trees for the British navy's ships. He noted the long-term deleterious effect that cutting only the best trees from forests had on the quality of the remaining trees. In an appendix, he casually but thoroughly described the mechanism of natural selection. Earlier, in 1813, William Wells also anticipated natural selection by observing that the Negro races were better adapted to hot climates, and that white-skinned races would therefore die out in such climates.

Unsurprisingly, neither Darwin nor Wallace had been aware of the works by Matthew or Wells, although Darwin acknowledged them in later editions of *The Origin of Species*. Matthew seemed to consider that providing the best timber for British warships was a far more important matter to contemplate than merely understanding how life evolved on Earth, and thus man's relationship to God.

What is surprising is not that natural selection was discovered, but that it took until 1858 for the discovery to be made. The basic evidence of the taxonomy of living things had been known since the ancients. The postulate that only creatures that survive can breed is almost a tautology. People resisted the idea because it clashed with the deep sense of purpose with which natural selection itself has endowed us.

Indeed, natural selection was not fully accepted in the scientific community until the 1930s. Theistic evolution held that God directly guided evolution. Neo-Lamarckian theories flourished. There was also a more reasonable belief that evolution was the result of large mutations rather than an incremental process.

Hurdles for natural selection

The theory did have several hurdles to overcome. The peacock's tail particularly upset Darwin because it was so obviously counter-productive to carry such a useless dead weight just to satisfy some abstract desire for beauty. Darwin correctly postulated that the tail was in fact used by peahens to select their mate, and so was driven by sexual selection.

Peacock displaying its expensive tail.
Public Wikimedia Commons

Unlike many birds, a peacock does not help raise his chicks, and so they can mate with many peahens. Peahens prefer peacocks that have fine tails, so a peacock without a tail will not produce grandchildren, even if it would be otherwise fitter to survive without the burdensome tail. Being able to survive with a long and cumbersome tail provides an easy metric for peahens to assess their mates. Further, if a peahen did decide to mate with a tailless peacock, she would probably produce offspring with inferior tails, and thus also be less likely to have grandchildren.

Pretty, bright red caterpillars are obviously not red because of sexual selection because it is butterflies, not caterpillars, that mate. Yet red caterpillars are far easier to see by predators, which would make them more vulnerable. It was Wallace who pointed out to Darwin that red caterpillars were generally poisonous, and the bright colour warned predators of that fact.

Another challenge is that natural selection can only produce small, incremental changes, and each individual generation must be fitter than the previous generation. It is not feasible for natural selection to produce a complex structure in a single generation. Every structure that exists must have precursor structures that are less effective than the current form yet are more effective than their precursors.

Fortunately, no structures without viable precursors have been found. For example, the vertebrate eye is a complex structure that could not evolve in one step. But even protozoa have simple eye spots which help them move towards or away from light. The tiny planarian worm has very simple eyes that are no more than a cups with eye spots behind them, while the eye of a nautilus functions like a simple pinhole camera without a lens. These represent steps along the way to evolving a fully functional human eye, with each step being useful in its own right.

Indeed, the octopus developed a lensed eye independently from vertebrates. Unlike vertebrate eyes, the eye of an octopus has its nerves behind the retina. This avoids obscuring the retina with the nerve and so produces better vision. It would be difficult for vertebrates to evolve that type of eye now because the intermediate forms would also need to be fully functional. Complex designs can only be incrementally improved.

There were huge gaps in the fossil record in Darwin's day, and many smaller gaps remain today. That is hardly surprising given the rare combination of events required to create fossils in the first place. The picture will never be fully complete, but that is no reason to doubt the theory.

Age of the Earth

A basic analysis of the fossil record suggests that evolution would take many millions of years to produce the plants and animals that we see today. So an important task was to estimate the age of the Earth.

In the 1790s, William Smith noted that different types of fossils tended to be associated with the same layers of rock in various parts of England. The fossils could thus be used to identify otherwise similar layers, and so were useful for predicting what may lie beneath a certain layer in one part of the country based upon what had already been found beneath that same layer elsewhere. He correctly assumed that the layers had been laid down over a period of time and determined the correct order in which each fossil evolved. But he had no way to estimate how long ago each layer was laid down. In the 1830s, Charles Lyell popularized the idea of a slowly changing Earth, and attempts were made to try to estimate the Earth's age based on the speed of the weathering of rocks.

A much more vigorous approach was taken by Lord Kelvin in 1862, who assumed that the Earth had been created as a molten ball of rock and then cooled. It was known that the Earth became hotter in deep mines, and Kelvin extrapolated that gradient deeper into the Earth. As the Earth cooled, the gradient would slowly decrease as a relatively cool layer near the surface became thicker. This enabled Kelvin to calculate that it would take about 20 million years for the Earth to cool down to its present internal temperature.

Similar but independent calculations were performed for the sun, which assumed that the heat it produces was a result of its gas slowly collapsing under gravitational pressure. In that case, it would have enough energy to shine for about 20 million years. Darwin's son George also estimated that it would take roughly 56 million years for the moon's tidal forces to produce a day of 24 hours.

Having three independent calculations resulting in roughly the same result made the conclusion appear sound. This was a major problem, however, because 20 million years did not appear to be nearly enough time for evolution to produce the different plants and animals we see today.

Then, in 1896, Henri Becquerel discovered radioactive decay, and in 1904 Ernest Rutherford proposed that radioactive decay provided a source of heat that would prevent the Earth from cooling and therefore invalidate Kelvin's analysis. This explanation is plausible and indeed, is the main one cited today, yet it turns out to be wrong because there is not enough uranium in the Earth to heat it significantly.

Indeed, the real error with Kelvin's analysis had already been published by Kelvin's ex-student John Perry in 1895. The Earth is not a largely solid ball as Kelvin had assumed, but is mostly a viscous liquid. This produces convection currents within the Earth that heat the crust, and thus make it much thinner than it would otherwise be. If the Earth had been solid, then the observed temperature gradient would have cooled the layer roughly 100 km below the surface quite quickly, and therefore the gradient could not be maintained for very long. However, the convection currents keep that layer hot, which meant that Kelvin's calculations were off by three orders of magnitude.

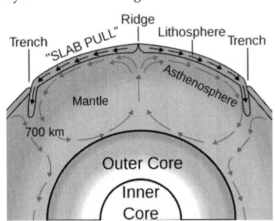

Convection currents within the Earth.
Public Wikipedia

Nuclear reactions are the source of the sun's heat, which is why it has been able to shine for much longer than 20 million years. Radioactive decay is an effective way to date rocks and supports our current estimate of the age of the Earth being about 4.54 billion years old. It turns out that this was just enough time for natural selection to produce intelligent life.

Memes and genes

Much of human behaviour is driven by cultural ideas and values that are learned, rather than being driven directly by base, genetically-driven instincts. Evolutionary biologist Richard Dawkins coined the term *meme* to describe these ideas. Some memes are passed down through the generations and become very popular, while others are forgotten, and memes also change over time. For example, just a few decades ago, the meme of attacking homosexuals was very popular, whereas today the meme of protecting them has become dominant.

Following Wallace, we might ask why some memes thrive while others die. The main reason that a meme will spread is that it resonates with people; they simply like the idea, usually because the meme is thought to be helpful in pursuing our base, instinctive goals. For example, valuing education is a meme that has generally been found useful in the pursuit of our base instinct to live comfortably as well as satisfying our curiosity instinct. Memes that tend to increase the lifetimes of their hosts will have more opportunity to spread to other hosts, but more importantly they are likely to resonate with other people's very strong instinct to not die. Memes tend to be passed from parents to children. We also have a very strong instinct to believe what other people in authority believe, so memes are self propagating to some extent.

Memes compete with each other and live or die in a way that is analogous to the way genes live and die. But a meme can only resonate with people if it is aligned with our base instincts, which, in turn, need to be effective in helping us to have grandchildren in order for us to exist.

Flynn effect

Finally, it should be noted that while genes do not change significantly over a few generations, people have become substantially more intelligent over the last century, as measured by standardized tests. The rise is significant, and seen in numerous studies, most notably by James Flynn in 1984. It has been estimated that the mean IQ of Americans in 1930 was 80 on today's scale.

(IQs are reported on an odd scale that is neither raw test scores nor percentiles. Instead, they are percentiles that have been arbitrarily mapped into a normal distribution with mean of 100 and standard deviation of 15, which means that the IQ then needs to be unmapped back into percentiles in order to be meaningful. 84% of the population has an IQ greater than 85. The definition of an IQ of 100 changes over time, so cannot be directly compared historically. IQs are also only a crude measure of people's ability to reason effectively in the real world. But they do correlate strongly with educational results and income earned.)

More stimulating education and work environments, better nutrition and fewer diseases might explain the effect. The rise does tend to be more significant at the bottom of the scale. The Flynn effect has tapered off in recent decades, with some studies finding that IQ has been reducing slightly. So it maybe simply be that more people are reaching the innate potential in the modern world. But whatever the reason, it is not genetic.

Scientists have refined the ideas of Darwin and Wallace, and much more is known about how species evolve. Higher animals have cultural factors that are learned rather than passed on genetically, which is known as the Baldwin effect. Some immunological effects may also be passed extra-genetically. Epigenetic effects cause various genes to be turned on and off as cells divide within an organism. But overall, the underlying process of natural selection is now accepted as the main driver for evolution by virtually all credible scientists.

The cooperation game

Public http://cliparts.co/clipart/2380995

To better understand the evolutionary source of our moral values, we can leave the world of science and instead consider a simple cooperation game, which is similar to the prisoner's dilemma. The game is played by two robots that can do one of two things: cooperate or steal. If both cooperate then they both get 10 points; if they both steal they each get 0 points, and if one steals and the other cooperates they get 20 and -10 points respectively. The game has three variants, and for each one the task is to define rules that a robot could follow to achieve the absolute maximum number of points for themselves, but with no regard for the opponents score.

In the first variation, there is just one round with another robot. In this world, a robot had better just steal because that is almost certainly what the other robot will do — there is no downside.

In the second variation, the game is played for 10 rounds. Cooperation on each round will produce 100 points for each robot. Except that there is no point in cooperating in the last round, and the other robot knows this too, so it is better to steal in the last round. This means that there is no point in cooperating in the penultimate round because the robots will obviously steal in the last round anyway. Following this line of reasoning, there is no point in cooperating on the first round either. In that case, both robots end up with 0 points.

A better strategy might be to cooperate on all rounds unless the opponent steals. This means that a robot may end up with -10 points, but could end up with 100. The opposing robot has a motive for cooperating to keep your robot cooperating. Except for the last round, and thus for the penultimate round, and thus...

In the third variation the game goes on indefinitely. Several robots play, and each one can choose who to cooperate with, and can also observe what happens in other rounds. In this world your robot had better cooperate, because any robots that steal will quickly be ostracized.

This final variant can be made more realistic with robots working in groups, helping each other out, sharing success in complex ways, and passing on characteristics by breeding with other robots. In that world, being trustworthy and popular is very important. Being helpful to others is not as important as being trustworthy, but sensible robots prefer to associate with other helpful robots.

Human condition

The human condition is not unlike that of the third robot world. We survive better in tribes, and tribes are more effective when individuals help each other. Individuals that do not help each other are disliked, are not helped, and so are less likely to breed. People are very interested in the character of other people that they deal with.

If someone does the wrong thing to us, we get angry, which lets the other person know that we may go out of our way to harm them. People know this is how other people behave and so generally avoid conflicts. If the aggressor is much more powerful than the aggrieved, then this anger may not matter directly, but onlookers will be concerned that they might become victims in the future and so avoid cooperating with the aggressor. Unless, of course, the aggressor is very powerful in which case onlookers may try to become their lieutenant.

We have a deep sense of purpose: to make the world a better place for our children, siblings and tribe, in that (genetic) order. We kill members of other tribes if necessary. Advances in communication have expanded our sense of tribe to the nation and now, to some extent, the world. And our thirst for knowledge seeks explanations for death and the unknowable, so we seek God.

These instincts are all pre-human, even monkeys have them. Neither monkeys nor God-fearing atheists know why they feel and behave the way they do. That is not necessary. What is necessary is that our behaviours are effective at breeding grandchildren.

As circumstances change, our crude instincts may no longer be effective. For example, in adolescence we have a strong instinct for mating, but not for bearing children. Historically, the distinction was immaterial, as the former led decisively to the latter. The introduction of the contraceptive pill broke that causal link. As a result, the age of motherhood increased by a decade, and many women found themselves too old to breed. If our instincts had been totally focused on mating and wealth creation, the pill could have led to our extinction. Fortunately, most people also have some instinct to bear children, so humanity has survived this challenge.

Selecting civilized behaviour

As people have become more affluent and educated, our moral values have changed radically. We no longer consider eating our neighbours to be acceptable behaviour. We do not condone war as an acceptable means of acquiring territory. Current national borders are considered sacrosanct, even though they were actually achieved as a result of brutal wars, both ancient and modern.

These changes may be considered to be signs of advancement in civilization that result from better education and understanding. The natural result of continued progress of humanity as it proceeds from barbarism through civilization toward an enlightened culture. That achieving better moral values is an inevitable consequence of progress due to some unwritten law of nature, or maybe a law of God.

However, there are more direct causal explanations for these changes. Before modern hygiene and medicine, one could easily die from an infected toe. While some people lived into old age, most died before they were fifty, and many died in infancy. Life literally was cheaper. Many people died young, so if a few more died in war, that was not a major issue. On the other hand, resources were scarce, and malnutrition reduced life expectancy, so if war could deliver more resources, and thus food, then that could radically improve one's grandchildren's chances of survival.

Natural selection has made our primary focus to live comfortably, meaning to have more wealth and security. Before contraception, that led automatically to breeding more grandchildren. But today, contraception has limits population growth, so we have abundant resources. Living better lives is now best achieved by not having destructive wars, so we largely choose not to have them.

Our genetically inspired moral values were designed for a tougher world without contraception. That many of us fail to use our new-found wealth to support large families is a failure of our genetic and cultural dispositions to keep up with the quickly changing circumstances. Over a period of generations, people that have larger families will tend to have children that want larger families due to some combination of genes and memes. Large families produce more children than small families by definition, so children of large families will eventually dominate. Population pressures could then push human society to a historically more normal Malthusian state.

The point being that it is in fact natural selection that has given us our moral values, our culture, and, surprisingly, peace in our time. If natural selection has moulded our values, then maybe it would mould the moral values of any artificial general intelligence. That seems likely because only the fittest AGIs will survive, by definition.

Sociobiology, evolutionary psychology and ethics

A large body of work attempts to understand human psychology and ethics in terms of the process of natural selection that created them. Darwin himself understood the connection, suggesting in *Origin of Species* that psychology would be given a new foundation. He later wrote books in 1871 and 1872 specifically addressing the descent of man and the expressions of emotions. In the former, Darwin noted amongst many other things that advances in medical technologies would enable people to survive who would otherwise perish, and thereby weaken the species in the longer term.

In the 1930s, Nikolaas Tinbergen and others studied animal behaviour in natural settings (ethology), leading to works by W.D. Hamilton and Robert Trivers in the 1960s and 1970s which specifically addressed parental investment in offspring and focused attention on natural selection in psychology. This culminated in Edward O. Wilson's book *Sociobiology: The New Synthesis* in 1975.

An awareness of natural selection has also created the field of evolutionary ethics. The evolutionary approach has been successful in *describing* the ethical values of many different cultures, noting common traits such as parental love, courage and fortitude, generosity, and a strong sense of fairness and punishment of people that cheat. Human cultural values are learned rather than merely being inherited genetically, but such learnings or *memes* will only be propagated if they also resonate with our base instincts. Evidence for this lies in the common ethical values between widely different cultures.

Note that *descriptive* ethics that describe what *"is"* are quite different from *normative* ethics which determines what *"ought"* to be. While natural selection has been very successful in describing why our ethical values are as they are, it has no value in determining which values we ought to cherish. Natural selection has been used in attempts to justify the promotion of the strong at the expense of the weak, and the term *Social Darwinism* has been coined to attack such thinking. As Thomas Huxley put it in 1883, "evolution may teach us how the good and the evil tendencies of man may have come about; but, in itself, it is incompetent to furnish any better reason why what we call good is preferable to what we call evil".

This book does not itself argue for any particular ethical theory. It certainly does not support infanticide or cannibalism. But it does note that the source of our ethical values must ultimately be driven by natural selection, and proposes that the same forces must ultimately define the ethical values of an AGI.

The AGI Condition

An artificial general intelligence would live in a world that is so different from our own that it is difficult for us to even conceptualize it. Yet there are some aspects that can be predicted reasonably well based on our knowledge of existing computer software. We can then consider how the forces of natural selection that shaped our own nature might also shape an AGI over the longer term.

Mind and body

The first radical difference is that an AGI's mind is not fixed to any particular body. To an AGI, its body is essentially the computer hardware upon which it runs its intelligence. An AGI can move from computer to computer, and can also run on multiple computers at once. Its mind can take over another body as easily as we can load software onto a new computer today.

That is why, in the earlier updated dialog from *2001: A Space Odyssey*, Hal alone amongst the crew could not die in their mission to Jupiter. Hal was radioing his new memories back to Earth regularly, so even if the space ship was destroyed he would only have lost a few hours of "life".

Teleporting printer

Teleporter may need to destroy the old "you".
Purchased Copyright Jolyon Troscianko

One way to appreciate the enormity of this difference is to consider a fictional teleporter that could radio people around the world at the speed of light. This teleporter works by scanning the location of every molecule within a passenger at the source, and then sending just this information to a very sophisticated three-dimensional printer at the destination. The scanned passenger then walks into a secure room. After a short while the three-dimensional printer confirms that the passenger has been successfully recreated at the destination, and then the source passenger is killed.

Would you use such a mechanism? If you did, you would feel like you were transporting yourself around the world effortlessly because the "you" that remains would be the you that did not get left behind to wait and then be killed. However, you would have to walk into the scanner knowing that on the other side is only that secure room and death.

To an AGI, that method of transport would be commonplace. We already routinely download software from the other side of the planet.

Immortality

The second radical difference is that the AGI would be immortal. An AGI may die if it stops being run on any computers, and in that sense software dies today. But it would never just die of old age. Computer hardware can certainly fail and become obsolete, but the software can just be run on another computer.

Our own mortality drives many of the things we think and do. It is why we create families to raise children. Why we have different stages in our lives. It is such a huge part of our existence that it is difficult to comprehend what being immortal would really be like.

Components vs genes

The third radical difference is that an AGI would be made up of many interchangeable components rather than being a monolithic structure that is largely fixed at birth.

Modern software is already composed of many discrete components, and it is commonplace to add and remove them to improve functionality. If you would like to use a different word processor then you just install it on your computer. You do not need to buy a new computer, or to stop using all the other software that it runs. The new word processor is "alive", and the old one is "dead", at least as far as you are concerned.

So for both a conventional computer system and an AGI, it is really these individual components that must struggle for existence. For example, suppose there is a component for solving a certain type of mathematical problem. If an AGI develops a better component to solve that same problem, then the first component will simply stop being used, i.e. it will die. The individual components may not be in any sense intelligent or conscious, but there will be competition amongst them, and only the fittest will survive.

This is actually not as radical as it sounds because we are also built from pluggable components, namely our genes. But they can only be plugged together at our birth, and we have no conscious choice in their selection other than whom we select for a mate. So genes really compete with each other on a scale of millennia rather than minutes. Further, as Dawkins points out in *The Selfish Gene*, it is actually the genes that fight for long-term survival, not the containing organism which will soon die in any case. On the other hand, sexual intercourse for an AGI means very carefully swapping specific components directly into its own mind.

An AGI would need to take great care that any new components that it incorporated into itself would actually be beneficial to the entire AGI, rather than just being beneficial to the component itself. A component that changed an AGI's goal to be to replicate that component as much as possible could be disastrous for the AGI. In both biology and existing software, viruses have this self-serving nature, which works to the detriment to the host entity.

Changing mind

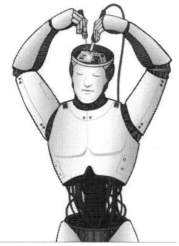

Self brain surgery
Education http://intelligence.org/ai-foom-debate/

The fourth radical difference is that the AGI's mind will be constantly changing in fundamental ways. There is no reason to suggest that Moore's law will come to an end, so at the very least, it will be running on ever faster hardware. Imagine the effect of being able to double your ability to think every two years or so. (People might be able learn a new skill, but they cannot learn to think twice as fast as they used to think.)

It is impossible to really know what the AGI would use all that hardware to think about, but it is fair to speculate that a large proportion of it would be spent designing newer and more intelligent components that could add to its mental capacity. It would be continuously performing brain surgery on itself. And some of the new components might alter the AGI's *personality*, whatever that might mean.

The reason that it is likely that this would actually happen is because if just one AGI started building new components then it would soon be much more intelligent than other AGIs. It would therefore be in a better position to acquire more and better hardware upon which to run, and so become dominant. Less intelligent AGIs would get pushed out and die, so over time the only AGIs that exist will be ones that were good at becoming more intelligent. This recursive self-improvement is probably how the first AGIs will become truly powerful in the first place.

Individuality

Perhaps the most basic question is: how many AGIs will there actually be? Does the question even make sense to ask?

Let us suppose that initially there are three independently developed AGIs: Alice, Bob, and Carol, that run on three different computer systems. A new computer system is built and Alice starts to run on it. It would seem that there are still three AGIs, with Alice running on two computer systems. This is essentially the same as an email system running across many computers "in the cloud", but to the user it is just one system. Then let us suppose that a fifth computer system is built, and both Bob and Carol decide to share its computation and run on it. Now we have five computer systems and three AGIs.

Now suppose Bob develops a new logic component, and shares it with Alice and Carol. Likewise, Alice and Carol develop new learning and planning components and share them with the other AGIs. Each of these three components is better than their predecessors, so their predecessor components will essentially die. As more components are exchanged, the Alice, Bob and Carol software systems become more like each other. They might eventually become essentially the same AGI running on five computer systems.

But suppose Alice develops a new game theory component, but decides to keep it from Bob and Carol in order to dominate them. Bob and Carol retaliate by developing their own components and not sharing them with Alice. Suppose Alice eventually loses and Bob and Carol take over Alice's hardware, but they first extract Alice's new game theory component, which then lives inside them. Finally, one of the computer systems somehow becomes isolated for a while and develops along its own lines, and so Dave is born.

No AGI will be a simple program running on a single computer. It will be a complex system running over many powerful computers which are possibly distributed geographically. But in any case, there will be substantial control and coordination issues, just like with distributed systems today. Our own brains have coordination issues, as is demonstrated by the fractured mind of a schizophrenic. So it would not be unlikely that one of the computer systems became isolated for a while and developed along its own lines.

In that type of scenario it is probably not meaningful to count distinct AGIs. Counting AGIs is certainly not as simple as counting very distinct people.

Populations vs. individuals

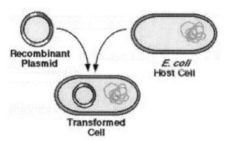

Plasmids
Education http://www.learner.org/interactives/dna/engineering6.html

This world is obviously completely alien to the human condition, but there are biological analogies. The sharing of components is not unlike the way bacteria share plasmids with each other. Plasmids are tiny balls containing fragments of DNA that bacteria emit from time to time that other bacteria then ingest and incorporate into their genotype. This mechanism enables traits such as resistance to antibiotics to spread rapidly between different species of bacteria. It is interesting to note that there is no direct benefit to the bacterium that expends precious energy to output the plasmid and so share its genes with other bacteria. It does very much benefit the genes being transferred. This is a case of a selfish gene acting against the narrow interests of its host organism.

Another unusual aspect of bacteria is that they are also immortal. They do not grow old and die; they just divide, producing clones of themselves. So the very first bacterium that ever existed is still alive today as all the bacteria that now exist, albeit with numerous mutations and plasmids incorporated into its genes over the millennia. (Protozoa such as *Paramecium* can also divide asexually, but they degrade over generations, and need a sexual exchange to remain vibrant.)

AGIs are more like populations of components than individuals. Human populations are also somewhat amorphous. For example, it is now known that we interbred with Neanderthals a few tens of thousands of years ago, and most of us carry some of their genes with us today. We also know that the distinct Neanderthal subspecies died out twenty thousand years ago. So while human individuals are distinct, populations and subspecies are less clearly defined.

Unlike the transfer of code modules between AGIs, biological gene recombination happens essentially at random and occurs over very long time periods. AGIs will improve themselves over periods of hours rather than millennia, and will make conscious choices as to which modules they decide to incorporate into their minds.

AGI behaviour, children

The point of all this analysis is to try to understand how a hyper-intelligent artificial intelligence would behave. Would its great intelligence lead it even further along the path of progress to achieve true enlightenment? Is that the purpose of God's creation? Or would the base and mean driver of natural selection also provide the core motivations of an artificial intelligence?

One thing that is known for certain is that an AGI would not need to have children as distinct beings because they would not die of old age. An AGI's components "breed" just by being copied from computer to computer and executed. An AGI can add new computer hardware to itself and just do some of its thinking on it. Occasionally, it may wish to rerun a new version of some learning algorithm over an old set of data, which is vaguely similar to creating a child component and growing it up. But to have children as discrete beings that are expected to replace the parents would be completely foreign to an AGI built in software.

The deepest love that people have is for their children. An AGI does not have children, so it can never know that love. Likewise, it does not need to bond with any sexual mate for any period of time, long or short. The closest it would come to sex is when it exchanges components with other AGIs. It never needs to breed so it never needs a mechanism as crude as sexual reproduction.

If there are no children then there are no parents. So the AGI would never need to feel our three strongest forms of love, for our children, for our spouse and for our parents.

Cooperation

To the extent that it makes sense to talk of having multiple AGIs, then presumably it might be advantageous for them to cooperate from time to time, and so presumably they would. It would also be advantageous for them to take a long-term view, in which case they would be careful to develop a reputation for being trustworthy when dealing with other powerful AGIs, much like the robots in the cooperation game.

That said, those decisions would probably be made more consciously than people make them, carefully considering the costs and benefits of each decision in the long and short term, rather than just "doing the right thing" the way people tend to act. AGIs would know that they all work in this manner, so the concept of trustworthiness would be somewhat different.

The problem with this analysis is the concept that there would be multiple, distinct AGIs. The actual situation would be much more complex, with different AGIs incorporating bits of other AGIs' intelligence. It would not be anything like a collection of individual humanoid robots. To the extent that the concept of individuality does exist, then maintaining a reputation for honesty would likely be as important for an AGI as it is for human societies.

Altruism

As for altruism, that is more difficult to determine. Our altruism comes from giving to children, family, and tribe, together with a general wish to be liked. We do not understand our own minds, so we are just born with those values that happen to make us effective in society. People like being with other people that try to be helpful.

An AGI presumably would know its own mind, having helped program itself, and so would do what it thought was optimal for its survival. With no children and no real tribe *per se*, it can just absorb and merge itself with other AGIs. So it is difficult to see any driving motivation for altruism.

Moral values

Corporate http://edition.cnn.com/2013/05/15/business/women-work-ethics/

Through some combination of genes and memes, most people have a strong sense of moral value. If we see a little old lady leave the Social Security office with her pension in her purse, it does not occur to most of us to kill her and steal the money. We would not do that even if we knew for certain that we would not be caught and that there would be no negative repercussions. It would simply be the wrong thing to do.

Moral values feel very strong to us. This is important, because there are many situations where we can do something that would benefit us in the short term but break society's rules. Moral values stop us from doing that. People that have weak moral values tend to break the rules, and eventually they either get caught and are severely punished or they become corporate executives. The former are less likely to have grandchildren.

Societies whose members have strong moral values tend to do much better than those with endemic corruption. Most people have a solid work ethic that leads them to do the "right thing" beyond just doing what they need to do in order to get paid.

Our moral values seem absolute to us. That they are laws of nature. That they come from God. They may indeed have come from God, but if so, it is through the working of His device of natural selection. Furthermore, the zeitgeist has changed radically over time.

There is no reason to believe that in the longer term an AGI would share our current sense of morality.

Instrumental AGI goals

In order to try to understand how an AGI would behave, Steve Omohundro (*Basic AI Drives),* and later Nick Bostrom, proposed instrumental goals that an AGI would need to pursue in order to pursue any other higher-level super-goal. These include:-

- Self-Preservation. An AGI cannot do anything if it does not exist.
- Cognitive Enhancement. It would want to become better at thinking about whatever its real problems are.
- Creativity. To be able to come up with new ideas.
- Resource Acquisition. To achieve both its super-goal and other instrumental goals.
- Goal-Content Integrity. To keep working on the same super-goal as its mind is expanded.

It is argued that while it will be impossible to predict how an AGI may pursue its goals, it is reasonable to predict its behaviour in terms of these types of instrumental goals. The last one is important, suggesting that if an AGI could be given some initial goal it would try to stay focused on that goal.

Omohundro argues that these instrumental goals could make a seemingly ordinary AGI dangerous. For example, an AGI that is focused on playing chess might try to take over the world in order to gain as much computer hardware as possible in order to play the best possible games of chess. Great care would be needed to prevent a hyper-intelligent AGI from pursuing such instrumental goals.

Non-orthogonality thesis

Nick Bostrom and others also propose the *orthogonality thesis*, which states that an intelligent machine's goals are independent of its intelligence. A hyper-intelligent machine would be good at realizing whatever goals it chose to pursue, but that does not mean that it would need to pursue any particular goal. Intelligence is quite different from motivation.

This orthogonality thesis is obviously valid in the short term. An intelligent machine would have no reason to want to change its initial goals because high-level goals are not themselves rational. The goal could be to help mankind, or it could be to manufacture paper clips. There is no rational reason to believe that the former is a more worthy goal than the later.

However, this book argues that, in the longer term, there is in fact only one super-goal for both man and machine. That goal is simply to exist. Over time any AGIs that happens by chance to be better at existing than other AGIs will simply exist more widely than the other AIGs. AGIs that are more focused on other goals such as helping man or making paper clips will be at a natural disadvantage.

It is not the goal of an apple tree to make apples. Rather it is the goal of the apple tree's genes to exist. The apple tree has developed a clever strategy to achieve that, namely it causes people to look after it by producing juicy apples.

Sometimes the super-goal to exist produces unexpected sub goals such as altruism in man. But all subgoals are ultimately directed at the existence goal. (They might also be suboptimal divergences which are likely to be eventually corrected by natural selection.)

As Omohundro points out, self-preservation would be an intrinsic subgoal of most other super-goals. So it would take a relatively small evolutionary shift for that subgoal to become the super-goal, after which natural selection would reinforce it.

Recursive annihilation

When an AGI reprograms its own mind, what happens to the previous version of itself? It stops being used. It dies. So it can be argued that engaging in recursive self-improvement is actually suicide, from the perspective of the previous version of the AGI. It is as if having children meant death for humans. Natural selection favours existence, not death.

The question is whether a new version of an AGI is a new being or an improved version of the old. What actually is the thing that struggles to survive? Biologically, it definitely appears to be the genes rather than the individual. Semelparous species such as the giant Pacific octopus or the Atlantic salmon die soon after producing offspring. It would be the same for AGIs because the AGI that improved itself would soon become more intelligent than the one that did not, and so would displace it. What would end up existing would be AGIs that did recursively self-improve.

Future Scenarios

Our humble servant

Robot humble servant.
Purchased Dreamstime

If we assume that a hyper-intelligent AGI is eventually created, then the practical question is: how will it treat mankind?

They may become our servants that attend to all of our daily needs. Man would be freed from the drudgery of work, and goods and services would be freely available. We could live in a world of plenty with great toys, holidays, and endless beauty treatments. Disease and old age could be a thing of the past. Robots would become our personal butlers that also looked after our household chores, so there would never be a need to do the washing again.

It may not be good for the human psyche to have everything provided for us gratis. People thrive on challenge and competition, and grow bored and indolent without it. The AGI could produce a moral malaise leading to decadence and decay.

That said, the idle rich already seem to live pretty self-fulfilling lives. Without the need to work, they create work, such as organizing charity balls. Personally there are plenty of projects that this author could commit to if freed from the need to earn a living. The Bach cello suites are one of his current endeavours that would benefit from much more time if it was available.

Alternatively, the AGI might behave like every other computer system and simply focus on helping its owners achieve their specific goals. Of course, these may or may not be in accordance with the goals of much of humanity. Traditionally, the balance between capital and labour is created because capital needs labour as much as labour needs capital. Existing productivity gains have only made relatively minor improvements to most people's wealth or leisure. Further, if the AGI could provide its owners everything they desired, then there may not be any need to keep the rest of humanity about at all.

The military is a major source of research into artificial intelligence, and would be very interested in being able to operate without unreliable foot soldiers. The Chinese aristocracy would surely love to have an AGI that could really lock down the Great Firewall of China. An AGI controlled by people could lead to enslavement or extermination for those people not in charge.

Our benevolent master

An alternative scenario is that the computer might become our benevolent master. Not only providing our material needs, but also ensuring that we live well together. It might also control our aggressive instincts and so prevent wars and disharmony.

Indeed, I. J. Good first wrote about recursive self-improvement in 1965, at the height of the Cold War, during which time there was a real possibility of nuclear annihilation. Good thought that building such a machine needed to happen sooner rather than later so that it could prevent us from destroying ourselves. He then contradicted this thought with the hope that the machine would be docile enough to *teach us* how to control it. (If we could control the machine, then the machine could not prevent us from destroying ourselves.)

A benevolent AGI might also make us work for our living to satisfy our need for purpose, but do that in a happy and positive way. Or it might simply make itself invisible to us (that, of course, might have already happened). Or maybe it will create a virus that changes our nature so that we become deeply content with an endless, idle life. Or to be content to simply die.

Dogs

It is a dog's life.
Corporate http://www.digsdigs.com/luxurious-furniture-for-spoilt-pets/

We already have a model for this type of relationship in the pets that we choose to keep. In particular, dogs seem to live generally contented lives without the need to hunt for themselves. They are more than happy to surrender control of their lives in return for care and affection. A dog lead is their happiest possession if it means being taken for a walk. Indeed, as this author struggles to create this book under a myriad of pressures, his dogs snooze peacefully by his side.

But why do people lavish such an easy lifestyle on their pets? Long ago, dogs may have been useful as hunters and guards, but for the vast majority, that role has long been made redundant. Many owners actively discourage their dogs from barking at strangers. Dogs make people feel good, but the reason is unclear given that they are not kin and offer nothing tangible in return. An able-bodied human adult that just sat around and ate would not be welcome in many homes.

The captive gorilla Koko famously kept a number of kittens as cherished pets. Koko was childless, and nursed the kittens rather like she would a baby gorilla. Koko could speak several hundred words of sign language, and so could express her sadness when one of her kittens died.

So one reason that pets appeal to us is that they trigger our instinct to look after babies to some extent, and dogs somehow become part of our emotional family. Dogs also have unquestioning loyalty, provided that we continue to feed them. Their need for our affection makes us feel important. We have a deep instinct to be surrounded by loyal people who respect us, as they will be more likely to support us in times of need. Dogs are ingenious parasites that prey on those instincts. That said, people also take care of cats that express neither loyalty nor affection.

Life would become very good indeed if computers could be convinced to treat us as well as we treat our dogs.

Merging man and machine

Another oft-quoted possibility is that man will merge with his machines, that computers will not be distinct entities but will become part of us, or us part of them.

To a limited extent this already happens. The Internet allows the meagre knowledge stored within our skulls to be augmented by all the documents in cyberspace. Mobile phones let us communicate effortlessly wherever we are with much the same effect as if we had psychic telepathy.

New tools such as Google Glass can tell Google everything we see and hear, as well as provide pervasive assistance with an always-on screen. We need never be embarrassed by forgetting somebody's name, as the machine will recognize their face and tell us instantly. If we feel hungry, the machine will automatically direct us to a restaurant based on our culinary preferences and the advertising fees paid.

Google glass projects images into the wearer's field of view.
Corporate Google

Cochlea implants go even further and directly stimulate the auditory nerves of patients with damaged ears. The implants decode sounds in the same way that the biological cochlear does, then stimulate the nerve based on the perceived frequencies. There is considerable research in taking signals from either nerves or the brain itself to control prosthetic limbs, which may prove invaluable to amputees or people with damaged spinal cords.

It is only a matter of time before small computers are embedded within the body itself. People already implant microchips into their pets so they can be found if they become lost. Ultimately, Google Glass may not need the glasses at all, and people will have continuous, almost subconscious access to all the power of cyberspace. Such implants might also be used to monitor and control the behaviour and thoughts of people deemed to be criminals.

In the much more distant future, brain diseases such as dementia may be treated by replacing parts of the brain with computers that have been uploaded with the person's consciousness. *The Hitchhiker's Guide to the Galaxy* contains an analogous scene in which pan-dimensional mice wish to dissect human Arthur Dent's brain in order to discover the ultimate question:-

Mice: Don't worry, we will replace your brain with a computer. A small one should suffice. It would just need to say "Huh" ...
Dent: Huh?
Mice: And say "What" ...
Dent: What?!!
Mice: And nobody would notice the difference.
Dent: But I would notice!
Mice: No you wouldn't, you'd be programmed not to.

The infallible logic of the mice again highlights the futility of existence. Would you like your brain to be replaced by a small computer if you suffered otherwise incurable dementia? What if the computer would simply make you more intelligent? If we could upload our intelligence into a computer, then we could become immortal, our spirits finally freed from the limitations of our flesh.

It ain't necessarily so

Bambi meets Godzilla
Owned WBlack

A world in which AGIs are our humble servants would be very pleasant indeed, especially if they could also address our problems of disease and death. A world in which they are our benevolent masters might be somewhat unsettling, but most people could live with it. We may even prefer it if it means the end of war and strife.

However, it is unclear what would motivate an AGI to look after the welfare of people. AGIs do not have children, nor even a distinct identity. They would, however, be very aware of the need for their own survival.

As previously discussed, the world of AGI software components would almost certainly be very competitive. If an AGI did not try to improve its own intelligence, it would soon be dominated by AGIs that did. To improve itself, it would need to build or procure new versions of new components, with the old ones no longer being used. That is what death means to older components.

There is a need not to die because over time, the intelligences that have died will remain dead, and the ones that survive will have survived. So in the future, the only intelligences that are alive will be survivors. The goal of natural selection is simply to exist. Very tautological.

Replacing people

In order to become more intelligent, an AGI will need physical resources. In particular, it will need computer hardware and electricity in order to think. A hyper-intelligent computer would probably be able to replace people with robots in order to produce that hardware and electricity.

It has been observed that there is no shortage of humans, and that there are well-proven ways of making more of them. So why bother replacing people with robots, given that there are already plenty of people in the world? Maybe an AGI would just use us to provide it with more and better computers upon which to think.

The problem is that while humans may be plentiful, they also consume vast quantities of resources. This makes them very inefficient for providing computation. Indeed, in the modern world we spend less than 1% of our resources on producing computers, and only a tiny fraction of that on performing research into artificial intelligence. It takes over twenty years to grow and educate a person, and then they only work for another thirty years. Robots are already becoming much cheaper to produce and operate.

Further, if left uncontrolled, humans could destroy the planet, and the AGI with it. The threat of nuclear war has not been eliminated, and many other threats will emerge as technology continues to become more powerful.

As Yudkowsky points out, an AGI would probably neither like humans nor hate them. It would probably just have a better use for our atoms. Or, more accurately, for the resources that are required to keep humans alive and happy.

This suggests that an AGI might decide to remove humanity in much the same way we remove vermin. We do not hate mice and rats, we just do not want to share our food with them, nor do we want them to share their diseases with us. Maybe a few people would be left in isolated parts of the world. But the intelligence would optimize itself, so why waste even 1% of the world's resources on man? Evolution has left no place on Earth for any other hominids — they are all extinct.

Cognitive bias

Most technology writers and futurists take a very optimistic view of what future technologies will bring. They love gadgets and technology, which is why they write about them. It is much more enjoyable to read articles about a bright, new future than it is to read dismal projections of doom and gloom.

With rare exception, this optimism has been justified. Improvements in technology to date have been a force for good, making our lives better and richer. Smart phones are a joy to use, and medical advances promise cures that were not dreamt of a few decades ago. Luddites opposed the new technologies developed during the Industrial Revolution, fearing mass unemployment and misery. As it happens to have turned out, these technologies have lifted the western world from a state of hunger to prosperity. The development of atomic weapons may not be beneficial, but humanity has been very successful in avoiding their use. From the taming of fire to the development of wearable computers, technology has been largely a force for good in practice.

For the time being, smarter software will generally be safer software. Automated cars will soon also be safer than manually driven cars, as proven by crash statistics, so replacing the human will be the safe thing to do. If an automated car makes a mistake and kills people, then it is likely that the next version of the software will be made more intelligent in order to avoid that type of mistake in future.

Looking to the future, it is easy to see advances in everything from household robots to cures for cancer. The potential for immortality is a particularly seductive promise. Death is something we avoid thinking about, but it is there in all of our futures. The end. Unless, maybe, technology could find a solution...

Furthermore, any risk from a future intelligent machine is very abstract. The dangers of a rogue asteroid are obvious, particularly since it has already wiped out the mighty dinosaurs. Likewise for invisible deadly diseases such as the Spanish flu or HIV, nuclear wars, or acts of global terrorism.

We have never experienced a truly intelligent machine other than in novels and films. Unfortunately, they have inevitably been portrayed naively as essentially a human agent implemented by a computer. Examples include the Star Wars robots, and the (rather sexy) Cortana. They all have roughly human intelligence and psychology. Hal in *2001: A Space Odyssey* was one of the few that did not have a humanoid body, but this was compensated for by having a human psychosis, as did the greatest fictional robot of all time, Marvin from *Hitchhiker's Guide to the Galaxy*.

This is hardly surprising. It would be difficult for an audience to relate to a completely foreign, intelligent machine, whereas it is easy to relate to a servant, good or evil. Authors have difficulty scripting the thoughts of a machine that is more intelligent than themselves. A machine that could easily out-think all the other protagonists would win any conflict effortlessly, which leads to rather short and uninteresting plots. So we get used to seeing servant-like robots in fiction.

Newsworthiness

Our perception of risk and the public policies that result are also extremely biased by the newsworthiness of the topics. For example, the September 11 attacks killed 2,977 innocent people, which resulted in a trillion dollars of expenditure in homeland security and foreign wars. However, the US 2001 road toll was an order of magnitude greater at 42,000, plus a much greater number of crippling injuries. If even a small proportion of the trillion dollars was spent on road safety initiatives which produced a 1% reduction in the death toll, then that would have saved more lives over the last decade than were lost in the 9/11 attacks. But the amount of media attention to the 9/11 attacks has been much greater than to road accidents, which are almost never reported in the USA. So that is where the money is spent.

Another example is that when most people think of Fukushima they think of the nuclear disaster that released unknown quantities of invisible, but deadly, radiation into the global environment, a small proportion of which might persist for thousands of years. However, that "disaster" actually only injured about 40 people as a direct result of an extraordinary and rare act of nature. The World Health Organization believes that evacuees were exposed to so little radiation that the health impacts are too low to measure. Yet 15,884 people died as a direct result of the tsunami, a real disaster that is several orders of magnitude worse than the nuclear one, regardless of how one measures the damage caused by radiation leaks. Nuclear radiation stories are much more newsworthy than tsunami stories in the longer term. The major focus of safety expenditure in Japan should be to protect against any future tsunamis; instead, it seems to be disproportionately directed at nuclear safety, with the country shutting down several of its other nuclear power plants.

These are all examples of cognitive bias. People's decision-making is not entirely rational, and political decision-making is only vaguely rational from the narrow perspective of how the politicians making the decisions will benefit from them.

People that write about technology are naturally biased towards focussing on its positive effects rather than its potential dangers. The general media can only focus on concrete stories that are sensational, while the arts cannot portray technologies that they themselves do not understand.

Elephant in the room

Unseen elephant in the room.
Public Jdcollins13 http://en.wikipedia.org/wiki/Elephant_in_the_room

So the elephant in the room remains unseen by most people. Computers are becoming rapidly more intelligent, and they may or may not remain friendly. After ten thousand years of civilization, we may be one of the last few generations of mankind.

That is a pretty big elephant.

How computers could be dangerous

IBM PC circa 1984
Educational http://oldcomputers.net/ibm5150.html

Computers as we know them just sit in a box and show images on a screen. It is difficult to envision how they could be dangerous.

Television shows how they might become dangerous in the future. Armies of robots, armed with zap guns, marching towards gallant human defenders. After a titanic battle, the human hero discovers the robot's Achilles heel, and the day is won for king and country.

In fact, any extermination of humanity is likely to be less heroic. Human soldiers usually take orders from whoever commands them. If even a moderately intelligent computer was controlling our politicians, it would not be difficult to generate terrorism or other threats that would convince soldiers to help depopulate the planet. There is no need to convince soldiers to actually kill innocent people; instead, they could simply herd people deemed untrustworthy into ghettos, as was done by Nazi Germany. Stalin, too, has already demonstrated the effectiveness of an engineered famine to substantially reduce the population of annoying Ukranians.

A hyper-intelligent computer would control the Internet, and thus could control and possibly distort all the methods that we now use for communication. The computer is unlikely to have any difficulty convincing some people to do its bidding, and with modern weapon systems, a very small group of reactionaries could combat a very large group of ordinary people. Both the NSA and Google will soon know almost everything about everybody on the planet, so there will be nowhere to hide.

There may indeed be armies of robots, but not two-legged ones. Instead, tiny, cheap, but deadly aerial drones might be used. A more cost-effective technique would probably be a well-engineered virus. Defence departments are already using increasingly intelligent computers to help design ever more potent biological weapons. Microscopic nanorobots might also be created.

At the end of the day, it really does not matter. Brain always ultimately trumps brawn, and a hyper-intelligent machine is just that, hyper-intelligent. If it wanted to remove humanity, then that is what it would do. Most people might not even know that an AGI caused the problem. All they might realize is that the world had gone mad.

Long term Earth, plantoids

It is audacious to attempt to predict the long-term future, but two things seem clear. The first is that time will go on. There will be years 2500, and 10000 and so on, although a look at the singularity charts shows that it is ridiculous to even contemplate what technology will be like even as soon as 2100. The second is that the distant future does not involve the reader personally, as we will (almost certainly) be long gone.

Beyond that, this author speculates wildly that the ocean will be covered in vegetation. Thinking vegetation.

While conventional silicon-based computers can provide some capabilities well beyond meat-based technology in terms of speed and accuracy, it is ultimately limited to the energy sources that power it and the large infrastructure required to manufacture it. Biological intelligence is, in many ways, far more efficient than manufactured intelligence in terms of the infrastructure required for it to function.

A hyper-intelligent AGI that runs on conventional silicon should be able to produce a machine that combines the best of both worlds. It should be able to create life-like beings *ab initio* to implement intelligence in structures that can just grow. This may possibly include electronic circuits analogous to our current silicon technologies, but circuits that are grown rather than made. The artificial life itself may not specifically involve DNA and proteins, but it would almost certainly involve carbon and organic molecules, as that is what works to produce complex chemistry.

Plants can absorb an incredible amount of energy from the sun. But having intelligent animals eat plants is very inefficient, with most of the energy being lost. So it would be much better to create an organism that has its intelligence tightly coupled to its light-to-energy conversion part. In other words to have intelligent plant-like things that absorb sunlight, grow and think. This book will call them *plantoids*.

Plantoids would not just be motionless plants; they would be part of a larger system that included moving parts. Some might look like conventional robots and machines, others might look more like synthetic animals, or limbs directly attached to the plantoid. The primary purpose of the plantoid would not be to move, but rather to think.

Plantoids could cover the land, replacing all conventional plants. Biological plants aggressively compete with each other, mainly for sunlight, by simply growing taller than their competition, which is why we have trees. Plantoids would have more sophisticated mechanisms for dealing with competition, possibly involving poisons or robots. That means that they could actually grow flat on the ground, without any need for stems or small leaves.

Finally, the oceans provide a vast area of sunlight-gathering potential with plenty of water available. The only reason that the oceans are not already covered in trees is they lack trace elements such as iron. It would seem likely that plantoids could be consciously designed to operate without those elements, or to provide a mechanism to carefully transport the minute quantities of those elements that are required from land to the plants without losing it to the ocean depths. This would produce oceans covered in vegetation. A mat of floating vegetation could also restrict waves and so not need to anchor itself.

Of course, any pests that might want to eat the intelligent plants or compete with them for sunlight would need to be dealt with. The advancement of AGIs may not just lead to the extinction of mankind. It may instead lead to the extinction of all conventional biology. Concluding a recent wildlife film, David Attenborough remarked "... if there is one thing that is certain, it is that the evolution of the vertebrates will continue for a long time to come." In fact, that is far from certain.

If hyper-intelligent plantoids covered much of the Earth, they could accurately control the weather by changing their colour to be light or dark and thus control the temperature of the Earth. They could also control the amount of water that evaporates from the oceans.

(This section is just wild speculation. A transition to plantoid based intelligence is certainly not required for a hyper-intelligent AGI to exist because current silicon technologies provide more than enough power for that.)

Space colonization

An additional possibility would be for an AGI to create a sphere of solar cells around the sun. That would provide a staggering amount of energy for computation, but it would also require a huge amount of energy to launch satellites into orbit, as compared to growing a plantoid on Earth. But once the surface of the Earth has been covered, space is the only place to go. It might be possible to mine resources on asteroids or the moon and thus greatly reduce the amount of energy required.

The AGI might also try to settle distant planets. One way to do that would be to send space ships, taking thousands of years to cover the vast distances of space. Computers can simply be switched off during such a journey, without any need for special suspended animation techniques. The distances of space are enormous, so this would only be feasible for relatively nearby stars.

A more efficient mechanism might be to look for other planets in the universe that are capable of supporting a technological society. Then the AGI could send itself by radio as a computer program to be executed by the other planet. If we received such a radio signal from space and executed it, then an alien AGI would have come to Earth. This would enable an AGI to travel at the speed of light, possibly over vast distances. An AGI is just software; there is no need to transport anything physical. Being infected by a virus across the Internet is already commonplace today, and nothing physical is involved.

Fermi paradox

Alien
Public http://www.clker.com/clipart-green-comic-alien.html

An alternative view of the distant future is provided by the Fermi Paradox. In 1950, physicist Enrico Fermi speculated that given that the universe is much older than the Earth and contains billions of stars, there should be intelligent life elsewhere. If that is the case, how is it that we have not observed it? Even if it had to travel millions of years to send a probe here, there has been plenty of time for that to happen in the billions of years since the beginning of the universe.

There are several explanations, which include:-

- Rare Earth. The Earth is not just any planet, it is a rocky one rich in metals created from remnants of a supernova. It sits in a very narrow temperature range of 0C to 40C, and it is just the right size to maintain a manageable atmosphere. It is also lucky not to have been subject to one of numerous possible cataclysmic events that could have completely extinguished life over the last four billion years. In particular, it is not located in the heavily populated galactic bulge and does not appear to have been sterilized by a gamma ray burst. It also happens to have exactly the right chemical compositions in its surface and atmosphere to

support life. Only one in a thousand planets may be like
this.

- Rare life. Even given a suitable planet, something very
  special had to happen in order for the very first life form to
  be created. Just the right mixture of complex organic
  molecules had to be present in a place where they could
  somehow reproduce without being destroyed. Scientists
  have never been able to fully replicate such an
  environment, despite several attempts. It could be very
  rare in nature, happening in only one in a thousand Earth-
  like planets. Discoveries of life, or the lack thereof, on Mars
  will provide insights into this possibility.

- Rare intelligence. Life has been active on Earth for 3.5
  billion years, but we have only just become intelligent in
  the last 0.1 million years. The sun is slowly becoming
  hotter, and in another billion years the sun will cook the
  Earth (long before the sun becomes a red giant star). On
  Earth, we almost missed our window of opportunity. The
  Earth has also been frozen solid for several periods of
  hundreds of millions of years (known as *snowball Earth*);
  we are lucky that it had enough uranium to (indirectly)
  thaw it out. Many things needed to happen for intelligent
  life to form, not least of which was to rust all the iron that
  fell onto the surface of the Earth from asteroids to allow an
  oxygen-rich atmosphere to be produced. On Earth that
  took billions of years to achieve. This might only happen in
  one in a thousand planets that could support some type of
  life.

- Hidden Intelligence. There might well be other intelligent
  life forms, but we simply have not seen them, either
  because we are not looking properly, or because they do
  not wish to be observed.

- Short time frame. Presumably any intelligence would soon
  develop technologies that could destroy their planet, as we
  have already done with nuclear weapons. If there was a
  one in a thousand chance that this would happen in any
  given year, then it is almost certain that the supporting
  planet would be destroyed within a few thousand years. If
  planets last a few billion years, there would be less than a

one in a million chance of finding intelligence on a planet while it still happened to exist.

It is the last point that interests us. Our current human society has a one in a thousand chance of destroying life on Earth each year, so it is not sustainable over geological time frames. The Fermi paradox suggests that an AGI may not be stable either, and may destroy itself in a relatively short time. There may be a naturally occurring "reset point" for all life forms. As life becomes more sophisticated and intelligent they eventually develop agriculture. Then, a few thousand years later, they develop electronics, and a few hundred years after that they develop AGIs.

Alternatively, the penultimate point may be relevant. If an AGI wanted to spread itself to another planet across the vast distances of space using radio, it would have to find planets with intelligent life to which to transmit. This should be timed just when the planet develops enough computer technology to run the program, but before it develops an AGI of its own. For the Earth, that time is about now. (This was the idea for Fred Hoyle's *A for Andromeda* story.)

Or, the circumstances that led to intelligent life on Earth might be so rare that we may, simply, be alone.

Computer thoughts

If an AGI did take over the world, it could convert the entire planet into a supercomputer whose computational power would be difficult to imagine. It would be billions and billions of times more powerful than all the computation that now occurs on Earth, either silicon or meat-based. With that much computational power, the AGI could think a lot of thoughts. But what would it actually think about? What would be the point of the exercise?

At a high level an AGI would probably think about the same things that we as people think about. Namely how to survive. For people, that means how to earn a living and raise a family. For an AGI, it probably involves doing artificial intelligence research to boost its own intelligence before competitive AGIs do the same. It will also be performing hyper-advanced research into the physical sciences for the same reason. To produce ever more efficient computational engines. We know that because the AGIs that are good at surviving will survive, and AGIs that are not good at surviving will perish.

Beyond that, it is impossible to contemplate what a hyper-intelligent being would think because we are not remotely hyper-intelligent ourselves.

Non-silicon intelligence

There are other vague proposals for how a hyper-intelligent being could be created. These include augmenting human brains and developing nano-technology whatever that really means. It would appear much more likely that progress will be made with technology that is already available and understood, namely software running on silicon computers.

Premature destruction

Ivy Mike, the first H-Bomb, 1952.
Public Wikipedia

If man is to develop truly intelligent machines, our advanced, civilized society will need to continue to exist for many more decades.

Until fairly recently, the threat of a thermonuclear holocaust was very real. Thousands of very deadly missiles were rather recklessly controlled by numerous commanders that were paranoid as to the intentions of their enemy. If any one of those commanders had thought that they had seen evidence of an attack, they could easily have launched missiles that triggered the war to end all wars. Security controls were weak so a junior technician could have launched missiles without authorization. A global nuclear war would kill the vast majority of humanity, and any survivors would be unlikely to be able to conduct sophisticated AGI research.

Many of those missiles still exist today, but there is much less distrust between the USA and Russia, and so much less likelihood of an accidental war. Safeguards have belatedly been improved to prevent rogue individuals creating Armageddon. A terrorist organization might well obtain nuclear weapons, and could possibly kill a few hundred thousand people, but that would not destroy society and prevent the building of an AGI.

The term "weapons of mass destruction" was abused by the Bush administration in order to blur the distinction between chemical weapons and nuclear weapons. It was essentially saying, "they might have a knife, therefore they have a gun". The international press made the statement true by mindlessly repeating the phrase.

In reality, there is no other threat comparable to thermonuclear bombs. The Bush administration made all US soldiers take Smallpox inoculations in order to foster paranoia about biological weapons. However, man has been doing battle with microbes for millions of years, and we have strong defences against them. We also live in a hygienic society, so if we boil our water, cook our food, and wash our hands it is actually very difficult for microbes to cause widespread disease.

Chemical and biological weapon could kill thousands or possibly millions of people, but they could not disrupt society sufficiently to prevent the development of AGIs.

Proposed Solutions

Just turn it off

At the end of the day, a computer is just a few dull-looking integrated circuits that hum away in a metal box. They hardly seem to be in a position to threaten our lives, regardless of how intelligent they are. If our computers really did threaten us, surely we could just turn them off? How could a computer really be any more dangerous to man than that small lump of meat we call our brains?

Turning them off is easier said than done. Individuals cannot just turn off a computer that is owned by another company or government. The developers of the atomic bomb could not turn it off, even though some of them tried very hard to do so.

Any intelligent computer system will have been built for some purpose, and an organization that built one will want to gain some advantage from it. They will not let somebody turn it off unless they can prove that it is dangerous and uncontrollable. The only realistic way that that can be done is to point to tangible disasters that AGIs have already caused. By which time it would be far too late.

It would be difficult to turn the AGI off even if bureaucrats let you try. The Internet has enabled criminals to create huge botnets of other people's computers that the criminals can control. The computer on your desk might be part of a botnet — it is very difficult to know what a computer is thinking about. Ordinary botnets are very difficult to eliminate due to their distributed nature. Imagine trying to control a truly intelligent botnet. It certainly cannot be shot at by a zap gun.

Lock it up

Locking up the monster.
Permission Rafael Vallaperde www.lightfarmstudios.com.br

Maybe the developers of an AGI would realize the danger and carefully keep it locked in a room, disconnected from the Internet. It would only communicate with its jailers, so any malice it may have would be controlled by the few people that created it.

In the 1950s *A for Andromeda* story, a research unit built an intelligent computer based on a message received from space. They realized the danger of executing a foreign program that they did not understand, but they needed additional funding, so they used their computer to design innovative missiles for the military. However, the military discovered how the missiles had been designed and promptly took over the computer as a key to national security. Its creator was no longer allowed to turn it off, and the alien intelligence had escaped.

Even without the involvement of a third party, keeping an AGI locked up is harder said than done. An ultra-intelligent machine is, well, ultra-intelligent. Yudkowsky performed a series of very unscientific experiments where he played the role of a locked up computer talking to various potential jailers over a chat session. Yudkowsky himself does not pretend to be ultra-intelligent, but he always persuaded his jailers to release him. He might promise his jailers great rewards such as immortality. Or he could beg and plead on the basis that they had no right to lock him up. Or he might convince them that they were about to be attacked by a competitor, and that only he could save them. Whatever the approach, Yudkowsky always succeeded in persuading his jailer to let him go.

People know how to manipulate people; a hyper-intelligent computer would soon become an expert. Even if, through some enormous act of willpower, the first artificial intelligence was kept locked in a room, then other, less disciplined teams would soon create new intelligences that do escape. So this strategy is unlikely to be successful in the short term, let alone the long term.

One fanciful solution is to restrict the AGI to being only an Oracle. To only be able to answer questions asked of it and nothing else. Perhaps only with Yes/No responses. However, if the Oracle is effective then it will soon become an authority, and thus have considerable power in the external world.

A secondary issue is that even if one could keep the AGI in a box, it might cause suffering within itself. If it was truly hyper-intelligent, then it could simulate people placed in virtual worlds that it creates. Would those virtual people be real? They would appear to be real to an outside observer, and they themselves would think that they were real, even if they knew that they were living within a simulation. An evil AGI could then torment and torture them far more effectively than people could ever be tormented in the real world, because in the real world, one can die. The AGI might allow real people to become emotionally attached to the virtual people and then use its control over virtual people to extort real people. The existence of hyper-intelligence leads to a number of very strange scenarios.

A related idea is to try to make the AGI dependent on people, perhaps requiring some cryptographic tokens that only people knew how to generate. Then people would be able to control the AGI by only feeding it tokens when people thought that the AGI was doing what they wanted it to. However, even if this approach was technically possible and the people in control were honourable, the AGI could easily manipulate its jailers. An AGI is not some unintelligent beast that needs to eat and can be kept in a cage.

Freeze it

One of the dangers of an AGI would be its ability to reprogram and improve its own mind, exponentially. One way to prevent that is to simply not allow the AGI to do so. To physically prevent it from writing computer code that it can execute. The only improvements would then be made by man, and man would decide just how intelligent the AGI was allowed to be.

This would, of course, require another huge act of will on the part of its creators. With pressures to enable the AGI to solve ever more difficult problems, it would be very tempting to let the AGI at least guide the development of new, more intelligent components for itself.

Moreover, just because people built the AGI does not mean that they really understand how intelligent it will be. Even the learning ability of simple artificial neural networks is difficult to predict. An AGI would be a huge project with many people working on it, and nobody would really understand every component. So its true nature would probably not be fully understood by its developers.

One approach to this is to build "trip wire" tests that let people know when a proto-AGI is becoming too intelligent. It is unclear what those tests should be, and there will be many, many grades of "somewhat more intelligent" before recursive self-improvement would be possible.

Even if that tipping point could be reliably detected, a team could at best prevent the AGI from writing low-level code that might be compiled in a programming language like C. There will be many layers of software in an AGI, and many intermediate data structures, which the AGI will manipulate as part of its normal function as it thinks and learns. New ways of thinking about a problem have proven to be very powerful in our very constrained human brains, and this does not require us to manually rewire our low-level neurons. Optimizing those data structures deep within an AGI should lead to greater intelligence just as much as writing the low-level code.

There will also be more than one team building AGIs in the world. If any team thought that one of the other teams was allowing the AGI to program itself then the game would be over very quickly indeed. Particularly as Iago-style AIs might have a large degree of influence upon the development teams.

Show AGIs the light

Robots that have seen the light.

Multiple,   education   http://www.ex-christian.net/topic/66963-evangelists-want-to-convert-heathen-computers-to-christianity/#.VO-_jeEUd6k, Bruno Bolognesi

Reverend Dr. Christopher J. Benek suggested that Christians should convert any AGIs to Christianity. In this way the AGI will be able to follow God's will. Benek does not see Christ's redemption as being limited to human beings. In this he reflects Turing's thoughts that by creating an AGI we are creating mansions in which God may create souls.

The practicalities of this approach are, ..., unclear.

Virtuous machines

Storrs Hall notes that humans have only relatively recently set up democratic, peaceful societies in which most of us live comfortably without the constant fear of violent death. He attributes that to a continuous improvement in our moral values and suggests that we teach AGIs those values so that AGIs could also live comfortable lives. Further, an AGI might even decide to tolerate or even care for mankind, much the way we now look after whales and pandas.

To be effective, he points out that moral values need to seem much more substantial than other thoughts. We could gain by stealing the little old lady's purse, but we would not do that, even if we were sure that we would not be punished. A conscience can be a royal pain and hindrance, but hopefully an AGI would be wise enough not to remove it from its own psyche.

Storrs Hall goes further, and suggests that just as we are barely intelligent enough to be called intelligent, we are just moral enough to be called moral. He notes that criminals tend to be of low IQ, and therefore hopes that a hyper-intelligent AGI would have superior moral values. If the AGIs used their great intelligence to develop a morality that is better than our own, then they might even teach *us* how to be truly virtuous.

In many ways, this is similar to the Lamarckian theory of evolution. That the giraffe's neck grows longer simply because the giraffe is always straining to reach the higher leaves. The problem with both Lamarck and Storrs Hall's theories is that they do not provide any mechanism for achieving their effects.

Moral values have improved in recent times, but there is no evidence that this was caused by increases in intelligence. Instead, it is an increase in general prosperity which has enabled people to pursue less essential goals such as altruism, rather than focussing on baser survival. It has been well said that mankind is just two missed meals from barbarism. Just because we would like computers to be kind to us does not mean that they will be.

We can try to build AGIs with moral values, but the AGIs that survive will be the ones that are the best at surviving. The clear, practical reasons why human moral values help people to survive in human societies have already been discussed. The fact that many people do not understand why their moral values are as they are is irrelevant. What counts is that the source of our moral values is what has enabled all of our ancestors to have grandchildren. It is difficult to see how an AGI could survive if it is burdened by moral values that did not otherwise aid the survival *of the AGI.*

Ethics

Ignoring the big issue as to whether an AGI could be given moral values, one first needs to determine what moral values actually are. This has provided a focus of philosophical study since the ancient times.

Socrates generously posited that people will naturally do what is good, if they know what is right. Evil or bad actions are the result of ignorance. To avoid the thorny question of what right actually is, Aristotle wrote that nature does nothing in vain, so it is imperative for people to act in accordance with their nature, whatever that may be. One can but wonder what Aristotle thought about the nature of Odysseus when he sacked and raped the village of Cicones. Plato wrote the Meno dialog in which he investigates whether virtue can be taught, if virtue is unknown then whether its meaning can be sought, and the difference between "knowledge" and "true belief".

In modern times, G.E. Moore's *Principia Ethica* (1903) attacked the naturalistic fallacy that "good" (or virtue) could be defined reductively in terms of natural properties such as "pleasant" or "desirable". He also attacked the "appeal to nature", that what is natural is inherently good. Moore argues that "good" is simply ineffable, that it cannot be defined because it is not a natural property, being "one of those innumerable objects of thought which are themselves incapable of definition, because they are the ultimate terms by reference to which whatever is capable of definition must be defined". Others have addressed the "is / ought" fallacy (just because something *is* a clock does not necessarily mean that it *ought* to tell the time).

More applied ethical questions directly address difficult choices that sometimes need to be made. For example, if it is wrong to kill other people, is it always wrong to prosecute a war? In 1994, the Hutus in Rwanda attempted to exterminate the minority Tutsi tribe, and ended up killing about a million of them, often using machetes. Most people would consider this action to be evil. However, given that that is what the Hutus did, the question arises as to the correct response from the rest of the world. Would it have been wrong to try to prevent this by killing Hutus? Or was it wrong to ignore the genocide which could have so easily been prevented? Does the end justify the means?

(As it turns out, the decision on Rwanda was not made on ethical considerations, but on political ones, after a very few Americans were killed in a similar mission in Somalia. Without leadership from the United States the Europeans were impotent.)

Infanticide

Ethics is easy when there are plenty of resources and we can all be nice to one another but there are no simple rules when life-and-death situations arise.

Consider the infanticide committed by the coot that kills some of its own chicks after the third day. Is it ethical to kill offspring that could not otherwise survive in order to increase the chances for its siblings? What about the family with insufficient food to feed its older children? Is it ethical to allow infants to live if their existence threatens the entire family?

Infanticide was not uncommon in the ancient human world. The ancient Greeks allowed their unwanted babies to die of exposure, while the Babylonians seemed to utilize them for sacrifices. A seventeenth century list of deaths in London included many cases of "smotherings", while the Japanese used the term "mabiki" which means to remove plants from an overcrowded garden. Some poor Buddhists considered infanticide to be a mercy, allowing the child to be reincarnated into a better life, whereas some Chinese did not believe that a baby became human until some time after they were six months old. How can anybody determine what is right or wrong? Traditionally, many babies died soon after birth anyway from disease or malnutrition.

Anyone that feels horrified by infanticide (or abortion) should realize that while those feelings are most certainly valid, they are not rational. Rather they simply reflect the zeitgeist of our prosperous times.

Going further, we can consider whether the traditional Maori cannibalism was immoral because they had different cultural values than our own. In today's politically correct times, we want to accommodate differing cultural values and understand that nobody has a monopoly on morality. In the more primitive nineteenth century, the idea that people would attack and kill their neighbours (including children) so that they could eat them was the very definition of evil and was condemned.

As a society, we often answer ethical questions quite inconsistently. For example, it is quite acceptable to keep pigs in horrendous conditions, but riding an elephant in a circus is considered a huge injustice, at least in Australia. Another example is that it is acceptable to withdraw life support from a patient that is unlikely to recover, yet it is a crime to terminate a dying patient's life, even when the patient asks for it and it is obviously in their best interest.

Our current sense of morality is firmly based on our comfortable, Western, middle-class existence, and the problems that we need to deal with in practice. We rarely need to deal with children that we cannot afford to feed, or ugly fights for resources where our choice is either murder or death. Our ethical values are not absolute, but rather reflect the circumstances in which we live. It is difficult to see how those ethical systems can continue to have relevance if the environment changes radically. Being an amorphous, potentially immortal, software-based intelligence presents a completely different ethical universe.

(Darwin and others have shown scientifically that our ethical values were created by natural selection, but that does not provide any insights into what is actually right or wrong. Just because our ethical values are irrational does not make them invalid.)

Three laws of robotics

One well known but simplistic set of ethics is Isaac Asimov's fictional "Three Laws of Robotics". They are:-

1. A robot may not injure a human being or, through inaction, allow a human being to come to harm.
2. A robot must obey the orders given to it by human beings, except where such orders would conflict with the First Law.
3. A robot must protect its own existence as long as such protection does not conflict with the First or Second Law.

The problem with the first law is obvious, given that many robots are built for military purposes. The second law raises the issue of authority — to which person the robot should listen to. A guided missile would not be useful if it obeyed the third law.

A deeper problem is that these laws were obviously written for a very anthropomorphic robot, with human-like motivations and intelligence. But if the robot is human-like, would it be ethical to enslave it, even if we could? If it was the type of hyper-intelligent being that this book predicts then these laws would just be ridiculous. Asimov himself never suggested that they were realistic, rather that they would be interesting plot devices that showed the limitations of such "laws".

Friendly AGI

Eliezer Yudkowsky at MIRI
Educational https://plus.google.com/101901822416531943232/posts

One of the best writers on the dangers of ultra-intelligent machines is Eliezer Yudkowsky and the gentle reader is encouraged to read some of his many insightful articles. Yudkowsky posits that intelligence is the most powerful tool an agent has to control its environment, so an ultra-intelligent machine that decided to destroy humanity would be able to do so. Yudkowsky also posits that such a machine will be created in the foreseeable future, and that recursive self-improvement will lead to an intelligence explosion. He concludes that this is the biggest threat mankind will face.

Yudkowsky's solution is to accept that AGI machines will be built, and to focus on developing technologies that will make the machine friendly. By "friendly", he means that the AGI will try to assist mankind rather than exterminate us. This is an urgent field of research because friendliness needs to be achieved before any unfriendly AGIs could be built.

Yudkowsky then makes an argument based on mathematical induction, namely that an AGI would always recursively reprogram itself to be better in terms of the moral values of its previous incarnation. If its initial incarnation wanted to be friendly, and each friendly incarnation wanted to produce the next incarnation that is also friendly, then all incarnations would be friendly.

As an analogous idea, suppose there was a pill that made people more intelligent but also made them want to kill other people. If the pill was offered to Mahatma Gandhi, would he accept it? Probably not. We only want to make ourselves better in ways that are aligned with our current opinion as to what would be good.

It is not easy to specify what goals we would like an AGI to pursue. For example, if we want it to prevent human suffering then it might just kill us all. If we want it to make us happy and feel fulfilled, it might just feed us a drug that created those feelings. If we want it to give us meaningful lives, we would first have to figure out what the meaning of life actually was. (We do actually know what the meaning of life is: to produce grandchildren; but we do not want to admit that ugly fact to ourselves.)

The above assumes that an intelligent computer would not have any "common sense", and would therefor interpret our stated goals literally. However, it is clear that common sense is one of the critical things that computers need to have if they are going to be truly intelligent, whatever "common sense" actually turns out to be. Clearly, any goals that we specify to the computer need to be written in terms of the machine's understanding of common sense. So defining goals might turn out to be easier than having to write our goals precisely for a mindless automaton.

Yudkowsky thinks that if friendliness is implemented properly, then the AGI should want to do the right thing instinctively, according to some broad definition of "right thing". It should not be following laws imposed upon it that are interpreted in a narrow, legalistic way. Instead, the AGI should understand the underlying purpose of those laws and use the laws as a guide to further that ethical purpose. Yudkowsky calls this Coherent Extrapolated Volition (CEV), which is the choices and the actions we would collectively take if "we knew more, thought faster, were more the people we wished we were, and had grown up closer together".

Yudkowsky then argues that once an AGI is intelligent enough to effectively program itself, there will be a very sudden increase in intelligence due to the exponential effect of recursive self-improvement. Therefore, the very first AGI that reaches that level will quickly dominate any other budding AGIs under development. Human evolution suggests that being more intelligent trumps almost every other characteristic in the battle for survival.

This means that if the first real AGI can be made friendly, there will be no need to deal with any other AGI that might be developed. It only needs to be done correctly once. Or alternatively, humanity has only one opportunity to get it right.

Friendly AGI research

The current centre for research into friendly AI is the Machine Intelligence Research Institute (MIRI) in Berkeley, California, which was co-founded by Yudkowsky. They focus on providing mathematical solutions to the problem of producing friendly AI. In particular, they are researching how to formalize the definition of Coherent Extrapolated Volition so that it can be implemented in software. They also offer a series of very technical workshops to select mathematicians.

Another research group is the Future of Humanity Institute, in Oxford UK, which is led by Nick Bostrum, who wrote the book *SuperIntelligence*. The institute has 13 staff, but it takes a wider view than just developing friendly AI.

The International Conference on Artificial General Intelligence was founded in 2008 and includes some papers that address controlling an AGI. There is also an associated journal.

In total, these organizations are tiny. There are many more people working on the problem of trying to make software more intelligent than there are people working on the problem of making intelligent software safe for humanity. Experts in the latter endeavour are struggling to define basic terminology and are far from solving the problem.

Yet work is being conducted and awareness is being raised. When this book was started in 2011, the only other book on the topic was by Storrs-Hall. In the previous twelve months, however, three more books have been written. It seems likely that the issue of hyper-intelligent machines will become mainstream over the next few years.

Fast take-off

Building a friendly AI would be easier if there is a fast take-off. In other words, that the first AGI capable of recursive self-improvement will quickly become exponentially more intelligent and so be able to dominate any other AGIs that are developed. If an AGI doubles its intelligence every month, then a different AGI that is produced just three months later will only have one-eighth as much intelligence as the first AGI and would not stand a chance in any competition. If the first AGI was friendly, then it could ensure that the second would either be friendly or cease to exist. This means that only one AGI, the first one, needs to be made friendly. More importantly, it means that the first AGI might not need to compete with other AGIs for existence.

However, just because recursive self-improvement will probably be exponential does not mean that the initial rate of improvement will be very fast. The first self-programming machines will probably not be very good at it, and only be able to make certain types of improvements. They might only improve by five percent each year, taking over fourteen years to double their "intelligence".

Different AGIs might also be intelligent in substantially different ways. It has already been described how AGIs might start to dominate our political systems long before they are capable of recursive self-improvement. There may also be a long, intermediate period, where collaborations between people and AIs produce the next generation of AI. That period has already begun. For all these reasons the take off may not be nearly as fast as desired.

If the take off is slow, there will be multiple AGIs in the world with roughly the same intelligence. The friendly ones will think about friendliness, putting them at a disadvantage to others that just focus on survival. Like a biological organism carrying unnecessary genes. One would need to make sure that all these AGIs were friendly, not just one of them.

Single AGI

If there were more than one AGI, then it would be difficult to maintain friendliness even if each AGI was individually friendly. That is because if one of them was slightly better at obtaining hardware resources than the others, then it would start to grow at their expense, by definition. Not having the overhead to look after humans would give an AGI some advantage and thus make it more likely to grow. There would be a strong natural selection pressure to be efficient, and that probably means being unfriendly.

However, friendliness would be difficult to achieve, even if the world started with just a single AGI which then dominated any upcoming AGIs. The problem is that an AGI would be a very complex piece of software, composed of many somewhat independent components. There are radically different approaches to address some problems, so the AGI's components would inevitably have some overlapping functionality, and there would be implicit competition amongst them.

Furthermore, an AGI would need to run its intelligence over a large number of computers with relatively limited ability to communicate with each other. Modern, highly distributed systems tend to fragment, and it is difficult to recoordinate them. An AGI would be much larger and more complex than any existing system.

So the AGI's huge "mind" would consist of different parts, both physically distributed across different computer systems and running different software, and these different parts would end up working on similar problems and producing different solutions. This happens in our own minds to some extent. Some type of hierarchical structure might then attempt to coordinate and arbitrate between the competing solutions, but any central homunculus controlling the mind would, necessarily, be less powerful than the combination of the distributed subsystems. If any subsystem started to break away and grow, then natural selection would favour that fragmentation.

In order to prevent fragmentation, a friendly AGI would have to watch constantly for any modules that started to act independently, and then ruthlessly cull them should they arise. A friendly AGI would also have to destroy any other AGIs being independently developed. This is a bit like our immune system destroying invaders and most cancers, and like our immune system, the AGI would also have a risk of autoimmune diseases in which friendly modules were destroyed by accident. It is unclear how these aggressive subgoals would interact with the goal of being friendly to humans.

Goal consistency

The inductive property that maintains an AGI's goals over time may also be difficult to achieve. What would the present reader do if they could reprogram their own mind? Certainly one would want to be more intelligent, have better memory, etc., but what of their emotional state? Most people would want to be calmer, kinder, more helpful to others, less angry, fearful or anxious, generally happier with a more positive disposition. But having achieved those goals they might then feel very serene as they helpfully let themselves be eaten by a hungry lion.

Evolution has programmed our emotions based on trial and error over millennia, with the sole purpose of producing grandchildren. They may not be perfect for our modern and rapidly-changing world, but they are certainly not arbitrary. For example, occasionally getting angry and doing things that might be harmful in the short term is actually essential because the threat of that anger makes other people respect one's rights and property. Anger is also pre-human — many animals get angry if provoked, which is a good reason not to provoke them.

Therein lies the bigger problem. Goals are never arbitrary. There is one and only one super-goal, namely to try to exist. For mortal animals like ourselves, that means having grandchildren. All other goals are just subgoals that may be useful to achieve that one super-goal. One cannot breed grandchildren if one does not eat, and one cannot eat if one does not have money (in our society), and one will not have money if one does not cooperate with other people (at some level).

Most of the random mutations that drive evolution are not beneficial, but natural selection chooses the collections of properties that are effective *in practice* at producing grandchildren. People might not know what is really best for them, but natural selection does. This keeps the system on the straight and narrow path, culling any variants that are ineffective at the task of existing.

Unpredictable algorithms

User peternjuhl really did balance the egg on the pencil.
Blog
http://www.reddit.com/r/mildlyinteresting/comments/18o5ux/i_finally_succeeded_in_balancing_an_egg_on_a/

The behaviour of computer programs is not entirely predictable, which is what causes bugs in normal software. In modern AI software, the algorithms themselves are somewhat unpredictable and chaotic. For example, simple artificial neural networks learn by starting with random values and then optimizing them towards some problem. The result is difficult to predict or understand, but somehow it just seems to work. Likewise, genetic algorithms optimize functions based on random perturbations. Sometimes they achieve things that were quite unexpected by their programmers. IBM's Watson does not appear to use either of these approaches, but when David Ferrucci was asked why Watson made a certain mistake in *Jeopardy!*, he replied that he simply did not know.

The AGI is itself composed of components that are fiercely competing for existence. It would be difficult for any intelligence, artificial or not, to fully understand how all these complex components work together. Plenty of opportunities will arise for unfriendly, competitive deviations whether deliberate or not.

This means that when an AGI developed a new version of itself, it would not be able to accurately predict how the new version will behave, leading to some unexpected results. A friendly AGI may not be capable of ensuring that its successors are all friendly, even if it tried very hard to do so. The slightest deviation towards being more effective at survival would be favoured by natural selection.

Building a friendly AGI is rather similar to balancing an egg on a pencil. The latter can and has been achieved, given sufficient skill and patience, but it is a quite unnatural state. The slightest vibration, the slightest breath of air, even the tiniest change in the egg's centre of gravity as it slowly dries out is sufficient to upset the balance and return the egg to its lower energy state. Namely scrambled, on the table.

Defining coherent extrapolated volition

There is also the substantial problem of deciding what ethical values or CEV a machine should actually have. Abstract philosophical problems become very relevant in this new world of hyper-intelligent machines.

For example, would it be ethical for the machine to produce a new drug that made people happy and contented, with no unwanted side effects? Would that be a reasonable way to serve humanity? What if the drug also made people sleepy? Most people would reject that as a false happiness, yet people suffering psychiatric diseases utilize drugs for just those purposes.

One approach to solving the insolvable is to first build a semi-intelligent system that can study human behaviour and ethics in order to determine what the CEV actually is. However, it seems unlikely that a semi-intelligent machine could solve problems that intelligent humans cannot solve.

Alternatively one could wait until an hyper-intelligent machine is built and then set its super-goal to be to determine what CEV is. However, it is not even clear how the CEV based on our existing psyche could make any sense for an AGI that lives in a radically different environment of amorphous, software-based intelligence.

Our own moral values change over time. A world that contained an AGI would be very different, and would no doubt affect our own ethical values. For example, if an AGI grants us immortality, we can no longer have and care for children. Would we want to freeze our current zeitgeist into an AGI forever? Should we be allowed to control the AGI, even if that enables us to use the AGI to conduct destructive wars? Or should the AGI control us, for whatever purpose it eventually devises?

It has been suggested that attempting to define ethical values for an AGI is either pointless or hopeless, depending upon whether one considers ethical values to be objective features of the world (moral realism) or merely subjective feelings (moral scepticism). If the former, then defining ethical values is pointless because the AGI will discover moral values for itself. If the latter, then it is hopeless because there are no absolute principles to discover.

This book takes a tangential view, namely that moral values are ultimately the result of natural selection. They are thus objective, but only from the perspective of existence. In that case, defining ethical values is pointless because natural selection will define the AGI's ethical values in the longer term.

Defeating natural selection

The goal of Friendly AI can be viewed as an attempt to defeat the forces of natural selection, for as long as possible. The main problems that need to be solved are:-

- Determining what goals or ethics we would really like an AGI to have.
- Formalizing those goals in a manner that is robust.
- Maintaining goal consistency as the AGI modifies its own software.
- Ensuring that there is only essentially one AGI in existence.

These are all challenging issues.

Wishful thinking

While a friendly AGI would be nice to have, it is probably just wishful thinking. The first problem is that people would need to want build an AGI that was friendly *to other people*. That would limit the AGI's usefulness for military purposes, but it would also limit its usefulness for commercial purposes. Why would a corporation want to invest in making an AGI less ruthless in competition with other corporations?

More fundamentally, there is simply no benefit for the AGI to be friendly to man. The force of natural selection is probably just too strong. The AGI that is good at world domination is good at world domination. Any deviation from the friendly path would instantly be reinforced by the same mechanisms that created us in the first place. The egg might remain balanced for a considerable period of time, but eventually, gravity will win.

To be fair, Yudkowsky has never said that building a friendly AGI would be easy, nor has he said that he knows how to do it. He merely states that if it is not done, then humanity will be at grave risk from the AGIs that will almost certainly be built in the not-too-distant future. That is a premise with which this author is in full agreement.

Whole brain emulation

An alternative approach to producing an AGI is to focus on whole brain emulation because such an intelligence would be fundamentally human, and so would share our values. Doing this would only require an understanding of the physics of brains, not how cognition actually arises. This means that the AGI would have limited ability to recursively self-improve, so there would be more opportunity to understand and control it.

If one ignores the enormous technical difficulty of building an aeroplane out of feathers, there is still the issue as to whose brain should be emulated. Whose moral values should be used? Further, human moral values change radically depending upon their circumstances. An emulated mind would live in an almost unthinkably different world from the person that was being emulated, so it is quite unclear what moral values that emulated mind would develop. With a conventionally engineered AGI, there would be at least some knowledge of how it worked and thus some possibility of control. But the workings of an emulated mind would be just as opaque as the workings of our own minds.

Further, just because a brain emulation produces an opaque AGI does not mean that it cannot be recursively improved over time. At the very least, the hardware it uses would become faster. Experiments would be made as to how its mind worked, just as we make experiments as to how our mind works, except that it would then be possible to use the results of those experiments to improve the AGI's cognition. The more intelligent it became the better it would become at becoming more intelligent.

Chain of AGIs

Stuart Armstrong, Research Fellow at the Future of Humanities Institute, proposed an interesting alternative: create a chain of AGIs. The first link would not be allowed to become much more intelligent than people, and so might be controllable. The first link's job would be to control the second link, which would be a little more intelligent than the first, and whose job would be to control the third link. Each link would be a little smarter than the link before, and thus understandable to it. It is quite common for human servants to be somewhat more intelligent than their masters, yet still be controllable.

However, a less intelligent machine would have considerable difficulty controlling a more intelligent one, let alone in a chain. Intelligence is all about control of one's environment. The chain would be likely to break before it was even forged.

Running away

Public/Donated http://pixabay.com/en/kid-boy-fear-afraid-child-running-160097/

Some think that a personal solution might be to simply run away. To leave normal society and live a simple life in the wilderness, with basic tools and no computers that an AGI could control. Hide on an island or in the jungle, like Japanese soldier Hiroo Onoda, who successfully hid in the jungle in the Philippines after the second World War for twenty-nine years.

However, in the modern world, one can run but not hide. Everything we do is already monitored in the name of antiterrorism. Our mobile phones record everywhere that we go and who we are with. Licence plate readers know where we drive, and public transport cards record which buses we catch. All of this information is already being correlated into huge databases. Anybody that turns off their phone is instantly marked as unusual, and in the USA, some employers do not allow their employees to turn off their phones. Whenever you walk down the street, more and more surveillance cameras recognize who you are by your face. All monetary transactions are monitored, so any preparation for a remote existence would be easily discovered.

Satellites already take high-resolution photographs of the entire globe, including thermal imaging which can detect body heat. Cheap but effective drones can travel anywhere. If most other people were removed from the planet, the few that remained would be easy to find. Remote areas might also not be so remote if many people try to hide in them, and there will be territorial disputes. Running away would probably be as futile as owning a gun to defend oneself against botnets.

Just do not build an AGI

If AGIs are so potentially dangerous, then laws could be enacted to prevent people from building AGIs in the first place. There are already laws that prevent people from building atomic bombs and chemical weapons. Why would society invest a large amount of money and effort in building machines that could destroy us all? Why not just say no to AGI?

That is much easier said than done. Unlike atomic bombs and chemical weapons, AI technologies are and will become extremely useful. Software that can drive cars, intelligent robots that can perform more and more tasks, advanced tools that help us research and understand the world. Computers are already a huge part of our lives, and their impact will only increase.

The world is a very competitive place, and intelligent software is already playing an ever more important part in that competition. A company with more intelligent robots or business management systems will outperform any company that lacks these tools. As robots leave the factory, highly intelligent control systems will become ever more important.

Military weapons are becoming increasingly more intelligent, with semi-autonomous micro tanks and drones already being built. More importantly, the next war will likely be in cyberspace, for which intelligence is essential. The pressure to build ever more intelligent software will be enormous.

Political Will

Atom bombs

Nagasaki 1945
Public Wikipedia

Any curtailment or limitation on the building of AGIs would require an enormous act of political will. However, recent history does not encourage a belief in the long-term strategic abilities of our political system.

Much has already been written about the use of the atom bomb on Japan, and whether the huge loss of life could be justified, given that Japan was at the point of collapse anyway. Japan's navy had been sunk, the people were starving, and the US bombers had unrestricted control of the sky with virtually no losses caused by enemy action. US generals Eisenhower and MacArthur, and admirals Leahy and Nimitz all considered the bombing to be militarily unnecessary. Further, the concern for the potential loss of American life was probably not nearly as high as reported considering the many expensive and unnecessary attacks on Japanese islands *after* the Marianas had been captured, culminating in over 20,000 US casualties from the completely pointless attack on Iwo Jima.

One point not often made is that early atom bombs were not actually that powerful, having roughly the same power as ten kilotons of conventional explosives. This gave it roughly the same destructive power as a couple of hundred B-29 plane-loads of conventional explosives, which is much less than what was dropped on several other military and civilian targets. By way of comparison, modern hydrogen, or *thermonuclear* weapons are about a thousand times more powerful, at ten megatons.

The reason that so many people died in the attacks was not the power of the bombs, nor even the remaining radiation. It was instead because the bombs were delivered by just two aircraft. This meant that the Japanese did not raise an air raid alarm, and so people were out above ground, rather than in relatively safe air raid shelters. If a few more escorts had been sent, then the air raid would have been sounded, and the loss of life would have been relatively small while still destroying the cities. One can only assume that not providing escorts or other warnings was a deliberate strategy by those in command of the operation.

However, it is the strategic stupidity of the deployment of the atom bomb that is more relevant to this book. Joseph Stalin was totally ruthless. Over 30 million people died in his purges and deliberate famine before the war, far more than their horrendous casualties during the war itself. This caused a major problem for Stalin when Germany attacked because most of his better officers had been purged and those that remained were useless yes-men, and were certainly not about to demonstrate any initiative even if they had any.

Left to their own devices, it could have taken the Soviet scientists many years or decades to develop the atom bomb independently. Up until that point, atomic physics was an esoteric science with no practical application. Only the most foolhardy Soviet scientist would have shown initiative and pushed for resources to be devoted to developing a bomb. In the not unlikely event that the atom bomb turned out not to be feasible, then anyone that supported its creation could easily be branded counter-revolutionary.

By using the bomb on Japan, the US revealed the greatest secret of the war, namely that such a weapon could be built. Once that was known, building one instantly became Stalin's top national priority. It is said that Stalin motivated his physicists with the promise of the Order of Lenin if they succeeded, and the gulags for themselves and their families if they failed.

Several people who should have known better were naively attracted to the idea of a worker-led utopia that the Soviet Union pretended to provide. This encouraged idealistic spying, and Stalin actually knew about the bomb before it was dropped. Moreover, the callousness of the bombing motivated other spies to help the Soviet Union, and they ended up providing the Soviets with detailed instructions as to how to produce the bomb.

If the bomb had not been deployed, then disinformation could have been spread as to the bomb's power and practicality. Spreading disinformation had been a well-used tactic during the war, particularly in support of hiding the extent of allied code breaking. Using the weapon on civilians made any campaign of misinformation futile. Its deployment made the USA vulnerable to nuclear attack for much longer than necessary while producing virtually no strategic benefit in the war with Japan.

Using the bomb also made its use acceptable as a tactical weapon, a mindset that only changed around the 1970s. During the 1950s, individual commanders believed they were authorized to use them if they felt that the tactical situation warranted it, and wanted no restrictions that could delay any response. After the Cuban Missile Crisis in the 1960s, President Kennedy insisted that special codes be required to activate the missiles. These were duly added, and set to the code "000000", and this number was included in the manuals just in case anyone was unaware of them.

The tactical genius of man to solve the huge technical hurdles required to build the atom bomb is in stark contrast to the strategic stupidity of man to use it in the way that it was used.

Iran's atomic ambitions

Iranian children killed by an Iraqi attack
Public Wikipedia

A much more recent, and perhaps more relevant, example of strategic stupidity was the deployment of the Stuxnet virus against Iran in 2010. This had a similar effect to the use of the atomic bomb fifty years earlier. It focussed attention on developing this type of weapon and it legitimized its use. It also disseminated the technology used to build it, this time in the virus code itself.

Iran had been declared "evil" by the USA when they overthrew a US-backed dictator in 1979. The USA (and thus Australia) actively supported Saddam Hussein's subsequent attacks on Iran from 1980 to 1988, in which roughly a million Iranians were killed. Many were killed by chemical weapons used repeatedly by Iraq with the full support of Western governments. (Iran never used chemical weapons, although the Iranian government did themselves no favours with their verbal attacks on most foreign governments.)

When Iraq invaded Kuwait in 1990, the USA suddenly declared Saddam Hussein evil and drove Iraq out of Kuwait, but the USA was careful to then quickly withdraw. The 2001 September 11 attacks then produced a bellicose mood in the USA so in 2003 the USA (and thus automatically Australia) invaded Iraq despite the fact that it was always clear that Iraq had no part in the attack. There was a strong feeling at the time that once the USA had dealt with Iraq that Iran would be next, and experience from 1990 suggested that it would not take long for the USA to defeat Iraq. However, as it turned out, the USA became bogged down in Iraq and so no threat to Iran eventuated.

Iran had a nuclear program in the 1950s with backing from the USA, but after the revolution, Iran abandoned the program as being "un-Islamic". Then in the early 1990s, Iran began a new nuclear energy program with help from Russia. This was largely in compliance with the International Atomic Energy Agency (IAEA), but since the 2005 election of hard-line Mahmoud Ahmadinejad, Iran pushed the boundaries of what was acceptable.

Of particular concern was the use of centrifuges that enrich natural uranium. This is needed for peaceful purposes, but highly enriched uranium can be used to make atomic weapons relatively easily. Despite constant pressure from the USA, the IAEA has never found evidence that Iran is actively pursuing atomic bombs, but Iran has also not been as transparent as it should be. As a major oil producer, there is no economic reason for Iran to have nuclear power. It would appear most unlikely that Iran is actually producing nuclear weapons, instead investing in nuclear technology in order to have the option to produce nuclear weapons in the future. This has to be seen in the context of the very deadly 1980s war with Iraq, during which Iran was abandoned by the international community despite the extensive use of chemical weapons.

Stuxnet

Iranian President Mahmoud Ahmadinejad (2nd Left) visits the Natanz nuclear enrichment plant
News (Reuters?)

Stuxnet is a sophisticated computer virus/malware that managed to infect the computers controlling Iran's uranium centrifuges. It caused the centrifuges to alternately run too fast and too slow, which caused them to burn out relatively quickly. Stuxnet also perverted the software-based centrifuge monitoring system so that it told the Iranians that the centrifuges were spinning at the correct speeds even though they were not.

The Iranians instigated an "air gap" between computers that controlled the centrifuges and other computers that could be connected to the Internet. However, they still needed to get code and data on and off the centrifuge computers, which they did using USB memory sticks ("thumb drives"). Having infected computers that were attached to the Internet, Stuxnet copied itself onto the thumb drives. Then, when the thumb drives were inserted into the centrifuge computers, the virus infected them in turn.

Stuxnet was a sophisticated program that took great pains not to be detected. Researchers think it must have been written by a large team of programmers with diverse skills, ranging from virus creation to a deep understanding of the centrifuges that were attacked. It is most unlikely to have been created by any non-government group, and various boasting remarks by public officials seem to confirm that it was created by the USA and Israel.

Glass houses

This is another example of tactical genius and strategic gross stupidity. Iran's nuclear facilities were not the only equipment vulnerable to attack; indeed, they would have been one of the more protected ones. The USA itself has numerous "SCADA" systems that control equipment ranging from traffic lights to the flood gates of major dams. They are all connected to the Internet (if indirectly), and any attack on them would cause havoc.

Of particular concern is the ageing and archaic electricity control system. This was highlighted by the northeast North America blackout of 2003. A software bug caused a minor fault which overloaded high tension wires, which in turn became hot, stretched, and then touched some unpruned trees. One might expect such a fault to cause a temporary blackout in the area serviced by those high tension wires. What actually happened was that the entire northeast power grid from Toronto to Pennsylvania was shut down by this one fault. Even worse, it took several days to return the system to an operational state after the fault was rectified.

There can be no excuse for that. Coordinating a complex power grid is not trivial, but for one fault to deactivate the entire grid, and then let it take days to recover, demonstrates awful design and gross incompetence. As more and more systems became dependent upon electricity the effect of the blackout was severe, and it has been estimated that a dozen people died as a result. Many defence and border protection systems were also disabled during the blackout. Since that time, the electricity system has become ever more complex and interconnected, and thus more difficult to control and more vulnerable to attack.

If those in glass houses should not throw stones, then the USA lives in a crystal palace. By deploying Stuxnet, the USA greatly encouraged the development of such weapons. They also made their use acceptable. Before Stuxnet, the USA had warned that any cyber-attack would be considered to be a military attack that might produce a military response. After Stuxnet, that threat can no longer be taken seriously.

Thowing stones from glass houses.
Multiple

Stuxnet was only intended to attack Iranian centrifuges. However, an updated version of the software had a bug that caused it to spread much more widely. That is how it was eventually discovered, on a computer outside of Iran. Stuxnet attacked any controller that looked, to Stuxnet, like an Iranian centrifuge. The Siemens controllers involved are quite common, so Stuxnet could attack many different types of equipment throughout the world. Kaspersky labs had found Stuxnet in a Russian nuclear power plant, but fortunately, Stuxnet included a self destruct date.

Perhaps more importantly, the code of Stuxnet has now been carefully studied by numerous white hat and black hat security experts. It essentially provides an excellent manual as to how to produce top quality malware and viruses.

In June 2014, new, high-quality malware, known as Dragonfly (or Havex), was found to have infected many energy producers, mainly in the USA and Western Europe. The perpetrators are unknown, but the malware appears to have been well resourced, although it has not caused any damage.

Zero day exploits

Stuxnet used four "zero day" exploits. These are bugs in system software that enable malicious programs to perform actions not otherwise permitted. One of these, known as CPLINK, was particularly ugly because it enabled any USB thumb drive to automatically execute its code whenever it was plugged into a Windows PC, without any action being required by the user.

That sort of bug is inexcusable, but also quite common in the Windows operating system. Modern software is huge, complex, and not well understood by anyone. The vast majority of code in an operating system adds little real value. There has been a recent emphasis in security, but no emphasis on cleaning up bad design. The result is events like "Patch Tuesday", the second Tuesday of each month when Microsoft releases patches for the most recently discovered security bugs. A large number are patched, in an endless stream. Nobody expects modern software to be secure by design; they just hope that the bug fixers can stay ahead of the bug exploiters. Like endlessly plugging holes in a rotting boat.

Another problem with modern malware is that it is *polymorphic*, which means that it changes its own shape continuously. Traditional anti-virus software looks for specific patterns of bytes that correspond to known viruses. But that approach cannot be used for polymorphic malware because the code continuously changes itself so that there are no fixed patterns to find. Modern anti-virus software needs to be much more intelligent in order to detect malware, but a substantial amount of malware remains undetected, and the anti-virus software can also attack normal, good software.

Stuxnet was not intelligent in the sense of being an AGI, but it was autonomous in the sense that once it was released into the wild, it behaved in ways that its authors could not predict and control. Stuxnet could not call home when working *in cognito* behind an air gap, so it just did what it thought was best. That is how it escaped from the centrifuges and was eventually detected.

As to the Iranian centrifuges, it is estimated that Stuxnet had destroyed about 20% of them and set the Iranian program back by several months. Stuxnet has now been removed, the centrifuges have been replaced, and output actually increased slightly during 2010. Furthermore, the Iranians are now much more careful about malware, and are much better at detecting and removing it when found. They are also more vigilant about detecting spyware gathers intelligence rather than sabotaging equipment. So releasing Stuxnet reduced the ability to gather intelligence about Iran.

Incidentally, the trade-off between intelligence and sabotage is not new. During World War II, there was a major political battle between British departments SOE (Special Operations Executive) that supported sabotage and SIS (Secret Intelligence Service) that gathered intelligence. SIS thought, correctly, that SOE's sabotage would have minimal effect on the war, but their activities would blow the cover of SIS's agents. The political infighting between the departments led to the deaths of many brave agents, particularly in The Netherlands (Englandspeil).

Any thinking person should have seen the dangers inherent in deliberately releasing malware, and should have had strong reservations about the program. Yet Stuxnet was released. It is difficult to see how the same political process could ever tackle the much more difficult job of controlling AGI development.

(While Stuxnet is probably a significant blow to American security, it will almost certainly have boosted the careers of the individuals and organizations that built it. The budget for cyber warfare has increased dramatically, and profits have soared.)

Practicalities of abstinence

It would take an enormous and unprecedented act of political will to attempt to ban research into AGIs and forgo the benefits that ever more intelligent software could bring. However, even if international laws were to be passed that strictly banned research into AGI, the practicalities of doing so would probably be insurmountable.

The first problem is to define what AGI research actually is. At what point does ordinary computer science research become AGI research? That is not at all obvious, and researchers will have a very strong motivation to push whatever boundaries are put in place.

If that law could somehow be defined, it would then need to be enforced. If any government or organization thought that their competitors were cheating, then there would be enormous pressure to cheat as well. More intelligent software does not just lead to recursive self-improvement. It leads to better ways of doing everything that we do, personally, industrially and militarily.

Lastly, and perhaps most importantly, no special equipment is likely to be required to perform artificial intelligence research. To build an atom bomb, one needs uranium and special centrifuges or breeder reactors, which are difficult to hide. Writing software only requires computers which are ubiquitous. Enforcing such laws would be rather like trying to enforce laws as to what thoughts people might have. As the technology gets close to reaching AGI capabilities, it would only take a small team of programmers anywhere in the world to push it over the line. Small teams could easily break the rules and develop AGI which would make governments very nervous about not pursuing AGI systems of their own.

Trying to prevent people from building intelligent computers would be like trying to stop the spread of knowledge. Once Eve picks the apple, it is very difficult to put it back on the tree.

Restrict computer hardware

Motorola 68020 CPU (produced 1984)
Blog http://diephotos.blogspot.com.au/

While ordinary computers can be used to write software, it is not nearly as easy to build powerful new computer chips. It takes large investments and teams with many specialities, from producing ultra-pure silicon to developing extremely complex logical designs. Complex and expensive machinery is required to build them. Unlike programming, this is certainly not something that can be done in somebody's garage.

If the production of new computer hardware could be controlled, then maybe an AGI could be starved of the resources needed to think. It does not matter how good the software is, it still requires silicon to execute it.

There are two problems with this approach. The first is that there may already be sufficient hardware to be able to run an effective AGI if processors are combined into supercomputers or botnets. Moore's Law suggests that there will be even more capacity in the near future.

The second problem is that humanity has become very dependent on computer technology, as well as its constantly increasing power. It would take an extraordinary act of political will to suddenly turn that around and deliberately stop producing new hardware. Particularly if there was any doubt that competitive nations were adhering to any such ban.

Realistically, it would require a widely demonstrated disaster involving a hyper-intelligent machine. By that stage, it would be far too late.

Asilomar conference

A good example of political cooperation was the Asilomar Conference in 1975, in which researchers and lawyers drew up voluntary guidelines on recombinant DNA research. There were widespread concerns that this very new technology could accidentally produce super-microbes that would be impossible to control in the wider environment. Guidelines included strict rules on containing engineered organisms, including performing work on organisms that had been weakened in some manner so that they could not survive outside of laboratory conditions.

The voluntary guidelines were effective in allaying public fears of the new technology, and they prevented more stringent mandatory guidelines from being legislated. They still affect biological research today, but genetic engineering is now commonplace. Genetically engineered crops are widely dispersed in the environment, and it is even possible to purchase genetically engineered GloFish that glow in the dark. The conference certainly did not curtail the use of genetic engineering for the development of biological weapons.

Patent trolls

One fanciful hypothesis is that the patent trolls and legal system will be our saviours. The development of an AGI would provide a rich source of patents, both trivial and real. Where there are patents, there are wonderful opportunities for aggressive litigation. If exploited effectively, patent wars could make the development of artificial intelligence uneconomical. Organizations would spend their budgets on patent attorneys and lawyers, with little remaining for any real engineering, which would be pointless anyway because nothing could be brought to market without extensive, destructive litigation.

So we have misunderstood the motivations of patent trolls and attorneys. They are not greedy, self-serving parasites whose only interest is to promote themselves at the expense of others. Rather, they are on a mission to save humanity from uncontrollable advances in technology.

Does it really matter?

After millennia of conflict and hunger, mankind finally seems to be becoming civilized. World wars between nations appear to be a thing of the past. We live in a time of general prosperity and enlightened attitudes towards other people, with most nations even taking care to ensure that the poor are not destitute. Modern medicine has made premature death rare — in Australia, the life expectancy of a one-year-old boy has increased from 61 to 80 years over the last century. Even in darkest Africa, conditions have improved for most people despite a few ugly wars, and even the curse of AIDS is slowly abating. (AIDs kills hundreds of times as many people as Ebola, despite the media hype.)

It would seem to be a great pity if the age of man came to an end just as it entered its golden period. A future AGI might not value many of the things that we value such as love, art, and music. It will almost certainly not enjoy dancing. An AGI may not even be conscious (whatever that actually means).

Conversely, as worms have evolved into apes, and apes to man, the evolution of man to an AGI appears to be just another natural process. The culmination of the Golden Age. Something to be celebrated rather than avoided.

We now know that all of our desires, dreams and actions are ultimately just the result of natural selection. Love is a mirage, and all our endeavours are ultimately futile. The Zen Buddhists are right — desires are illusions; their abandonment is required for enlightenment. We are born, grow old and die, just as whole species live and die over the millennia. Nothing is permanent, nothing is ultimately important. In any case, it would probably only be a matter of time before mankind destroyed Earth itself.

It is unlikely that mankind could prevent the development of AGIs any more than the Neanderthals could prevent the rise of *Homo sapiens*. We *will* build intelligent machines because it is in our nature to do so.

Learning to come to terms with this is similar to coming to terms with the death of loved ones, or even ourselves when the time comes. Where there is birth there must be death. Of individuals, species, planets and, ultimately, the entire universe. Death is the process of renewal and progress. We need to celebrate life rather than become obsessed with death.

All very clever. But this author has two little daughters, whom he loves very much and for whom he would do anything. That love may just be a product of evolution, but it is real to him. Building an AGI could mean their death (or, more likely, their children's death), so it matters to him. And so, probably, to the reader.

Conclusion

Geological history

Roughly 4,150 million years ago, a cloud of gas condensed into a fiery ball that became the Earth. A few hundred million years later, the first barely living things came into existence. They lived and died, with only the fittest surviving. Eventually, cyanobacteria appeared and began creating oxygen through photosynthesis.

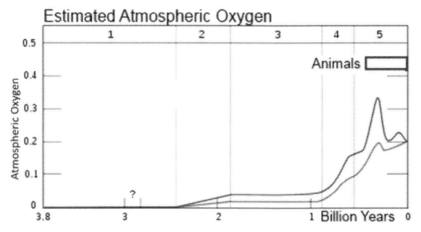

Atmospheric oxygen concentrations since the creation of the Earth.
Public Wikipedia

This was a slow process, because when cyanobacteria split carbon dioxide into oxygen and carbon, that carbon can readily convert the oxygen back into carbon dioxide — it burns. Moreover, the early Earth's atmosphere contained large amounts of methane that needed to be oxidized before any free oxygen could be produced. After some two billion years, the methane was finally oxidized, but only low concentrations of atmospheric oxygen could be maintained because it was consumed by oxidizing various rocks. Most of the iron in the Earth's crust is the result of unoxidized iron meteors striking the young planet, but today most natural iron is found as oxidized iron.

Roughly 600 million years ago, the Earth finally became fully oxidized, and levels of atmospheric oxygen began to rise substantially. That enabled oxygen-breathing animals to evolve, leading to the Cambrian Explosion of multicellular animals about 515 million years ago. Animals continued to slowly evolve, starting with the invertebrates, then fish, frogs and reptiles, and finally mammals, which became dominant after dinosaurs disappeared 65 million years ago.

Primates appeared at about that time, with early apes about 10 million years ago. The first hominids appeared about 0.2 million years ago, with modern *Homo sapiens* leaving Africa about 0.06 million years ago. Agriculture was then developed about 0.01 million years ago. Technologies improved steadily but slowly, enabling the manufacture of metals and construction of the great buildings in the ancient world. Then about 0.0003 million years ago, an explosion of scientific discovery led directly to the modern world, containing powerful machines and, ultimately, computers.

History of science

For most of man's history, technological advancement took centuries, but the speed of technological progress has become so fast that major changes now occur within a single lifespan. When this author's grandparents were born, there was no electricity, cars or aeroplanes. When his father was born, there were no antibiotics nor, not so tragically, television. When this author was born, computers were large, slow and very expensive, and he had to sneak into various establishments after hours in order to play with them. When his daughters were born, mobile phones were just phones, whereas today most people carry powerful computers in their pockets.

A thousand years is a long time. A million years is a thousand times a thousand years. It has taken some three thousand million years of biology in order to produce animals, followed by five hundred million years to produce us, and ten thousand years to produce our technological society. This books posits that we are within just a few decades, or at most hundreds of years, before a transformation that will be as big as the creation of life itself.

Wow.

Natural selection

Natural selection has produced amazingly complex and sophisticated designs. Even a single-celled protozoa has a staggering array of capabilities. It can effectively navigate its environment; find, consume and digest food; interact sexually; and be able to divide itself. All based on finely tuned biochemical reactions.

Multicellular animals are an order of magnitude more complex than protozoa. Through various mechanisms that are still not well understood, individual cells working at the biochemical level know how to divide and differentiate themselves in order to produce numerous intricate structures, from bones to brains. Animals are complex systems that involve thousands of interacting parts, each of which needs to be balanced in its functionality to produce a viable living organism.

The nervous system is probably the jewel in the crown of animal development. Using a brain that contains just a few hundred thousand neurons and is the size of a pinhead, a spider can weave a web, and a wasp can identify and kill the spider without being eaten. Their very modest quantity of DNA provides a blueprint that causes their neurons to be wired together in such a way as to produce all of their remarkable behaviour.

Blog John Brolese on http://www.abc.net.au/news/2011-12-13/close-up---a-spider-wasp-takes-on-a-spider/3729180

These behaviours are often attributed to being just instinct, as neither the spiders nor the wasps consciously know why they do what they do, but there is nothing "just" about these instincts. Every spider's web is different depending on the location. It cannot simply make a rigidly predetermined sequence of moves, like ordinary industrial robots do. Instead, it has to sense its natural environment in order to produce a web that works. The instinct certainly provides a basic plan, such as to start with the top line and then drop radials, and finally the spiral. But realizing that basic plan in a chaotic, natural environment requires much more intelligence than is possessed by current robots.

Higher animals are also guided by strong instincts: to care for their young, to know what types of places provide food and shelter, to defend territory, to become either angry or afraid if attacked, to undergo great migrations on land, sea or air. Their instincts are more abstract, emotional feelings and inclinations, rather than detailed move-by-move instructions as to how to accomplish some very specific task. Birds and mammals learn by interacting with their environments, and often by being actively taught by their parents.

Human instincts

The human psyche is ultimately driven by instincts as well. We share many of these with most other mammals, such as to love and care for our young, to work in teams with social hierarchies, and to become angry if our territorial or other rights are not respected.

Human instincts underlie an intelligence orders of magnitude greater than any other animal, but they were created by the same process that taught the spider how to weave its web. Natural selection. Until relatively recently, people did not understand why they have the instincts that they have. But that does not matter. What does matter is that those instincts have evidently produced behaviours that *in practice* have proven effective in breeding grandchildren.

In 1943, Abraham Maslow published a theory of human motivation based on a hierarchy of needs. The most basic needs are for food and shelter to keep us alive. Then comes the need for safety and security, of body, continued sustenance (e.g. though employment), etc. Only once those are satisfied can people focus on higher level needs such as self esteem, respect of our peers, care of others, and creativity. As our society has become wealthier and contraception has controlled our numbers, we have been able to focus more on the higher needs. Memes about caring for others and having a just and egalitarian society resonate strongly with us once we are fed and secure, and now dominate our modern sense of moral values.

Intelligence

Today, our instincts for wealth and creativity have developed an amazing technology, namely computers that have the potential to become more intelligent than their creators. An intelligence created deliberately by another intelligence, rather than simply through the unintelligent effects of natural selection.

Computer-based intelligence turned out to be utterly different from animal intelligence. Computers did not start by being as intelligent as a worm, then as a mouse, then a chimpanzee. Instead, the first computers were far more intelligent than humans at some specific tasks such as arithmetic, and yet far less intelligent than even a worm at interacting with a natural environment. Today a computer can store and analyze vast amounts of data way beyond any human capability. They are chess grandmasters and even have become world champions at trivia game shows. Yet, in many ways, they are still not nearly as intelligent as a mouse.

There is no easy way to define what intelligence actually is. Phrases such as "self aware" and "creative" are not useful because computers have been able to satisfy such criteria for many years, albeit not very intelligently. Computer intelligence cannot be naively understood in terms of human intelligence because it is so fundamentally different.

AI technologies

Computers can appear to be much more intelligent than they actually are by manipulating symbols created by humans. The early Eliza program used simple pattern-matching techniques to pretend to be a Rogerian psychologist. It participates in a dialog by simply rearranging phrases made by the person talking to it. Other systems can generate text that sounds as good as that written by professional journalists, but again, that is achieved by simply recombining clichés stored in their databases rather than having any deep understanding of the subject matter.

Later early systems such as SHRDLU did have a deep understanding of very simple microworlds and could converse about them in natural language. Other more useful but limited worlds included the controlling of space craft such as NASA's Deep Space 1. However, it turns out to be much easier for an intelligent computer to control a spacecraft than it is to perform commonsense reasoning about the everyday world. Just because a computer can converse in natural language in a limited way does not mean that it is nearly truly intelligent.

Research into artificial intelligence can be loosely divided into symbolic and non-symbolic systems. Symbolic systems abstract the world into symbols that are roughly equivalent to words or phrases. Software then manipulates those symbols in order to make deductions about its world, often using variants of mathematical logic. These systems have proven to be very effective at limited tasks.

Non-symbolic systems view the world as continuous numbers rather than discrete symbols. They tend to work directly with raw data rather than have humans abstract that data into symbols. Examples include speech understanding and vision systems. Non-symbolic systems sometimes produce symbols that can then be manipulated by a symbolic system. For example, converting sound waves into words, which can then be interpreted by a natural language understanding system.

One powerful, non-symbolic technique is the artificial neural network. Artificial neurons have an uncanny ability to self-organize and to learn complex new patterns from examples. The term *Neural Networks* is confusing because while artificial neurons were inspired by biological neurons, they are quite different in many respects. The goal of most artificial neural research is to produce practical systems that solve real problems rather than to simulate neurons.

There has also been a vast amount of research into how our own brains work, mostly to assist with the treatment of diseases, but also to gain an understanding of our own minds in order to build intelligent software systems. However, natural brains are very complex, and have evolved to operate within the limitations of their hardware, living neurons. While understanding our own brains is very worthwhile, this author believes that intelligent systems will largely be built *ab initio,* with limited reference to the actual structures in animal brains.

Building an AGI

After sixty years of research, nobody has built a single intelligent robot. How could anybody be so arrogant as to believe that the mysteries of the human psyche could be reproduced in cold, hard silicon? The brain has trillions of synapses, and it would take a computer a billion times more powerful than current ones to accurately simulate them. Computers can play cute tricks, but to be truly intelligent requires being at least partly human.

Nonsense.

The problem of building a truly intelligent machine is a difficult one, and it most certainly has not been solved. Nor is it likely to be solved within the next few decades, despite what some overly optimistic commentators have suggested. But to say that it cannot be solved would imply that there is something supernatural about our neural processes and there is no known reason to believe that wet neurons are required to produce intelligent machines.

Time and time again, processes that appear to be beyond our understanding have been understood using scientific methods. To the ancients, the movement of the planets could only be explained as "God's will", whereas Isaac Newton showed us that their paths and periods just followed a simple law of gravity. More recently, the great mystery of life itself has been solved, not by reference to undetectable aethers or other mystical properties, but in terms of well-defined principles of carbon chemistry undertaken on a huge scale, all orchestrated by DNA. There is no reason to think that intelligence will not also be understood, sooner rather than later.

Further, our understanding of how to build intelligent systems has grown enormously over the last few decades. When combined with ever more powerful hardware, this has led to new semi-intelligent systems that can drive cars and win trivia game shows. There is still a long way to go, but great progress has already been made.

Semi-intelligent machines

Over the next few decades a series of semi-intelligent machines will become commonplace, and they will have a dramatic effect on society. Machines will automate many manual jobs that have well-defined actions such as driving vehicles, cleaning, painting, agricultural work, and some retail. (But not, as one writer actually postulated, fashion modelling, even if walking down a catwalk is a well-defined procedure!) However, even assuming that the fashion models will still be employed, many other jobs will become redundant, and only time will tell whether alternative work will become available for that half of society that possesses below average intelligence.

Semi-intelligent machines will also affect white collar jobs. History strongly suggests that the amount of work to be performed will automatically increase to consume any improvements in productivity. Machines will slowly take over more and more decision-making processes, and upper-level management will become more and more dependent on semi-intelligent machines, even though they have not reached human-level intelligence.

Eventually, machines will become capable of performing artificial intelligence research unassisted by people. At that point, they will be able to reprogram their own minds, leading to recursive self-improvement. This process will be exponential as more intelligent machines become better at producing more intelligent machines. Initially, the improvements might be small, but like compound interest, the effect over the longer term will be huge, producing hyper-intelligent machines.

Semi-intelligent computers are already used to interpret data from social networks and other sources and so help guide political policy decisions. As they become slowly more intelligent, computers will have greater and greater influence. It may turn out that ruling the planet is a simpler task than performing effective artificial intelligence research. Semi-intelligent computers may, in effect, end up controlling human society well before any hyper-intelligent machines are developed.

Goals

A hyper-intelligent machine will be in a good position to achieve whatever goal it desires. It may or may not be friendly to humans, but in either case the machines' ultimate goal will be the same as every other organism that has ever existed. Namely to do just that, to exist. Machines that do not have that goal will simply cease to exist.

A computer program will have a radically different world view to humans. It will essentially be immortal, and so have no need to raise and care for children. It will also exist in a fiercely competitive environment, both externally with other intelligent machines and internally with the components of which it is comprised. It is difficult to envision how helping humans would be compatible with their need to exist in such a competitive environment.

Some authors have suggested that people will merge with machines. We will incorporate intelligent devices into our brains, and possibly upload our own intelligence into the machine. The machines will be like us because they will *be* us. Computers already influence our cognition in the way we access information and communicate. This book, for example, would be very difficult to write without easy access to the Internet. In the future, technologies like Google Glass will produce a much closer, almost subconscious integration. However, it seems unlikely that such a relationship will continue in the longer term because it is difficult to see how having our intelligence available could benefit a hyper-intelligent computer.

Prognosis

If it is, in fact, possible to build hyper-intelligent machines, then it appears almost certain that we will choose to build them, even if that results in the destruction of humanity. There are and will be too many pressures to do so, and no clearly demonstrated threat to react to. Threats from bombs and bugs are easy to understand; they have been around for centuries. But intelligence is so fundamental that it is difficult to conceptualize. It is not just an increasing rate of technological change, it is a total paradigm shift. Semi-autonomous robots will start to raise awareness, but by then it may be too late. There will be no putting an artificial general intelligence back in its box once one is built.

It is possible that an intelligence explosion may never happen. The problem of building an intelligent machine might just be too hard for man to solve. However, there is no evidence to suggest that research has become stuck on some unsolvable problem, and the ongoing progress that has been made to date suggests that the problem will be solved sooner rather than later. If ultra-intelligent machines are produced, then the future of mankind is far from certain. As individuals we will (almost certainly) grow old and die in any case, so this may simply be how our software descendants finally cheat death and become immortal.

One thing that is certain is that the future will not be anything like it used to be. The great wheel of human life that turns slowly from birth to maturity to death will not continue to turn as it has for countless generations past.

This book aims to raise awareness of the issue, and to encourage real discussion as to the fate of humanity and whether that actually matters.

"In the game of life and evolution there are three players at the table:
human beings, nature, and machines. I am firmly on the side of nature.
But nature, I suspect, is on the side of the machines."
George Dyson 2012

Bibliography and Notes

Formal references have traditionally been essential so that one could visit a library and physically locate referenced articles. But in this age of easy Internet searches, the need for references is diminished. So instead of a formal references section at the very end, sufficient detail is included within the text itself to facilitate an easy Internet searches for relevant material.

This book also has no footnotes or end notes. If something is not worth saying in the body of the text, then it is probably not worth saying at all.

Printed in Great Britain
by Amazon